The Justification of the Gentiles

Cain
by Fernand Cormon
Musée d'Orsay, Paris
©Service Photographique de la
Réunion des Musées Nationaux

". . . from the Gentiles, Sinners"

"and such were some of you! But you have been washed;
you have been sanctified; you have been justified in
the name of our Lord, Jesus Christ" (1 Cor 6:11)

THE
JUSTIFICATION
OF THE
GENTILES

PAUL'S LETTERS
TO THE GALATIANS
AND ROMANS

HENDRIKUS BOERS

In appreciation of

Mikhail Gorbachev

who transformed Paul's religious expectations
into political reality

Copyright © 1994 by Hendrickson Publishers, Inc.
P. O. Box 3473
Peabody, Massachusetts, 01961–3473
All rights reserved
Printed in the United States of America

ISBN 1–56563–011–4

Library of Congress Cataloging-in-Publication Data

Boers, Hendrikus
    The justification of the Gentiles: Paul's letters to the
    Galatians and Romans / Hendrikus Boers
        p. cm.
    Includes bibliographical references and indexes.
    ISBN 1–56563–011–4
    1. Bible. N.T. Romans—Criticism, interpretation, etc.
    2. Bible N.T. Galatians—Criticism, interpretation, etc.
    3. Justification—History of Doctrines—Early church, ca.
    30–600. I. Title
    BS2655.J8B64 1994
    227'.1066—dc20   93-47042
                                                                CIP

Quotations of the Greek New Testament are taken from *The Greek New Testament,* edited by Kurt Aland, Matthew Black, Carlo M. Martini, Bruce M. Metzger, and Allen Wikgren, Third Edition. ©1966, 1975, United Bible Societies. Used by permission.

Contents

Chapter 2
A Macro-Structure for Galatians

Chapter 3
A Macro-Structure for Romans

Chapter 4
A Macro-Structure for Galatians and Romans

Part Two
The Semantic Deep Structure of Paul's Thought

Chapter 5
Paul's System of Values

Chapter 6
Paul's Micro-Universe

Conclusion

Appendixes

Bibliography

Indexes

Abbreviations

BTB	Biblical Theology Bulletin
ChW	*Christliche Welt*
EKK	Evangelisch-katholischer Kommentar zum Neuen Testament
EVuB	*Exegetische Versuche und Besinnungen* (2 vols.; Göttingen: Vandenhoeck & Ruprecht, 1960 and 1964)
FoiVie	*Foi et vie*
GuV	*Glauben und Verstehen* (4 vols.; Tübingen: J. C. B. Mohr [Paul Siebeck], 1933–1965)
HThR	*Harvard Theological Review*
JAAR	*Journal of the American Academy of Religion*
JBL	*Journal of Biblical Literature*
JR	*Journal of Religion*
NovT	*Novum Testamentum*
NTS	*New Testament Studies*
SBLDS	Society of Biblical Literature Dissertation Series
SBLMS	Society of Biblical Literature Monograph Series
SEÅ	*Svensk exegetisk Årsbok*
ST	*Studia Theologica*
Tbl	*Theologische Blätter*
TTh	*Tijdschrift voor Theologie*
WUNT	Wissenschaftliche Untersuchungen zum Neuen Testament
ZNW	*Zeitschrift für die neutestamentliche Wissenschaft*
ZThK	*Zeitschrift für Theologie und Kirche*

Preface

In this study I do not presume to have come close to saying a final word concerning the interpretation of Paul's thought in Galatians and Romans, although I do claim to have made advances in understanding him. The most important distinguishing factor of the text-linguistic, semiotic method I have used, compared with the traditional methods, is that my primary concern is not with Paul's expressions, but with his underlying meanings. Thus, differences that I previously considered to be of fundamental significance, such as the difference between the understanding of the "seed of Abraham" as Christ in Gal 3:16 and as Isaac in Rom 4:13–21,[1] now appear to be of secondary importance. They appear rather to be merely different ways of expressing the same thing. In Romans Paul may have become persuaded that he could not maintain that the seed of Abraham in the Genesis story referred to Christ as he did in Galatians, and so he interpreted it as Isaac in Romans, but that is not necessarily a change in his meaning. The fact that he was able to interpret Abraham's seed so differently in the two letters in itself indicates that the figure[2] ("seed of Abraham") was not of fundamental importance for him.

---

[1]See my *Theology out of the Ghetto. A New Testament Exegetical Study Concerning Religious Exclusiveness* (Leiden: E.J. Brill, 1971).

[2]"Image" is probably a better term in English to convey what is meant here with the reference to "the seed of Abraham," but serious problems would arise if the French "figure" in the semiotics of A.J. Greimas were to be translated with "image," where the latter term has a different meaning. (See A.J. Greimas and J. Courtés, *Sémiotique: dictionnaire raisonné de la théorie du langage* [Paris: Classiques Hachette, 1979], under "Figuratif," "Figurativation," "Figure," and "Image." ET, *Semiotics and Language. An Analytical Dictionary* [by Larry Crist and Daniel Patte, and others, Bloomington, Indiana University Press, 1982]).

A distinguishing feature of my method of interpretation is that I take many of Paul's statements as not meaningful in themselves, even if he took them to be true, but as preparatory for a meaning towards which he was working. So, for example, what he wrote in Rom 4:6–8 was itself not his point, from which he then drew conclusions in verses 9–12; rather, the significance of verses 6–8 for Paul was to prepare for the point he makes in verses 9–12. To use William Wrede's formulation, one cannot "squeeze conceptual capital from every single phrase and every casually chosen expression used by an author."[3] The primary question in the interpretation of Paul is not whether his statements are true, but what he means by them.

In the study presented here I hope to open a window to a new understanding of Paul. The radical nature of the changes in the understanding of his thought, especially the rejection of the opposition between justification by faith and justification for good works, leaves me with no illusions about the difficulty of finding willing ears for this interpretation. An openness to this new approach is all I request, not acceptance of any particular insight, a willingness on the part of the reader to move to a level of understanding that is attuned to Paul's thinking process, rather than the means or products of his thinking.

In the semiotic part (Part II) I tried to reduce the formalization to a minimum, limiting myself to logical and semiotic squares that clarify the structure of Paul's thinking. I am aware of how difficult wading through such formalized material can be, but I hope the investigation in Part II, which demonstrates the complete consistency of Paul's thought, will make the effort worthwhile. The advantage of the formalization is that it minimizes speculation on possible meanings.

Due to the nature of this study, I refer only infrequently to the secondary literature on Paul, including commentaries on Galatians

---

"Figure" in the sense intended here is not the same as in the English phrase "figure of speech," which Webster defines as "*a form of expression* (as a simile or metaphor) used to convey meaning or heighten effect often by comparing or identifying one thing with another that has a meaning or connotation familiar to the reader or listener" (*Webster's Ninth New Collegiate Dictionary* [Springfield: Merriam-Webster, 1990], my emphasis). Only the italicized part of the definition is relevant here.

[3]William Wrede, *Über Aufgabe und Methode der sogenannten neutestamentlichen Theologie* (Göttingen: Vandenhoeck & Ruprecht, 1897). Repr. in Georg Strecker (ed.), *Das Problem der Theologie des neuen Testaments* (Darmstadt: Wissenschaftliche Buchgesellschaft, 1975) 81–154, see page 96. ET in Robert Morgan, *The Nature of New Testament Theology* (London: SCM Press/ Naperville, Ill: Alec R. Allenson, 1973) 68–116.

All translations are my own.

and Romans. That literature nevertheless functions as an essential background for the study. In a subsequent volume, "A Reading Through Galatians and Romans," in which I will utilize the insights gained in this study for an interpretation of Galatians and Romans, I will give critical recognition to that literature.

The manuscript for this book was essentially complete at the end of my sabbatical leave in August of 1990. Before publication, however, it seemed wise to subject the insights that had come to me during the final stages of my research to scrutiny in critical discussion. I was not able to profit from the reaction of colleagues, but I was confident that educational settings with critical young minds would provide a good forum. For that reason, I delayed the book's publication until I had the opportunity to teach a seminary course and conduct a graduate seminar on Galatians and Romans, respectively, in the spring and fall of 1991. In the fall I also taught a course on Pauline theology, in which implications of this study were examined in the context of all of Paul's letters. In that way I was able to refine a number of formulations and to reflect further on issues that arose from the more fundamental insights presented in this book. I was tempted to include some of these during the final editing of the manuscript, but found that such a procedure disturbed the integrity of the work, running ahead into what I intend to discuss in a subsequent volume. Some of those reflections are due to appear in the course of the year in the following publications, "We who are by Inheritance Jews; not from the Gentiles, Sinners,"[4] "Polysemy in Paul's Use of Christological Expressions,"[5] "Paul and the Canon of the New Testament," and "A Context for Interpreting Paul."[6]

The contributions of the students, especially in these two courses and in the seminar, as well as in courses and seminars over a period of almost three decades, through thoughtful, critical, inquiring participation in the study of Paul, provided the atmosphere in which this study grew and came to fruition. To all of them I express my sincere thanks.

Of great significance in the graduate seminar was our realization of how deeply Paul's understanding of salvation is grounded in the Christ-event. At places in Paul's writings one might gain the impression that Abraham's faith in God's promise is more fundamental than the coming of Christ. According to Rom 15:8 Christ's mission

---

[4] *JBL* 111 (1992) 273–81.
[5] See Abraham J. Malherbe and Wayne A. Meeks (eds.), *The Future of Christology: Essays in Honor of Leander J. Keck* (Minneapolis: Fortress Press, 1993) 91–108.
[6] The latter two to appear in collections of essays in honor of two distinguished colleagues.

was to secure the promises of the Fathers, which can only mean the promise to Abraham that in him all the gentiles will be blessed (Gal 3:8, cf. Rom 4:17), making the promise to Abraham more fundamental than Christ's action in service of it. Romans 4 presents faith coming to parallel expression in both Abraham's faith in God's promise (4:5 and 17–22) and in the Christian's faith in God who raised Jesus from the dead (4:24). In Gal 3:29 Paul explicitly subordinates belonging to Christ to being a child of Abraham, "If you are of Christ, then you are children of Abraham, [and so] inheritors according to the promises." Our reflections on Paul's thought nevertheless convinced us that just as the meaning of Christ in these letters cannot be understood without its grounding in the promise to Abraham, so also the promise to Abraham has no meaning except in relationship to its fulfillment in Christ. The Christ-event thus has to be understood comprehensively in terms of the promise to Abraham that in him many gentiles would be blessed, and in terms of the fulfillment of that promise in Christ. This will become clear throughout the following study.

In this light it appeared to me that taking the formal step of becoming a Christian may after all merit serious consideration. What finally persuaded me that such a move would be contrary to Paul's understanding of salvation in Christ was 1 Cor 7:19, which I give here in a contemporizing translation, "Neither being formally a Christian counts for anything, nor not being formally a Christian, but keeping the commandments of God." The alternatives have equal validity. Christians too can be children of Abraham if they do not rely on being Christian as the means of their justification, as Paul understands the Jews to have done by relying on being Jews; Christians too can be children of Abraham if they follow in the footsteps of his non-Christian faith (cf. Rom 4:12). What being Christian beyond these distinctions meant for Paul becomes clear when we consider how he interpreted being a Jew in more than a formal sense in Rom 2:25–26. To make the point clear I once more give a contemporizing translation. "Being a Christian has meaning if you 'do' the Law; if you are a transgressor of the Law, your being a Christian has become non-Christian. If thus a non-Christian keeps the just requirements of the Law, will his [or her] not being a Christian not be counted as Christian?" I hope that this study will demonstrate that to keep the commandments of God and to believe in Christ Jesus as the one in whom God's promise to Abraham (Gal 3:6, Rom 4:17) was fulfilled, far from being contraries, are for Paul the same. I thank in particular Katrina Poetker for her contributions to these reflections, with which she most certainly does not agree in detail.

I came across the painting of Cain by Fernand Cormon (1845–1924) for the first time a few years ago during a visit to the Musée d'Orsay in Paris. Its sheer size[7] is overwhelming—although it is not the largest in the Orsay collection—but what remained with me as a lasting impression was the disheartening cheerlessness of this band of outcasts fleeing through the desert like driven animals with neither hope nor future. The size of the painting enhances the impression on the viewer. Standing at almost any point one sees Cain leaving the scene at the right with a large part of the group still approaching from the left.

From Paul's secure, Pharisaic point of view, a group such as this represents the quintessence of what he refers to as "gentiles, sinners" in his sarcastic remark to Peter in Gal 2:15: "We who are by heritage Jews, not from the gentiles, sinners." Note, especially Rom 1:18–32. Cain is the primordially accursed: "The Lord said, 'What have you done? Hark! your brother's blood that has been shed is crying out to me from the ground. Now you are accursed, and banished from the ground which has opened its mouth wide to receive your brother's blood, which you have shed. You shall be a vagrant and a wanderer on earth' " (Gen 4:10–11 [RSV]). And yet Paul, with supreme irony, states that it is the Jews who are cursed by the very Law on which they rely for privilege: "Those who are from the Law are under a curse" (Gal 3:10). It is a curse from which Christ alone is able to free them (v. 13) in order that salvation could become available to the gentiles (v. 14), the likes of Cain and his band of outcasts.

All the translations in this study, except where noted, including those from modern languages, are my own, with added references to English translations where they exist. The subject matter of chapter 1 is drawn largely from an article which appeared in *Studia Theologica* under the title, "The Foundations of Paul's Thought: A Methodological Investigation."[8] That material is used here with the approval of the editor of the journal.

The completion of this study was made possible by grants from the Association of Theological Schools and from the Emory University Research Committee. I acknowledge their support with sincere appreciation. Special thanks are due to Jim Waits, many years dean of the Candler School of Theology, for his support and encouragement, not only for this work, but also for my research and other academic activities in general. It gives me particular pleasure to acknowledge here my indebtedness to him for everything he has contributed to my work through the years.

---

[7]380 x 700 cm., or 12.5 x 23 ft.

[8]The full title is, "The Foundations of Paul's Thought: A Methodological Investigation—The Problem of the Coherent Center of Paul's Thought," *ST* 42 (1988) 55–68.

Colleen Grant edited the manuscript for style, with keen sensitivity and an excellent understanding of the subject matter. I extend to her special thanks. With the generosity typical of John Hayes, he went to the utmost limits of friendship and collegiality in his careful reading and editing of the manuscript. I can only depend on that same friendship for him to accept that I do not have words to express my appreciation. Finally, I would like to express sincere thanks to Patrick Alexander of Hendrickson Press for the keen sensitivity to content and style with which he did the final editing of the manuscript. His friendship, encouragement, and collegiality remain cherished memories of the final stages in the completion of this book.

With special appreciation I recognize Paul-Gerhard and Margret Schoenborn for the constant interest and encouragement, the repeated critical discussions, with which they followed the course of this investigation.

Gerhard Dautzenberg may have been the first colleague to read through the entire manuscript. For his thoughtful comments, my sincere thanks.

This study is the fruit of research and reflection on Paul's thought spanning decades; it was completed at the Philipps University in Marburg, an academic environment that excels in a hospitality that does justice to the agreeableness of its setting. I thank specifically the Fachbereich Evangelische Theologie for its hospitality, in particular the colleagues in New Testament, Wolfgang Harnisch, Dieter Lührmann, and Gerd Schunack, who treated me as if I were one of them, allowing me to participate in their academic deliberations, tempered by consideration for my time.

It was a remarkable year. As one after another of the East European nations were able to reclaim responsibility for their own political destinies, I became increasingly aware of the degree to which the political program of the one man who made that possible was based on a conception of human relationships similar to what emerged in this study as fundamental to Paul's thinking in Galatians and Romans: that privilege and condescension are the root causes of mistrust and insecurity among peoples. In recognition of what he has done to make a reality of some of Paul's deepest concerns, I dedicate this volume to Mikhail Gorbachev.

Much has happened in the meantime, heartbreakingly disappointing as well as encouragingly positive. On the one hand, the civil war in former Yugoslavia is not a direct result of the Gorbachev revolution, but is part of an explosion of formerly repressed national enmities, of which others have erupted and threaten to do so in the former Soviet Union as well. It is a heavy price to pay for the removal of repression, but there can be no going back on the fundamental changes that have been made. On the other hand, what Gorbachev set in motion created the atmosphere in which two desperately hopeless situations now have the promise of a solution: South Africa and the Israeli–Palestinian conflict.

The values of the promised new world order in the period subsequent to the demise of the Soviet domination of Eastern Europe are embodied in Vaclav Havel. In a speech at Lehigh University, he formulated a fundamental principle of the anticipated new world order, and, at the same time, what was at the heart of Paul's surrender of Jewish exclusiveness, and so all religious and every other privilege, in the following words: "no member of a single race, a single nation, a single sex, a single religion may be endowed with basic rights that are any different from anyone else's."[9]

---

[9]*The New York Times*, July 26, 1992, section 4, page 7.

Introduction∾

The Macro-Structure of
Galatians and Romans

> ". . . semantic macro-structures are
> necessary to explain in sufficiently
> simple terms how it is possible that
> throughout a text the selection of
> lexical items and underlying for-
> mation of semantic representations
> is heavily restricted by some global
> constraint."
>
> Teun van Dijk[1]

INTRODUCTION

It is common knowledge that Paul was not a systematic
thinker. This viewpoint determines the macro-structure with which
one approaches a Pauline text. A macro-structure in the sense of
Teun van Dijk's can be described in non-technical language as follows: In order to interpret a text we are dependent on some overall
understanding of its meaning that enables us to make sense of the
individual parts and the way they are structured. According to van
Dijk, every reader approaches a text with her or his own macro-structure.[2] That does not mean that we approach a text with a fixed
macro-structure; it will change as we deepen our understanding of
the text's meaning. Rudolf Bultmann, following Martin Heidegger,
refers to the same phenomenon as the hermeneutical circle. In a
non-linguistic way, Bultmann draws attention to the role played by

---

[1] *Some Aspects of Text Grammars. A Study in Theoretical Linguistics
and Poetics* (Janua Linguarum, Series Maior 63; The Hague/Paris: Mouton,
1972) 160.

[2] "[E]verybody will construct the macro-structure for a text which is
relevant to him, personally, and these macro-structures will be different for
the same text" (*Some Aspects of Text Grammars*, 161).

a macro-structure in the understanding of a text with his statement that we do not approach a text without expecting something from it.

The purpose of the first part of this study of Galatians and Romans is to develop a macro-structure for reading these letters. That will mean more than expecting something of the text. In that regard, the procedure I will follow in this first part can be understood as a thinking through of Bultmann's hermeneutical circle. It will be not a theoretical thinking through of the phenomenon in general, but an attempt to describe concretely the macro-structure of Galatians and Romans. These letters have enough in common at a fundamental level to allow us to approach them with a single macro-structure. Within this macro-structure certain individual features—such as the actual figures Paul uses to convey his meaning, and the way the letters are structured—can be understood as two variants of the same macro-structure. Accordingly, Part I will conclude with a chapter on the common features of their macro-structure. The theme of Paul's thought in Romans, that the gospel is the power of God to salvation for all who believe, "to the Jews first, and to the gentiles" (Rom 1:16), expresses a theme also present in Galatians: "we who are by heritage Jews, and not from the gentiles, sinners, . . . we too believed in Christ Jesus in order to be justified from the faith of Christ" (Gal 2:15–16). That theme is a determining factor in Paul's thinking in both letters.

Unlike *Neither on this Mountain nor in Jerusalem. A Study of John 4*,[3] this volume is, to be precise, not a study in semiotics, but a semiotic study of Galatians and Romans. By that I mean, I will not focus on semiotic methodology itself, but will investigate these two letters of Paul utilizing the methodological complex: text-linguistics, structuralism, and semiotics. I do not intend here to offer a quick course on text-linguistics, structuralism, or semiotics, but I would like to underscore how such methodological considerations aided my investigation of Paul's thought. This methodology will be clarified where necessary, but it will be self-explanatory most of the time.

THE ANTICIPATION OF CERTAIN INSIGHTS OF LINGUISTICS IN WREDE AND BULTMANN

The methodological configuration which I have referred to as text-linguistics–structuralism–semiotics is not completely new, especially not in the way I use it as an aid in the interpretation of texts. The primary significance of this configuration is that features tradi-

---

[3]SBLMS 35; Atlanta: Scholars Press, 1988.

tionally recognized as part of the interpretation receive particular methodological attention before the actual process of interpretation begins. That this methodological configuration is not new, but a refinement of features of traditional New Testament interpretation, can be shown by two examples: the first is the anticipation of a structuralist understanding of meaning by William Wrede; the second is the anticipation of some of the insights of semiotics in the phenomenon that Bultmann refers to as *Sachkritik*. Here we note only a general feature or two of their thought which demonstrates how they anticipated later developments. More will be said about Wrede and Bultmann in the next chapter.

A structuralist understanding of meaning originated in the linguistics of Ferdinand de Saussure, the father of structuralism.[4] According to this view, the meaning of individual words is determined by their relationship to all other words in a given language. A simple way to explain this is illustrated by colors. The meaning of the word *green* in a given language is determined by the other words used in that language to give expression to the color spectrum. As a result, the color range referred to by the word *green* may differ from language to language. The only way to determine the meaning of *green* in a particular language is by establishing which other colors are differentiated in that language and how they relate to *green*. Similarly the meanings of words for *dwelling* in various languages differ according to the range of words used to distinguish various types of dwellings. Compare, for example, the English range: castle, palace, mansion, house, home, apartment (or flat), cottage, hovel, hut, shack, shanty, or the German: Festung, Burg, Schloß, Palast, Haus, Wohnung, Schuppen, Hütte, Bude, with what is available in Indian, Asian, African, American Indian, or Eskimo languages.[5]

---

[4]In his lectures, *Cours de linguistique générale* (ed. Charles Bally and Charles Albert Sechehaye; Paris: Payot 1916). ET, *Course in General Linguistics* (by Wade Baskin, New York: Philosophical Library, 1959).

[5]What can be achieved in this way is shown by Johannes P. Louw and Eugene A. Nida's *Greek-English Lexicon of the New Testament Based on Semantic Domains* (2 vols.; New York: United Bible Societies, 1988). In this lexicon words are not listed alphabetically followed by definitions: all the words in the Greek New Testament are arranged in a first volume in what are called semantic domains and subdomains of related meanings, for example, "Geographical Objects and Features," or "Body, Body Parts, and Body Products." A second volume lists the New Testament Greek words alphabetically, indicating where they can be found in the first volume. In this way it becomes possible to determine where in the spectrum of meaning in New Testament Greek a word like σάρξ has its place, and to what other words it is closely related. It takes little imagination to realize that σάρξ will be found in that spectrum of meaning in the area of the physical body as well as in the area of moral qualities, to mention only two.

This understanding of meaning in language was anticipated by William Wrede in his famous essay, "The Task and Methods of New Testament Theology,"[6] in which he protested against the "wrong-headed" approach of squeezing "as much conceptual capital from every single phrase and every casually chosen expression used by an author" as possible. According to him, the sense of a term "has rather to be oriented on a few decisive conceptions of the author, so that the main lines of its meaning can be given. In the case of the concept πίστις, this will involve the characteristically Pauline view of its object and in the case of σάρξ, what he says about ἁμαρτία, δικαιοσύνη, νόμος, θάνατος, αἰών οὗτος, πνεῦμα, etc."[7] This is not yet an advanced linguistic view, but Wrede understood clearly that in ordinary language the meaning of words is not inherent in the words themselves but is determined by their relationships to other words.

In his theory of *Sachkritik*, Bultmann anticipated semiotics and some of its insights. There is hardly anyone who has not experienced the functioning of *Sachkritik* in daily life. A person tries to say something but is not quite able to bring her or his point across, and then the listener suggests, "Is this not what you are trying to say?" The listener then proceeds to say what the other was trying unsuccessfully to communicate. What we try to communicate and the way we express it are hardly ever in complete agreement, and the listener or reader is sometimes able to discover our meaning, not in the expressions themselves, but, so to speak, by penetrating to the intended meaning *through* the expressions. There are few people who can put their thoughts on paper in a first attempt. I have been told that Bultmann was able to do that, and I remember Martin Noth in Bonn, lecturing "publication-ready" with nothing more than a fascicle of the Kittel text of Exodus in front of him. Most of us discover that our first drafts inadequately convey the meanings we intend.

An ancient example of this same phenomenon in a positive form is Socrates' masterful eliciting of correct mathematical (geometric) answers from Meno's uneducated young servant in Plato's dialogue of the same name. That an uneducated person can give answers that agree with fundamental geometric principles proves that those principles are not products of education, but inherent in human thought.

[6]ET in Robert Morgan, *The Nature of New Testament Theology* (London: SCM Press/Naperville, Ill.: Alec R. Allenson, 1973) 68–116. *Über Aufgabe und Methode der sogenannten neutestamentlichen Theologie* (Göttingen: Vandenhoeck & Ruprecht, 1897). Repr. in *Das Problem der Theologie des neuen Testaments* (ed. Georg Strecker; Darmstadt: Wissenschaftliche Buchgesellschaft, 1975) 81–154.

[7]"The Task and Methods of New Testament Theology," 77; *Über Aufgabe und Methode der sogenannten neutestamentlichen Theologie*, 96–97.

A major aspect of the task of semiotics is to clarify how the phenomenon that Bultmann referred to as *Sachkritik* functions: how do we express meaning in language, and how is meaning communicated in language? How do we understand meaning as expressed in a language?

A step in the direction to this understanding of language was also made by Karl Barth when he insisted that the task of interpretation was not complete with the mere commenting on what "stands there" but had to proceed to the question about what is meant. Bultmann's *Sachkritik* was a further, more radical step along the way proposed by Barth.

1 ～

Towards a Semiotic, Text-Linguistic, Method of Interpretation

INTRODUCTION

This chapter will take a first step toward developing an interpretive framework, a macro-structure, for interpreting Paul's letters to the Galatians and the Romans. Before taking that step, however, I must clarify certain methodological features employed in this investigation referred to earlier as the methodological configuration, text-linguistics–structuralism–semiotics. The three components of this configuration are closely related and cannot be separated. Nevertheless, they may be distinguished as follows: Text-linguistics is primarily concerned with the syntactic linkage of sentences in a discourse—written as well as oral—and with the way language functions in the communication of meaning.[1] The specific emphasis of structuralism in this configuration is related to the fact that meaning does not reside in words themselves, but is an effect that arises from the way words are structured and interrelated in a language, and that depends on the ways in which words are linked syntactically to express meaning in a discourse. Text-linguistics and structuralism are both concerned with how meaning transpires in language, which is what I understand to be the specific concern of semiotics: Language as the system of signs through which meaning is expressed.

As I indicated in the Preface, I do not intend here to offer a quick course on text-linguistics, structuralism, or semiotics, but to clarify how those three disciplines assisted my investigation of Paul's thought in Galatians and Romans. In this chapter I will do so

---

[1]A fine, readable, interesting introduction to text-linguistics is the work by Robert-Alain de Beaugrande and Wolfgang Dressler, *Introduction to Text-linguistics* (London: Longmans, 1981).

by showing how the problem of the interpretation of Romans 2 within the structure of Romans poses a challenge to semiotics. I will then proceed to the main task of taking a first step toward a macro-structure for Galatians and Romans by considering the insights of a number of interpreters of Paul. This will allow us to focus on what is at issue in the apostle's thinking.

I. ROMANS 2 AS A PROBLEM OF INTERPRETA-TION AND AS A CHALLENGE TO SEMIOTICS

It is well-known that Romans 2, either as a whole or parts of it, does not fit well with the meaning of the letter as it is generally understood. In Rom 2:13 Paul writes, "Not the hearers of the Law are just before God, but the doers will be justified," and then, in 3:20, "through works of the Law no one will be justified before him, for through the Law is the recognition of sin." The two verses apparently contradict each other: the doers of the Law will be justified (2:13), but through works of the Law no one will be justified (3:20).

Not only Rom 2:13 stands in opposition to what is generally perceived as a central feature of Paul's thinking, namely, justification sola fide. This verse is but the tip of an iceberg. All of chapter 2 stands out as an admirable apology for justification through works. According to Rom 2:7, God will reward "those who, through the patience of good works, seek glory and honor and immortality" with "eternal life," and according to verse 10 there will be "glory and honor and peace for everyone who does good." The chapter ends with Paul's assurance that the gentile who carries out τά δικαιώματα τοῦ νόμου will receive "praise, not from human beings, but from God" (2:29).

In a linguistic sense, interpreters throughout the history of the interpretation of Paul have resolved the problem of Romans 2 by taking the rest of the letter, understood in the traditional sense of a negation of justification through the doing of good works, as the main text which determines the meaning of the entire letter. Romans 2—or the parts that do not fit that meaning—is then read in a way that is consistent with the rest of the letter. In that way, before the process of interpretation begins, the reading of Romans is predetermined in such a way that one part of the letter determines how another is to be read. In reality this predetermination of how chapter 2 is to be read also determines the meaning of the rest of the letter. By leaving out of consideration the possible influence of chapter 2 on the meaning of Romans, the traditional understanding is reinforced. Our understanding of the letter would be different if chapter 2 were allowed to co-determine its meaning.[2]

By subordinating chapter 2 of Romans to what is perceived as the meaning of the rest of the letter, the traditional interpreter of Romans, without being aware of it, constructs the text of Romans before beginning the process of interpretation. This may be formulated text-linguistically: Out of the series of sentences in the letter a text is constructed. Such a construction of the text of the letter was recently carried out with clarity and a new consistency by

---

[2]What takes place linguistically in these procedures can be clarified by the following considerations. The basic truth about semiotics which concerns me in the interpretation of texts is that a text is not something solid, but dynamic. Take the sentence, "That is the man." Four words linked by a syntactic structure: a demonstrative pronoun, a verb, an article and a noun. It says nothing. To put it simply, it is not a text, but, as I said, four words that are syntactically linked. But it has the potential of saying something, of becoming a text. I will illustrate how this can happen. My illustration will not make this sentence into a text, but will show how it could become a text.

To begin with, the textual potentiality of this sentence is not single but multiple; it could be a number of completely different texts. Let us try just two:

That is the man.
That is the *man.*

Even with this way of placing the accent on different words in the sentence we have not limited its potential meanings to two. Each of these two accented forms of the sentence could themselves still have a number of meanings. Let us nevertheless limit ourselves to two possibilities: In the first case we identify a man as the one we are looking for. I will give the meaning of the second by adding a second clause, "but where is the woman?" What we did text-linguistically in this way was to show how two texts could be constructed from the meaningless, but potentially meaningful sentence, "That is the man."

This is an exceedingly simple example, but if there is such a great potential of textuality in such a simple sentence, how much more exists in longer stretches of sentences, such as we find in Paul's letters to the Galatians and to the Romans.

One might say that we have always been aware of this in the interpretation of texts. But have we? In the history of interpretation we have been aware that written documents can have different meanings, but have we been aware that what we have in the strings of sentences in a single version of the New Testament is not a single text, but a potential variety of texts? An awareness of what is at issue is reflected in the rule of interpretation that a verse or a passage has to be interpreted in its context. What semiotics does is to investigate in a separate methodological step what appears here as part of the process of interpretation already in progress. Whereas the rule of interpretation that a passage has to be interpreted in its context is already part of the method of interpretation, semiotics understands such an issue as something that needs to be considered separately, before the process of interpretation begins.

E. P. Sanders in *Paul, the Law, and the Jewish People*. Recognizing
the unsatisfactory nature of the attempts to reconcile chapter 2 with
the rest of the letter,[3] Sanders constructed the text of Romans by
excluding that chapter from consideration in his interpretation,
discussing it separately in an appendix, because what "is said about
the law in Romans 2 cannot be fitted into a category otherwise known
from Paul's letters."[4]

It should be clear that, whether one subjects the interpretation of chapter 2 to the accepted meaning of the rest of Romans, or
removes the chapter from the letter in the process of interpretation,
the interpreter *constructs* a text from the written document before
beginning the process of interpretation. There is no other way of
proceeding. The text-linguist merely turns this procedure into a
conscious process for which the interpreter is methodologically
answerable. Sanders' removal of chapter 2 from consideration was a
step toward such a conscious move.

From a semiotic point of view, the tension between Romans
2 and the rest of Romans should be considered, not as a problem to
be avoided, but as a promising starting point for deepening our
understanding of the letter and, in addition to that, of Paul's thinking. Even if we were to assume that chapter 2 is not Paul's own
formulation but was drawn from a Diaspora synagogue tradition as
Sanders proposes,[5] we still must ask how Paul perceived justification by faith apart from works, his supposed main topic, since he was
able to write what stands in the chapter. In a semiotic approach the
interpreter would not try to reconcile the chapter with the rest of
what is considered normative in Paul's thinking by a prior interpretive decision; neither would the interpreter completely eliminate it
from consideration. Rather, such an approach would construct the
text of Romans by including chapter 2 before beginning the process
of interpretation.

One way of doing this would be to interpret Paul not as a
theological thinker for whom contradictions in thought are intolerable, but as a religious thinker for whom contradictory statements
and the way of coping with them are part of the thinking process, as
Claude Lévi–Strauss, the French structural anthropologist, suggested

---

[3]Sanders lists a number of these proposals and concludes that none
is satisfactory (*Paul, the Law, and the Jewish People*, 125–27). His own
solution is that Rom 1:18–2:29 is a Diaspora synagogue sermon (129), but he
is unable to give more than tentative explanations as to why Paul used
this material that, according to Sanders, does not fit into his own thinking
(131–32).

[4]*Paul, the Law, and the Jewish People*, 132.

[5]*Paul, the Law, and the Jewish People*, 129.

for religious texts.[6] In that case Paul's thinking would take place within the field of tension created by the contradictory statements. Paul proclaims both justification by faith apart from works and the opposite doctrine of justification though works as two poles within which his thinking takes place, neither of which, by itself, expresses his intended meaning.[7] I remain convinced that Paul's thinking is grounded in irreconcilable oppositions, but further work in interpreting him, still using text-linguistic–structuralist–semiotic methods of interpretation, has convinced me that whatever contradictions may exist in Paul, the contradiction between justification by faith and justification through works is not one of them.

II. TOWARD A MACRO-STRUCTURE FOR GALATIANS AND ROMANS

As I indicated above, the main purpose of this chapter is to take a first step toward developing a macro-structure, an interpretive framework, for understanding Paul's letters to the Galatians and the Romans. This first step will not yet focus specifically on Galatians and Romans, but on Paul's thought in general. To use Bultmann's formulation, we will determine what we are going to look for in our interpretation of these letters. To do this, I will concentrate on some of the fundamental issues in recent scholarship. I will not rehearse the history of the interpretation of Paul; my concern is not with Pauline scholarship in general, but with those issues in Pauline scholarship that can help focus our investigation in such a way that we can enter into it with an informed idea of what it is we seek. In a second step, in chapters 2 and 3, respectively, I will identify a specific macro-structure for Galatians and Romans. These letters have so much in common semantically that, in addition to the specific macro-structures which relate to the particular features of

---

[6]To be more precise, Lévi–Strauss discovers this type of thinking in mythical texts. See, for example, "The Structural Study of Myth," *Myth, A Symposium, Journal of American Folklore* 78 (1955) 428–44. Translated with some additions and modifications as "La Structure des mythes," *Anthropologie Structurale* (Paris: Plon, 1958), vol. 1, 225–55. ET, *Structural Anthropology* (by Claire Jacobson and Brooke Grundfest Schoeps, New York: Basic Books, Inc., 1963; paperback: Doubleday Anchor Book, 1967) vol. 1, 202–28.

[7]I have tried to show how such an interpretation could be explored in "Interpreting Paul: Demythologizing in Reverse," in *The Philosophy of Order. Essays on History, Consciousness and Politics in Honor of Eric Voegelin* (ed. Peter J. Opitz and Gregor Sebba; Stuttgart: Klett-Cotta, 1980) 153–72.

each letter, one can speak of a common semantic macro-structure for both letters, which is the topic of chapter 4.

I am inclined to begin the investigation in this chapter where my own interest in New Testament scholarship found fruitful soil, namely, with the *religionsgeschichtliche Schule*. The concerns of that "School" dominate this study: uncovering the sources in human experience from which Paul's thinking arose. According to the *religionsgeschichtliche Schule*, New Testament thought was grounded in the developing Christian religion, as reflected in all the documents of New Testament times, not only those that became part of the New Testament canon. A significant feature of the *religionsgeschichtliche Schule* from a semiotic point of view comes to expression in Wrede's understanding that the location of meaning in the New Testament is not in the New Testament text itself, but in the living, developing religion of which the New Testament was a partial expression. According to Wrede, "In a living religion almost every significant shift in outlook is determined by religious historical processes, and only in a minor way by literature."[8] The New Testament literature is an expression of meaning: the location of that meaning is in the living religion of New Testament times.

The dialectical theology movement initiated by Barth's interpretation of Romans ended prematurely the *religionsgeschichtliche Schule*'s approach to the interpretation of the New Testament. The early deaths of eminent New Testament members of that "school," William Wrede (1859–1906), Johannes Weiß (1863–1914), Wilhelm Heitmüller (1869–1926) and Wilhelm Bousset (1884–1920), contributed significantly to the extent to which dialectical theology came to dominate theology in the second quarter of this century. After the appearance of Barth's *Der Römerbrief* in 1919, only Bousset and Heitmüller of those mentioned above remained briefly on the scene. How little the questions of the *religionsgeschichtliche Schule* remained part of New Testament scholarship during the period that followed is shown by a remark by that eminent second generation member of the "School," Rudolf Bultmann, in the fifth edition of Bousset's *Kyrios Christos*. "In conclusion a word is necessary concerning the *religionsgeschichtliche Schule*'s objective to present the *religion* of primitive Christianity and to use the New Testament for that purpose. Today we would ask whether this objective could do justice to the New Testament; whether we should not return to the earlier question concerning the *theology* of the New Testament."[9]

---

[8] *Über Aufgabe und Methode der sogenannten neutestamentlichen Theologie*, 102. ET, "The Task and Methods of New Testament Theology," in Robert Morgan, *The Nature of New Testament Theology*, 68–116.

[9] *Kyrios Christos*, VI.

Even though Bultmann defends the school in its objective, he does so in the sense of a theology of the New Testament: "It should be borne in mind that the goal of investigating the religion of the New Testament instead of the theology of the New Testament was grounded in the opposition of the *religionsgeschichtliche Schule* to the dominant conception of the time (when one leaves out of consideration the exception of [Adolf] Schlatter) . . . to investigate the so-called doctrines. In that regard the *religionsgeschichtliche Schule* is a decisive step towards a better understanding of the New Testament. The question concerning the religion [of the New Testament] is fundamentally to ask for the existential meaning of the *theological* statements in the New Testament."[10] Bultmann's own work, culminating in his two-volume *Theology of the New Testament*, is a fitting example of such a transition from the religion of the New Testament to its theology.

Every religious historical approach to the study of the New Testament, that is, every study of the religious thought of the Hellenistic period as a means of shedding light on the New Testament, does not bear a specific relationship to the *religionsgeschichtliche Schule*. Such work could be theological, as the example of Bultmann shows. The specific understanding of the *religionsgeschichtliche Schule* was that the New Testament was the product of a religion, not of theological reflection. Crucial for the "School" was a new understanding of history under the influence of the rise of sociology. The New Testament was understood as rooted in human history.

I have nevertheless found that the most fruitful approach for our purpose here—the interpretation of Galatians and Romans—is to begin not with the *religionsgeschichtliche Schule*, but at that great turning point in the interpretation of Paul that was signalled by Karl Barth's interpretation of Romans. Barth's concern for an overall meaning goes beyond mere comments on individual words, sentences and groups of sentences, thus anticipating some of the text-linguistic, structural, and semiotic concerns fundamental to the present investigation.

Recognizing that Paul was not a systematic thinker forces us to focus on the center of his thought rather than on systematic coherence as the means of understanding him. This concern characterizes in one way or another the views of the scholars I would like to consider in this first step toward developing a macro-structure for the study of Paul's thought in Galatians and Romans: Karl Barth, Rudolf Bultmann, Ernst Käsemann, J. Christiaan Beker, and Daniel Patte.

---

[10] *Kyrios Christos*, VI (my emphasis).

Barth is important for a contemporary understanding of Paul, not merely because *Der Römerbrief* marks the beginning of dialectical theology, but because his interpretation of Romans was not a series of comments on individual verses, but an attempt to understand what Paul was trying to bring to expression in this letter. As Barth writes, the task is "to press forward to *understand* Paul, that is, to find out how what stands written could be, not merely somehow repeated in Greek or German, but *thought*; [to find out] how it could have been *meant*."[11] Bultmann took a step beyond the distinction between what is written and what is meant in his critique of Barth. Believing that Barth stopped short, Bultmann maintained that the only way to understand Paul was by a consistent practice of *Sachkritik* which distinguishes between what Paul means and his expression of that meaning in words and concepts.[12] The importance of Käsemann is that he called attention back to a feature in Paul which Barth implicitly and Bultmann explicitly considered as a mere form of expression, Paul's apocalypticism. Käsemann considered apocalypticism as the expression of a crucial meaning in Paul. In that way Käsemann drew attention back to the question of the meaning expressed in Paul's apocalyptic statements. The methodological question concerning the interpretation of Paul was addressed with unequalled clarity by Beker. Most significant is his distinction between a coherent center of meaning in Paul's thinking and the contingent expressions of this meaning as Paul addressed concrete issues in his letters. This methodological problem was then addressed by Patte with a structural approach that enabled him to distinguish between the deeper level of the system of beliefs in which Paul's thinking is grounded, and Paul's argumentation as the means of communicating concretely with his readers. To each of these we now turn our attention.

A. *Karl Barth*

In his commentary on Romans, Barth advanced greatly the interpretation of Paul by focussing on a single, central idea, which he took over from Kierkegaard. "If I have a 'system' it would be that I keep in mind what Kierkegaard called the 'infinite qualitative difference' between time and eternity. 'God is in heaven and you are

---

[11] *Der Römerbrief*, X; ET, 6.
[12] See especially Bultmann's review of Karl Barth's interpretation of 1 Corinthians in "Karl Barth, 'Die Auferstehung der Toten,' " *TBl* 5 (1925) 1–24; repr. in Rudolf Bultmann, *GuV* (Tübingen: J. C. B. Mohr [Paul Siebeck], 1958), vol. 1, 38–64; ET, "Karl Barth, The Resurrection of the Dead," *Faith and Understanding* (by L. P. Smith; New York: Harper and Row, 1969) 66–94.

on earth.' The relationship of *this* God to *this* human being, and the relationship of *this* human being to *this* God is for me at the same time the theme of the Bible and the sum of philosophy."[13] Barth was persuaded that this relation was also fundamental for Paul.[14] According to Barth, Paul understood God's judgment to have ended all of history. There was no continuity of the present history on the other side of God's judgment. "God's judgment is the *end* of history, not the beginning of a new second history. It is finished with history; [history] does not continue. What lies on the other side of [God's] judgment is not relatively, but absolutely different and separated from what is on this side."[15] It was a resurrection from death, as he eloquently argued in *Die Auferstehung der Toten*. Death was a zero point from which resurrection was an entirely new beginning. Barth eloquently expressed this relationship between time and eternity by commenting on Paul's simile in 1 Cor 15:36–38, cf. 42–44a, of the seed which grows into a plant. "But in between [the seed and the plant] there is somehow a critical point at which the seed itself has to die and pass over in the totality of its being into the developing plant. Does it mean decay? Certainly, but equally certainly also becoming! That is the critical point we have in mind when we interpret seed and plant as identical, even if all the predicates of the seed are abandoned here; all the predicates of the plant are assumed, even though this permutation of predicates is completely incomprehensible, for us the same as total discontinuity. The zero point is at the same time the synthesis of the positive and the negative sides."[16] Barth's was a more radical dehistoricizing of eschatology than Rudolf Bultmann's. Faith meant recognizing the complete lack of personal value before God and before fellow human beings. "Nothing human remains which claims to be more than a vacuum, privation, possibility and illusion, as the least impressive of all phenomena in this world, as dust and ashes before God, like everything [else] in the world. Faith remains only as faith, without personal value (also without the personal value of self-denial), without personal power (also without the personal power of humility!), without trying to be somebody, neither before God nor before fellow human beings."[17]

What is appealing about this aspect of Barth's interpretation of Paul, in Romans as well as in 1 Corinthians, is his consistency in applying his proposed fundamental principle. However, one cannot

---

[13] *Der Römerbrief*, XIII; ET, 10.
[14] "Daß ich weiß, daß Paulus dies weiß, das ist mein 'System' " (*Der Römerbrief*, XIV; ET, 11).
[15] *Der Römerbrief*, 51; ET, 77.
[16] *Die Auferstehung der Toten*, 111; ET, 187.
[17] *Der Römerbrief*, 84; ET, 110.

escape the sense that it was a principle which Barth did not derive from the text, but rather imposed on it. That does not mean that what he described as the "infinite qualitative difference between time and eternity" was not a factor in Paul's thinking. It is indeed an important feature in his letters, but it is not the center from which everything else becomes meaningful. The problem surfaced in Bultmann's argument that Barth's interpretation left certain features of Paul's thinking beyond comprehension, for example, his apocalyptic statements. The problem with Barth's interpretation was the single-mindedness with which he applied the proposed principle in his interpretation of Paul. The very strength of his interpretation, its consistency, was also its weakness. Nevertheless, he showed that one could interpret Paul by focusing on a single central conception, rather than by attempting to interpret him as if he were a systematic thinker.

Barth understood clearly what can now be formulated text-linguistically and semiotically: the meaning of a text cannot be found in the words or even sentences themselves, in what "stands there" in the text, as he formulates it, but in what is brought to expression in them and in their interrelatedness, that is, in what is meant by the text. Barth affirms the importance of historical inquiry, but he is amazed at how little meaning was sufficient to satisfy the historical-critical interpreters who preceded him. "Indeed, I object to the recent commentaries to the Epistle to the Romans, but certainly not only to the so-called historical-critical ones, but also, for example, to Zahn and Kühl. But what I disapprove in them is not historical criticism, the validity and necessity of which I once more affirm explicitly; [what I disapprove of is] that they end with an interpretation which I cannot recognize as an interpretation, but only the first primitive attempts at [an interpretation], namely, the establishment of 'what stands there' through translation and description of the Greek words and phrases in corresponding German. . . ."[18] He recognizes that these interpreters "did actually want to move beyond that primitive level to [where they could] *understand* Paul, that is, to detect how what is written could, so to speak, not only be repeated in Greek or German, but also *thought* ('nach-*gedacht*') in terms of what might be *meant*. And *here* the disagreement begins, not in the undisputed use of historical criticism in preparing for the interpretation that needs to follow. Whereas I pay careful attention to the historians, with gratitude, as long as they are involved in those primitive interpretative attempts; whereas I would not in the wildest dreams have dared to do anything else than to sit, simply listening, at the feet of such learned men as Jülicher, Lietzmann, Zahn, Kühl, and their predeces-

---

[18] *Der Römerbrief*, X; ET, 6.

sors, Tholuck, Meyer, B. Weiß, and Lipsius, when it concerned the determination of 'what stands there,' I am ever again amazed about the modesty of their expectations when I consider their attempts to move forward to actual *understanding* and *interpreting*. Actual understanding and interpretation I call that activity which Luther practiced with intuitive command, which Calvin evidently systematically set as the objective of his exegesis, and which was clearly at least the aim of Hofmann, J.T. Beck, Godet, and Schlatter among the more recent interpreters."[19]

From a linguistics point of view, Barth's criticism shows that the historical commentaries are closer to dictionaries of words and phrases than to the interpretation of texts, except that these commentaries do not discuss the words and phrases alphabetically, but as they occur in the biblical writings. The meaning of a text is not the sum of the meanings of the individual words and phrases, but an effect that arises from the way in which words, phrases, sentences, and even paragraphs are structured, text-syntactically and semantically. We will return to the textual understanding in more detail below. At this point it is important to note that Barth already recognized that meaning comes to expression in a text as an effect that is more than the sum of the meanings of the individual words and phrases. What he did not see was that meaning is not bound to the verbal expressions in the text, but sometimes has to be discerned by penetrating beyond the expressions. This became the crucial issue in the controversy concerning *Sachkritik* between Barth and Bultmann.

B. *Rudolf Bultmann*

In his insistence on *Sachkritik* Bultmann took an important step beyond Barth towards an interpretation of Paul that sought a level of meaning more fundamental than the concreteness of Paul's actual expressions. While agreeing with Barth on what was central to Paul's thought in Romans and in 1 Corinthians, he argued that there was not always complete agreement between *what* Paul tried to express and his *means* of doing so. "Does Paul in 1 Corinthians 15 speak about the *last* things in this [Barth's] sense? Of the end of history ('Endgeschichte')?"[20] he asks; and replies, "He does indeed do so; but he does so by speaking of the last *things*, of the 'final history' ('Schlußgeschichte'), which Barth correctly distinguishes from the end of history in the above-mentioned sense. Final history is, quoting Barth, 'history at the conclusion of history . . . at a point

---

[19] *Der Römerbrief*, X–XI; ET, 6–7.
[20] "Karl Barth, *Die Auferstehung der Toten*," 51; ET, 80.

beyond the possibilities known to us, but nonetheless as a new, unknown, further possibility, linked to the former in an unbroken series, even when, as a result of unheard-of catastrophes, [this final history] may surpass and continue [the present] at a higher level.' It appears to me as certain that Paul speaks of such a history in 1 Corinthians 15 as it is that he cannot and does not want to speak of it. In other words one cannot avoid *Sachkritik* in 1 Corinthians 15 (and not only occasionally, as Barth after all does, for example, in verse 29)."[21]

This central feature of Paul's thinking, according to Bultmann, was not bound to his expressions, but was articulated through them, and not always with equal success. Paul brought his thoughts about the end of history to expression by writing about the last events in history. The apocalyptic-mythological means of expressing his thoughts did not have as its objective the mythical ideas themselves, but was a form of thinking which was available to Paul and his readers within their religious culture. "For as little as Paul proclaimed a 'world view,' so completely was he, like everybody else, bound to say what he had to say in the concepts of his world view. And it is not appropriate to declare the elements of the world view, which is in this case mythological, simply as 'symbolic' ('Gleichnis') and to remove them by reinterpretation ('Umdeutung'). What Barth concedes for later Christian eschatologists—that they construe out of the biblical materials a final history which was in truth not an end of history at all ('eine in Wahrheit nicht endgeschichtliche Schluß-geschichte')—applies to Paul as well, who takes his material from Jewish or Jewish-gnostic Apocalypticism."[22] Thus Bultmann exposed a methodological weakness in Barth's approach. Barth was not able to cope with expressions of Paul's thought that did not fit his proposed fundamental principle, specifically the apocalyptic conceptions. Bultmann too was unable to make sense of the ideas in themselves, but he was at least able to recognize their presence and the necessity of dealing with them. In that way, he allowed his own interpretation to be questioned, as was subsequently done by Käsemann.

The distinction between *what* was expressed and the *means* of expressing it lies at the root of Bultmann's program of demythologizing. With his famous statement that the myth did not want to provide an objective world view, but expressed the way in which human beings understood themselves in the world, Bultmann moved from the expressions to what was behind them, giving coherent meaning to Paul's thought notwithstanding its frequent lack of cohe-

---

[21] "Karl Barth, *Die Auferstehung der Toten*," 52; ET, 80–81.
[22] "Karl Barth, *Die Auferstehung der Toten*," 52; ET, 82.

sion. "The real sense of the myth is not to provide an objective world view; rather, in the myth comes to expression how a person understands [her- or] himself in [her or] his world. The myth does not want to be interpreted cosmologically, but anthropologically—better still, existentialistically."[23] This was an important interpretive principle for Bultmann, not only concerning Paul, but also concerning all the New Testament. Unlike Barth's center, however, it was not a systematic *idea*, but an understanding of the way in which meaning was conveyed in Paul's writings. Bultmann's principle of interpretation was universal and free of value. He could use it to interpret texts relating contrary points of view as well.

By distinguishing between meaning and expression, Bultmann was better able than Barth to deal with the apocalyptic conceptions in Paul without abandoning Barth's dehistoricized eschatology. More importantly, Bultmann's method did not allow the expressions that contradicted what he thought was Paul's meaning to recede from the interpreter's view. The question that remained, however, was: what in Paul's writings was meaning, and what was merely the means of expression. Like Barth, Bultmann did not attribute to the apocalyptic expressions the significance they deserved, but methodologically he opened the way for them to assert themselves and to serve as the basis for a critique of Bultmann's own understanding of Paul's meaning.

C. *Ernst Käsemann*

It was Käsemann who carried out that critique most consistently. The basis for his critique was not primarily methodological, but was rooted in his conviction that history was decisive for the interpretation of the New Testament. He first formulated his views in connection with the issue of the quest for the historical Jesus, initially, in 1954, with "Das Problem des historischen Jesus,"[24] and again, ten years later, in 1964, in his assessment of the so-called new quest of the historical Jesus, with "Sackgassen im Streit um den historischen Jesus."[25] The same concern was expressed in connec-

---

[23] "Neues Testament und Mythologie," *Kerygma und Mythos* (ed. H.-W. Bartsch; Hamburg: Herbert Reich, vol. 1, 1948, 2d ed. 1951) 22. ET, "The New Testament and Mythology," *Kerygma and Myth* (by Reginald Fuller, London: SPCK, 1953) 10.

[24] *ZThK* 15 (1954) 125–53; repr. in Ernst Käsemann, *EVuB* (Göttingen: Vandenhoeck & Ruprecht, 1960) vol. 1, 187–213; ET, "The Problem of the Historical Jesus," *Essays on New Testament Themes* (by W. J. Montague, London: SCM Press Ltd.) 15–47.

[25] *EVuB*, vol. 2, 1964, 31–69; ET, "Blind Alleys in the 'Jesus of History' Controversy," *New Testament Questions of Today* (by W. J. Montague, London: SCM Press Ltd., 1969) 23–65.

tion with apocalypticism in the New Testament in two essays, "Die Anfänge christlicher Theologie" (1960),[26] and "Zum Thema der urchristlichen Apokalyptik" (1962).[27]

Käsemann's concern for history sought to recognize the historical-apocalyptic dimension of Paul's thinking without surrendering the existential-eschatological dimension which had been so crucial for Barth and Bultmann. This is apparent in the following statements which emphasize the same break in eschatological continuity which Barth perceived in 1 Corinthians 15: "The conception of an immanent continuity of life is alien to Paul. Wherever we speak of development he reaches for the idea of a miracle which bridges the gap between oppositions. So baptism marks the death of the old person and the miraculous beginning of a new life under the sign of the resurrection. Accordingly Gal 2:20 declares, 'It is not I who still live; Christ lives in me.' "[28]

Käsemann was able to maintain both dimensions, the existential-eschatological and the historical-apocalyptic, in the single Pauline formula, "justification of the ungodly." According to him, in the existential-eschatological dimension, the expression refers primarily and concretely to the believer, but it would lose its meaning if it were restricted solely to that dimension and did not also pronounce salvation in an historical-apocalyptic dimension. "Justification of the sinner in the first place certainly concerns me concretely. But this formula loses its significance when it does not announce salvation for every human being and the entire world. For the ungodly too is found only in the entanglement of everything earthly in sin and death. . . ."[29] The justified sinner does not escape from the world, but remains part of it. This is signified by the meaning of "body" in Paul, which Käsemann defines as "dieses Stück Welt das ich bin," "this piece of the world that I am," that is, the human necessity to participate in creation. Ontologically, "one can state that having a body ('Leiblichkeit') is essential to the human being in its necessity to participate in creatureliness, and in the ability to communicate in the widest possible sense, that is, in its dependence on the world as presented to it in every given moment."[30] In that sense justification of the sinner functions as a powerful center in Käsemann's interpretation of Paul's thought, holding together its existen-

---

[26] *ZThK* 57 (1960), 162–85; repr. in *EVuB*, vol. 2, 1964, 82–104; ET, "The Beginnings of Christian Theology," *Questions*, 82–107.

[27] *ZThK* 59 (1962), 257–84; repr. in *EVuB*, vol. 2, 105–31; ET, "On the Subject of Primitive Christian Apocalyptic," *Questions*, 108–37.

[28] *Paulinische Perspektiven*, 20; ET, 8.

[29] *Paulinische Perspektiven*, 138–39; ET, 78.

[30] *Paulinische Perspektiven*, 43; ET, 21.

tial as well as its historical dimensions. "Paul does not have a fixed exegetical method and did not develop a closed dogmatic system. But he does have a theme which controls his entire theology: the doctrine of justification. Not only did that give him a 'hermeneutical starting point'; it determined his interpretation of Scripture throughout, that is, critically from the perspective of the antithesis of Law and Gospel."[31]

Like Barth and Bultmann, Käsemann thus also interpreted Paul in terms of a center of his thought, but for Käsemann that center was not limited to the existential dimension of the believer's relationship to God; it included the historical dimension of being bound to the world, in which salvation through the death of Christ signified God's kingdom on earth. "For Paul justification of the sinner is the fruit of the death of Jesus: nothing more. But that means the Regnum Dei on earth."[32]

The center out of which Käsemann interpreted Paul enabled him to take up positively Paul's expressions concerning the world and history, but his interpretation was not without its limitations: it did not go far enough in affirming the historical dimension. Käsemann was unable to interpret positively Paul's statements concerning justification through works of the Law. According to his interpretation the true meaning of the Law was disclosed only within the framework of faith. The Jews perverted the Law. There was no justification through the Law in the sense of Moses. "According to its origin and intention, the Law is the divine will, which does call to obedience, and in that sense it is, according to Rom 3:21, a witness for the gospel of the justice of God, and so of the *nova oboedientia* which it establishes, but which could be perverted by Judaism to a demand to achieve. . . . The letter is what Jewish interpretation and tradition made of the differently intended divine will. . . ."[33] This forced Käsemann to interpret Paul's affirmation of a justification through doing what the Law required in Romans 2 as applicable only to Christians. In that way it was incorporated into the existential-eschatological dimension of faith. I quote Käsemann's formulation extensively because of its importance for this study. "It was undoubtedly not meant hypothetically when it is conceded to the gentiles [in Rom 2:13ff.] that their consciences have a link to the Jewish law when they actualize, and even to a certain extent, evidently mainly morally, fulfill the demands of the Mosaic law. One must bear in mind the remarkable movement from verses 13ff. to verses 25ff. to recognize clearly the problem raised by the notion of a circumcision

---

[31] *Paulinische Perspektiven*, 282; ET, 164.
[32] *Paulinische Perspektiven*, 84; ET, 46.
[33] *Paulinische Perspektiven*, 251–52; ET, 146–47.

of the heart, not of the letter. Such a circumcision is certainly not a fiction for the apostle. There is a presence of the Spirit and a dominion of the letter, and the irreconcilable opposition between the two. There are indeed Christians in whom the Spirit realized its work specifically as a circumcision of the heart. Thus we see Paul move from what is initially a hypothetical consideration to the description of an actual occurrence. The otherwise superfluous repetition and intensification of verses 13ff. at the end of the chapter has the purpose of presenting the Christians as recipients and models of a circumcision of the heart."[34] With that Käsemann reached the limits of his interpretation of Paul. He does not allow for a positive meaning of the world, except insofar as it is incorporated into the meaning of justification by faith. Paul's statements about the Law do not have meanings of their own. Their only meaning is as expressions of that single "theme which controls [Paul's] entire theology: the doctrine of justification [by faith]."[35]

D. J. Christiaan Beker

The most systematic clarification of the methodological problem of interpreting Paul was given by Beker in terms of the contingency and coherence in the apostle's thought. Beker formulates the problem of the center of Paul's thought sharply in his criticism of Käsemann: "Käsemann identifies *one* theme as *the* theme and does not distinguish the primary language of the symbolic structure (the Christ-event in its apocalyptic meaning) from the *variety* of symbols that interpret it. Thus, righteousness must be viewed as *one* symbol *among* others and not as *the* center of Paul's thought."[36] I will leave aside for the time being the question of whether this criticism of Käsemann is valid. The point is well taken. It is similar to making a single apple the essence of apple, to making a single *expression* of Paul's meaning his meaning *itself*. However, as I will show, it is Beker himself, more than Käsemann, who makes "one symbol among others" the center of Paul's thinking.

The complexity of the issue became clear in discussions that followed my paper at the 1986 SBL meeting in Atlanta in which I discussed the present subject.[37] The main question became whether one should speak of a "unifying *center*" at all. The objection was that

---

[34] *Paulinische Perspektiven*, 242–43; ET, 141.
[35] *Paulinische Perspektiven*, 282; ET, 164.
[36] *Paul the Apostle*, 17.
[37] "The Foundations of Paul's Thought: A Methodological Investigation—The Problem of a Coherent Center of Paul's Thought," subsequently published in *ST* 42 (1988) 55–68.

a center suggested some kind of a central idea.[38] Daniel Patte illustrated what he thought was wrong with a unifying center by referring
to the elevator shaft as what might be considered the unifying center
of the hotel, making a single part representative of the whole. Patte's
example reveals what is at issue. A unifying center cannot be a part
which stands for the whole; it should be conceived as a fundamental,
abstract structure which makes the whole understandable. Architecturally, the unifying center of the building would have to be found
in the fundamental principles which governed its construction: the
architect's design, including an idea of the purpose of the building,
physical factors and skill in its construction, etc. The building's
architecturally unifying center is also not identical with what the
architect intended. There would certainly be many points at which the
architect could recognize that what happened in the construction of
the building was not what he or she intended, and that not solely
because of construction failures. In interpreting the building architecturally the architect too would have to abstract from the actual building.

The same is true in the interpretation of Paul. The unifying
center of his thought is to be found at the deepest, most abstract,
syntactic and semantic levels out of which the expression of his
thought is generated, not in the sense of a single fundamental idea
to which he gives expression, but of a generative structure, a grammar, in the sense of the generative trajectory of A. J. Greimas and
J. Courtés.[39] I will not try to clarify the functioning of such a generative grammar at this point, but will do so in the course of this
investigation by showing how it contributed to my understanding of
Paul's thinking.[40]

According to Beker, "Paul's coherent center must be viewed
as a symbolic structure in which a primordial experience (Paul's call)

---

[38] The expression "unifying center" comes from Christiaan Beker,
but, in view of those discussions, he decided to abandon it because it did not
adequately express his understanding.

[39] See *Sémiotique* under "générative (parcours)" and "générative
(grammaire)"; ET under "generative grammar" and "generative trajectory."
According to Greimas and Courtés, "Les structures sémio-narratives, qui
constituent le niveau le plus abstrait, l'instance ab quo du parcours génératif,
se présentent sous forme d'une *grammaire sémiotique et narrative* qui com-
porte deux composantes—syntaxe et sémantique—et deux niveaux de pro-
fondeur: une *syntaxe fondamentale* et une *sémantique fondamentale* (au
niveau profond), une *syntaxe narrative* et une *sémantique narrative* (au
niveau de surface)" (*Sémiotique*, 159; ET, 133). The "starting point of the
generative trajectory" of the English translation may not render the full
meaning of the crucial "l'instance ab quo du parcours génératif" in the French.

[40] I did show how such a grammar could function in the interpretation of the New Testament by abstracting it from the text of John 4:4–42 in
Neither on this Mountain, nor in Jerusalem. A Study of John 4.

is brought into language in a particular way. The symbolic structure comprises the language in which Paul expresses the Christ-event. That language is, for Paul, the apocalyptic language of Judaism, in which he lived and thought."[41] This last sentence is reminiscent of Bultmann's statement that "as little as Paul proclaimed a 'world view,' so completely was he, like everybody else, bound to say what he has to say in the concepts of his world view."[42] The difference is that Paul's apocalyptic language, which Bultmann understood as a means of expression for Paul, not what Paul intended, is taken by Beker as the coherent center of the Apostle's thought.

In his 1986 SBL seminar paper[43] Beker made it clear that in his understanding of what he terms Paul's hermeneutic he operates with three levels. At the most fundamental level there is the Christ-event, also called "a primordial experience (Paul's call)." The second level is the symbolic structure in which Paul brings his primordial experience into language. It is the language in which Paul expresses the Christ-event. For Beker that language is the apocalyptic language of Judaism in which Paul lived and thought, as he states in the preceding quotation. The other characteristic feature of Beker's understanding of Paul, the interface between contingency and coherence, is a third step in Paul's hermeneutic, the step which mediates between the apocalyptic symbolic structure and the situations in which Paul became involved in his activity as an apostle.

Confusion arises in Beker's interpretation when, for example, he fails to keep these three levels distinct. "The most striking aspect of Paul's thought is his hermeneutic, that is, the interface between contingency and coherence. I called Paul's coherent center a symbolic structure that contains a 'deep' structure of Christian apocalyptic and a 'surface' structure of a variety of symbols. The 'surface' structure now operates as an interpretive field that mediates between the coherent center and its relevance to contingent situations, that is, the authentic truth of the coherent center aims at relevance according to the demands of the dialogical situation."[44]

There is an inconsistency between Beker's statement that Paul's coherent center is "a symbolic structure that contains a 'deep' structure of Christian apocalyptic *and* a 'surface' structure of a variety of symbols," and his subsequent formulation: "The 'surface' structure now operates as an interpretive field that *mediates* between the coherent center and its relevance to contingent situations, that is, the authentic truth of the coherent center aims at relevance

---

[41] *Paul the Apostle*, 15–16.
[42] *GuV*, vol. 1, 52; ET, 82.
[43] "The Method of Recasting Pauline Theology."
[44] *Paul the Apostle*, 17.

according to the demands of the dialogical situation."[45] First the 'surface' structure is part of the coherent center, but then it operates as an interpretive field, mediating between the coherent center and its relevance to contingent situations. If I have understood him correctly here, the first statement should read, "I called Paul's *hermeneutic* center a symbolic structure that contains a 'deep' structure of Christian apocalyptic and a 'surface' structure of a variety of symbols." Then it would become clear, keeping for the time being to his own formulations, how it is that the 'surface' structure mediates between the coherent center, i.e., the 'deep' structure, and its relevance to contingent situations.

The problem arises not only because Beker refers only to the second and third levels, but also especially because he refers to the structure of Christian apocalyptic as a 'deep' structure, whereas in his own sense it is in reality an intermediate structure. He may not be willing to recognize structure in the Christ-event or the "primordial experience" of Paul's call, but if they do not provide coherence to Paul's thinking, nothing that Beker's proposed symbolic structure can do will rescue Paul from incoherence. Exactly the opposite is the case. Coherence in Paul's thought depends on that deepest level, not Beker's intermediate level. Even if what he calls Paul's "symbolic structure" lacks coherence—and I have no doubt that it does—the coherence of his thought could still be guaranteed by the deepest level of the Christ-event and Paul's primordial experience of it. *That* is where the issue of coherence in Paul's thought must be addressed.

Beker nowhere shows how he came to conclude that God's apocalyptic triumph was the center of Paul's thinking. He posits it already in the preface of *Paul the Apostle*, at the beginning of the book: "I posit the triumph of God as the coherent theme of Paul's gospel; that is, the hope in the dawning victory of God and in the imminent redemption of the created order, which he has inaugurated in Christ. Moreover, I claim that Paul's hermeneutic translates the apocalyptic theme of the gospel into the contingent particularities of the human situation."[46] I have already noted that Beker has in the meantime clarified his position by pointing out that he does not intend a central core, which he refers to here as the "coherent theme." But that is not the problem. The problem is the short vision which is reflected in his formulation of the center, as if Paul's hermeneutic begins at the level of the apocalyptic symbolic structure.

---

[45] Both emphases are mine.
[46] *Paul the Apostle*, ix.

Beker himself in effect admits that the "apocalyptic symbolic structure" does not unify Paul's thought. He admits that in Galatians coherence is virtually absent, and he does not even try to show that the letter depicts the apocalyptic triumph of God. "The situation also dictates the virtual absence of an otherwise central feature in Paul's letters—the future apocalyptic dimension of the gospel. Apart from Gal. 5:1, 5:21b, and 6:6–8, this topic is completely ignored."[47] Thus he continues: "Galatians threatens to undo what I have posited as the coherent core of Pauline thought, the apocalyptic coordinates of the Christ-event that focus on the imminent, cosmic triumph of God. Indeed, the eschatological present dominates the letter."[48]

In a footnote Beker points to structuralism as a possible means of engaging with the problem of the center of Paul's thinking. He understands his own work as coordinate with it. "The language of structuralism," he writes, "may be helpful to clarify the delineation of Paul's coherent core."[49] I will return to this later.

E. *Daniel Patte*

Patte is the scholar to whom we can appropriately look for a structural interpretation of Paul. According to him we can have our best access to Paul's thinking through an understanding of his system of convictions. Patte's purpose is not specifically to find the center of Paul's thinking, but to understand the system of beliefs underlying the apostle's theology: "I choose to focus our reading on Paul's faith because, in my view, faith is the most central and fundamental dimension of a religion."[50] He does so by comparing and contrasting it with opposed systems of belief. "The primary goal of our reading of Paul's letters is to elucidate what *characterizes* Paul's faith. This implies that our reading will be aimed at providing a description of Paul's faith so that it might be compared and contrasted with other types of faith."[51] In his view the system of beliefs is fundamental: "Elucidating the characteristics of Paul's faith we are compelled to ask: What did the Apostle to the Gentiles view as self-evident? What did he take for granted and as absolutely true?"[52]

Patte distinguishes between two levels in the expression of meaning in a text. At one level are the ideas expressed in a text and

---

[47] *Paul the Apostle*, 58.
[48] *Paul the Apostle*, 58.
[49] *Paul the Apostle*, 16.
[50] Daniel Patte, *Paul's Faith and the Power of the Gospel: A Structural Introduction to the Pauline Letters* (Philadelphia: Fortress Press, 1983) 7.
[51] *Paul's Faith*, 6.
[52] *Paul's Faith*, 11.

the way these function in its argumentation. At another level are the convictions on which the argumentation is based, even though these are less obvious. "Because convictions are self-evident and because they cannot be demonstrated by argument, they remain in the background of a discourse."[53] The distinction between convictions and arguments can be illustrated by means of a negative example, Paul's futile attempt in 1 Cor 11:3–12 to argue on religious-ethical grounds that women should be veiled at prayer. In the end he himself is not able to conceal that his religious-ethical arguments merely serve his attempt to prove an unwavering bourgeois conviction, when he asks: "Is it proper for a woman to pray to God unveiled?" (11:13). The phenomenon is conspicuous when Paul's reasoning brings him to a point where he has to draw a conclusion which is contrary to his deepest convictions, to which he typically responds with his well-known μὴ γένοιτο, "by no means!" followed by a simple statement of the conviction; for example, Rom 3:5–6, "If our wickedness co-establishes the justice of God, what shall we say? Is God who inflicts wrath not unjust? . . . By no means! In that case, how would God judge the world?" (cf. Gal 3:21, Rom 3:4; 3:31; 9:14).

Patte distinguishes two basic patterns of conviction, those concerning the existential problems of life and death, and those concerning the relationship of the human community to nature or other crucial problems posed by human existence, such as injustice and violence in society. Regarding the former he states, "The convictional pattern which characterizes a faith is first established around the elements of human experience which pose the most difficult existential problems for an understanding of the meaningfulness of human experience. For instance, what is the meaning and purpose of life since it ends up in death? For certain religions this is the fundamental problem."[54] Concerning the second pattern Patte notes, "In other religions the central issue is that concerning the relationship of the human community to nature or other crucial problems posed by human existence, such as injustice and violence in society. The convictional resolution of these problems establishes the fundamental conditional pattern in terms of which the entire semantic universe is organized."[55] These two basic patterns of conviction represent, respectively, the existential and the social semantic universes of Paul's thinking.

Patte points out that a simple list of convictions does not provide an understanding of what is characteristic of faith. Such an understanding becomes possible only through recognizing the sys-

---

[53] *Paul's Faith*, 12.
[54] *Paul's Faith*, 24.
[55] *Paul's Faith*, 24.

tem in which the ideas are organized. He continues, "what is truly characteristic of faith is not the number of convictions or even the specific kind of convictions they involve, but rather the way in which the convictions are organized to form a system."[56] He distinguishes two sets of conviction: those which establish what is good and those which establish what is real, which he understands to be interrelated as two steps in a single process of understanding. The first step is the establishment of what is real. Only when that is established can the second step be taken—the establishment of what is desired.[57] Such a system of convictions can be termed a semantic universe, which is "organized according to a certain fundamental law which characterizes a given faith. This law establishes the convictional pattern according to which all the elements of the semantic universe are interrelated."[58]

The system of convictions is organized in a hierarchy in which the pattern of religious elements is fundamental and is applied or duplicated non-religiously in new situations and experiences. "We commonly acknowledge that [a system of convictions] is organized hierarchically; we view certain convictions as more basic or central than others. This is implied in the legitimate distinction that we make between 'religious' and 'nonreligious.' Often we use the term 'religious' to designate basic parts of a system of convictions in which the fundamental convictional pattern is *established*. Similarly, we use the term 'nonreligious' to designate secondary parts of this system in which this convictional pattern is *applied* or duplicated. The semantic universe can thus be viewed as ever-expanding, framing every new situation and new experience according to the pattern of its core (the religious core)."[59] We are reminded of Beker's coherence and contingency. The religious elements constitute the core, the "fundamental convictional pattern," which is "applied or duplicated" in "every new situation and experience," except that for Patte the contingent situations become part of an ever expanding semantic universe.

The problem with Patte's investigation with regard to our topic is that he never moves beyond identifying Paul's convictions and their arrangement. What he provides is not significantly more than lists of convictions. He writes only in general terms about the existential and social semantic universes in Paul's thought. It never becomes clear how these universes are transformed grammatically out of their deeper, more abstract levels, first into systems of values,

---

[56] *Paul's Faith*, 20.
[57] Cf. *Paul's Faith*, 21.
[58] *Paul's Faith*, 23.
[59] *Paul's Faith*, 23–24.

and then into convictional patterns. What we do find is a description of how the convictional patterns become transformed into the concrete figures of Paul's writings. In that regard too his work is methodologically similar to Beker's. Both work from an intermediate level, except that Patte begins with patterns of convictions whereas Beker begins with Paul's apocalyptic symbolic structure.

Investigating Paul's patterns of convictions is of course what Patte set out to do; he does not promise to do anything else. It is nevertheless frustrating that he has at his disposal a method that could do so much more. The closest he comes to identifying a deeper, more abstract level out of which it could become possible to understand how meaning is generated in Paul's more concrete formulations is when he establishes that Paul's system of convictions is dynamic when compared with the static system of those whom Paul opposes. As in the case of Beker, he never shows how he comes to this understanding, but merely posits: "Usually a system of convictions is static in the sense that the cluster of fundamental convictions which establishes its convictional pattern is set once and for all. The believers express this by affirming in one way or another that they have the complete and final revelation. In such a case the believers' identity, the purpose and meaning of life, the view of society and of the world, and so on, established by such a system of convictions, is perceived as permanently true, as something which cannot change without losing its truth."[60] According to Patte, "For Paul, the Hellenistic religions (i.e., the pagan religions) and also Judaism belong (rightly or wrongly) to this type of faith."[61] Then he suggests that Paul's system of convictions is of the dynamic type. "By contrast other systems of convictions can be said to be dynamic in the sense that the clusters of fundamental convictions which establish their convictional pattern are not taken as set once and for all. . . . Could it be that Paul's Gospel is a system of convictions of this type?"[62] As in the case of Beker, he describes how this works in Paul's writings, but not how it is the central core on which the meaning of Paul's statements depend.

As promising as the approach to Paul's thought in terms of a system of convictions is, the fact that Patte does not clarify the structural integrity of Paul's convictions as a system, the fact that he provides as little a grammar of Paul's thought as Beker does, makes him subject to a criticism of Käsemann. "Even if [Paul] did not write a Summa theologica, it is going too far when one sets in its place a series of interwoven thoughts concerning the encounter with God."[63]

---

[60] *Paul's Faith*, 64.
[61] *Paul's Faith*, 64.
[62] *Paul's Faith*, 64.
[63] *Paulinische Perspektiven*, 237; ET, 138.

This fits almost to a "T" what we encounter in Patte, a number of intertwined convictions without a controlling center.

CONCLUSION

Cumulatively, these studies contribute to the study of Paul by clarifying one of if not *the* most fundamental problems in Pauline interpretation, namely, that the coherence of Paul's thought cannot be found in his expressions, in "what stands written" (Barth), but at a deeper level of meaning. None of them succeeds in clarifying that deeper level by identifying a center which makes it possible to integrate the diversity of the apostle's thinking into a coherent whole. Such a center cannot be found in any particular Pauline expression, such as Beker's eschatological triumph of God, or Patte's patterns of convictions. The root of the problem is that in the history of the interpretation of Paul justification by faith is taken with few exceptions without question as the coherent center of his thought. This is determined not as the product of critical investigation, but as an assumption controlling almost every aspect of the interpretation. For our investigation of Galatians and Romans the question is whether in these and Paul's other letters the opposition between justification through works of the Law and justification by faith constitutes the coherent center of his thought, or whether this opposition is only one form in which a more fundamental meaning comes to expression in response to a contingent issue which he encountered in his ministry to the Galatians. An interpretation of Paul's thought which follows the probable chronological sequence of his letters (excluding Philemon)—1 Thessalonians, 1 and 2 Corinthians, Philippians, Galatians and Romans—which does not impose the opposition found in Galatians and Romans between justification through works of the Law and justification by faith on the rest of letters will discover that the earlier letters can be interpreted successfully without relying on that opposition as the fundamental principle of interpretation.[64]

---

[64] This is the procedure I followed in the course on Pauline theology to which I referred in the Preface. What emerged as a more probable coherent center in the earlier letters was 1 Cor 7:19, "Circumcision counts for nothing, and not being circumcised counts for nothing, but keeping the commandments of God." What is stated with calm assurance in 1 Corinthians became a critical issue in Galatians, followed by Romans, as a result of the contingency of the Galatians' suggestion that they should submit to circumcision in order to participate in God's covenant with Abraham.

In planning the course I had been uncertain of what to do about Philippians: Should it come before or after Galatians and Romans? In due course it became clear that Philippians must have been written before the

This is not a new insight, but I had to re-discover it for myself. Wrede already understood what was at issue with unsurpassed clarity: "It is indeed possible to present Paul's religion in its entirety without taking note of the doctrine of justification, except when discussing the Law. It would indeed have been strange if Paul's supposed main doctrine were to have been present only in a minority of his letters. It is present only where there is a struggle with Judaism."[65] It is developed fully only in Galatians, Romans, and "in the equally polemical" Phil 3:6–9. The polemical context in which the doctrine occurs signifies its real meaning. It functions as a polemical doctrine (*Kampfeslehre*), understandable only in the context of his controversies with Judaism and Jewish Christianity, and it is intended only for that purpose, which makes it "historically of great importance and characteristic of [Paul]."[66]

The center of Paul's thought transcends every instance of its expression. The most fruitful attempt at resolving the relationship between a coherent center in Paul's thought and its diverse expressions is Käsemann's suggestion, because justification of the sinner as he understands it connotes the fundamental opposition between the believer and the world. "Justification of the sinner in the first place certainly concerns me concretely. But this formula loses its significance when it does not announce salvation for every human being and the entire world. For the ungodly is to be found only in the intertwining of everything of the world in sin and death. . . ."[67] The ultimate challenge for an understanding of Paul is to find a center which allows us to understand how he could say, on the one hand, "Not the hearers of the Law are just before God, but the doers of the Law will be justified" (Rom 2:13), expressing the social dimension of this thought, and, on the other, "Through works of the Law no one will be justified before him" (Rom 3:20), representing the existential dimension.

I would like to take Beker's structuralism footnote to which I referred earlier as my point of departure for an understanding of

---

other two. It is inconceivable that in combating the appeal to Jewish privilege in Phil 3:2–11 Paul would have left no trace of the essentials of his reasoning concerning the same issue in Galatians and Romans, if he had already developed the argument in those letters, in particular, that it was as a gentile that Abraham was justified by faith.

[65] *Paulus* (Religionsgeschichtliche Volksbücher I 5–6; Gebauer-Schwetschke: Halle, 1904) 72. Repr. in K. H. Rengstorf (ed.), *Das Paulusbild in der neueren deutschen Forschung* (WF 24; Darmstadt: Wissenschaftliche Buchgesellschaft, 1964) 1–97, see page 67. ET *Paul* (London: Philip Green, 1907) 123.

[66] Ibid.

[67] *Paulinische Perspektiven*, 138; ET, 78.

Paul, indicating how I understand it: "The language of structuralism may be helpful to clarify the delineation of Paul's coherent core. The symbolic structure can be called the paradigmatic structure that contains the totality of the syntagmatic symbols. In other words, the traditional symbols that are juxtaposed to each other in Paul's letters (syntagmatic) constitute in their totality the paradigmatic structure of Paul's thought, just as all the elements of language are contained in its basic grammar. In this sense, the 'coherent center' is the synchronic-paradigmatic structure of Paul's thought, which should not be splintered into its diachronic and syntagmatic elements if we intend to understand the coherence of Paul's thought."[68] The only emendation I would make is to substitute "figurative trajectory," or even better, "configuration," for his "symbolic structure." The meaning is essentially the same. It refers to a series of repeated figures—or symbols, to use his term—that recur in Paul's letters. They do not have to be linked *syntactically*, but they recur in such a way that they build up *paradigmatically* to create a thematic meaning-effect. Such a figurative trajectory *could* be Paul's apocalyptic statements or his statements concerning justification.

The "coherent center" of Paul's thought would then be what links all the themes structurally. What holds everything together, syntactically and paradigmatically, is the grammar of his thought, constituted, in the sense of Greimas, by its syntactic and semantic components. The structure of Paul's thought is constituted by all the elements of meaning linked syntactically and paradigmatically. From his writings it should be possible to abstract a fundamental system of thought, a system of values, which gives meaning to his concrete expressions, what Beker correctly refers to as contingent. The system of values does not necessarily have to do with aesthetics or ethics, even though that may be involved, but refers to what, at a deeper level, undergirds the expression of his thought, undergirds his arguments in Patte's sense. The system of values is in turn rooted at an even deeper level in what Greimas refers to as the micro-universe of a text,[69] such as the existential and the social semantic universes which Patte identified in Paul's thinking.

I propose that Paul's thought is grounded in the opposition between the existential and the social micro-universes, what Barth refers to as the opposition between eternity and time, Bultmann as eschatology and history, Käsemann as the believer and the world; it comes to expression in the opposition between justification by faith and justification for the doing of good works in Paul. Characteristic

---

[68] *Paul the Apostle*, 16.
[69] See *Sémiotique* under "micro-univers" and "univers"; ET under "micro-universe" and "universe."

of Paul's thought is affirmation of both sides of the opposition, requiring that one interpret him eschatologically, existentially, as Bultmann had done, and at the same time socially, historically, as Käsemann demanded. Paul's thinking on the basis of the opposed micro-universes, the existential and the social, is the coherent center of his thought. The fact that he thinks on the basis of an irresolvable opposition at the deepest level of his thought explains why he falls into contradictions at the surface level when he engages with different concrete issues. That is the contingency in which his thinking becomes involved, as Beker correctly states. It is the setting of his thought in both universes which is at the root of his proclamation of justification of the sinner, if one takes justification radically, more radically than Käsemann does. It should be recognized that with the formula "justification of the sinner" we have already left the abstract level of his thought by making use of one of his actual expressions. In that sense Beker is correct in his criticism of Käsemann. The failure to recognize that justification of the sinner is a concrete expression and not an abstract universal is what I would call a fallacy of misplaced abstraction, inverting Whitehead's famous expression,[70] but I hope remaining true to what he intended with it. Where Beker is not correct is that he does not recognize that the formula as Käsemann understands it brings to expression both sides of the fundamental polarity which lies at the roots of Paul's thinking. In that sense it is not a single theme in Paul's thinking, to use Beker's expression, but rather Käsemann's attempt to bring to expression what he understood to have been at the roots of Paul's thinking, even if he did so by using a single crucial expression. Its value is that it acknowledges that the Apostle's thinking was rooted in a contradiction at the most fundamental level, the affirmation of both poles of the opposition between the existential micro-universe and the social micro-universe. That fact explains the contradictions in Paul's writings. Thus we end with the paradox that what gives *coherence* to Paul's thought appears to be at its most fundamental level a *contradiction*.

---

[70] "The fallacy of misplaced concreteness," for example, Alfred North Whitehead, *Process and Reality: An Essay in Cosmology* (New York: Harper and Row, 1960) 11.

Part One ✑

Macro-Structures for Galatians and for Romans

INTRODUCTION

In the Introduction the macro-structure of a text was spoken of in non-technical language as follows: in order to be able to interpret a text we are dependent on an overall understanding of its meaning which permits us to make sense of the individual parts and the way they are structured. According to van Dijk, "semantic macro-structures are necessary to explain in sufficiently simple terms how it is possible that throughout a text the selection of lexical items and underlying formation of semantic representations is heavily restricted by some global constraint."[1] One might refer to a macro-structure as a basic grid into which one fits the individual sentences to form a coherent whole as one reads a text. Van Dijk notes that every reader approaches a text with her or his own macro-structure.[2]

We are hardly ever aware of a macro-structure when we read, and yet it is a powerful "tool" without which we would be unable to understand what we read. A macro-structure is an abstraction, similar to a grammar. We are hardly ever aware that we rely on a grammar, except when we learn a foreign language or run into problems with a difficult sentence, or when we specifically study grammar. That a grammar is an abstraction and yet the abstraction of something that actually plays a decisive role in the use of a language is easily seen when a cultural linguist tries to write a grammar, more specifically a syntax, for a language which does not yet have one. Such a linguist questions native speakers about how they use the language; for example, how do they formulate certain kinds of sentences? In due course the linguist is able to develop rules for that

---

[1] *Some Aspects of Text Grammars*, 160.

[2] "[E]verybody will construct the macro-structure for a text which is relevant to him, personally, and these macro-structures will be different for the same text" (*Some Aspects of Text Grammars*, 161).

language and to verify them with native speakers. With this, users of that language are made aware of rules governing its use of which they were never consciously aware. Those rules are abstractions from the way language functions—they do not exist concretely—and yet without such a control there would be no language, but merely strings of sounds or series of letters.

Let me illustrate this with a simple example: Consider a sentence in English, "You must work harder," and in German, "Sie müßen fleißiger arbeiten." It would not occur to an English speaker to say: "You must harder work," or for the German to say, "Sie müßen arbeiten fleißiger." Neither the native English nor the German speaker need to be aware of syntactic or stylistic rules which say that in English the adverb has to follow the verb and in German it has to precede it, but if they studied syntax they would be able to recall that there are such rules.

Take as another example the sentence, "I care for you." The reader or hearer has to arrange the words into the syntax of a sentence. This is done with such self-evidence that he or she is not even aware of it. But try to do it with a string of words in a language you do not know. The string of words *as such* does not provide its own syntax; it must be furnished by the speaker/writer and then again by the hearer/reader. Similarly, the reader or hearer notes whether the sentence is addressed to her or him, or to some other person. That is also relevant for the meaning of the text. Finally, the hearer or reader has to contextualize the sentence, either from its "co-text" (i.e., if it appears in a discourse), or from the setting or context in which the sentence was formulated. And what applies to a single sentence is equally true for a series of sentences in a discourse.

In contemporary linguistics this phenomenon is studied by abstracting transformational rules in a transformational grammar rather than by means of the abstracted static rules of traditional grammars.[3] Irrespective of the syntax used to study the way a language functions, the users of a language must employ some kind of a grid by means of which series of sounds in a spoken language and

---

[3] See the analysis of the ambiguous sentence number 10 in Appendix I, "flying airplanes can be dangerous," and the transformational diagrams 12–15.

The originator of transformational grammar was Noam Chomsky. See, for example, his *Aspects of the Theory of Syntax* (Cambridge: Massachusetts Institute of Technology, 1965), and *Syntactic Structures* (Paris: The Hague, 1971). For the universality of transformational rules, see Charles J. Fillmore, "The Case for Case," in Emmon Bach and Robert T. Harms (eds.), *Universals in Linguistic Theory* (New York/Chicago/etc.: Holt, Rinehart and Winston Inc., 1968) 1–90.

strings of letters in a written language are recognized as words and sentences. The same applies to lengthier sounds or strings of letters in a discourse, even though this aspect of language has only recently come into focus in text-linguistics.

Many of us have experienced picking up a book and not being able to make heads or tails out of it. Every word and sentence may be individually understandable, and yet what the author is trying to articulate remains incomprehensible. And then, after having studied the subject of the book, we may come across the book again, and discover that it reads as something completely familiar, so that we can hardly imagine that we could not have understood it in our first attempt to read it. What happened at our first reading was that we did not have a functioning macro-structure, to use van Dijk's term, which could serve as a grid into which we could fit the individual sentences to form a coherent whole. Further study of the subject matter gave us that grid, even though the book itself may never have played a role in the development of the grid.

Recently, van Dijk, in collaboration with W. Kintsch, performed some experiments that revealed in a dramatic way that macro-structures do not depend entirely on the syntactic linking of sentences in a discourse. In this experiment, one half of a group read texts with the sequence of the paragraphs intact and the other half with the sequence scrambled. Although it initially took much longer to read the stories with the scrambled paragraph sequences, the time it took those readers to produce summaries of the stories was not significantly longer than for those who read the texts with the paragraphs intact. The summaries made by readers of the scrambled texts could not be distinguished (by other readers) from the summaries of the readers of the intact texts.[4] The experiment shows that the readers did not depend on the sequence of the paragraphs to make sense of the stories, but arranged what they read into a grid which made that possible.

The power of the macro-structures with which we approach material is what frequently makes communication between opposed groups of interpreters so difficult. We keep arguing about the material without realizing that it is not the material—on which we can frequently agree—that is at issue, but the way in which the

---

[4]W. Kintsch and T. A. van Dijk, "Comment on se rapelle et on résume des histoires," *Langages* 40 (1975) 98–116; W. Kintsch, "On Comprehending Stories," in Marcel Adam Just and Patricia A. Carpenter (eds.), *Cognitive Processes in Comprehension* (Hillsdale, New Jersey: Lawrence Erlbaum Associates, 1977) 33–62. For a summary, see Lynne M. Reder, "The Role of Elaboration in the Comprehension and Retention of Prose: A Critical Review," *Review of Educational Research*, 50 (1980) 27.

material is arranged into the macro-structures with which we approach it. This can be shown by the way Judaism of New Testament times is widely understood in Christian interpretation. Sanders demonstrates this with the two contrasting descriptions by H. A. A. Kennedy: "it must not be forgotten that the conception of the revealed legal system presupposed the existence of the Covenant. It is given to the community as standing *within* the Covenant. And that relationship in turn presupposed what we can only call faith in the mercy and goodness of God. So that all that is done by the worshipping people in the later ritual is not for the purpose of reaching fellowship with God: its aim is to maintain the fellowship unbroken."[5]

Kennedy argues that in New Testament times the covenantal understanding became overshadowed by a legalism: "But for [the later] period, the crowning proof of Israel's election is its possession of the Law. Obedience to the Law, therefore, is the chief token of its acknowledgement of the Divine grace. But as this obedience came to involve the observance of minute regulations, the notion of merit was bound to insinuate itself, and so the rigid contract-conception overshadowed that of the Covenant, which rested on the mercy of God."[6] The same contrast is maintained by Käsemann in his description of the Jewish perversion of the Mosaic law noted in the previous chapter: "According to its origin and intention, the Law is the divine will, which does call to obedience, and in that sense it is, according to Rom 3:21, a witness for the gospel of the justice of God, and so of the *nova oboedientia* which it establishes, but which could be perverted by Judaism to a demand to achieve. . . . The letter is what Jewish interpretation and tradition made of the differently intended divine will."[7]

Against this misrepresentation of the Jewish understanding of the Law, Sanders states, referring to the two quotations from Kennedy: "I have maintained, and I hope demonstrated, that this rests on a misreading of the later Jewish material and that the *first* description of the covenant conception given by Kennedy was maintained in Israel, not excluding the Rabbis, who supposedly are the best representatives of a petty legalism which supplants the idea of the covenant by God's grace and Torah obedience as man's proper response within the covenant."[8]

---

[5] "The Significance and Range of the Covenant Conception," *The Expositor* 10 (1915) 389; cf. Sanders, *Paul and Palestinian Judaism*, 419.

[6] "The Significance and Range of the Covenant Conception," 392; cf. Sanders, *Paul and Palestinian Judaism*, 419–20.

[7] *Paulinische Perspektiven*, 251–52; ET, 146–47.

[8] *Paul and Palestinian Judaism*, 420.

This misunderstanding of the Jewish attitude to the Law was so universal in Christian theological circles until recently that it never occurred to scholars that it could be different. The Jewish texts which could have exposed this error were available and read, but the bias in the understanding of Judaism in New Testament times functioned as a macro-structure that prevented the texts from being read differently.

With regard to Paul's letters to the Galatians and the Romans, a similarly powerful bias reveals itself in the almost universal assumption that the main theme of Romans is justification by faith. This understanding, this component in the macro-structure with which Romans is approached, is so entrenched that it hardly ever occurs to interpreters to question it. This is true even though the assumption that justification by faith is the main theme of the letter creates great difficulties in its interpretation, some of which I mentioned in the previous chapter. There are similar problems in the interpretation of Galatians, though these are not as dramatic as in Romans.

The absence in New Testament scholarship of an awareness of the role played by a macro-structure in the reading of a text appears in a comment by Hans Dieter Betz concerning Galatians. He states that his work "is the preliminary outcome of asking too many questions about how to arrive at an 'outline' of the letter to the Galatians. Nearly all the commentaries and *Introductions to the New Testament* contain such an outline, table of contents, or paraphrase of the argument. However, despite an extensive search, I have not been able to find any consideration given to the possible criteria and methods for determining such an outline."[9] In a series of articles preceding the publication of his commentary on Galatians, Betz addressed these issues methodically and directly.[10] In trying to find an appropriate macro-structure for Galatians, Betz relied on classical rhetoric. This anticipates the first main issue in the present chapter. Our ultimate task will be to see if we can abstract macro-structures for Galatians and Romans from these letters themselves, but first we should review briefly steps toward a better understanding of the structure of Paul's letters.

---

[9]"The Literary Composition and Function of Paul's Letter to the Galatians," *NTS* 21 (1975) 353–79, see page 351.

[10] In addition to the above-mentioned "The Literary Composition and Function of Paul's Letter to the Galatians" see, "Geist, Freiheit, und Gesetz. Die Botschaft des Paulus und die Gemeinde in Galatien," *ZTK* 71 (1974) 78–93; ET, "Spirit, Freedom, and the Law. Paul's Message to the Galatians," *SEÅ* 39 (1974) 145–60; "In Defense of the Spirit. Paul's Letter to the Galatians as a Document of Early Christian Apologetics," in Elisabeth Schüssler-Fiorenza (ed.), *Aspects of Religious Propaganda in Judaism and Early Christianity* (Notre Dame, Ind.: University of Notre Dame Press, 1976) 99–114.

One important step was made in the SBL seminar on "The Form and Function of the Pauline Letters," organized in 1970 and chaired by Nils A. Dahl.[11] Before then important work had been done by John L. White in his M.A. thesis[12] and Ph.D. dissertation,[13] and Chan-Hie Kim in his dissertation,[14] all under the guidance of Robert W. Funk, as well as in Funk's own, "The Apostolic *Parousia.*"[15] The work of the SBL seminar was heavily indebted to three crucial studies, one by Paul Schubert on the thanksgiving sections of the Pauline letters,[16] another by Heikki Koskenniemi on the idea and phraseology of the Greek letter,[17] and a third by Carl J. Bjerkelund on the introduction to the paraenetic sections.[18]

The range of contributions to this seminar was far-reaching, including the crucial formal studies by White,[19] Dahl's famous, unpublished, but much quoted paper on Galatians,[20] the identification of the genre of the Pauline letters as paraenetic by Abraham J. Malherbe, illustrated with a study of 1 Thessalonians,[21] the discus-

---

[11] The principles on which the seminar was based were formulated in a working paper by Dahl, "The Pauline Letters: Proposal for a Study Project of an SBL Seminar on Paul," and a response by Robert W. Funk, which formulated the title of the seminar, "The Form and Function of the Pauline Letter: A Response to the Seminar Proposal by Nils A. Dahl."

[12] *The Form and Structure of the Official Petition* (SBLDS 5; Missoula: Society of Biblical Literature, 1972).

[13] *The Body of the Greek Letter* (SBLDS 2; Missoula: Society of Biblical Literature, 1972).

[14] *The Familiar Letter of Recommendation* (SBLDS 4; Missoula: Society of Biblical Literature, 1972).

[15] *Christian History and Interpretation: Studies Presented to John Knox* (ed. W. R. Farmer, C. F. D. Moule and R. R. Niebuhr; Cambridge: Cambridge University Press, 1967) 249–68.

[16] *Form and Function of the Pauline Thanksgiving* (*ZNW* Beiheft 20; Berlin: Alfred Töpelmann, 1939).

[17] *Studien zur Idee und Phraseologie des griechischen Briefes bis 400 n.Chr.* (Annales Academiae Scientiarum Fennicae, Sarja-Ser. B, Nide-Tom. 102, 2; Helsinki, 1956).

[18] Παρακαλῶ: *Form, Funktion und Sinn der* παρακαλῶ-*Sätzen in den paulinischen Briefe* (Bibliotheca Theologica Norvegica 1; Oslo: Universitetsforlaget, 1967).

[19] For example, "The Structural Analysis of Philemon: A Point of Departure in the Formal Analysis of the Pauline Letter," *The Society of Biblical Literature One Hundred Seventh Annual Meeting Seminar Papers* (Society of Biblical Literature, 1971) 1–47. See also William G. Doty's unpublished, "Response to 'The Structural Analysis of Philemon,' by John L. White."

[20] "Paul's Letter to the Galatians: Epistolary Genre, Content, and Structure."

[21] "I Thessalonians as a Paraenetic Letter" (unpublished). See also his earlier article, "'Gentle as a Nurse.' The Cynic Background to I Thess ii," *NovT* 12 (1970) 203–17.

sion of the structure of that letter by John C. Hurd,[22] and finally
Wilhelm Wuellner's rhetorical study of Romans.[23] Very significant in
this context are also the preparatory articles and subsequent commentary on Galatians by Hans Dieter Betz, to which I referred above.

Those studies offer a kind of map for finding one's way
through Paul's letters. Through them it was possible to see for the
first time how one could distinguish between the meaning of Paul's
individual statements and the way they function in his letters. What
is relevant about those studies in the present context is their recognition that Paul's letters could not be read without attention to how
he uses his language. This applies in general to the question concerning the genre of a letter, whether it is (or all the letters are) paraenetic,
as Malherbe maintains in the works mentioned above, or whether
a letter is rhetorically an apology, as Betz argues with regard to
Galatians.

Another development worth noting before we analyze the
structures of Galatians and Romans is the move in linguistics beyond
the level of the sentence in what is referred to as discourse analysis.
The first step in that direction as far as I know appeared in two
articles by the linguist Zellig S. Harris,[24] who limited his investigation to syntactic questions. In New Testament studies the most
important work was done in South Africa in a group associated with
Johannes P. Louw.[25] For Louw the ultimate concern is not syntax, but
semantics, as revealed in the title of his main work on the subject,
Semantics of New Testament Greek.

Our concern in the following two chapters will be the structural features of Galatians and Romans individually. In chapter 4 I
will give attention to those features of the two letters which bring
to expression a common meaning, suggesting a common macro-
structure for both letters.

---

[22] "Concerning the Structure of 1 Thessalonians" (unpublished). See
also my "The Form Critical Study of Paul's Letters. I Thessalonians as a Case
Study," *NTS* 22 (1976) 140–58, which contains references to earlier work on
various structural features of the Pauline letters.

[23] "Paul's Rhetoric of Argumentation in Romans. An Alternative to
the Donfried-Karris Debate Over Romans," in Karl P. Donfried (ed.), *The
Romans Debate* (Minneapolis: Augsburg Publishing House, 1977) 152–74; 2d
rev. and expanded ed. (Peabody, Mass: Hendrickson, 1991) 147–71.

[24] "Discourse Analysis," *Language* 28 (1952) 1–30, and "Discourse
Analysis: A Sample Text," *Language* 28 (1952) 474–94.

[25] See Louw's "Discourse Analysis and the Greek New Testament,"
BT 24 (1937) 101–18, and *Semantics of New Testament Greek* (Philadel-
phia/Chico: Fortress/Scholars Press, 1982).

2 ∼

A Macro-Structure for Galatians

I. FORMAL ANALYSES OF THE STRUCTURE OF GALATIANS

Betz analyzed Galatians as an apologetic letter with the following rhetorical sections:[1]

1:1–5	Prescript—This is part of the epistolary framework, and not specifically rhetorical.[2]
1:6–9	*exordium* or *prooemium*—Statement of the *causa*, the reason for writing.[3]
1:10–11	*transitus*—Transition from the *exordium* to the *narratio*.[4]
1:12–2:14	*narratio*—Statement of the facts that have a bearing on the case.[5]
2:15–21	*propositio*—A summing up of the points made in the *narratio*.[6]
3:1–4:31	*probatio, confirmatio* or plainly *argumentatio*—According to Betz the most decisive section because here the proofs are offered.[7]

---

[1]For a complete discussion, see "The Literary Composition and Function of Paul's Letter to the Galatians." Most of the material from this article is incorporated into *Galatians* as indicated below. See also *Galatians*, 14–25, and "In Defense of the Spirit," 103–4.

[2]*Galatians*, 37.

[3]*Galatians*, 44–46.

[4]*Galatians*, 46.

[5]*Galatians*, 58–62.

[6]*Galatians*, 113–14.

[7]*Galatians*, 128–30. Betz admits, "an analysis of these chapters in terms of rhetoric is extremely difficult. One may say that Paul has been very successful—as a skilled rhetorician would be expected to be—in disguising his argumentative strategy. This is to say that, in spite of the apparent confusion, there is to be expected a clear flow of thought" (*Galatians*, 129).

5:1–6:10   *exhortatio* or *paraenesis*—A characteristic feature of philo-
            sophical literature, especially the diatribes of the Hel-
            lenistic period.[8]
6:11–18   Postscript—This is also part of the epistolary framework,
            which at the same time functions rhetorically as a *per-
            oratio, conclusio* or *recapitulatio*, in which a last appeal
            is made to the readers.[9]

Betz' rhetorical analysis has encountered a great deal of
critical objection, particularly his understanding of the letter as an
apology. A number of critics, some of them independently of each
other, have argued that Galatians is rhetorically not an apology, but
a deliberative speech.[10] According to Joop Smit the question is

> whether this narration [Betz' *narratio,* 1:12–14] is presenting facts
> about which the Galatians as a judicial body have to pronounce
> judgment. The story does not confront them with a precise legal
> question, but rather proposes two courses of action from which they
> should choose. Paul recounts the facts from the past to recommend
> his own course of conduct and to discourage them from introducing
> the changes his opponents are urging upon them. This would mean
> that the speech Paul sent to the Galatians more probably belongs to
> the *genus deliberativum* than to the *genus iudicale.*[11]

Smit analyzes Galatians as follows:

1:6–12   *exordium*—"The purpose of the *exordium* is to make the
            listeners well-disposed, attentive and receptive."[12]
1:13–2:21   *narratio*—Exposition of the facts.
3:1–4:11   *confirmatio*—Confirmation by proof.
4:12–20   *conclusio,* part 1: *conquestio*—An appeal to pity.
4:21–5:6   *conclusio,* part 2: *enumeratio*—A summing up to refresh
            the memory.

---

[8] *Galatians,* 253–55.
[9] *Galatians,* 312–13.
[10] The most significant of these may be Joop Smit's, "The Letter of
Paul to the Galatians: A Deliberative Speech," *NTS* 35 (1989) 1–26, and
G. A. Kennedy's *New Testament Interpretation through Rhetorical Criticism*
(Chapel Hill: University of North Carolina Press, 1984). See also, among
others, Robert G. Hall, "The Rhetorical Outline of Galatians: A Reconsideration," *JBL* 106 (1987) 277–87, François Vouga, "Zur rhetorischen Gattung des
Galaterbriefes," *ZNW* 79 (1988) 291–92, and Benoît Standaert, "La Rhétorique
antique et l'épître aux Galates," *FoiVie* 84 (1985) 33–40. In addition see the
further analysis of the structure of 1:6–2:14, agreeing with Betz, by James C.
Hester, "The Rhetorical Structure of Galatians 1:11–2:14," *JBL* 103 (1984)
223–33.
[11] "The Letter of Paul to the Galatians," 3.
[12] "The Letter of Paul to the Galatians," 9.

5:7–12   *conclusio*, part 3: *indignatio*—Inciting the listeners to great hatred of some persons.

6:11–18   *amplificatio*—A part that is added because the speech is sent in the form of a letter. It is an elaboration of the line of thought of 5:11.

Smit does not include the prescript, 1:1–5, in his analysis, obviously since it has a purely epistolary function. Even though that section is included in Betz' outline, he too does not consider it part of the rhetorical structure. "The epistolary framework of the Galatian letter can be easily recognized and separated from the body—in fact it separates so easily that is appears almost as a kind of external bracket for the body of the letter. However, several interrelations between the epistolary framework and the body of the letter indicate that both elements are part of one and the same composition."[13] Note also his remark: "As a rhetorical feature, the postscript of Galatians serves as the *peroratio* or *conclusio*, that is, the end and conclusion of the apologetic speech forming the body of the letter."[14]

Smit also does not include 5:13–6:10 in his analysis. He notes that Betz was faced with an "unsolvable problem; namely, his [Paul's] *paraenesis* (Gal 5.1–6.10) has no place within the compass of classical rhetoric,"[15] and he obviously does not accept Betz' appeal to philosophical diatribes to justify its inclusion. According to Smit, "In classical rhetoric an exhortative passage such as this is completely unknown as a separate part of a normal speech."[16] On the basis of these, as well as other considerations, he considers this part of the letter an addition "at a somewhat later time."[17]

Neither Betz nor his critics have shown conclusively that Galatians was actually structured by Paul as a rhetorical speech with an epistolary prescript and conclusion. What they have shown, with varying degrees of success, is that Galatians can be analyzed rhetorically in terms of the structure of either an apologetic or a deliberative speech. They have shown convincingly that Paul's letters were influenced by rhetoric, either formally or as part of Paul's involvement in the general culture of his time. This realization can contribute in an important way to the interpretation of his letters. Furthermore, these studies have shown that if the letter was structured rhetorically, the evidence clearly favors a deliberative speech.

---

[13] *Galatians*, 15.
[14] *Galatians*, 313.
[15] "The Letter of Paul to the Galatians," 8.
[16] "The Letter of Paul to the Galatians," 4.
[17] "The Letter of Paul to the Galatians," 9.

These analyses provide a kind of map to guide one's reading, alerting one linguistically to the function of Paul's language in the various sections of the letter. They do not yet provide a full macro-structure for interpreting the letter, but they are important first steps towards such a macro-structure since they clarify features of the letter's formal structure. Text-linguistically one might compare these analyses with the letter's formal grammatical structure (syntax), without a methodological concern for its semantics, the meaning conveyed through the syntactic structure. In other words, they both focus on the letter's formal structure but direct little attention toward its meaning. Nonetheless, there are, at times, hints as to its meaning, for example, in the following, where Smit clarifies why he favors a deliberative speech:

> Paul does not confront the Galatians here with the question whether a certain course of action is legitimate or not, but he makes the reproach that they would be acting foolishly and harming them-selves if they change their behaviour. Honour and advantage, or shame and disadvantage, however, are at stake in the *genus de-liberativum*. An argumentation starting with the exclamation, 'O foolish Galatians' almost certainly belongs in that genre.[18]

The meaning of a text would be different depending on whether it is intended as a defense or as a reproach.

Most of Betz' critics do not move beyond the issue of the letter's formal structure or rhetorical type to a consideration of its meaning, although Smit's analysis is based on previous work in four articles in the *Tijdschrift voor Theologie* and *Bijdragen*.[19] According to Smit, the research in those articles "convinced me that it is not justifica-tion by faith but the fact that in Christ the Jews are called to unite with the Gentiles which is the real issue of the letter,"[20] for which he appeals to the work of K. Stendahl, E. P. Sanders and F. Watson.[21]

For Betz the rhetorical analysis was a first step towards a complete interpretation of Galatians, not only in his commentary, but already in his article "Spirit, Freedom, and the Law: Paul's Message to the Galatians." In the case of the *peroratio* he explains the relation-

---

[18] "The Letter of Paul to the Galatians," 4.
[19] "Hoe kun je de heidenen verplichten als joden te leven? Paulus en de torah in Galaten 2,11–21," *Bijdragen* 46 (1985) 118–40, "Naar een nieuwe benadering van Paulus' brieven. De historische bewijsvoering in Gal. 3,1–4,11," *TTh* 24 (1984) 207–34, "Paulus, de Galaten en het judaisme: een narratieve analyse van Galaten 1–2," *TTh* 25 (1985) 337–62, and "Redactie in de brief aan de Galaten: retorische analyse van Gal 4,12–6,18," *TTh* 26 (1986) 113–44.
[20] "The Letter of Paul to the Galatians," 8.
[21] "The Letter of Paul to the Galatians," 7, n. 4.

ship between his formal rhetorical analysis and what could be a semantic macro-structure for the letter as follows: "Seen as a rhetorical feature, the *peroratio* becomes most important for the interpretation of Galatians. It contains the interpretive clues to the understanding of Paul's major concerns in the letter as a whole and should be employed as the hermeneutical key to the intentions of the Apostle."[22]

On the whole his understanding of the meaning of Paul's reasoning and his proposed rhetorical structure, except for the fact that he understands it as an apology, do not appear to be closely interrelated. The rhetorical analysis appears merely to pose the question in the following way: "When we move from the form of the letter to its content, two basic questions have to be raised: What is it that Paul is defending? How can it be defended?"[23] For an answer to the second question one would probably have to point to the letter itself. Betz' subsequent formulation of the second question a few pages later reveals that it already presupposes an answer to the first: "*How* can the Spirit be defended?"[24] This is a question which concerns Betz throughout. "How can an irrational experience like the ecstatic reception of the divine Spirit be defended as legitimate if the means of such a defense are limited to those available in the apologetic letter?"[25]

What remains methodologically unclear is whether his understanding of what is at issue in the letter leads to his understanding of its rhetorical genre, or is it the other way around? Or is the relationship reciprocal? In "In Defense of the Spirit" his investigation of the situation in Galatians is presented after his analysis of the structure of the letter and as an answer to the question, "What is it that Paul is defending?"[26] whereas in the commentary the events in Galatia which led to the writing of the letter are investigated before the structural analysis of the letter.[27] In both cases Betz seeks a reconstruction of the events to which the letter is a response.

According to Betz,

> Most commentators argue that the Apostle defends his apostolic office and his gospel. The literary analysis has shown that he defends primarily his gospel, that is "the gospel of uncircumcision." This gospel is of course intimately connected with his own vocation and apostolic office, so that his apostolic authority depends entirely on the outcome of the defense of the gospel.[28]

---

[22] *Galatians*, 313.
[23] "In Defense of the Spirit," 104.
[24] "In Defense of the Spirit," 108.
[25] *Galatians*, 25.
[26] "In Defense of the Spirit," 104–8.
[27] *Galatians*, 8–9.
[28] *Galatians*, 28.

The question then becomes, against what does he defend the gospel? "Paul's letter was the reaction to the fact that the Galatians had changed their mind about him, about his message, and about themselves."[29] This raises the question: What went wrong in the relationship between Paul and his gospel on the one hand and the Galatians on the other?

Betz' main evidence for what went wrong is a "number of passages in Galatians [which] suggest that [the Galatians] had a problem with the 'flesh' "[30] (5:13, 16, 17, 19; 6:12, 13). The Galatians, who had undergone a radical transformation from their previous existence in slavery to the elements of the universe into the freedom of the Spirit,[31] now experienced problems with the flesh which they were unable to solve through participation in the Spirit alone.[32] They became easy prey to the legalistic missionaries who offered the supplementary way of the Law as a means of overcoming their moral difficulties. "According to Paul's opponents' theology, Christian existence takes place within the terms of Jewish Torah covenant. . . . As long as they stand firmly in the Torah covenant, the Christians are under the protection of Christ."[33] Thus, in Betz' interpretation circumcision as such was not the issue, even though he understands Paul's proclamation as "the gospel of uncircumcision."[34] In his understanding circumcision was merely the means of appropriating the Law. The emphasis is not on circumcision, but on the Law as a moral code.

From a textual point of view Betz' evidence is limited. Although he speaks of a "number" of passages which point to a problem with the flesh, there are actually only two, 5:13–26 and 6:12–16. The theme of the first is given in 5:13: "For you are called to freedom, brothers, but not the freedom which provides occasion for the flesh, but that which serves each other in love." The rest of the passage is exposition. The theme is general enough not to have been the specific reason for the writing of the letter, but a relevant admonition which flows from it. The second passage concerns not the moral trepidation of fleshly behavior at all, but circumcision as a boasting in the flesh. "Those wishing to make a nice appearance in the flesh are the ones who force you to become circumcised . . . ; they want you to become circumcised in order to boast in your flesh" (6:12–13). In his commentary on 6:12–13 Betz himself understands these verses, not in the

---

[29] *Galatians*, 8.

[30] *Galatians*, 8; cf. "In Defense of the Spirit," 105–6; "Geist, Freiheit, und Gesetz," 86.

[31] Cf. esp. "Geist, Freiheit, und Gesetz," 83–84.

[32] "Geist, Freiheit, und Gesetz," 86–88; "In Defense of the Spirit," 105–7; *Galatians*, 8–9.

[33] *Galatians*, 8–9.

[34] *Galatians*, 28.

sense of "a problem with the 'flesh,' "[35] but as verses in which "Paul delivers a sharp attack against his opponents. The attack is supposedly descriptive and is intended to disclose the real goals of the adversaries."[36] Actually Betz had already developed the idea of the issue in Galatians in connection with 2 Cor 6:14–7:1, which he considered an anti–Pauline fragment representing the view of Paul's opponents.[37]

The "story" which Betz reconstructed for Galatians on the basis of his understanding of 2 Cor 6:14–7:1 and Gal 5:13–26 (6:12–16 is clearly not relevant), combined with his analysis of Galatians as rhetorically an apologetic letter, functions as the macro-structure for his interpretation. The evidence for this story is exceedingly scant, and depends more on imagination than on textual evidence. Betz has become so convinced of his macro-structure as to make it impossible for him to read the letter in any other way. His interpretation of the letter has become the means of reinforcing his proposed macro-structure. Even though the evidence in favor of a deliberative speech seems overwhelming, there is no reason why Betz' analysis cannot provide insights into the letter. What prevents this from happening is the rigidness with which he forces the letter into the mold of his macro-structure. There is no place for a hermeneutical circle in the sense of Bultmann; everything moves from the theory concerning the letter's meaning to the letter. The letter itself, the subject-matter of the interpretation, is left no opportunity to correct and refine the theory. Betz no longer appears to approach the letter with a question; all questions appear to have been answered.

At the same time that Betz was developing his understanding of the "story" and structure of Galatians, I had come to a different understanding of the structure of the letter in terms of the conventions of Hellenistic letter writing, as that had been investigated in the SBL seminar on "The Form and Function of the Pauline Letters" to which I referred above. My analysis of the letter had convinced me of a structure similar to what I had identified for 1 Thessalonians,[38] except that Galatians has what Dahl referred to as an "ironic rebuke"[39] instead of the usual thanksgiving section in the other letters. My understanding was that only 1:11–2:21—the "ironic rebuke"—constituted an apology, a section in which he establishes his authority in the gospel before

---

[35] *Galatians*, 8.

[36] *Galatians*, 314.

[37] See "2 Cor 6:14–7:1: An Anti–Pauline Fragment," *JBL* 92 (1973) 88–108; also *Galatians*, 217, 261, 310.

[38] "The Form Critical Study of Paul's Letters. I Thessalonians as a Case Study," *NTS* 22 (1976) 140–58.

[39] "Paul's Letter to the Galatians: Epistolary Genre, Content, and Structure." The phrase was coined by Terence Y. Mullins.

proceeding to the main purpose of his writing. In the case of Galatians, the main purpose of the writing is the contrast between justification through circumcision and the Law and through the Gospel (3:1–5:12), a topic Paul had already hinted at in the "ironic rebuke."

In my study of 1 Thessalonians I had concluded from a comparison with other letters that the apostolic apology was a discrete formal section within most of the Pauline letters: 1 Thess 2:1–12; Gal 1:10–2:21; Phil 1:12–26, 2:2–14; 2 Cor 1:12–17, continued in 7:5–16, and 10:7–12:13. Apologetic matters are strongly hinted at in Rom 1:14–16a, and missing in a formal sense only in 1 Corinthians and Philemon. The apostolic apology stands in the tradition of Socrates' apology as presented by Plato in his dialogue with that name, including its character of a defense not of the apostle personally, but of the gospel (philosophy), as Betz had shown in his study of 2 Cor 10–13.[40] Abraham Malherbe has conclusively demonstrated that 1 Thess 2:1–12 is an apology similar to, for example, Dio Chrysostom's *Oration* 32. The parallel in Dio reveals that we do not need to take Paul's apology in 1 Thessalonians as a reply to a personal attack.[41] According to Malherbe, "Paul's description of himself is therefore not to be viewed as a personal defense. In keeping with his paraenetic intent, he reminds his μιμηταί of the qualities they should imitate in their model. . . ."[42] The identification of the apologetic section appeared to me to be no longer in doubt. In most of Paul's letters, the thanksgiving section ("ironic rebuke" in the case of Galatians) is characteristically followed by the apostolic apology, a discrete section in which the Apostle presents himself and the gospel he proclaims, in order to establish or reaffirm himself and his proclamation in the eyes of his readers.[43]

On the basis of these considerations I proposed the following structure for Galatians. For easy comparison with Betz' proposal, I place them side by side:

Rhetorical Structure (Betz)	*Epistolary Structure*
Prescript 1:1–5	Salutation 1:1–5
exordium, incl. *transitus* 1:6–11	Ironic rebuke 1:6–10
narratio 1:12–2:14	Apostolic apology 1:11–2:21
propositio 2:15–21	
probatio 3:1–4:31	Central section 3:1–5:12
paraenesis 5:1–6:10	Exhortation 5:13–6:10
Postscript 6:11–18	Conclusion 6:11–18

---

[40] *Der Apostel Paulus und die sokratische Tradition.*
[41] "Gentle as a Nurse," 217. See now George Lyons, *Pauline Autobiography: Toward a New Understanding* (SBLDS 73; Atlanta: Scholars, 1985).
[42] "I Thessalonians as a Paraenetic Letter," 14.
[43] See "The Form Critical Study of Paul's Letters," 153.

Some of the differences are relatively insignificant, for example, the beginnings of the *narratio* and the "apostolic apology" and the *paraenesis* and the "exhortation." The place of 1:10–11 and 5:1–12 in the structure of the letter is ambiguous. Decisive, however, is Betz' understanding of 1:6–6:10 as the body of the letter and his interpretation of it as an apology. In my interpretation of the letter in terms of its epistolary form, I recognize only 1:11–2:21 as an apology, distinct in function from the "central section" (3:1–5:12) and the "exhortation" (5:13–6:10). The meaning of the letter, based on the analysis of the Pauline letter-form in my study of 1 Thessalonians,[44] would have to be found in the "central section" in conjunction with the "exhortation."

Both proposed structures appear to fit the letter formally, and could function well as macro-structures for its reading. (When I first proposed the above epistolary structure, the criticism from a rhetorical point of view of Betz' interpretation of the letter as an apology had not yet been mounted.) It had become evident to me that in order to negotiate between the two proposed structures, both based on "form critical" considerations, it would be necessary to employ a method other than a form-critical one. With that in mind I engaged in a basically text-linguistic analysis of the letter.[45]

II. A TEXT-LINGUISTIC ANALYSIS OF THE STRUCTURE OF GALATIANS

In a text-linguistic analysis it is fundamental to proceed, not from given forms suggested by rhetoric or letter-writing conventions, but from the elements of the letter itself. It presupposes that in order to structure a discourse sensibly an author is governed by certain rules of language function. I tried to discover how Paul organized the sentences in the discourse in order to express his thoughts. Moving gradually from the most elementary syntactic relationships between sentences, to more complex paragraph relationships, to the discourse structure of the letter as whole, it became possible to uncover its meaning as well. The principles and procedures involved are discussed in Appendix I, "Principles and Procedures in Discourse Analysis." The method is based on the analysis of discourse structure along the lines developed by Louw.[46] It also reveals

---

[44] "The Form Critical Study of Paul's Letters."

[45] Our opposed understandings of the structure of Galatians were subsequently discussed in a special session of the Pauline seminar, "The Structure of Galatians: Rhetorical or Text-linguistic Analysis."

[46] See his "Discourse Analysis and the Greek New Testament" and *Semantics of New Testament Greek.*

similarities to the methods proposed by Eugene A. Nida,[47] and by John Beekman and John Callow,[48] although I encountered those works after completing my own analysis. Only after I analyzed the letter's textual syntax and its semantic coherence did I again consider the possible influence of the conventions of Hellenistic letter writing.

A. *The Primary Sentence Groupings*

The first step in the inquiry was to identify the individual simple and complex sentences in Galatians as basic components of the letter. The individual sentences can by analyzed further in terms of noun and verb phrases, into which further phrases and even sentences are incorporated,[49] but I did not find such detailed procedures useful for analyzing the macro-structure of the letter. At the same time, I did not find it possible to take compound sentences as basic units because the relationships between the clauses combined in a compound sentence, unlike a complex sentence, remain undetermined. Those relationships are more like the relationships between independent sentences in a discourse than like the relationships between clauses in a complex sentence, as the analysis of 1:10a–c, 12, and 13b–14 below shows. The next step was to establish how the simple and complex sentences are grouped in longer units in the discourse. I present only the first 14 verses of Galatians on page 53 in order to clarify the procedure.

I will first discuss the groupings as individual sentences and their conjunctions, that is, not from the conception of the whole. I should point out, however, that in a few cases revisions were called for by a conception of the whole, but in no case were considerations from the point of view of the whole imposed on those derived from the point of view of the individual sentences. The considerations from the point of view of the whole should be considered as mere aids, as scaffolding so to speak, which helped determine the fundamental groupings. Even where the groupings were discovered with the help of such aids, they can stand on their own and can be discussed without considering the "scaffolding" which helped to identify them.

---

[47] See especially, "Grammatical Meaning and Secondary Semantic Configurations," *Exploring Semantic Structures*, 50–65.

[48] *Translating the Word of God*, 287–432.

[49] See the analysis of the sentence "The man who was angry kicked the dog" in Appendix I (pp. 229–40).

¹ Paul an apostle—not from human beings nor through a human being, but through Jesus Christ and God the Father, who raised him from the dead—² and all the brothers [and sisters] who are with me, to the churches of Galatia.

³ Grace to you and peace from God the Father and our Lord Jesus Christ, ⁴ who gave himself for our sins to deliver us from the present evil age, according to the will of our God and Father; ⁵ to whom be glory for ever and ever.

Amen.

⁶ I am *astonished* that you are so quickly deserting him who called you with the kindness of Christ and turning to a different gospel, ⁷ which is not another gospel, except that there are some who trouble you and want you to pervert the gospel of Christ.

⁸ However (ἀλλά) even if we, or an angel from heaven, should preach to you a gospel contrary to that which we preached to you, let him be accursed.

⁹ As we have said before, and (καί) now I *say* again:

If anyone is preaching to you a gospel contrary to that which you received, *let* him *be* accursed.

¹⁰ For (γάρ) now I *obey* human beings,
or (ἤ) is it God?

or (ἤ) I *try* to please human beings!

If I were still pleasing human beings, I *would* not *be* a servant of Christ.

¹¹ For (γάρ) I would have you *know*, brothers [and sisters], that (ὅτι) the gospel which was preached by me *is* not a human gospel

¹² For neither (οὐδὲ γάρ) *did* I *receive* it from a human being, nor (οὔτε) *was* I *taught* it,

but (ἀλλά) it came through a revelation of Jesus Christ.

¹³ For (γάρ) you *have heard* of my former life in Judaism,

that (ὅτι) I *persecuted* the church of God violently
and (καί) *tried* to destroy it,

¹⁴ and (καί) I *advanced* in Judaism beyond many of my own age among my people, so extremely zealous was I for the traditions of my fathers.

The groupings are on the whole self-explanatory; nonetheless, in order to appreciate fully the structure of the letter, attention should be given to the structural details. The following is intended merely as a guide. The analysis itself proceeded from the smallest groupings and progressed to the larger ones. For the sake of simplicity, the discussion below proceeds from larger groupings, with a clarification of all the subgroupings contained in the larger groupings.

1:3–5. As in the case of 1:1–2, the verb is presupposed in the first sentence (v. 3). One may differ on whether "amen" also presupposes a verb, or whether it is a sentence without a verb. In any case, "amen" forms a group with what precedes it. It is the affirmative conclusion of the latter.

1:6–9. The relationship between 9a and b[50] is of a particular kind: an announcement plus direct/indirect reason. The structural relationship between sentences in direct or indirect reason and those that introduce them is unique and is indicated here by an unclosed bracket. From the point of view of the announcement in verse 9a, "As we have said before, and now . . . say again," the sentence is not complete without 9b. From the point of view of what is actually said, however, 9b itself is a complete sentence. As such, structures such as these do not have to concern us here. For a discussion, see the analysis of sentences 5–9 in Appendix I (pp. 229–40).

Verses 8 and 9 stand in opposition to the statement of verses 6–7, marked by ἀλλά = *however*. The statement of verse 9 is added to the contrasting one of verse 8.

1:10a–c. This part of the verse is a grouping of two sentences, 10a and c, by means of the conjunction ἤ = *or*, with 10b first joined to 10a in a separate grouping, also by means of ἤ = *or*.

1:10d–2:21. Verse 10d replies to the accusation of 10a–c, and 1:11–2:21 substantiates the reply. All of this is not presented on the diagram. This is an example of Paul's expansion at its best. Verses 11–12 give an initial substantiation of the reply in verse 10d. This is in turn substantiated by a series of further points: The way in which he came to the gospel (1:13–2:10); the vindication of the gospel as preached by him in the incident in Antioch (2:11); and finally the reasoning of 2:12–20. To these are added two further statements (2:21a and b), which conclude the entire reasoning.

---

[50] Latin letters—a, b, c, etc.—after a verse number in this inquiry will always refer to the individual sentences in a verse.

The argument in verses 11–12 is expanded by the contrast between Paul's life as a Jew (1:13–14) and what happened after that (1:15–2:10). Galatians 1:15—2:10 is comprised of four separate parts marked by the threefold repetition of ἔπειτα = *then*, 1:15–17, 18–20, 21–24, and 2:1–10. The identification of these larger groupings derives not from considerations of the whole, but from the attempt to answer the question concerning the extent of the substantiation of the reply in 1:10d which begins with 1:11–12. Each of these groupings is itself composed of smaller groupings. The structure of the section as a whole (1:10d–2:21) suggests that Paul gives an answer (1:10d); expands on it (verses 11–12), and then expands on that again (1:13–2:10); adds to it (2:11–14); and again (2:15–20); until he can finally conclude with 2:21.

In more detail these sections can be analyzed as follows:

1:11–12. Verse 11 constitutes a first substantiation, which is then in turn substantiated by the statements of verse 12. However, verse 11 is more than a simple substantiation of verse 10d. γάρ = *for*, followed by the announcement, "I would have you know, brothers [and sisters]," introduces the entire series of arguments (1:11–2:20) which substantiate verse 10d.

The sentences in verse 12 are grouped like those in 10a–c. Two sentences, 12a and c, are grouped by means of the conjunction ἀλλά = *but*, with 12b first joined to 12a in a separate grouping, by means of οὐτέ = *nor*. The differences are not grammatical, but semantic: 10a and c are parallel statements, whereas 12a and c are contraries. Verses 10a and b, however, are contraries, whereas 12a and b are complementary.

1:13–14. The relationship between 13a and 13b–14 is similar to that of an announcement plus direct/indirect reason, except that verse 13a can be considered a complete sentence. It nevertheless anticipates what follows in 13b–14. One could just as well insert a colon after "You have heard of my life in Judaism" (13a). Then 13b would begin with the direct reason: "I persecuted the church etc." What the readers heard (13b–14) is formulated once more in a sentence grouping of the type found in 10a–c and 12a–c. The two complementary statements (13b and c) are in turn grouped with verse 14, in both cases by means of καί = *and*. The pattern in 10a–c and in 12 is that Paul makes a statement (10a and 12a), then adds another to it (10b and 12b) before he joins the first with a third (10c and 12c). It should be noted that the third statement in both cases is grouped with the first only, the second being a type of parenthesis. If this pattern also applies in the case of verses 13b–14, verse 13c should be translated "and I tried to destroy it," giving it greater independence. In the Greek (ἐπόρθουν) it is not possible to determine whether or not the subject "I" is explicit.

What happens in these three formulations, verses 10a–c, 12a–c, and 13b–14, is that Paul makes a statement (10a, 12a, 13b), and then dwells on it for a moment by means of another contrasting (10b) or complementary statement (12b and 13c), before he proceeds to the next statement (10c, 12c, 14). It seems to indicate a reflective mood, and may be due to the pause he makes after each statement while the scribe writes down what he had just dictated.

The γάρ = *for* of verse 13a introduces the substantiation for the assertions of verses 11–12. The substantiation in this case continues through 2:14. When Paul begins to respond to the proposed accusations against him in 10d, he already aims at the final formulation in 2:21, "[So you see,] I do not nullify the grace of God (οὐκ ἀθετῶ τὴν χάριν τοῦ θεοῦ) by the gospel as proclaimed by me; for if justification were to be through the Law, then Christ died in vain (εἰ γὰρ διὰ νόμου δικαιοσύνη, ἄρα Χριστὸς δωρεὰν ἀπέθανεν)."

After the entire text of Galatians was analyzed in this way, identifying the primary groupings of sentences and how those groupings of sentences form larger groups in paragraphs, and how those in turn formed sections of the letter, the task became to consider the analysis from the point of view of the whole. The analysis revealed the letter to be *syntactically* completely *cohesive*; the question then became whether it was also *semantically coherent*. Did Paul express a coherent meaning, or a number of more or less related meanings?

B. *The General Structure of Galatians*

There is no problem with the prescript and blessing (1:1–5) which conforms with conventional letter salutations. The qualification of "apostle" as "not from humans nor through a human being, but through Jesus Christ and God the Father, who raised him from the dead" anticipates a central theme of the letter. In Paul's mind it already addresses the accusation, imagined or real, as formulated in verse 10, and stands parallel to verses 11–12. If the readers knew that such an objection had been made against Paul's proclamation, they would have recognized the polemical nature of the qualification.

1. *Galatians 1:6–2:21*

The most difficult problem in understanding this section concerns the function of γάρ = *for* in 1:10. No commentary offers a satisfactory solution. The closest parallel seems to be 1 Cor 11:22, about which Walter Bauer writes, "oft in Fragen, wo wir ein nachgestelltes *denn auch* gebr[auchen]. . . . μὴ γὰρ οἰκίας οὐκ ἔχετε εἰς τὸ ἐσθίειν καὶ πίνειν; Habt ihr denn keine Häuser?"[51] In English one might formulate, "So, don't you have houses in which to eat and to drink?" The sense of Paul's remark comes out even better if one does not take it as having the form of a question but rhetorically as a sarcastic statement with interrogatory import, in Greek as well as in English: "So, you don't have houses in which to eat and to drink."

With that as an example we can translate in the same sarcastic sense the accusation, "So now I am obedient to human beings." Its function is that, after the "rebuke" in verses 6–9, Paul takes up the supposed or real accusation that in his proclamation he ceased to be obedient to God because he no longer adheres to the Law, but has become subject to human interests. This also sheds light on the ἄρτι = *now* with which verse 10 begins, which coordinates his proclamation with his past life in Judaism referred to in verses 13–14. The formulation of the accusation is Paul's own. In the sense of the charge as formulated, his ἀναστροφήν ποτε ἐν τῷ Ἰουδαϊσμῷ = his "former life in Judaism" could not have been considered as obedience to human beings, but that is precisely what he will argue.

The problem with taking verse 10a as having the form of a statement rather than a question is that, although it gives a satisfactory meaning for γάρ = *for*, it makes the relationship of 10a to 10b difficult, since 10b is clearly a question ἢ τὸν θεόν; = "or God?" Verse 10b in the form of a question as an alternative to 10a suggests that 10a is part of the same question: "Do I now obey human beings or God?" An alternative solution is to take 10b as having a syntactically loose connection to 10a: "So now [it is said] I obey human beings!" to which Paul counters with "or [is it] God? [We shall see!]." The question then leads to the alternative which expands on 10a, ἢ ζητῶ ἀνθρώποις ἀρέσκειν = "or I try to please human beings." Only ἢ τὸν θεόν *has to be* in the form of a question. Also 10c could be taken as having the form of a sarcastic statement. The same relationship applies to 1 Cor 11:22. "So, you don't have houses in which to eat and to drink" does not have to be taken as having the form of a question, but what follows on it clearly is: "Or do you frown on the churches of God and put to shame those who have nothing?" The looseness of the connection of 1:10b to 10a finds many parallels in Paul, notably, as already discussed, in 1:12a and b, where the thought of 12a is continued in 12c, with b as a parenthetic statement; similarly the thought which occurs in 13b and c is continued in 14. For an analysis of the structures of these verses see diagrams 7–11 in Appendix I (pp. 229–40).

---

[51] *Wörterbuch zum Neuen Testament*, s.v. γάρ, 1f.

Gal 1:6–9 thus appears to introduce the topic under discussion, namely, the "gospel" now being "heard" in Galatia as opposed to the gospel proclaimed by Paul. Having set the theme—and twice pronounced an anathema on the other "gospel" (vv. 8 and 9)—Paul takes up the stated accusation against his proclamation of the gospel: "So now I am obedient to human beings in my proclamation—or is it God [to whom I am obedient? We shall see]—or I try to please human beings." To this he gives a preliminary, but conclusive reply: "If I were still pleasing human beings, I would not be a slave of Christ!" The ἔτι = *still* is important, contrasting an earlier time with the present. To what Paul refers concretely is not clear. Does he mean that his ἀναστροφήν ποτε ἐν τῷ Ἰουδαϊσμῷ = his "earlier life in Judaism" (vv. 13–14) had not been to please God but human beings, that rather than please human beings now, he did so earlier when he was under the Law? Probably. He may not have the incident in Antioch specifically in mind, but that incident could be revealing with regard to the issue. In Antioch he certainly did not make himself pleasing to human beings.

The section 1:11–2:21 substantiates the reply in 1:10d to the accusation of 1:10a and c. As I indicated above, when Paul begins to substantiate his reply to the accusations against him in 10d, he already aims at the final formulation in 2:21, "I do not nullify the kindness of God; for if justification were through the law, then Christ died to no purpose." Since he can assume that his readers accept the proposition that Christ did not die to no purpose, he can consider it a telling argument for his readers that justification cannot be through the Law. That argument at the same time suggests a theme he will argue more fully in connection with Abraham's two sons in 4:21–5:1.

Before Paul can say what he wants to say in 2:15–21—comments that refer back to the accusations of 10a and c, and the reply of verse 10d—he first gives proof that the gospel that he proclaimed is not a human gospel: He received it through a revelation of Christ. The argument has the following structure. He first states the case as a substantiation of the reply of 10d in verses 11–21, and then in turn he substantiates that with two further arguments: (i) he contrasts his life as a Jew (vv. 13–14) with the events following his conversion, which culminate in the confirmation of his gospel by the "pillars" in Jerusalem (1:14–2:10); and (ii) he points to the vindication of the gospel as he proclaimed it in the controversy that arose in Antioch (2:11–14). Upon the completion of this reasoning he is ready to conclude with the statements of 2:15–21.

In the series of four events (1:15–17; 18–20; 21–24; 2:1–10), introduced with ὅτε δέ = *but when*, and marked in each subsequent case by ἔπειτα = *then*, it is necessary to recognize the continuity of 2:1–5 and 6–10. The latter five verses do not make a separate point, but round off what was at issue in Jerusalem. This unity is somewhat disturbed by the incidental remark that Titus had not been circumcised, an issue which is not under discussion at this stage. Paul interjects it as something "by the way." That he does so at this point may reveal its importance for him, and calls for our attention.

It is well known that Gal 2:2–5 is riddled with syntactic as well as semantic difficulties. To what does Paul refer when he writes, "lest I run or ran in vain," at the end of verse 2? How do verses 4–5 relate to what precedes, and what do they mean? If these verses (4–5) are taken as part of a new sentence, as the introductory conjunction δέ = *and* in verse 4 suggests, they remain syntactically incomplete. The entire section, verses 3–5, seems to be parenthetic. It is not an entirely coherent part with the rest of the narrative.

The ambiguity at the end of verse 2, "lest it be in vain that I run or ran," is due to the lack of a context which would clarify its meaning. It coheres with what precedes, explaining why Paul did what he states in the beginning of the verse, but there is no context to illuminate its own meaning. One may sense some relationship to what follows in verses 3–5, but the relationship remains vague. In any case, as the text now reads, the phrase stands on its own as if meaningful by itself. The διὰ δέ = "*and* because of" which introduces verses 4–5 seems to begin a new sentence, but it too remains incomplete. There are many anacolutha in Paul, but usually it is clear why he does not complete what he says, for example, a thought intervenes in the form of a parenthesis. Here in verses 4–5 he seems to break off what appears to be a parenthetic statement for no reason, to return to the main trend of his thought in verse 6. If one does not attach too much weight to the δέ, verses 4–5 may be taken as the reason why Titus was not circumcised, but that gives the impression of very incoherent thoughts. It was not because of the false brothers that Titus was not compelled to become circumcised, but as a rejection of their demands.

However one interprets 2:1–5, the coherence between verses 3 and 4–5 is problematic. Verse 3 also does not cohere with what precedes. It is clearly parenthetic. The only question is how far the parenthesis reaches. The problematic nature of the connection between verse 3 and verses 4–5 and the already parenthetic nature of verse 3, suggests that possibly only that verse is parenthetic. If so, Paul resumes his thoughts from verse 2 in verses 4–5. The syntactic structure of 2:1–5 would then appear as diagrammed below. Verse 2a is clearly parenthetic. In this case a branching display can serve our purpose better than bracketing. The broken lines in the schematic indicate parentheses.

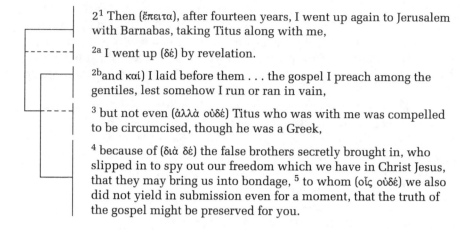

2¹ Then (ἔπειτα), after fourteen years, I went up again to Jerusalem with Barnabas, taking Titus along with me,

²ᵃ I went up (δέ) by revelation.

²ᵇand καί) I laid before them . . . the gospel I preach among the gentiles, lest somehow I run or ran in vain,

³ but not even (ἀλλὰ οὐδέ) Titus who was with me was compelled to be circumcised, though he was a Greek,

⁴ because of (διὰ δέ) the false brothers secretly brought in, who slipped in to spy out our freedom which we have in Christ Jesus, that they may bring us into bondage, ⁵ to whom (οἷς οὐδέ) we also did not yield in submission even for a moment, that the truth of the gospel might be preserved for you.

Verses 2b and 4–5 form a single complex sentence, a single colon, which is interrupted by the parenthesis of verse 3. That Paul frequently interrupted his thoughts in the middle of a sentence is well-known, for example, in Gal 2:6, "From those who are esteemed to be something—whatever they once were does not matter to me; God does not look at appearances. For those in esteem did not expect additional requirements of me." In the case of Gal 2:6 Paul had to start the sentence all over again after the parenthesis. He was unable to continue the formulation he started before the parenthesis because he did not provide the main verb before the interruption. (Note also 2 Cor 5:6–8.)

Thus, underlying the broken syntactic structure of Gal 2:1–5 is a recognizably smooth semantic structure (a structure of meaning) in which the last clause of verse 2 and verses 4–5 provide contexts for each other, leaving little difficulty in interpreting their meaning. Paul obviously operated with a well-formed semantic structure which did not, however, ensure an equally well-formed syntactic structure, particularly as a result of the second parenthesis (v. 3). In this case the broken syntactic structure did not disturb the semantic structure as in Gal 2:6 or 2 Cor 5:6–8, where he had to revert back to his intended meanings with new formulations. If this had not been a written discourse, Paul would probably not have been able to take up the trend of his thought again in verse 4 after the parenthesis of verse 3. In an oral discourse he would have had to revert to the procedure which he used in 2:6 and in 2 Cor 5:6–8, i.e., by starting the sentence all over again after the parenthesis.

In Gal 1:20 we have a parenthetic statement that is syntactically and semantically ambiguous. As the analysis in diagram 16 in Appendix I (p. 240) shows, any one of three semantic structures could have produced the ambiguous syntactic structure of 1:18–24 in which the parenthesis occurs. The situation in connection with the parenthesis of 2:3 is more extreme. It is, from a syntactical point of view, completely without context. The reason why Paul introduced it at this point is not at all clear. Semantically it appears to be a disconnected remark. There may have been something in the preceding clause, "lest somehow it is in vain that I run or ran," which prompted him to introduce it, but what remains unclear at present. We will come back to this later.

The point of the section as a whole is the argument that, contrary to the assumed accusation, it is not in the proclamation of the gospel that Paul is subservient to human beings, but that he could previously have been as a zealous observer of the Law. That he persecuted the church of God, trying to destroy it, could certainly not have been in obedience to God. The events subsequent to his conversion prove that it was as a proclaimer of the gospel that he acted in obedience to God, including resistance to human beings when obedience to God demanded it of him, as in the Antioch incident. He went up to Jerusalem to lay his understanding of the gospel before the "pillars" in order to make sure that his proclamation was not in disaccord with the gospel as they proclaimed it. There is only one gospel, that which Peter *and* he proclaimed, each with a distinct area of responsibility. The leadership in Jerusalem recognized that it was the same God "who worked through Peter for the mission to the circumcised, who also worked through [Paul] for the gentiles" (2:8). That "those in repute" added nothing to what he proclaimed affirms that there was nothing missing in his understanding of the gospel.

This oneness in the understanding of the gospel, and the Jerusalem leaders' agreement with his proclamation, was put to the test in Antioch. From Paul's point of view Peter, as well as Barnabas and the others, could not deny the truth of the gospel as he (Paul) proclaimed it. The truth of his proclamation was affirmed in that incident, including the demand to be obedient to God even when it was not pleasing to human beings, who are represented not only by "certain men (who) came from James," but also by Peter, Barnabas, and the others in Antioch.

The section 2:15–21 distinguishes itself by its discursive character compared with the reporting character of the verses that precede. Syntactically it continues what Paul said to Peter in Antioch, although only 14b is unequivocally recognizable as such. Verses 15–21 may be taken as an exposition of the gist of what he said then, but they apply equally well in the present situation. Verses 15–21 bring Paul's present argumentation, the substantiation of the reply in 1:10d to the accusations of 1:10a and c, to a preliminary conclusion: "I do not nullify the grace of God" with the gospel free from the Law,

but am obedient to God in doing so. With the final statement of verse
21b, "if justification is through the Law, Christ certainly died for
nothing," he sums up the entire argument.

2. Intermediate considerations

a. We have noted that 2:3, the statement that Titus was not
circumcised, is so loosely connected to what precedes and what
follows that it may well be considered as without either a syntactic
or a semantic context. However, circumcision, which appears to have
been at issue in that parenthesis, comes up two more times in the
letter, in 5:2–12 and at the very end of the letter in 6:12–15. It is
noteworthy that in 6:12–15 Paul brings up the subject again after he
had already prepared to conclude the letter with his autograph in
6:11. The subject seems to have been very much on his mind, but up
to this point it has not become clear how it relates to what appears
to have been the main purpose of the letter as expressed in 1:6–5:1, and
specifically in the section to which we now turn our attention, 3:1–5:12.

The answer to the question of how circumcision relates to the
discussion in 1:6–5:1 can be found in the solution to a problem in
the heart of the letter, namely, the relationship between the quotation
of Gen 15:6 in 3:6, and the conclusion which Paul draws from it
in verse 7.

> As (it is written): "Abraham believed in God, and it was reckoned to
> him as justification."

> Therefore you should recognize that it is persons of faith who are
> children of Abraham.

The conclusion is unwarranted by the quotation of Gen 15:6
as it stands. There is nothing about being children of Abraham in the
statement that Abraham "believed in God, and it was reckoned to
him as justification" which could lead to the conclusion that "it is
persons of faith who are children of Abraham." Something must have
been presupposed as the link between the statement and the conclusion drawn from it, something which Paul as well as his readers
would have been able to take for granted. That something was
probably Gen 17:1–12 which reads in abbreviation as follows:

> (God said to Abraham): I will make my covenant between me and
> you, and will multiply you exceedingly. . . . Behold, my covenant is
> with you, and you shall be the father of a multitude of nations. . . . I
> will establish my covenant between me and your offspring through-
> out their generations. . . . And this is the covenant which you should
> keep between me and you and your offspring: You should circum-
> cise all your males. . . . It will function as a sign of the covenant
> between me and you.

That the covenant between God and Abraham was at issue in Galatians is indicated by 3:15–18 where Paul explicitly refers to it. He discusses the relationship between Abraham's trust in God and circumcision at greater length in Rom 4:3–12. The issue and the way it is discussed in Romans and in Galatians are very similar; this should be borne in mind in considering the relationship between the two letters.

Genesis 17 provides the perfect context for the reasoning of Gal 3:6–7. What was at issue in Galatians was the understanding of the covenant and of being a child of Abraham. The Galatians appear to have become persuaded that participation in the covenant included circumcision as was demanded by God in Genesis 17. To combat this Paul quotes Gen 15:6, "(Abraham) believed God and it was reckoned to him as justification." To this statement Paul added nothing. Abraham's trust in God was in itself sufficient for his justification. In Romans 4 in the same connection he emphasizes that Abraham received circumcision only afterwards as a sign of his justification by faith. Thus, according to Paul, one might conclude, "It is persons of faith who are children of Abraham, and not those who are from circumcision" (Gal 3:7).

In the controversy between Paul and the Galatians the meaning of circumcision had become ambiguous. The Galatians apparently understood it as a confirmation of the covenant between God and Abraham. As a Jew, Paul understood circumcision as the ritual by means of which one became subject to the Law, which is what he assumed the Galatians had in mind. Furthermore, for Paul, obedience to the Law as the means of justification, signified by circumcision, was contrary to faith in Christ. "Look, I, Paul, say to you that if you receive circumcision, Christ will be of no advantage to you, and I testify again to everyone who receives circumcision that he [or she] is bound to keep the whole Law" (5:2–3). Note that this comes immediately after the conclusion of his main argument, "For freedom Christ has set you free. Stand firm therefore, and do not submit again to a yoke of slavery" (5:1).

To take circumcision in the above-mentioned sense as the central issue in the macro-structure of Galatians goes a long way towards providing the means "to explain in sufficiently simple terms how it is possible that throughout the text the selection of lexical items and underlying formation of semantic representations is heavily restricted by some global constraint."[52] To begin with, as we noted above, it provides the context within which the parenthesis in 2:3 becomes clear. The reason why the statement that Titus had not been

---

[52] Van Dijk, *Some Aspects of Text Grammars*, 160.

circumcised is introduced without syntactic cohesion at that point is because the issue of circumcision is the semantic context of the discourse. The purpose of 2:1–10 is to introduce the apostles in Jerusalem as unbiased witnesses for the fact that circumcision was not an added requirement to justification by faith. Gal 2:6, "those in esteem did not expect additional requirements of me," is semantically closely related to 2:3, "Titus was not compelled to be circumcised."

The purpose of the reasoning in 2:11–5:1 is to make clear the intolerable implications of circumcision as Paul understood it. Circumcision meant becoming a Jew through submission to the Law, which was contrary to the justification of gentiles by faith. That reasoning provides an appropriate base for Paul's conclusions about circumcision in 5:2–12. Understanding circumcision as the dominant issue in the macro-structure of Galatians also explains why Paul came back to it in the conclusion of the letter in 6:12–15. Briefly formulated, the semantic macro-structure of Galatians was Paul's attempt to explain why the Galatians should not accept circumcision. It was not the means of being true to the covenant between God and Abraham, but the ritual through which one became a Jew by subjecting oneself to the Law. The Law came much later and was contrary to the covenant with Abraham that in him the gentiles would be justified by faith, faith which had its fulfillment in Christ.

b. That this was not the first time the problem of circumcision had been discussed is indicated by the πάλιν = *again* in 5:3, and probably also by 4:16, "Have I then become your enemy by telling you the truth?" This may be exactly what had been at issue. The question of circumcision had previously been raised, and Paul had expressed his fundamental opposition. The Galatians remained unconvinced, arguing on the basis of Gen 17:11–12 that circumcision was the sign of belonging to God's covenant with Abraham. The issue had evidently reached a critical stage, as indicated by Paul's frustration in 3:1–5; 4:11, etc. It is in this situation that he asks the question of 4:16.

c. The apostolic apology (1:10–2:21) appears to be dominated by the issue of circumcision, implicitly in Paul's report of his visit to Jerusalem where his gospel to the uncircumcised was accepted without additions by the Jerusalem leaders (2:6), and explicitly only in the reference to Titus in 2:3. The same issue dominates the report of the Antioch incident with Paul's rejection of the demand that the gentiles should become Jews (2:14), that is, become circumcised.

d. It nevertheless remains clear that for Paul the issue was not circumcision per se (cf. 5:6; 6:15), but the significance of circumcision for the believer. By showing that the inheritance promised to Abraham was intended for those who are in Christ (3:6–14), and that the other son, i.e., Ishmael, representing circumcision and the Law, cannot inherit with the children of the promise (4:21–31), Paul expects that his readers would understand that there can be no supplement to faith, particularly not circumcision and the Law.

3. Galatians 3:1–5:12

In 1:6–2:21 Paul's concern was with the gospel as he preached it. That part of the letter is an apology, introduced by the "ironic rebuke" (1:6–9) in which he establishes the authority with which he preached the gospel. The last, conclusive apologetic statement is 2:21a; in 3:1–5:12 apostolic apology is no longer a concern. Only in 5:10–12 might there be again a hint at an apology. Despite this shift, a consistent theme runs through the entire first part of the letter (1:6–5:12) including the "ironic rebuke" and "apostolic apology," namely, the alternatives of obedience to the Law or freedom from the Law, specifically, whether gentiles have to be circumcised, that is, become Jews, in order to participate in Christ. It is discussed under the aspect of an apology in 1:10–2:21, and in a more straightforward manner, partly paraenetic, in 3:1–5:12.

In a preliminary way the following alternation between sections which function as interactions with the readers and those which function to provide information can be perceived in 3:1–5:12; what M. A. K. Halliday distinguishes as the "interpersonal" and "ideational" components of a discourse.[53]

3:1–5	Interpersonal
3:6–22	Ideational = Exposition
3:23–4:20	Interpersonal
4:21–31	Ideational = Exposition, but with an interpersonal conclusion (v. 31)
5:1–12	Interpersonal

The respective points of the two expositions are: (i) those who believe are the children of Abraham, not those who are under

---

[53] *Explorations in the Functions of Language* (London: Edward Arnold, 1973). Halliday also distinguishes a third, "textual" component. "The ideational component is that part of the grammar concerned with the expression of experience, including both the processes within and those beyond the self—the phenomena of the external world and those of consciousness—and the logical relations deducible from them. The ideational component thus has two sub-components, the experiential and the logical. The interpersonal component is the grammar of personal participation; it expresses the speaker's role in the speech situation, his personal commitment and his interaction with others. The textual component is concerned with the creation of the text; it expresses the structure of information, and the relation of each part of the discourse to the whole and to the setting" (99).

the Law (3:6–22) and (ii) the children of the slave woman cannot inherit with those of the free woman (4:21–31).

Within the interpersonal section 3:23–4:20, a more personal appeal characterizes 4:12–20. It appears as a type of parenthesis between the application of the first theoretical exposition (3:6–22) to the readers (3:23–4:11) and the second exposition (4:21–31). The second and third interpersonal sections (3:23–4:11 and 5:1–12) are paraenetic. The readers are no longer appealed to as judges, as in 1:10–2:21; they are exhorted on the basis of the expositions. The first interpersonal section (3:1–5) provides the introductory setting for the entire section, calling forth the expositions as well as the exhortations.

Although the expositions in 3:6–22 and 4:21–31 are bound by the common theme of Law and Gospel, as well as by the figure of Abraham and his sons, they appear as separate treatises. This is shown by the different word usages. Of the terms that are dominant throughout the first exposition (3:6–22)—*law* (11 times) and *faith* (9 times)—only *law* occurs in the second, and then only 4 times. Inversely, the dominant terms in the second exposition (4:21–31), *son(s)* (14 times), *slave* (8 times) and *free* (7 times), do not occur at all in the former.

On the other hand, there is a close thematic relationship between 4:1–11 in the second interpersonal section, and the second exposition in 4:21–31, both being marked by the theme of slavery and freedom. A significant difference, however, is that in the interpersonal section the contrast is between slavery and sonship whereas in the exposition it is between sonship of the slave woman and that of the free woman, representing two covenants. The same term, υἱός = *son*, which is used as the contrary of δοῦλος = *slave* in the former passage, is used for the son of the slave woman as well as for the son of the free woman in the latter. The sections thus do not appear to be directly related to each other at the concrete, surface level of the text, but only through the theme of "sonship." Thematically, in Paul's mind the two sections may actually have been more closely related than appears on the surface.

The determining issue is what Paul intends with this part of the letter. Are the expositions his primary purpose, or are the exhortations? Is he still concerned with a defense of the gospel (no longer specifically of his apostleship) in the expositions, with the interpersonal sections applying the defense to the situation of the Galatians? Or is his purpose to exhort the readers, for which the expositions serve as theoretical bases?

In one case at least the relationship between exposition and exhortation is clear. In the interpersonal section 4:1–11, an exposition of the conception of inheritance (vv. 1–5) is directly related to the exhortation which follows (vv. 6–11), with the exposition clearly intended as support for the exhortation, the primary objective of the section.

With regard to the relationship of the exposition in 3:6–22 to the exhortation which follows in 3:23–29, one does not get the impression that the exposition concerning Abraham was formulated with the exhortation in mind. Instead, it appears that the exhortation is a conclusion drawn from the exposition for the sake of making it concrete in the situation of the readers. In this case the exhortation seems to serve as a conclusion drawn from the exposition. On the other hand, the connection, καθώς [γέγραπται] = *as* [*it is written*] (3:6), with which the exposition begins suggests that it serves to substantiate the final statement of the preceding interpersonal section, connecting it with the entire preceding section. "Does he who provides you with the Spirit and works powers in you, do so through works of the Law or the obedience of faith; as [it is written], Abraham believed in God and it was reckoned to him as justification" (3:5–6).

In the exposition concerning the two sons (4:21–31), the argument is twice applied to the readers, "But we, brothers [and sisters], are children in accordance with Isaac's promise" (28) and "Therefore, brothers [and sisters], we are not children of the slave woman, but of the free" (31). The introduction to the section, "Tell me, you who want to be under the Law, do you not hear the Law?" (4:21), which ties in with the concluding statement at the end of the section (v. 31), suggests that the entire exposition serves the exhortation. This impression is strengthened by the way in which the introductory sentence follows the very personal exhortation of 4:12–20. The abruptness of verse 21 suggests that the exposition which it introduces is embedded in what precedes. The connection is similar to that between 3:5 and 3:6. The exhortation which begins in 5:1 is also clearly a conclusion drawn from the exposition of 4:21–31.

Apparently the expositions do not stand on their own. They do not have independent meanings, but argue their points for reasons that are beyond themselves. The question is whether those reasons are the exhortations, i.e., that this part of the letter is fundamentally paraenetic, or are the expositions a continuation of the reasoning concerning the Law and faith in 2:15–21? Could not 3:1–5 be taken as a type of paraenetic parenthesis with the reasoning of 2:15–21 continuing in 3:6–22?

It may be best first to try to determine as far as possible the significance of the exposition in 3:6–29. It commences with the statement that it is through trust in God that Abraham was justified (3:6), adding immediately that it should thus be clear that the gentile believers are the children of Abraham (vv. 7–8). The specific emphasis on "those who believe" as the ones who are blessed in Abraham

(v. 9) coordinates with verse 6. The section concludes with the same point (v. 29), except that it now has a christological emphasis added to it, "If you are of Christ, then you are seed of Abraham, inheritors according to the promise." What lies between this verse and the opening verse of the section (v. 9) is devoted to providing this christological emphasis: (i) Christ redeemed "us" from the curse of the Law (vv. 10–14); (ii) Christ is the one offspring in whom the promise to Abraham is fulfilled (vv. 15–18); (iii) the Law had only an intermediary function until the coming of Christ (vv. 19–25), which is partly a continuation of a related theme of (ii) that the Law came in between; and (iv) in Christ we are all united as children of God without distinction (vv. 26–28). It is important to note that this christological exposition is not an end in itself, but shows that the ultimate meaning of being "of Christ" in this context is to be a child of Abraham (v. 29).

The thematic overlapping of (ii) and (iii) may justify considering them as a larger grouping. However, they do not make quite the same point: (ii) argues that the Law which came in between could not affect the promise which was made to Abraham and "to his offspring," whereas (iii) indicates that the intermediary function of the Law was ended by the coming of Christ. In that regard (iii) is more closely related to (i). Thus one may consider all of (i)–(iii) a larger grouping which is supportive of, and thus subservient to, the argument of 3:6–9, with 26–29 relating the christological emphasis explicitly to the argument of verses 6–9. It is interesting to note that although Paul was able to affirm the higher category of being a child of God through the christological point in verse 26, he does not forget that the point of the argument as a whole is being a child of Abraham, "If you are of Christ, then you are seed of Abraham, inheritors according to the promise" (v. 29, cf. 9). Belonging to Christ thus enables one to become a child of Abraham. This reaffirms that being a child of Abraham is the point of the entire section (3:6–29), and that one could consider the main argument to be contained in verses 6–9 and 26–29, with verses 10–25 having an expanding, supportive function.

The argument could be considered complete, but what follows indicates that Paul thought there were still some loose ends. In 4:1–11 he argues that "we" were formerly enslaved under the elemental powers, but "we" have now received the inheritance of children. The crucial reasoning in verses 4–5 is remarkable. Verse 5 contains two final clauses, both introduced by ἵνα = *so that*, "in order to redeem (buy free) those who are under the Law, in order that we receive the gift of the Spirit." One gets the impression that the second follows from the first. That could not be possible, unless "those who were slaves to the elemental powers" are the same as "those who were under the Law." Indeed, in 3:19–20 Paul may have come close to saying that the "angels" who gave the Law are to be taken as having some relationship with the elemental spirits. This impression, however, is contradicted by the more positive function of the Law as (protective) custodian in the time when "scripture consigned all things to sin" in 3:22–25.

In verses 23–25 Paul says that "we" were under the custody of the Law; ὑπὸ νόμον ἐφρουρούμεθα συγκλειόμενοι . . . = "we were confined under the Law, kept under restraint . . ." (v. 23). Is this what is referred to in 4:5a, "so that he might redeem those who were under [the custody of] the Law?" But can being *redeemed* (ἐξαγοράσῃ = *purchase, buy off*) from the Law be considered the same as "no longer (being) under a custodian"? The expression recalls 3:13, "Christ redeemed (ἐξαγόρασεν) us from the curse of the Law." The correlation of 4:1–11 with 3:10–14 is unmistakeable: those who were formerly enslaved under the elemental powers, but have now received the inheritance of children, correlates not only with those who were redeemed by Christ from the curse of the Law, but also with 3:23–25, until faith came we were under the Law. The beginning of 4:1–6 repeats in a different form and at a different level the same point as 3:23–25: being under a custodian before the coming of faith. Does 4:5, "in order to redeem those who were under the Law, in order that we should become children," then not also correlate with 3:10–14, "Christ redeemed us from the curse of the Law" (v. 13) and with 3:23–25, "so that we might receive adoption as children," as two successive events? The "us" of 3:13 does not refer to the gentiles, but specifically to the Jews, those who were under the Law. Thus Paul appears to say, "Christ redeemed us [Jews] from the curse of the Law . . . , in order that the blessing of Abraham might come upon [you,] the gentiles in Christ Jesus, in order that we may receive the promise of the Spirit through faith" (3:13–14). Note that also in 3:14 a second final clause follows the first, but in this case it is expository of the first, probably in the sense of "in order that [all of us together, Jews as well as gentiles] may receive the promise of the Spirit through faith," a meaning that would also make sense of 4:4–5. We will encounter the same sequence again in Rom 15:8–9a, "Christ became a servant of circumcision for the sake of the truth of God in order to secure the promises to the Fathers, and the gentiles glorify God because of mercy." It is a telling argument. Christ freed those who were under the Law from the Law in order that those who are not under the Law, the uncircumcised, could participate in the blessing of Abraham. Now the Galatians want to reverse the process by being circumcised, that is, becoming subject to the Law. It is understandable that Paul chides them, "Having begun with the Spirit, you now want to end with the flesh!" (3:3), and "not to become subject once more to a yoke of slavery" (5:1), the statement with which he concludes this part of the discussion.

If one were to ask why the Jews had to be redeemed from the Law in order for the gentiles to participate in the blessing of Abraham, the answer would probably be that as long as the Jews understood being under the Law as the only means of participating in the promise to Abraham they were not able to recognize that the promise was something in which the gentiles could also participate.

In 4:1–11, Paul relates the redemption of those who were under the Law (Jews) and those who were subject to the elementary spirits of the universe (the gentiles) by means of the one act of God in Christ. He seems to have been distracted from his concern with the Law and faith by the points he makes concerning the elemental powers in verses 3–10, unless it can be argued that the rituals of verse 10 refer to Jewish feasts. If that were the case he would effectively have equated being under the Law with servitude to the "elemental spirits," obliterating every distinction between Jew and gentile, a view for which no support can be found elsewhere in Paul. In these verses he tries to establish a parallel between the Jews under the Law and the gentiles under the elementary powers. The section may thus have a strongly paraenetic function. And if verses 3–10 are a distraction with paraenetic emphasis, it may also explain the somewhat unrelated and very personal remarks in verses 12–20.

With the sharp transition in 4:21, Λέγετέ μοι = "Tell me," Paul returns to the main thread of the argument after the distraction which began with verse 3. This final reasoning may then also culminate the argument. One cannot participate in faith and in the Law at the same time. The two are mutually exclusive. That is what Paul intended in 3:6 when he introduced Abraham as the example of the obedience of faith without works of the Law. The argument concludes with the introduction of the two sons of Abraham in 4:21–31, leading to the final statement of 5:1.

Before the specific mention of circumcision in 5:2 (cf. the parenthesis concerning Titus in 2:3), the full significance of this issue could not have been recognized before one had read the entire letter, unless, like the Galatians, one had been familiar with the circumstances under which it had been written. But now with a strong call to attention, Ἴδε ἐγὼ Παῦλος λέγω ὑμῖν = "Look, I, Paul, say to you" (5:2), Paul makes explicit what the original readers understood as central all along: circumcision. That circumcision is what concerned him throughout the letter is also suggested by the fact that he comes back to it in 6:12–16, after his autograph in 6:11. But the strongest indication that circumcision was the fundamental issue in the letter may be his taking for granted as shared information the reasoning concerning Abraham in 3:6–7. It is evidently also the context for the remark in 2:14, "if you, a Jew, live like a gentile and not a Jew, why do you want to force the gentiles to become Jews?" Circumcision was the ritual through which one became a Jew.

Paul's purpose with the letter appears to have been to re-affirm and outline his opposition to circumcision. Everything preceding 5:2 prepares for his reassertion of the rejection of circumcision in 5:2–12. One should bear in mind that Paul himself had been circumcised. His point is that it had been precisely from circumcision and all it involved that he had been freed through Christ in order to proclaim the gospel to the uncircumcised, "in order to redeem those who were under the Law, in order that we should become children" (4:5). For the Galatians to become circumcised signified for Paul a reversal of the sequence expressed in the reproach, "having begun with the Spirit, are you perfected (ἐπιτελεῖσθε) in the flesh?" (3:3). In the contrary movements in these two verses (4:5 and 3:3) Paul's frustration with the Galatians is revealed, and in these movements lies the key to the understanding of the letter.

C. *The Argument of Galatians in Outline*

The structure of Galatians is more similar to the other Pauline letters, e.g., 1 Thessalonians, than might appear at first sight. The letter does not have the typical thanksgiving section; the "ironic rebuke" of 1:6–9 functions in its place. The exhortation section commences in an atypical way in 5:2. It is atypical in two ways:

1. It does not begin with the usual Λοιπὸν οὖν, ἀδελφοί, ἐρωτῶμεν ὑμᾶς καὶ παρακαλοῦμεν = "For the rest, brothers, I ask you and admonish you" (1 Thess 4:1), or Παρακαλῶ οὖν ὑμᾶς, ἀδελφοί = "Therefore, I admonish you, brothers" (Rom 12:1), but with the much sharper Ἴδε ἐγὼ Παῦλος λέγω ὑμῖν = "Look, I, Paul, say to you . . . " The untypical beginning of the admonition section reveals that as useful as formulas are for identifying the various periods of the letters, they are not the sole means for doing so. At times they fail.

2. The introductory formulation is atypical partly because the main purpose of the letter is explicitly stated only now, in the first part of the admonition section (5:2–12). Thus, in a sense the introductory formulation is still part of the preceding reasoning of 3:1–5:1, all of which prepared for the admonition. Actually a move toward the exhortation section is already made in 5:1, which is a paraenetic conclusion to the reasoning of 4:21–31. The introduction is at the same time sharper, calling the reader more strongly to attention, and smoother, with less of a turn in the discourse than, for example, 1 Thess 4:1 or Rom 12:1. The very abruptness of Gal 5:2 reveals the presence of this part of the admonition in what precedes, drawing the conclusion from it. Nevertheless, 5:2 does introduce the

admonition section. Gal 5:2–12 thus belongs at the same time to the
central section of the letter (3:1–5:12) and to the admonition section
(5:2–6:10). As the conclusion of the reasoning that begins in 3:1, it
ties in with what precedes in 3:1–5:1, and at the same time introduces the admonitions that follow in 5:13–6:10.

Bearing this in mind, it is possible to identify the following
revised conventional structure of the letter. Note the overlapping of
5:2–12 in sections (d) and (e).

> (a) Prescript (1:1–5)
> (b) "Ironic rebuke," in place of the usual thanksgiving (1:6–9)
> (c) Apostolic apology (1:10–2:21)
> (d) Main argument of the letter (3:1–5:12)
> (e) Admonition section (5:2–6:10)
> (f) Postscript (6:11–18)

Understanding circumcision as the issue which prompted
the letter and seeing that Paul wrote in order to state why he
was against it in principle enables us to outline the argument of
Galatians.

1:1–5. In the *prescript* there is already a hint at the theme of
the apology: "not from human beings, nor through human beings, but
through Jesus Christ and God, the Father" (v. 1).

1:6–9. In the *"ironic rebuke"* Paul in effect announces the
theme of the letter, the Galatians' turning away from the gospel for
the uncircumcised, as he proclaimed it, to another "gospel" which
evidently requires circumcision. He rejects the idea that there could be
any other gospel than the one he proclaimed. In the apologetic section
he will argue that the gospel which he proclaimed to the gentiles was
the same as that which Peter proclaimed to the circumcised.

1:10–2:21. Before pursuing the main theme in more detail, he
raises the question of his competence in the matter in the form of a
challenge against the accusation that in his proclamation he tries to
please human beings and to obey them instead of God (v. 10a–c). In
10d he rejects the accusation outright, and then proceeds to substantiate his rejection in 1:11–2:21.

He received his gospel through a revelation of Christ Jesus
(1:11–12); he gave up his life under the Law when it pleased God to
reveal Christ to him (1:13–16). The gospel he received through
revelation, without prior agreement with the apostles in Jerusalem,
was recognized by them as the same gospel which they too had
received before him (2:1–10). The gospel as he proclaimed it was for
the gentiles, for the uncircumcised, which was in no way inferior to

that for the circumcised for which Peter had the responsibility (2:8). He stresses that the Jerusalem leaders did not consider his proclamation of the gospel deficient in any way (2:6d), as if it needed to be supplemented with circumcision as proposed by some or someone in Galatia. Circumcision as an issue surfaces explicitly for the first time in the aside that on the occasion of his visit to Jerusalem it was not expected that Titus should be circumcised (2:3–4).

In the incident in Antioch the gospel as he proclaimed it was sustained in the controversy concerning the association between Jewish and gentile Christians (2:11–14). That it was fundamentally an issue of circumcision is clear from his reproach of Peter, "if you, a Jew, live like a gentile and not a Jew, why do you compel the gentiles to become Jews" (2:14), which means, in the present context, why do you insist that they be circumcised?

Remarkably, Paul reports on the council in Jerusalem in a way which does not support his view of the relationship between Jewish and gentile Christians, even though he may have thought it did. According to his account there were to have been two equivalent forms of the gospel (Gal 2:9). It seems that in recognizing two parallel, equivalent forms of the gospel, the council did not settle the relationship between them. In Antioch the brothers "from James" had opposing ideas of how the two groups were to relate to each other, specifically with regard to matters of food. According to the brothers from James, Jewish Christians remained bound to maintain kosher laws, whereas Paul was convinced that the laws did not apply. Peter, Barnabas, and the others, faced with the choice, agreed with the brothers from James.

Paul's view of the matter was not unequivocal. As late as in Rom 3:30 he could still reaffirm the parallel equivalence of Jewish and gentile Christians, "It is one God who justifies the circumcised out of faith and the uncircumcised through faith."[54] Moreover, 1 Cor 7:18 can give the impression that Paul wanted to maintain the equivalent distinctiveness of Jewish and gentile Christians, "Was someone circumcised when called? Do not try to reverse it! Was someone uncircumcised when called? Do not become circumcised!" However, the next verse reveals his complete devaluation of circumcision, "Circumcision counts for nothing, and not being circumcised counts for nothing, but keeping the commandments of God" (1 Cor 7:19). The statement may give the impression of affirming once more the equivalence of the two conditions, but in reality both parts of the

---

[54] The prepositions ἐκ=*from* and διά=*through* in themselves do not signify a difference in meaning. Paul evidently also does not intend that, but he makes use of the two distinguishable prepositions to indicate that there are two equivalent forms of justification by faith: a Jewish form and a gentile form.

parallelism effectively negate the value of circumcision. On the surface Paul evidently wanted to maintain Jewish and gentile as distinguishable identities, but at a deeper level he ignored the matter. Thus, notwithstanding Rom 3:30, he was at pains throughout Rom 1:18–4:25 to eliminate all meaning in the distinction, interpreting the meaning of circumcision in such a way in chapter 2 that Jews could be considered gentiles and gentiles Jews (cf. 2:25–29), and in chapter 4 making Jews depend on gentile faith for salvation: "[Abraham became] the father of the circumcised for those who are not only from the circumcision, but also followed in the footsteps of the trust while uncircumcised of our father Abraham" (Rom 4:12).

Paul's attitude towards his Jewish heritage probably remained ambivalent. When Jewish identity came in the way of his proclamation he reacted sharply against it, but at heart he probably remained a Jew. Rom 9:1–3 reveals his deep personal attachment to and appreciation of (vv. 4–5) his Jewish identity, notwithstanding his harsh devaluation of it in Phil 3:8. And note how sharply he turns against imagined gentile pride in Rom 11:17–24.

3:1–5:12. In the *main argument* of the letter he addresses the issue of circumcision directly, although not explicitly, with reference to Abraham. For the readers who knew the issue, he did not need to be explicit. His point is that it is through faith that one is a child of Abraham, not through circumcision (3:7–9) as some in Galatia assumed on the basis of Genesis 17. In what follows Paul discusses the meaning of being a child of Abraham, first by showing that those who were under the Law were under a curse from which Christ freed them (3:10–14), including Paul himself, and then by arguing that the Law which came 430 years after the promise could not affect the promise, which found its fulfillment in Christ. In Romans he will argue more to the point, by drawing attention to the fact that Abraham was circumcised after he had already been justified (Rom 4:10–11). The Law and the promise are contraries (3:15–18). The place of the Law in the scheme of things is as a mere custodian until the time of the promise, after which it could no longer have any function (3:19–25). He then underscores the opposition between the Law and the promise with the allegory of Sarah and Hagar (4:21–31). A recurring theme in this section in Galatians is that the Jews had to be freed from the Law in order for the gentiles to participate in the blessing of Abraham (3:1–13, 23–29 and 4:4–6), which means that circumcision had to become irrelevant for the Jews as a step towards the salvation of the gentiles.

In 5:2–12 Paul focuses on the main issue explicitly for the first time, introducing the matter with a sharp call to attention: "Look, I, Paul, say to you, if you become circumcised Christ is of no use to you" (5:2). The relationship between circumcision and the preceding argument concerning the Law becomes clear in the statement that everyone who receives circumcision is bound to keep the entire Law (v. 3), that is, he or she has become a Jew.

5:2–6:10. With his reference to circumcision, Paul already commenced the admonition section of the letter.

6:11–18. In the conclusion of the letter, after his autograph (v. 11), Paul expresses one final time his concern about circumcision (vv. 12–17).

CONCLUSION

There is no single, absolute, macro-structure for a discourse: thus there is none for Galatians. As van Dijk states, and as this study has shown, every reader approaches a text with her or his own macro-structure. What should commend the macro-structure I have proposed for Galatians is that it was developed with the closest attention possible to the text of the letter itself. The test of its correctness will be the subsequently more detailed interpretation of the letter; that is where its usefulness will have to be shown.

The semantic feature of my proposed macro-structure has found indirect confirmation in the studies by Sanders and Heiligenthal that have appeared in the meantime. Contrary to the almost universal view that Paul's opposition to Judaism was fundamentally an opposition to what is characteristically referred to as works righteousness, Sanders argues that works righteousness was never a feature of Judaism, not even of rabbinic Judaism. Thus, Paul's opposition to works of the Law "is not against a supposed Jewish position that enough good works earn righteousness. In the phrase 'not by works of law' the emphasis is not on *works* abstractly conceived but on *law*, that is, Mosaic law. [Paul's] argument is that one need not be Jewish to be 'righteous' and is thus against the standard Jewish view that accepting and living by the law is a sign and a condition of favored status."[55]

A work that is even closer to my specific concerns, and comes to a conclusion similar to Sanders', is the dissertation by Roman Heiligenthal, *Werke als Zeichen*. Heiligenthal understands the meaning of "works" in Galatians as signs of belonging to the people of the covenant. His understanding is "that 'works of the Law' in Galatians

---

[55] *Paul, the Law, and the Jewish People*, 46.

are signs of membership in a group, more precisely, visible signs of belonging to the Jewish people."[56]

As my linguistic analysis has shown, the favored status of membership in a privileged group to which Sanders and Heiligenthal refer is signified by circumcision in Galatians. It comes to its most succinct expression in Paul's sarcastic remark to Peter in 2:15, "We who are by heritage Jews, and not from the gentiles, sinners." That remark may be Paul's most explicit expression of the macro-structure which determined the writing of his letter to the Galatians. With that suggestion we move to a deeper level of his thought to which we will return later. The task to which we need to give attention now is the macro-structure of Romans.

---

[56]*Werke als Zeichen,* 128; cf. 127–34.

3 ～

A Macro-Structure for Romans

I. ANALYSIS OF THE STRUCTURE OF ROMANS

Constructing the epistolary structure of Romans poses no serious problems, except that it lacks a distinct "apostolic apology," although an "apology" is hinted at within the thanksgiving section (1:14–16). Furthermore, in its present form the letter has three concluding blessings in 15:33, 16:20, and 27b. For our purposes the much discussed question of the integrity of chapter 16 is of little significance. The evidence, although not conclusive, appears to favor the conclusion that chapter 16 was not an original part of the letter. Assuming that it ends with chapter 15, the letter reveals the following epistolary structure:

1. Prescript (1:1–7)
2. Thanksgiving (1:8–17)
3. Main argument (1:18–11:36)
4. Admonition (12:1–15:21)
5. Postscript (15:22–33)

A serious issue facing any interpreter of Romans concerns the structure of its main argument, 1:18–11:36. The macro-structure that currently almost universally controls the interpretation of the letter contends that its central point is expressed in 3:21–24, the announcement of justification by faith; for support this approach appeals to the discussion of Abraham's justification in chapter 4. The problem remains, however, how should one understand the relationship of the remaining chapters (5–11) to this central theme? Chapters 9–11 have long been recognized as problematic because of the break, or at least fracture, in the text-syntactic cohesion between 8:31 and 9:1. Because of this break, chapters 9–11 are typically taken as a kind of appendix to the main argument, or even as an independent argument. In chapters 5–8 textual *cohesion* poses no problem; the discussion flows fluently from one topic to the next. The difficulty is with the *coherence* of the various topics in relation to each other and especially in relation to the supposed main theme of justification by faith in 3:21–24. Conventional interpretations fail to recognize this lack of coherence as a problem. Commentaries typically focus on the meanings of individual verses and maximally groups of verses, and studies of individual parts of the letter (for example, the many studies of chapter seven). Such approaches prevent the macro-structure of the letter from emerging as a specific issue.

If justification by faith is accepted as the central theme of Romans, little can be done structurally with what follows 3:21–4:25. Unless chapters 5–8 are taken as a series of semi-independent topics, it is unclear what Paul intends in these chapters. But if these chapters are accepted as a series of discussions of individual topics, then justification by faith as the central theme in the macro-structure of Romans must be forsaken. In that case the letter would have one main theme, which would bring the discussion to a final high point in 3:21–4:25, followed anti–climactically by a series of more or less loosely related sub-themes. But chapters 5–8 do not seem to discuss individual topics. Paul appears to carry on a single discussion that moves from one related topic to another, as if together they constitute a coherent whole. From a text-linguistic point of view, concerned with the meaning of the letter as a whole, it becomes clear that we do not know what Paul is trying to say in chapters 5–8. Even though we are able to interpret the meanings of the individual parts in those chapters, we do not know what the entire letter means.

A. *The Rhetorical Questions in Romans 1:18–11:36*

My initial attempt to solve this problem by means of a discourse analysis, which had been so effective in Galatians, produced no results. With regard to the text-syntactic structure of the letter, Paul appears to move smoothly from one argument to another in chapters 5–8. A discourse analysis reveals text-syntactic breaks as the reasoning moves from one topic to another, but it remains insensitive to incoherence in the meanings of the topics. Thus, the discourse analysis of Romans reveals text-syntactical cohesion in Paul's reasoning through 8:31. It is not until the move from chapter 8 to chapter 9 that a break in syntax occurs. However, the discourse analysis could not identify semantic incoherence in the letter, leaving that problem unsolved. I had come to an impasse.

In one of a number of attempts to overcome the obstacle, I listed the rhetorical questions in chapters 1–11, including the two rhetorical statements in 11:7 and 19.

3:1	What then is the prerogative of the Jew, and what the use of circumcision?
3:3	What if some of them became distrustful? Will not their distrust destroy the trustworthiness of God?
3:5c	Is God unjust who transmits wrath?
3:9	What then? Do we have something to show?
3:27a	What then about boasting? It is excluded. By which Law? That of works?
3:31	Thus the Law is destroyed through faith?
4:1	What then shall we say did our forefather Abraham in accordance with the flesh receive?
4:9	This blessing, then, is it on the circumcised, or also on the uncircumcised? (cf. v. 10)
6:1	What then shall we say? Let us keep sin in order that mercy may become abundant? (cf. v. 2b)
6:15	What then? Should we sin because we are not under the Law, but under mercy? (cf. v. 16)
7:7	What shall we say? The Law is sin?
7:13	The good then became death for me?
8:31	What then shall we say about these things? If God is over us, who is against us? (cf. vv. 31–35)
9:14	What then shall we say? Is there injustice with God?
9:19	Now you will say to me: Why does he still find fault?
9:30–32a	What then shall we say? That the gentiles who did not pursue justice received justice, the justice of faith, whereas Israel who followed the Law of righteousness did not attain the Law? Why?
11:1	I say then: Did God reject his people?
11:7	What then? What Israel sought, it did not find, but the elect found it, and the rest were hardened.
11:11	Thus I say: Did they then stumble to fall?
11:19	You will say: Branches were cut out in order that I should be grafted in.

These questions reveal a remarkable thematic unity from chapter 3 through 11. They all concern problems of the Law and of Israel (the Jews). Note above the close thematic unity of the first two questions and two of the last three, all of which concern the election and rejection of the Jews.

The thematic unity of these questions (3:1; 3:3; 11:1; 11:7; 11:11) suggests a new way of approaching the meaning of the letter. If we consider not only these five, but all the rhetorical questions, it furthermore becomes plain that closely related to the theme of the election and rejection of the Jews is that of the Law (3:9, 27a, 31; 6:1, 15; 7:7 and 13), circumcision (4:1, and 9), and the salvation of the gentiles in relation to that of the Jews (9:30–32a; 11:7, and 19). To these we can add the following questions in chapter 2, all of which concern in one way or another the Jews' relationship to the Law.

2:3   Do you think, you who judge those who do these things, and do them yourself, that you will escape the judgment of God?

2:4   Or do you look down on his graciousness and his tolerance and broadmindedness, unaware that God's graciousness [is intended to] lead you to a change of heart?

2:21–23 You who teach another, you do not teach yourself? You who proclaim not to steal, you steal? You who say, do not commit adultery, you commit adultery? You who loath idols, rob temples? You who are proud of the Law, dishonor God by your transgression of the Law?

2:26   So, if an uncircumcised person observes the just requirements of the Law, will his lack of circumcision not be considered circumcision?

In themselves the questions in Rom 2–11 do not supply a new macro-structure for Romans, but they do suggest a new starting point, a consistent theme throughout the letter, from 1:18 through 15:8–12, namely, salvation of Jews and gentiles, and the relationship between them. Romans 15:8–9a can be viewed as a summary of the theme: "I say, Christ became a servant of circumcision for the sake of the truth of God, in order to secure the promises of the Fathers, and the gentiles praise God because of mercy."

B. *The Prerogative of the Jew*

On the basis of this thematic unity it becomes possible to recognize the theme of the letter in 1:16, "For I am not ashamed of the gospel, for it is the power of God to salvation for all who believe, to the Jews first, and to the Hellenes." The theme of the letter has been widely recognized as 1:16–17, but the emphasis has usually fallen on justification by faith in verse 17, "For God's justice has been revealed in [the Gospel] from faith to faith, as it is written, 'The just will live by faith.' " The thematic unity of 1:18–11:36, however, reveals that verse 17 is not itself the theme of the letter, but only a substantiation of the theme given in verse 16. That God's justice was revealed from faith to faith is not the theme of the letter, but an underscoring of the theme in verse 16 that the gospel is the power of God for all who believe, to the Jews first, and to the Hellenes. A strong thematic bond also becomes manifest in the relationship between the announcement of the theme in 1:16, "I am not ashamed of the gospel, for it is the power of God to salvation for all who believe, to the Jews first, and to the Hellenes," and its summary in 15:8–9a, "Christ became a servant of circumcision for the sake of the truth of God, in order to secure the promises of the Fathers, and the gentiles praise God because of mercy." Paul underscores this by citing scripture in verses 9b–12, "As it is written, 'For that reason I will profess you among the gentiles, and praise your name,' and again [scripture] says, 'Rejoice, O gentiles, with his people,' and again, 'Praise the Lord, all gentiles, and let all the peoples praise him,' and again Isaiah says, 'There will be the root of Jesse, and he who rises to lead the gentiles; in him the gentiles will hope.' " In its simplest form the same theme occurred earlier in 1 Cor 7:19, "Circumcision is nothing, and not being circumcised is nothing, but keeping the commandments of God."

In 1:16 Paul does not say "to the Jews first, and to the *gentiles*," but "to the Jews first, and to the *Hellenes*." What led him to this formulation is his statement in 1:14, "To Hellenes and barbarians, to the wise and the ignorant, I am in debt," a statement probably motivated by his intended visit to Rome where these distinctions would have been appropriate. After the formulation of the theme in 1:16, however, the distinction shifts to one between Jews and gentiles, the circumcised and the uncircumcised. Paul does distinguish between Jews and Hellenes a few more times in the first chapters, 2:9–10 and 3:9, and then again in 10:12. It is noteworthy that after 3:9 the contrast between Jews and Hellenes occurs again for the first time in 10:12. For the rest, the contrast is between Jews and gentiles, the circumcised and the uncircumcised, occurring already in 2:14, and continuing through 15:8–12.

"Hellenes" does not refer specifically to Greeks, but to the cultured and wise, as distinct from barbarians, the uncultured and ignorant. The two groups appear in a different context in 1 Cor 1:22–24, "For the Jews ask for a sign and the Hellenes seek wisdom, but we proclaim Christ crucified, to the Jews a scandal and to the gentiles stupidity, but to those who are called, Jews as well as Hellenes, Christ, the power of God and the wisdom of God." Here Paul moves from Hellenes to gentiles and back to Hellenes as if there were no difference. Although the contrast in Romans focuses on Jews and gentiles, the circumcised and the uncircumcised, the contrast between Jews and Hellenes that first brought him to the formulation of his theme in 1:16 may prove of great importance at a deeper level of his thinking. In his reasoning in Romans as a whole, however, even though he formulates it as a contrast between Jews and Hellenes in 1:16, the contrast is between Jews and gentiles.

It is important to note that the theme is not simply salvation to Jews as well as gentiles, but to the Jews *first*, and to the gentiles. Paul's formulation in 1:16, "to the Jews first, and to the Hellenes," repeated in 2:9 and 10, may be intentionally precise: The Jews are the first to receive salvation, and gentile salvation is grounded in that of the Jews. Gentile salvation is not independent of that of the Jews, nor a mere addendum to it, but an integral part of it. This is vivid in the metaphor of the wild branches grafted into the stem of the cultured olive tree, drawing sap from its roots, in 11:17–21, especially verses 17–18: "If some of the branches were cut out, and you, from a wild olive tree, were grafted into [their place], and became participant in the sap from the roots of the olive tree, do not boast against the branches. But if you do boast: it is not you who bear the roots, but the roots you!" Important as it is to note the warning against gentile arrogance here, Paul's formulation also attests that there is only one community of salvation, that of the Jews, into which gentiles are incorporated.

The only place where this order, the Jews first, and the gentiles, is reversed is in the discussion of the promise to Abraham in 4:10–12, "How was [Abraham's faith] reckoned [to him as justification]? When he was circumcised or uncircumcised? Not circumcised, but uncircumcised. And he received the sign of circumcision, a seal of the justification of faith while uncircumcised, so that he would be the father of all who believe while uncircumcised, that it would be reckoned to them, and the father of the circumcised for those who are not only circumcised, but also follow in the footsteps of the faith of the uncircumcised Abraham." Not only was Abraham justified as an uncircumcised Gentile, but as a result of his justification he became the father, in the first place of the uncircumcised who believe, and then also of the Jews.

Subordinate to the main theme of 1:16–17, to the Jews first, and to the gentiles, appears to be a counter theme in 1:18–2:25, namely, that there is no difference between Jews and gentiles. This counter theme dominates the discussion in 1:18–3:20, and is summarized in phrases, such as, "there is no favoritism with God" (2:11), and, "there is no difference" (3:22), and again explicitly in 10:12, "There is no difference between Jews and Hellenes." The problem posed by this counter theme is how one should understand the Jews being first (1:16) if there is no difference between Jews and gentiles. Paul was obviously aware of the problem, and addressed it squarely in 3:1 by asking, "What then is the prerogative of the Jew; what the use of circumcision?" and reaffirming that the Jews do have a prerogative because they were entrusted with God's revelation, τὰ λόγια τοῦ Θεοῦ: "Much in many ways, the first of which is that they were entrusted with God's revelation" (v. 2). Notwithstanding there being no difference between Jews and gentiles, it is still true that the Jews were the first to have received God's revelation. But that distinction, that prerogative, is threatened by the disbelief of some of the Jews, "what if some of them became distrustful?" (v. 3a). This question is complicated by a second which arises from it: "Will not their distrust destroy the trustworthiness of God?" (v. 3b). Paul does not answer the challenge to the prerogative of the Jews immediately, and only begins to answer, unsuccessfully, the question concerning God's trustworthiness, but returns to these issues as the central theme of chapters 9–11.

In 3:9 he turns once more to the counter theme of the lack of distinction between Jews and gentiles, "What then? Do we [Jews] have something to show? By no means! For we have already charged that everyone, Jews as well as gentiles, are subject to sin." After having affirmed the distinction of the Jews in 3:1–2, Paul now asks if as a result of that distinction Jews have anything to show *for themselves*, to which he replies in the negative. The privilege of having been entrusted with God's revelation does not mean that the Jews have something to show for themselves. In 11:20c–21 Paul says essentially the same to gentile Christians, "It is by faith that you stand; do not be arrogant, but fear; if God did not spare the natural branches, he will also not spare you." Receiving God's revelation by responding to it with trust does not make one person better than another.

The relationship between 3:1–2 and 3:9 reveals how the main theme—salvation for the Jews first, and for the gentiles—and what appears to be a counter theme—there is no difference between Jews and gentiles—relate to each other. The latter is not really a counter theme, but a sub-theme. It shows the fact that Jews and gentiles are equally in need of salvation, as Paul states in Gal 2:14b–16, "I said to Peter in front of everyone, 'If you as a Jew live like a gentile and not a Jew, why do you want to force the gentiles to become Jews? We who are by heritage Jews, and not from the gentiles, sinners, knowing that a person is not justified through works of the Law except through the faith of Jesus Christ, we too believed in Christ Jesus in order to be justified through the faith of Christ and not from works of the Law, for from works of the Law no one will be justified.' "

The threat which the distrust of "some" in Israel (3:3) poses for the thematic order of Jews first, then gentiles, prompts Paul to address the disbelief of the Jews as a separate issue in chapters 9–11. If the salvation of everyone is grounded in the salvation of the Jews, what if the Jews themselves do not believe? The disbelief of the Jews thus becomes an important sub-theme in the letter. That this sub-theme is integral to the main theme of the first part of the letter is shown by the way in which Paul raises it as a question in the discussion of the main theme in order to substantiate his affirmation of the distinction of the Jews in 3:2, "What then? If some of them became distrustful, will not their distrust destroy the trustworthiness of God?" (3:3).

That this issue does not come to mind incidentally is shown by chapter 2 where Paul argues conclusively that Jews and gentiles

are equal before the Law to such a degree that a gentile who observes
"the just requirements (τὰ δικαιώματα) of the Law" can effectively be
considered circumcised (2:26). The reasoning of chapter 2 stands in
such sharp opposition to Paul's main theme that salvation came to
the Jews first, and only then to the gentiles, that he is forced to ask
if there is then after all anything special to being a Jew: "What then
is the advantage of the Jew, and what the use of circumcision?" (3:1).
He reaffirms the sequence of the main theme by stating emphatically,
"much in many ways" (3:2a), and by pointing to God entrusting them
with his revelation as proof: "in the first place that they were
entrusted with God's revelation" (3:2b). This answer in turn raises
the unavoidable question concerning their disbelief. But having been
raised within the framework of the main theme, the question concerning Jewish disbelief immediately recedes into the background
because Paul's response to it changes the focus of the discussion to
a different theme, namely, God's trustworthiness (v. 4) and justice
(vv. 5–8). Paul cannot avoid the issue permanently, and so, after
rounding off the discussion of the main theme in 8:31–39, he raises
it to a thematic level in chapters 9–11.

   In Rom 1:18–3:20 Paul proves both positively and negatively
that there is no difference between Jews and gentiles, representing
the one component of his thesis, "to the Jews first, *and to the
Hellenes*," salvation is for Jews *as well as* gentiles. The gentiles are
depraved (1:18–32), but the Jews are condemned by the very Law on
which they rely for their privileged relationship to God (3:9–20).
Moreover, when the gentiles observe the just requirements of the Law
they fulfill what it means to be circumcised and a Jew (2:6–29). Rom
2:1–5 thus appears to be directed specifically to the Jews who condemn the gentiles, but are themselves guilty of what they condemn
in the gentiles. The challenge of the Jew who condemns the gentile
in 2:3, "Do you who judge those who do these things, and do them
yourself, think that you will escape the judgment of God?" recalls
Gal 2:14, "If you as a Jew live like a gentile and not a Jew, why do
you want to force the gentiles to become Jews?" That challenge
expresses in straightforward terms what he conveys with bitter sarcasm in Gal 2:15, "We who are by heritage Jews, and not from the
gentiles, sinners."

   Paul's challenge in Romans comes through as particularly
harsh after what he had written about the gentiles in 1:18–32. He
does not remain vague, but details his accusation in 2:16–25, giving
cruel substance to his sarcastic remark in Galatians,

> But you call yourself a Jew and depend on the Law and pride
> yourself in God, and know the [divine] will, and, instructed by the
> Law, examine the differences [between good and evil], confident

that you are a guide for the blind, a light in darkness, an instructor of the ignorant, a teacher of the young, having the appearance of the wisdom and the truth of the Law. You who teach another, you do not teach yourself? You who proclaim not to steal, you steal? You who say, do not commit adultery, you commit adultery? You who loath idols, rob temples? You who are proud of the Law, dishonor God by your transgression of the Law. As it is written, "For the name of God is blasphemed through you among the gentiles." Circumcision is useful if you practice the Law; if you are a transgressor of the Law your circumcision has become no circumcision.

Galatians sounds mild compared with Romans.

Romans 2:1–5 and 2:17–25 prepare for, respectively, 2:13–16 and 2:26–29, in which gentiles put Jews to shame concerning obedience to the just requirements of the Law. Paul's remarks in those passages cannot be considered generally true, either for Jews or for gentiles, but even if these are the exceptions, they prove the rule. In 3:9–20 Paul then thrusts home the condemnation of the Jews by means of the very Law on which they depend for their claim to a privileged relationship with God. In between, in 3:1–8, the other component of Paul's theme, "*to the Jews first*, and to the Hellenes," is apparent in his recognition that it was the Jews to whom God entrusted his revelation (3:1–3). Yet even that is muddled by the subsequent disbelief of some of them, which almost certainly refers to their rejection of Christ, as in 10:3–4, "Ignorant of the justice of God, and seeking to establish their own, they did not submit to the justice of God; the end of the Law is Christ for the justification of everyone who believes."

C. *The Complex Issue of the Law*

The component of Jewish priority and the inclusion of the gentiles in the main theme of Romans entails a second, highly complex, sub-theme: the Law. Its complexity is shown by the fact that, on the one hand, Paul expresses the conviction that the justification of Jews as well as gentiles cannot take place on the basis of the Law, "through works of the Law no one will be justified before him, for through the Law is the recognition of sin" (3:20). On the other hand, Paul states that no one should live in disobedience to the Law: "What then? Should we sin because we are not under the Law, but under [God's] kindness? By no means! Do you not realize that to whom you subject yourself as slaves, you are a slave to whom you are subservient, either of sin to death or of obedience to justice?" (6:15–16). Furthermore, according to chapter 2, justification can be achieved by obeying the Law (2:13), and a gentile can overcome what separates her or him from the Jew by observing the just requirements

of the Law: "So, if an uncircumcised person observes the just requirements of the Law, should his [or her] lack of circumcision not be
considered circumcision?" (2:26). Yet, in chapters 3 and 4 Paul is
emphatic that there is no justification through works of the Law,
either for the Jew or for the gentile. For example, in 3:20 he states,
"through works of the Law no one will be justified before God, for
through the Law is the recognition of sin." Even in these chapters,
however, Paul is unwilling to consider the Law and faith as contraries: "Do we destroy the Law with faith?" he asks, and replies, "By no
means! We affirm it" (3:21).

Only once does Paul take up the Law as a separate topic, in
7:7–8:4, where he repeats no less than five times that the Law is good
(vv. 12, 14a, 16, 22, and 25). He evidently hoped to have solved the
problem of his conflicting statements concerning the Law with formulas such as, "So, with regard to myself, I slave for the Law of God
with [my] mind, but with the flesh for the Law of sin" (7:25b), and
"The Law of the spirit of life in Christ Jesus freed you from the Law
of sin and death" (8:2). The sub-theme of the Law is so much an
integral part of the main theme of salvation to the Jews first, and to
the gentiles, that it is not always possible to distinguish it from the
main theme. Here in 7:7–8:4 is the one place where it becomes
thematic, that is, a topic in its own right. And yet, as a sub-theme the
problem of the Law weaves a powerful macro-structural thread into
the fabric of Paul's main argument.

It is important to note that in 3:27–30, when Paul prepares
for his decisive argument against the understanding that salvation is
limited to the Jews, in which he will appeal to Abraham's justification by faith, he realizes that this implies a challenge to the Law. In
3:28–30 he states his case against the limitation of salvation to the
Jews, "For we consider that a person is justified by faith without
works of the Law. Or is God of the Jews only? Not also of the gentiles?
Indeed, also of the gentiles, since it is one God who justifies the
circumcised out of faith, and the uncircumcised through faith." But
before he proceeds to prove that in chapter 4, he asks, "Do we destroy
the Law with faith?" and replies, "By no means! We affirm it" (3:31).
He does not clarify how this is the case. Only in chapter 6 does he
take up the issue again, insisting there on the validity of the Law also
for the believer, first implicitly, "Shall we sin in order that generosity
may abound?" (6:1b), and then explicitly, "Shall we sin because we
are not subject to the Law, but depend on generosity?" (6:15b). Just
as chapters 9–11 are the working out of the problem of 3:3, "what if
some of them became distrustful? Will not their distrust destroy the
trustworthiness of God?" so chapter 6 appears as an exposition of the
point of 3:31, "Do we destroy the Law with faith? By no means! We
affirm it." Paul's understanding in chapter 6 completely agrees with

chapter 2. Even though he nowhere addresses the issue squarely, he is evidently aware of the dilemma that he is at the same time denying and affirming the validity of the Law.

In 7:1 it may appear as if Paul does not address Jews, but gentiles who know the Law, "For I speak to persons who know the Law" (7:1b). Would he speak like that to Jews? It seems similar to Gal 4:21, "Tell me, you who want of be under the Law, do you not hear the Law?" However, what follows in 7:1c–6 could not have been addressed to gentiles; it concerns specifically those who are under the Law: "the Law rules over a person as long as he [or she] lives" (7:1c). Paul appears to be thinking through what it means to be liberated from the curse of the Law, as in Gal 3:10–14; 4:4–5, which suggests that he must be addressing Jews. Certainly what he says in 7:4–6 cannot apply to anyone other than a Jew. Thus, 6:16–23 appears to concern the sinful gentile who has been freed from the depraved existence as described in 1:18–32. Similarly, 7:1–6 concerns the Jew who is freed from the curse of the Law, the curse which Paul hammered home in 3:9–20.

In 7:7 Paul raises the issue of the Law explicitly, "What shall we say? The Law is sin? By no means!" Here the problem of the Law becomes an existential issue which moves beyond the question of its relationship to salvation in a positive (6:15–23) and in a negative sense (7:1–6). Paul's repeated affirmation that the Law is good in verses 12, 14a, 22, and 25 reveals how crucial it is that he not abandon the Law. One may ask whether this existential struggle with the meaning of the Law represents Paul's own deeply personal struggle with the Law. On the one hand, he is opposed to the limitations which the Law sets for salvation, that is, the obligation to prove one's membership in the community of salvation by carrying out the commandments. On the other, Paul's deep conviction that a life contrary to the Law must end up in the depravity of the gentiles. For the Jews, the Law was the pedagogue until the coming of faith (Gal 3:23–24), constraining them from lapsing, like gentiles, into an existence of sin. These alternatives are expressed respectively in 7:1–6, the Jew freed from the curse of the Law, and in 6:15–23, the gentile redeemed from depravation by a commitment to obedience. The alternatives recall once more the main theme, especially in its summary form in 15:8–9, "Christ became a servant of circumcision for the sake of the truth of God, in order to secure the promises of the Fathers," by freeing them from the curse of the Law, "and the gentiles praise God because of mercy," for having redeemed them from depravation.

When Paul continues his apology for the Law in 7:7–8:4, he is without question trying to distinguish between the Law as the representative of what is good (vv. 12, 14a, 22, and 25), and the Law as an oppressive force through sin (vv. 8, 11, 21, 23). In 7:25b he seems to think that he has resolved this existential issue by distinguishing between two Laws, which he evidently understands as two distinct sides of the one Law: "So, with regard to myself, I slave for the Law of God with the mind, but with the flesh the Law of sin." The distinction continues to concern Paul in 8:1–3, but then in verse 4 he moves to a formulation in which it becomes a distinction between the flesh and the spirit which continues in verses 5–17, leaving behind the problem of the Law in its positive and negative meanings. Note the transition in 8:3–4, "[Because of] the impotence of the Law in which it was weak because of the flesh, God, having sent his son in the similarity of the sinful flesh and because of the sin, condemned sin in the flesh, in order that the just requirement of the Law would be fulfilled in us who do not live in accordance with the flesh, but the spirit." Note especially in verse 4 the connection between "the just requirements of the Law" and "who do not live in accordance with the flesh, but the spirit," and then the statement in 8:15a, "you did not receive a spirit of slavery once more to fear," which almost certainly means the Law as a restrictive principle, the curse of the Law to which Paul refers in Gal 3:10–14.

Thus, even though one can subdivide 5:12–8:17 into a number of subsections, each with a unique emphasis (see immediately below), the problem of the Law affords semantic coherence to the entire section. Additionally, passages like 6:16–23 and 7:1–6 cohere with earlier parts of the letter, respectively, to 3:31 (cf. 1:18–32) and 3:9–20. At the same time, as a sub-theme, the problem of the Law integrates the section into the framework of the main theme, "the gospel . . . is the power of God to salvation for all who believe, to the Jews first, and to the Hellenes" (1:16).

D. *The Meaning of Faith in the Structure of Paul's Reasoning*

The importance of the Law as a sub-theme in Romans, apart from its pervasiveness in the main argument of the letter, is shown by the fact that, even though it is integral and thus subservient to the discussion of the main theme in most of the letter, the Law does become thematic in 7:7–8:4. By contrast, justification by faith never becomes thematic. When it comes into sharpest focus in 3:21–4:25 it is not as a separate topic, but as a means of showing that it is only through faith that the blessing of Abraham could become effective for all who believe, Jews as well as gentiles. The clearest statement of the theme of the section is 3:29–30, "Or is God of the Jews only? Not also of the gentiles? Indeed, also of the gentiles, since it is one God who justifies the circumcised out of faith, and the uncircumcised through faith." Equally conclusive for an understanding of the theme is 4:9–10, "This blessing, then, is it on the circumcised, or is it also on the uncircumcised? For it is said, Faith was reckoned as justice for Abraham. How was it reckoned? While circumcised or uncircumcised? Not circumcised, but uncircumcised."

Paul uses the story of Abraham, an essential foundation for the Jews' pride in their exclusive relationship with God, to show that it is through faith, through trust in God, that gentiles as well as Jews are justified, in contrast with circumcision and the Law which limit salvation to the Jews. Abraham received circumcision as a seal of his justification, but, Paul emphasizes, he received it after he had already been justified. And so gentiles as well as Jews can participate through faith in the justification of the uncircumcised Abraham, proving that God is not of the Jews only, but also of the Gentiles.

In 4:13–22 Paul then expounds the nature of Abraham's faith, and its relationship to that of the believer in general, and in verses 23–25 connects it with faith in Christ. Faith is not the theme in these verses, but serves to bring to expression the theme that God is not of the Jews only, but of Jews as well as gentiles. This theme dominates the Abraham discussion through 4:18, with faith functioning to underscore it, as Paul states in 4:16, "For that reason it is through faith in order that it would be a generosity, so that the promises would be secure for every seed, not only for someone who is from the Law, but also for one who is from the faith of Abraham, who is the father of all of us." Only in verse 18 does the faith of Abraham itself become briefly thematic, "who, with hope against hope, believed that he would become the father of many gentiles in accordance with the statement, 'So will your seed be.' " Abraham's faith is then applied as a model for the Christian faith in the God who raised Jesus from the dead (4:23–25). That salvation of Jews as well as gentiles is the theme also in verses 3:21–26 in the beginning of the section, is shown by verses 22–23, "(But now the justice of God has been revealed without the Law), the justice of God through the faith of Christ for all who believe. There is no difference, for all have sinned and fall short of the glory of God." When Paul states in 3:21a, "But now the justice of God has been revealed without the Law," his purpose is not to raise justification by faith to a thematic level, but to argue that the justification of Jews as well as gentiles was made possible "through the faith of Jesus Christ (διὰ πίστεως Ἰησοῦ Χριστοῦ)" (v. 22).

With regard to the structure of 3:21–4:25 it is important to note, on the one hand, the non-christological character of 3:27–4:22, and, on the other, how Paul coordinates Abraham's faith and the Christ-event in 4:23–25. The discussion of Abraham's faith in God is embedded in the two christological passages, 3:21–26 and 4:23–25. Thus, even though the discussion of Abraham's faith in God is remarkably non-christological, especially when compared with Galatians 3, in Paul's mind both discussions were equally christological. As different as Gal 3:16 and Rom 4:23–25 are in terms of the forms of expression, both presuppose the christological foundation of the faith of Abraham.

On the basis of these considerations it becomes possible to recognize that a single theme controls the semantic macro-structure of Romans—salvation for all, for the Jews first, and for the gentiles. That it is through faith that salvation becomes available is an important sub-theme, as is the problem of the Law, which in a negative sense restricts salvation to the Jews, but in a positive sense remains the norm of behavior for the believer.

E. *A Provisional Outline of Romans 1:18–11:36*

One cannot really subdivide the main argument of the letter (1:18–11:36) into separate parts, except that in chapters 9–11 the sub-theme of the disbelief of Israel emerges as the main theme, with the main theme of chapters 1–8 becoming a sub-theme. It may nevertheless be useful to attempt a preliminary arrangement in order to find a way through Paul's complex reasoning. Such a structuring can also reveal the intricate interrelationships of the parts, which may otherwise appear as separate topics:

1. 1:18–4:25—Faith as the means of justifying Jews as well as gentiles

The point of this section can be summarized by asking, as Paul did in Gal 2:14–16: Why judaize the gentiles if we Jews know that even as a Jew one is not justified except through the faith of Jesus Christ? The section can be divided further into two subsections:

1:18–3:20. There is no difference between Jews and gentiles, as Paul states in 3:23, "There is no difference, for all have sinned and fall short of the glory of God," drawing on his discussion in 1:18–3:20. One can subdivide this part further into the following three sections, taking 3:1–8 as a parenthesis:

    (i) 1:18–32, the depravity of the gentiles;
    (ii) 2:1–29, the equality of Jews and gentiles before the Law;
    (iii) 3:9–19, the guilt of the Jews before the Law.

The main point of the section is that with regard to both justification through works and condemnation as sinners, there is no difference between Jews and gentiles, with only a brief consideration of the priority of the Jews and the problems that arise from that in 3:1–8.

3:21–4:25. Faith as the means of salvation for Jews and gentiles. The key to this section is 3:28–30, "For we consider that a person is justified by faith without works of the Law. Or is God of the Jews only? Not also of the gentiles? Indeed, also of the gentiles, since it is one God who justifies the circumcised out of faith, and the uncircumcised through faith." The point of Paul's reasoning in this section is to deny the Jewish claim, based on the Law, that justification is limited to Jews, the circumcised.

Paul's fundamental purpose is not to oppose works of the Law and faith, but to show that it is only through faith that both Jews and gentiles can find salvation. Justification by faith does not stand in opposition to justification through the doing of good works, but to the Jewish claim of an exclusive relationship with God, based on the Law.

Transition: 5:1–11

Paul draws conclusions from the reasoning of the previous two sections, spelling out what they mean, and at the same time, he looks ahead to the discussions in 5:12–8:39.

2. 5:12–8:39—The new life in Christ

This part can be divided further into the following subsections:

5:12–7:6. Four models of transition from the earlier to the present existence.

> (i) the Adam-Christ type anti–type (5:12–21),
> (ii) participation in Christ through baptism (6:1–14),
> (iii) enslavement to sin or to justice (6:15–23),
> (iv) the metaphor of the married woman (7:1–6).

7:7–8:17. The Law of the flesh and the Law of Christ. This section continues the paraenetic application of the meaning of these models already begun in connection with the metaphor of the married woman in 7:4–6. Incorporated into this paraenesis is a semi-independent discussion of the problem of the Law (7:7–8:4). The section can be subdivided further into:

> (i) the conflict between the two sides of the Law (7:7–8:4),
> (ii) the conflict between the spirit and the flesh (8:5–17).

8:18–30. A look into the eschatological future. This section conveys the difference between the present unfulfilled situation and the future fulfillment.

8:31–39. Concluding expression of confidence in the new life in Christ.

Even though individual topics are identifiable in 5:12–8:17, they are all bound together semantically by a single theme, the transition from a previous existence under the Law and sin to the new existence in Christ. In 8:18–19 Paul shifts the focus from his main theme for the first time to look into the future, concluding with his praise of God for the salvation received.

3. 9:1–11:36—The problem of the disbelief of Israel

Paul picks up the issue that he raised in 3:3, the problem of the disbelief of some in Israel. This part can be subdivided into the following three subsections:

9:1–33. The doctrine of double election. Paul attempts to solve the problem of the disbelief in Israel by means of a doctrine of double election. It fails; even if it explains the disbelief of some in Israel, it does not resolve the problem. As the reasoning which follows makes clear, Paul is unwilling to accept the exclusion of even a part of Israel.

10:1–21. The Jews' attempting to establish their own righteousness. By attempting to establish their own righteousness, the Jews were prevented from submitting to the justice of God. The section ends with a strong reaffirmation of Israel's stubborn disbelief.

11:1–36. The ultimate redemption of all of Israel. The section ends with a doxology on the wisdom of God.

II. PAUL'S REASONING IN ROMANS 1:18–11:36

In this section I will try to chart Paul's reasoning, using the above outline as a guide. I will focus especially on Paul's own words, quoting extensively from the letter, in an attempt to avoid abstracting meanings from his formulations. A mere reference to a verse or section of the letter relies on an abstract, remembered meaning. The only way of really understanding Paul is to abstract general principles from the way in which these figures are interrelated in his thinking, for example, series of figures that relate a single theme, and the relationships between themes as the basis for relationships between individual figures.

What is involved methodologically can be illustrated by the discussion of Rom 7:7–8:4 on pages 120—32. In this section of Romans three series of figures denote three closely interrelated themes. The themes are abstractions which generalize the series of figures: α. the Law as a negative power; β. the rupture in human nature due to the power of sin; and γ. the fundamental goodness and holiness of the Law. The relationship between these three themes can be presented as a tension between the negative side of the Law and its fundamental goodness and holiness, which is made intelligible through the mediation of the rupture in human nature, as in the following diagram:

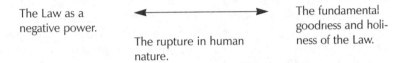

| The Law as a negative power. | ←————————→ | The fundamental goodness and holiness of the Law. |

The rupture in human nature.

Paul did not think consciously in terms of these abstract themes, but in terms of the figures, and even then not in terms of the three series, but of the individual figures and their interrelationships.

On the one hand, by listing the three series of figures and noting the interrelationships between them, it becomes possible to discover what Paul had in mind, even at a subconscious level. On the other hand, it is important to think in terms of Paul's own figures and not in terms of the abstracted themes. So, it is possible to abstract the interrelationships between the three series of figures expressing what I have abstracted as three distinct themes with the following observation: there is a recurrence of figures expressing the positive side of the Law as conclusions drawn from figures expressing its negative side in conjunction with figures that express the rupture in human nature. But to see how the interrelationships function in Paul's own thinking it is necessary to return to the concreteness of the figures themselves. One must note how the figures relate to each other in the connections which Paul himself establishes in the text, by listing the figures in which those relationships come to expression. Such a listing reveals that only the first four of the seven figures in the passage that express the positive side of the Law appear as conclusions from figures that express its negative side in conjunction with the rupture in human nature. The remaining three figures expressing the negative and positive sides of the Law are given in relationships of direct parallel opposition to each other, without the mediation of figures expressing the rupture in human nature. This latter theme is not abandoned, but absorbed into the parallel oppositions between the positive and negative sides of the Law. As a result, in 8:3–4 Paul is able to convert the conflict between the two sides of the Law into a conflict between the flesh and the spirit, with which he takes up again the topic of 7:4–6, which becomes the theme through 8:17. To see how all of this functions, I refer to the discussion of that section of the letter below on pages 120–33.

Listing the series of figures thematically, and the interrelatedness between the themes, provides an abstract structure, a grammar which controls my reading of this section of Romans. As Teun van Dijk points out, "everybody will construct the macro-structure for a text which is relevant to him, personally, and these macro-structures will be different for the same text,"[1] which obviously includes my proposed macro-structure. The crucial question is whether it is a structure abstracted from the text, or one that is brought to it. An abstracted syntactic and semantic "grammatical" structure has validity only as the means through which the text to which it is answerable becomes understandable. To read the text without abstracting such a "grammatical" structure for which the interpreter remains answerable to the Pauline text is the most certain way of imposing a given macro-structure on the text. Such is often the case when the text is read "simply as it stands."

In order to bring the danger of imposing a macro-structure on the text under control it has been my consistent concern to return to Paul's own figures, repeatedly quoting them, in that way ensuring a high degree of answerability to Paul's text itself in the interpretation of his thought. In that way I take seriously Barth's ideal, to write not "*on* Paul, but, certainly not without sighing and shaking one's head, as well as one can, to the last word, *with* Paul."[2] At the same time, by seeking to abstract a macro-structure from the letter itself, I avoid Barth's naïve assumption that he interpreted Romans without a macro-structure, a "system" as he called it, conceding that if he did have a "system" it would be that he kept in mind "what Kierkegaard called the 'infinite qualitative difference' between time and eternity."[3]

In the original form of my study the quotations are in Greek. For the sake of making the study available to a wider readership than those who read Greek, I give the quotations in translation. The translations are my own, as in the earlier parts of this study. Inevitably they represent my readings, and since they continually go back to the Greek, they are not always identical. In that way the reader, including the reader who knows Greek, can determine how I read the text at a given point.

---

[1] *Some Aspects of Text Grammars*, 161.
[2] *Der Römerbrief*, XX; ET, 17.
[3] *Der Römerbrief*, XIII; ET, 10.

As indicated above, the only part in Paul's argument that stands out separately is chapters 9–11, in which the sub-theme of the disbelief of some in Israel comes thematically into focus, while the main theme, salvation for the Jews first, and for the gentiles, recedes into the background as a sub-theme. The first part of the body of the letter, 1:18–8:39, constitutes a unity, in which it is nevertheless possible to *distinguish* two, *inseparable*, main parts: the reasoning that salvation for Jews as well as gentiles is possible only through faith (1:18–4:25), and a discussion of the nature of the new situation in which the believer is placed though faith (5:1–8:39).

A. 1:18–4:25—Faith as the Means of Salvation for Jews and Gentiles

As mentioned above, this entire section can be summarized with Paul's statement in Gal 2:14b–16: in 1:18–32 Paul extensively describes what it means to be "from the gentiles, sinners" (Gal 2:15); in 2:1–3:20 he outlines broadly and expands on his challenge to Peter, "If you as a Jew live as a gentile and not a Jew, why do you want to force the gentiles to become Jews?" (Gal 2:14); and in 3:21–4:25 he clarifies the meaning of "We who are by heritage Jews . . . , knowing that a person is not justified through works of the Law except through the faith of Jesus Christ, we too believed in Christ Jesus in order to be justified through the faith of Christ and not from works of the Law, for from works of the Law no one will be justified" (Gal 2:15–16). Paul's reasoning in this section can be divided further into two steps: 1. 1:18–3:20—Jew as well as gentile (Hellene) stand in judgment before the Law, and 2. 3:21–4:25—Through faith Jews as well as gentiles are justified.

1. 1:18–3:20—There is no difference between Jews and gentiles

The theme that there is no difference between Jews and gentiles occupies Paul's attention throughout this section. He argues first by emphasizing the depravity of the gentiles (1:18–32), then by showing that before the Law there is no difference between Jews and gentiles, because to be justified by the Law depends on observing its just requirements (2:1–29), and finally, by proving from scripture that the Jews too are under the judgment of God (3:9–19). In 3:20 he concludes: "Therefore, through works of the Law no one will be justified before him, for through the Law is the recognition of sin."

The way Paul arrives at this conclusion is complicated, because in his attempt to show that Jews and gentiles are equal before the Law in chapter 2 he does not prove that no one, neither Jew nor gentile, can be justified by doing good works; rather, gentiles who observe the just requirements of the Law are justified by the Law, and Jews who fail to do so are condemned. In 2:7–11 he not only states that one can gain eternal life through good works, but he also presents eternal life as the appropriate objective of such works. Moreover, God's wrath is the punishment for those who do evil: "to those who, with the patience of good works, seek glory and honor and immortality, eternal life, but to those who [live] from strife, and are disobedient to truth but obedient to evil, wrath and anger. Tribulation and pressure on every human being who does evil, on the Jew first, and on the gentile, but glory and honor and peace to everyone who does good, to the Jew first, and to the gentile. There is no favoritism with God."

In the conclusion of his reasoning in chapter 2, the question becomes what does it mean to be truly a Jew, that is, what is the true meaning of circumcision? According to 2:25–27 it is through works that one proves whether one is truly circumcised: "Circumcision is useful if you practice the Law; if you are a transgressor of the Law your circumcision has become no circumcision. So, if an uncircumcised person observes the just requirements of the Law, will his [or her] being uncircumcised not be considered as circumcision? And the by-nature uncircumcised person who fulfills the Law judges you who are through the letter and circumcision a transgressor of the Law." According to 2:28–29, the true Jew, the truly circumcised, will receive praise from God, "For one is not a Jew when it is in the open, nor is circumcision in the open in the flesh; one is a Jew when it is in secret, and circumcision is of the heart, in the spirit, not the letter, of whom praise is not from human beings, but from God." Romans 2 is in effect the apology for justification through works, comparable with Matthew's summary statement in Matt 7:21, "Not everyone who calls me 'Lord, Lord,' will enter the Kingdom of the Heavens, but he [or she] who does the will of my father who is in the heavens." It is not the claim to be circumcised which justifies a person, but observation of the just requirements of the Law.

Significantly, in his conclusion in 2:25–29 Paul is not merely concerned, as in 2:6–16, with gentiles who, "not having the Law by heritage, do what the Law requires,"[4] and so, "not having the Law,

---

[4] φύσει, "by nature, by heritage," is syntactically ambiguous in this verse. It can go with either μὴ νόμον ἔχοντα, "not having the Law," with the meaning that by their (non-Jewish) heritage they do not have the Law, or with τὰ τοῦ νόμου ποιῶσιν, "do the things of the Law," with the meaning that they do the things of the Law naturally. In 1:26–27 the related terms, φυσικὴν, παρὰ φύσιν, clearly refer to what is natural. In 2:27, however, φύσεως, and in 11:21 and 24, κατὰ φύσιν, παρὰ φύσιν, the meaning is clearly the contrasting heritage

are for themselves the Law" (2:14); in verses 25–29 he takes this reasoning a step further by asking, "if an uncircumcised [gentile] observes the just requirements of the Law, will his [or her] lack of circumcision not be considered circumcision?" (2:26). Even if Paul does not use the term, his question can be reformulated, do these gentiles not show by their actions that they are effectively judaized in a way that can be approved? In 2:29 he does refer to being "in secret a Jew" (ἐν τῷ κρυπτῷ Ἰουδαῖος) parallel to "circumcision of the heart, in the spirit, not the letter." Is a gentile who is considered circumcised by fulfilling the Law then not a Jew? What then is the difference between this form of being a Jew, and what Paul opposes so vehemently in his challenge to Peter in Gal 2:14b, "If you as a Jew live as a gentile and not a Jew, why do you want to force the gentiles to become Jews?"

Hermeneutically the questions in 2:25–29 are, what is Paul interpreting, and what are his means of interpretation? Does he interpret a gentile's obedience to the Law by means of circumcision and being a Jew, or does he interpret circumcision and being a Jew by means of a gentile's obedience to the Law? Put in another way, have the abstractly conceived works of 2:6–16 become concretized here as "works of the Law," that is, works on the basis of which a gentile can claim to be effectively a Jew; or is a gentile's obedience to the Law used to interpret circumcision and being a Jew in such a way that they become devoid of the claim to an exclusive relationship with God?

A similar hermeneutical issue arises in the interpretation of Matthew's "Description of the Last Judgment" (Matt 25:31–46). Does Matthew interpret the deeds of non-Christians, persons who do not know Christ but care for their fellow human beings, by attributing to them a crypto-Christian quality, "I was hungry and you gave me to eat; I was thirsty and you gave me to drink; a stranger and you welcomed me; naked and you fed me; sick and you cared for me; I was in prison and you visited me" (vv. 35–36, cf. 42–43), or does he interpret what it means to belong to Christ by means of deeds of caring for fellow human beings that were performed or left undone without Christ in mind? In Matthew's "Description" the king does not address non-Christians, but Christians who either cared for their fellow human beings, or failed to do so, without Christ in mind. Their replies make this clear: "Then the just answered him, saying, Lord, when did we see you hungry and we fed you, or thirsty and gave you to drink? When did we recognize you as a stranger and

---

of Jews and gentiles. The latter is also Paul's meaning here in 2:14. See also Gal 3:14, "We who are by heritage Jews," φύσει Ἰουδαῖοι.

welcomed you, or naked and we clothed you? When did we find you
sick or in prison and came to you?" (vv. 37–39, cf. also the reply of
the others in v. 44). The point of the "Description" is that it is the
deeds themselves that count, not whether they were done with Christ
in mind, that is, in the name of Christ, as in the statement in 7:21.
Not by professing to be a Christian will one enter the Kingdom of
God—"Not everyone who calls me, 'Lord, Lord' "—but by one's
deeds will one be judged—"but he [or she] who does the will of my
Father who is in the heavens." Matthew uses non-Christian deeds,
deeds performed or left undone by Christians without having Christ
in mind, to interpret what it means to belong to Christ.[5] So it is with
Paul in Rom 2:25–29 concerning circumcision and being a Jew.

At the surface level of his expressions in 2:25–29 Paul appears to say that gentiles who fulfill the Law are cryptically Jews,
and can be considered circumcised "of the heart, in the spirit, not
the letter" (v. 29). The question is whether this applies to gentiles as
such. Or does it apply to them by virtue of their being cryptically
Jews? In verse 26 he is explicit, even if it is in the form of a question,
"if an uncircumcised person observes the just requirements of the
Law, will his [or her] lack of circumcision not be considered circumcision?" But what does he mean? His main purpose in this chapter
is to show that before the Law there is no difference between Jews
and gentiles. But does he do so by making Jews of everyone who
obeys the Law, or does he strip circumcision and being a Jew of its
traditional meaning? Does the gentile of verse 26 become a Jew, or
has circumcision and being a Jew become meaningless? It is important to note that Paul does not address gentiles in chapter 2, but Jews,
already in verse 1, and explicitly beginning with verse 17 and
continuing in the second person singular all the way through verse
27, which should apply to verses 28–29 as well. Paul is not addressing gentiles in these verses, telling them how they can in a round-
about way effectively become Jews. He is addressing the Jews, telling
them that the true meaning of circumcision and being a Jew is not
the claim that through "works of the Law" an exclusive relationship
is established with God, but that one is truly a Jew "in secret," and
circumcision is not "in the open in the flesh," but "of the heart, in
the spirit, not the letter." In short, in these verses Paul appeals to the
Jews to obey the Law as if they were gentiles. As he will argue by
means of the Abraham story in chapter 4, the Jew too is justified, not
by virtue of being a Jew, but by trusting God, that is, on a basis which
is equivalent to being a gentile. Abraham, he writes, became the

---

[5]See my *Theology out of the Ghetto. A New Testament Exegetical
Study Concerning Religious Exclusiveness* (Leiden: E. J. Brill, 1971) 63–73.

father of the circumcised "for those who are not only circumcised, but also follow in the footsteps of the faith of the uncircumcised Abraham" (v. 12). The works in obedience to the Law in 2:25–29 are thus still the works of 2:7–10, works in general, so to speak, works of the uncircumcised, not "works of the Law" in the concrete technical sense of circumcision, the sign of being a Jew. And so, as Matthew after him in the "Description of the Last Judgment" interprets the meaning of belonging to Christ by means of non-Christian acts, Paul here in Romans 2 interprets the meaning of being a Jew and of circumcision by means of the works of the gentile who obeys the Law in the abstract sense of 2:6–11. Works in Romans 2 are not the "works of the Law" which Paul rejects so vehemently in Galatians and in Rom 3:20–4:16, but obedience to the Law for which "praise is not from human beings, but from God" (2:29c). It is the same kind of works to which Matthew refers in his "Description of the Last Judgment," and to which Paul encourages his readers in Romans 6.

Circumcision and being a Jew have lost their traditional, exclusive meanings so completely in Paul's reasoning in chapter 2 that he finds himself confronted in 3:1 with the question whether anything still remains which distinguishes Jews from gentiles: "What then is the prerogative of the Jew, and what the use of circumcision?" If the answer to this double question were to be negative, an important component of Paul's main thesis would be lost. It would certainly also be contrary to his own conviction concerning the Jews, as chapters 9–11 clearly show. In chapter 2 he demonstrated the one component of his thesis, that salvation concerns Jews as well as gentiles without distinction so comprehensively that it appears to leave no place for the other component, that salvation was offered "to the Jews first." Thus it is important for him to answer in the affirmative: "Much in many ways, in the first place that they were entrusted with God's revelation" (3:2). That answer will become important again in chapter 11 where Paul will point out to his gentile Christian readers that their salvation is not independent of, but grounded in, the salvation of the Jews. They should not boast against those in Israel who have been excluded through disbelief, because "it is not you who bear the roots, but the roots you!" (11:18c).

At the same time Paul still wants to maintain that the Jews, having been entrusted with God's revelation, are not thereby treated with favor. Thus he returns to the theme of equality of Jews and gentiles when he asks, "What then? Do we [Jews] have something to show?" (3:9ab), and replies emphatically with the negation, "By no means!" (v. 9c). In the substantiation of his negative reply Paul formulates the theme of 1:18–3:20 once more, the comprehensiveness of the need of salvation, "for we have already charged everyone, Jews as well as gentiles, to be subject to sin" (3:9d). The series of quotations from scripture that follow in 3:10–18 serve to underscore his point. These quotations do not prove the sinfulness of humanity in general, but specifically the sinfulness of the Jews, as Paul concludes in verse 19, "We know that what the Law says it says to those who are under the Law." He does not need to prove the sinfulness of the gentiles: in addition to what he wrote as common Jewish knowledge about gentile depravation in 1:18–32, we are reminded of his sarcastic Jewish self-identification in Gal 2:15, "We who are by heritage Jews, and not from the gentiles, sinners." Over against that self-identification the series of quotations from scripture in Rom 3:10–18 prove that the Jews have no advantage over the gentiles before God. They are condemned as sinners, equivalent to gentiles, by the very Law on which they rely to establish their privileged relationship with God. As Paul wrote in Galatians, those who are under the Law are under a curse (3:10). Rom 3:10–18 demonstrates that curse.

And so also the apology of justification through works in chapter 2 is shown to have been intended by Paul as a step in an argument that has as its ultimate purpose to prove that "through works of the Law no one will be justified before [God]" (3:20a). In this way Paul proves the point he made in Gal 2:15–16 that there is no value in judaizing the gentiles because, "We who are by heritage Jews, and not from the gentiles, sinners, knowing that a person is not justified through works of the Law except through the faith of Jesus Christ, we too believed in Christ Jesus in order to be justified through the faith of Christ and not from works of the Law, for from works of the Law no one will be justified."

In the question of 3:1, "What then is the prerogative of the Jew and what the use of circumcision?" Paul shifts the meaning of the terms "Jew" and "circumcision" from the abstract meanings of 2:25–29, being "in secret a Jew" whose circumcision is "of the heart, in the spirit, not the letter" (2:29), to the concrete, historical Jew and to the physical rite of circumcision. His reply in 3:2b, "they were entrusted with God's revelation," and the question which follows in 3:3a, "what if some of them became distrustful?" makes this clear. Thus, also the definition of "the use of circumcision" changes from fulfillment of the Law in 2:25, "circumcision is useful if you practice the Law; if you are a transgressor of the Law your circumcision has become no circumcision," to being entrusted with God's revelation, "they were entrusted with God's revelation" in 3:2b (cf. v. 1b). At issue for Paul is the problem of the historical Israel to which he will return extensively in chapters 9–11.

In the course of Paul's reasoning in Rom 1:18–3:20 the individual points, taken by themselves, do not always express his intended meaning. This is particularly true of chapter 2. The conclusion of his reasoning in that chapter, especially as formulated in verses 25–29, is obviously not what he was driving at in the chapter, as the conclusion of the entire section demonstrates: "through works of the Law no one will be justified before him, for through the Law is the recognition of sin" (3:20). He intended not an apology of justification for good works, but a denial of an exclusive Jewish relationship with God through "works of the Law." But in arguing that "through works of the Law no one will be justified before [God]" (3:20a) Paul could not avoid affirming the positive meaning of obedience to the just requirements of the Law, even if that was not his intent. It will however become his point in chapter 6.

That does not mean that the individual arguments or the larger complexes, such as chapter 2, have no validity in themselves, even if their meanings do not cohere closely with what Paul is trying to say. Therefore, in the interpretation of the letter the meanings of the individual arguments will have to be assessed separately, as will their relationships to Paul's reasoning as a whole. What significance could the tension between those arguments and the reasoning in Romans as a whole have for an understanding of the Apostle's thinking?

2. 3:21–4:25—God is not of the Jews only; also of the gentiles

The theme for this section is given in the question and answer of 3:29–30, "Or is God of the Jews only, not also of the gentiles? Indeed, also of the gentiles, since it is one God who justifies the circumcised out of faith, and the uncircumcised through faith." These two verses, combined with their introduction, verse 28, reveal how faith stands over against what Paul refers to as works of the Law, "For we consider that a person is justified by faith without works of the Law. *Or is God of the Jews only?*" (3:28–29a). Works of the Law here refers not to good works in general, as in chapter 2, especially in verses 6–10 and 25–29, but specifically to what restricts salvation to the Jews. Whatever doubt remains that "works of the Law" do not refer to good works in general is dispelled by 4:9–10 where it becomes clear what Paul means when he says that Abraham was not justified through works. Abraham's lack of a work was that he had not yet been circumcised when he was justified, "This blessing then was it on the circumcised [only]? Or on the uncircumcised as well? For we said, faith was reckoned to Abraham as justification. How was

it reckoned? While circumcised or uncircumcised? Not while circumcised but uncircumcised."[6]

That is not to deny that Paul also says that Abraham did not
have a good work on which he could rely, as he states explicitly in
4:5, "For the person who does not work, trusting instead in [God]
who justifies the ungodly, his [or her] faith is reckoned as justification." The next three verses reveal that Paul found it necessary to
argue that Abraham had been a sinner, "As David also pronounces
the blessing on the person to whom God attributes justice without
works: 'Blessed are those whose sins are forgiven, those whose sins
are concealed; Blessed is the person to whom God does not reckon
sin' " (4:6–8). There is no reason to doubt that Paul believed what he
wrote in these verses, but they may not express the meaning he
actually wanted to convey. If I were to say, "The Dutch are a stubborn
people," I could mean it, but that may not be my point. These words
may not be what I want to say, but rather, "That is why they presented
the Nazis with such formidable resistance." The general statement
about the Dutch is not my point, but preparation for what I want to
say about their resistance against the Nazis.

And so in Paul: Does what he wrote in 4:6–8 express his
point, or are those statements the means of saying something else?
What follows in 9 and 10 reveals his intent. In these verses Paul
clarifies what he had in mind when he presented Abraham as someone who could not rely on a good work, and proving from scripture
that he was justified as a sinner (4:6–8) by noting that it was as a
gentile that Abraham was justified: "This blessing then was it on the
circumcised [only] or the uncircumcised as well? For we said, faith
was reckoned to Abraham as justification. How was it reckoned?
While circumcised or uncircumcised? Not while circumcised but
uncircumcised" (4:9–10). Paul's concern in 4:6–8 is not primarily
with the fact that Abraham had been guilty of sin, but with Abraham's guilt as proof that he had been a gentile when he was justified.

Failure to recognize this leads to a misinterpretation of verse
11 that is devastating for an understanding of Paul, and equally
devastating for Christianity's self-understanding. In order to underscore his point that Abraham was still uncircumcised when he was

---

[6]The first part of 4:9 refers to Jews and gentiles in general, but the
second part of the verse shows Paul's purpose in quoting Ps 31:1–2. It is part
of his argument that Abraham was justified as a gentile, as a sinner. That what
is said in the Psalm applies to the uncircumcised as well as the circumcised
cannot be proven from the Psalm itself, but depends entirely on the reasoning
that follows in Rom 4:9c–11b. Verses 6–8, thus, cannot be interpreted as
having a meaning in themselves; they are subservient to the discussion of
Abraham's justification which begins in 4:1–5 and continues in 4:9c and the
verses which follow.

justified, Paul adds, "And he received circumcision as a sign, as a seal of the justification of faith of the uncircumcised" (4:11a). The problem arises because of Paul's unfortunate use of the ambiguous term "seal." Whereas circumcision as a "sign" unambiguously points beyond itself to Abraham's "justification by faith while uncircumcised," the term "seal," which has the same meaning for Paul, is taken by his interpreters as having a meaning in itself. "Seal" becomes a "hall-mark" (NEB), a "guarantee" (Jerusalem Bible) of Abraham's justification. In this way the term is allowed to usurp a meaning of its own which belies Paul's intent, much like the Jews who, according to Paul, tried to establish their own righteousness, and so did not submit to the justice of God (10:3). In Christian interpretation baptism is typically understood to have replaced circumcision in this sense of a seal of faith.[7] In that way, through the seal of baptism, Christianity is able to take over the Jews' privilege of an exclusive relationship with God, the very privilege which Paul denied the Jews in Romans, as he had previously done in Galatians. This becomes especially transparent in infant baptism, which becomes the basis for the claim to be "by heritage Christians, and not from the heathen, sinners" (cf. Gal 2:15). In believer's baptism this exclusive claim is not denied; it is merely interpreted differently.

Justification by faith means gentile salvation, justification of the ungodly, "For the person who does not work, but trusts in him who justifies the ungodly, his [or her] trust is reckoned as justice" (Rom 4:5). Justification through "works of the Law" is restrictively Jewish. It limits salvation to the Jews, as Paul's negation in 3:28–29 shows "For we consider that a person is justified by faith without works of the Law. Or is God of the Jews only? Not also of the gentiles? Indeed, also of the gentiles." For Paul, the Jew and the gentile are not

---

[7] So Ernst Käsemann, "Das Verständnis der Beschneidung und, davon allenfalls abgeleitet, der Taufe als 'Siegel' hat sich höchstens mit dieser älteren Tradition verbunden. Immerhin ist damit erntshaft zu rechnen, weil Kol 2,11ff. eine traditionelle Typologie von Beschneidung und Taufe in der Urchristenheit voraussetzt, 'versiegeln' in 2.K 1,22: Eph 1,13: 4,30 zur festen Terminologie der Taufe gehört. . . . Für Paulus ist Abrahams Beschneidung die Dokumentation und Legitimation der Glaubensgerechtigkeit." *An die Römer* (HNT 8a; 2d ed.; Tübingen: J. C. B. Mohr [Paul Siebeck] 1974) 108.
   Also Otto Michel, "Die Beschneidung ist nach Gen 17,11 'Zeichen des Bundes' (σημεῖον διαθήκης), nach den Targumen sogar 'Siegel Abrahams' (σφραγίς). Wir haben also eine durch das NT selbst gegebene Bestimmung der Beschneidung vor uns. Es liegt nahe, die urchristliche Bildsprache, daß die Taufe 'Siegel' (σφραγίς) sei, in Zusammenhang mit dem spätjüdischen Sprachgebrauch zu bringen (Barn 9,6). Im Bild des 'Siegels' drückt sich die Zugehörigkeit, die Beglaubigung, sowie die anschauliche bzw. legitime Anerkennung aus." *Der Brief an die Römer* (MeyerK 4. Abt.; 12th ed.; Göttingen: Vandenhoeck & Ruprecht, 1963) 119–20.

fundamentally opposed to each other, nor are good works and faith. The fundamental opposition is between salvation limited to an exclusive group and salvation for all. Salvation that is limited to an exclusive group is expressed concretely as a justification through "works of the Law," which means justification of the Jew only. Salvation for all is expressed concretely as justification by faith, which means justification of the ungodly, the gentile as well as the Jew (see especially 4:11c–12). That the opposition between good works and faith is not fundamental for Paul is shown by his positive estimation of obedience to the Law, not only in chapter 2, which concludes in verse 29 with God's praise for the true Jew who observes the just requirements of the Law without asserting it as a claim against non-Jews, but also in 6:15–23 with his question, "What then? Shall we sin because we are not subject to the Law, but depend on generosity?" and his emphatic denial, "By no means!" (v. 15).

That Jews and gentiles do not stand in fundamental opposition to each other is shown by their common participation in salvation, for example, in 3:29–30, "Or is God of the Jews only? Not also of the gentiles? Indeed, also of the gentiles, since it is one God who justifies the circumcised out of faith, and the uncircumcised through faith," a statement which is amply confirmed by the participation of Jews as well as gentiles in the inheritance of Abraham (4:11c–12). Indeed, to express this common participation was already the main purpose of Paul's reasoning concerning works and the Law in 1:18–3:20, culminating in the statement of 3:22b–23, "There is no difference, for all have sinned and fall short of the glory of God." That this applies to the gentiles is beyond dispute. Paul's point is that it applies to the Jews as well.

That is not to deny the significance of justification by faith in Paul's reasoning, but its significance in this part of the letter is as a means of expressing a deeper meaning, the salvation of gentiles as well as Jews. Paul's concern is that circumcision and the Law restrict salvation to the Jews, whereas faith makes it available to all who believe, "to the Jews first, and to the Hellenes." The opposition between justification through works of the Law and by faith is of great importance for him, but not as an issue in its own right. It arose from the question whether salvation was limited to the Jews, or was intended for the gentiles as well. That is the fundamental issue in Galatians and in Romans, and not the opposition between justification through works and justification by faith which brings it to expression. In both letters Paul argues that from the beginning salvation was promised to the gentiles as well. It is a point he is willing to argue, whether it is in terms of works of the Law (cf. Rom 2:13, "the doers will be justified"), or without them (cf. 3:20, "through works of the Law no one will be justified before [God]"). Thus it is not surprising, as is widely acknowledged, that the term "work(s)" (ἔργον/ἔργα) is extremely ambiguous in Paul, as are "circumcision" (περιτομή) and "Law" (νόμος).

As I have argued above, "works of the Law" in Galatians and in Romans 3 and 4 is close to being a technical term for Paul. The meaning of the phrase should be distinguished sharply from fulfilling the just requirements of the Law (2:26), for which a person receives "praise, not from human beings, but from God" (2:29). That "through works of the Law no one will be justified before [God]" (3:20) does not contradict "the hearers of the Law are [not] just before God, but the doers will be justified" (2:13), or Paul's commendation of good and condemnation of evil works in 2:7–10. All of this agrees completely with the admonition to his readers in chapter 6 not to think that they can do evil because they are not under the Law but beneficiaries of God's kindness, and with his strong defense of "the Law of God" in chapter 7. In Rom 3:20 works of the Law refers to works as the basis for the claim of privilege; in 2:13 it refers to the due reward for doing good in obedience to the Law.

Paul begins his reasoning in 3:21–4:25 by affirming that God revealed his justice through Christ for all who believe without benefit of the Law: "But now the justice of God has been revealed without the Law, witnessed to by the Law and the prophets, the justice of God through the faith of Christ for all who believe; there is no difference" (3:21–22). He does not present this as a new revelation, as something previously unknown. It was "witnessed to by the Law and the prophets" (3:21b). With that Paul reaffirms one of the two components of his main theme, "to the Jews first," which he referred to in 3:1 as "the advantage of the Jew" and "the value of circumcision," and explains further that the Jews "were entrusted with God's revelation" (3:2). It is the other component, "and to the Hellenes," meaning that salvation is not limited to the Jews, which makes him raise the question of 3:27a, "What then about boasting?" to which he replies "It is excluded. By which Law?[8] That of works? No, but by the Law of faith." That Paul intends here is not to negate pride for works in general, but specifically for works on which the Jew relies for her or his claim to an exclusive relationship with God, is shown by what follows in 3:28–29, "For we consider that a person is justified by faith without works of the Law. Or is God of the Jews only? Not also of the gentiles? Indeed, also of the gentiles." That

---

[8]Translating νόμος with "principle" may make Paul's meaning clear at this point, but it removes the ambiguity in the meaning of the term to which his reasoning is subject. I also retain the capitalized form because a lower case, even if correct, would introduce a distinction that is not present in Paul's usage.

"pride" (καύχησις) in verse 27 concerns pride in one's works is shown by 4:2, "For if Abraham was justified through works, he would have something of which to be *proud."*

There is a certain parallel to the concerns of 3:27–30 in the denial of Jewish privilege in 3:9, "What then, do we have something to show? By no means, for we have already charged everyone, Jews as well as gentiles, to be subject to sin." As Paul had negated Jewish privilege in 3:9, so here in 3:27 he negates Jewish pride in an exclusive relationship with God. In this case, however, it is with the qualification that their pride is excluded by the "Law of faith," not by the "Law of works," which allows it. Paul does not call to mind that in 2:1–3:20 he had argued that Jewish pride was excluded by the Law, culminating in the application of the list of condemnations in 3:10–19 to the Jews: "We know that what the Law says it says to those who are under the Law." But here in 3:21–4:25 his intention is to pose *faith* against Jewish privilege; in so doing he abandons the negation of the same privilege by the Law, as he had argued in 1:18–3:20.

Paul negates Jewish privilege twice in two independent sets of reasoning: In 1:18–3:20 he argues his case on the basis of the Law, and in 3:21–4:25 he does so on the basis of faith, revealing that the negation of Jewish privilege on the basis of the Law alone was insufficient for him. It was important to argue it on the basis of faith because that is where he found himself. For that reason, it appears that after he had negated Jewish privilege on the basis of the Law in 1:18–3:20, he may have, for the sake of his reasoning in chapter 4, conceded to a Jewish position which relied on the Law—the Law of works in his formulation—to affirm Jewish privilege.

As we have seen, Paul did write about the Law affirming works at a more abstract level, for example, in his statement in 2:6–11 that God "will reward each in accordance with his [or her] works: to those who, with the patience of good works, seek glory and honor and immortality, eternal life, but to those who [live] from strife, and are disobedient to truth but obedient to evil, wrath and anger. Tribulation and pressure on every human being who does evil, on the Jew first, and on the gentile, but glory and honor and peace to everyone who does good, to the Jew first, and to the gentile. There is no favoritism with God." And in 2:13 he affirms justification for works done in obedience to the Law, ". . . the doers of the Law will be justified." But in 3:27 he does not have in mind pride for good works in general, abstractly, but specifically works that represent the pride of circumcision and being a Jew, which he now maintains is allowed by "the Law of works," but denied by the "Law of faith."

Nowhere is the ambiguity in Paul's understanding of works more evident than here. The pride of works which the Law of faith excludes, that is, the Jewish claim to an exclusive relationship with God, is not quite the same as the pride which the Law of works allows, that is, justification for obedience to the Law, as in 2:13. Paul himself appears to have sensed a problem; after having stated in 2:27 that the Law of the faith denies the pride affirmed by the Law of works, he qualifies that denial parenthetically in 3:31, "Do we destroy the Law by faith? By no means! We confirm the Law." In that way he may have tried to avoid an understanding according to which the negation of pride by the Law of faith in 3:27 applies to the doing of good works as well. An indication that the understanding of pride of works in 3:27 is not exclusively an issue of Jewish privilege can be found in 4:4, "For the person who works the reward is not considered a generosity, but in accordance with what is due."

Paul does not appear to be aware of the ambiguity in his use of the expression "works of the Law," positively as works that are done in obedience to the Law, which he affirms in Romans 2, and negatively as works that establish Jewish privilege, which he negates in 2:1–3:20. He must have assumed that the distinctive meanings were self-evident; he does not think through the relationship between them—they were probably also not sharply distinguished in his mind—but he will take up the issue as a central theme in 7:7–8:4. In 3:27 he writes about pride of works in a way that overlooks the distinction implied by his reasoning in 2:1–3:20. In that way a certain tension between Rom 1:18–3:20 and 3:21–4:25 becomes manifest. In 1:18–3:20 he denied Jewish privilege purely on the basis of the Law: In 3:21–4:25 his intention is evidently to set Jewish privilege in opposition to faith.

New Testament scholars, including myself, are convinced that Paul was not a systematic thinker, and yet what we have up to this point in Romans is certainly a remarkably systematic achievement, notwithstanding the tension just mentioned. Paul builds his argument in 3:21–4:25 systematically on what precedes in 1:18–3:20. The depravation of the gentiles in 1:18–32 combined with the condemnation of the Jews in 3:9–19a enable him to conclude that the Law condemns every human being as a sinner, "So that every mouth will be shut and the entire world will be subject to God's judgment" (3:19b). In between, in chapter 2, he argued for a positive meaning of the Law, and justification for works done in obedience to it. The ultimate purpose of that reasoning is the equality of Jews and gentiles before the Law, but on the surface it already stands in a certain tension with his statement that "through works of the Law no one will be justified before [God]" (3:20).

The entire reasoning in 1:18–3:20 prepares for Paul's main point. Having proved that Jews and gentiles are equal before the Law, he is ready to argue that the difference between Jews and gentiles is also removed through faith, not by absorbing gentiles into Judaism, by judaizing them, but by the participation of gentiles as well as Jews in the promise of salvation to the uncircumcised Abraham, Abraham the gentile. Note the parallels: with regard to works in 2:11, "There is no favoritism with God," and with regard to faith in 3:22b, ". . . there is no distinction." But in his concern to focus on the negation of Jewish privilege by faith, he leaves his argument that that privilege is already negated by the Law (1:18–3:20) completely out of consideration. And so a certain incoherence in the relationship between 1:18–3:20 and 3:21–4:29 is revealed. It is most evident in the contradiction between 3:9, according to which Jews have nothing which makes them stand out, and 3:27, according to which the Law of works does not negate pride. The negation in 3:9 is supported by the entire reasoning of 1:18–3:20, according to which Jews and gentiles are equal before the Law. This thesis is argued negatively in 3:9–20, culminating in the statement in 3:20 that "through works of the Law no one will be justified before [God], for through the Law is the recognition of sin," and positively in 2:25–29, culminating in the statement in 2:29ab that "who is in secret is a Jew, and circumcision is of the heart, in the spirit, not the letter." According to 3:9–20 the Law does not allow pride because it condemns the Jews as sinners, and according to 2:25–29 it does not allow pride because, negatively formulated, "not who is in the open is a Jew, nor is circumcision in the open in the flesh" (2:28). Pride is excluded if one cannot be a Jew in the open and circumcision is not "in the open in the flesh," all the more so if a gentile who observes the just requirements of the Law can be considered circumcised, and so equivalent to a Jew (2:26).

By arguing that Abraham was justified as a gentile—"How was it reckoned? While circumcised or uncircumcised? Not circumcised, but uncircumcised" (4:10)—Paul comes close to saying that the Jews needed to become gentiles once more in order to participate in the promise to Abraham. Yet that is not his intention as becomes clear in his formulation in 4:11c–12, "so that he would be . . . the father of the circumcised for those who are not only circumcised, but also follow in the footsteps of the faith of the uncircumcised Abraham." The Jews as Jews, as the circumcised, also participate in the justification of Abraham as the father of all who believe, even if here the Jews are mentioned after the gentiles. The formulation in 3:30 is more succinct, making use of two prepositions that can lexically have the same meaning to express two realizations of justification by faith, ". . . since it is one God who justifies the circumcised out of (ἐκ) faith, and the uncircumcised through (διά) faith. Both statements, 4:11–12 and 3:30, recall his fine, balanced statements in 1 Cor 7:18, "If someone is called circumcised, do not try to reverse it; if someone is called uncircumcised, do not become circumcised."

Noteworthy about Paul's reference to the faith of Abraham in Rom 4:11a–b is that it reinforces at the same time the priority of the Jews—Abraham receives circumcision as the seal of his justification by faith, "he received the sign of circumcision, a seal of the justification of faith."—and confirms the salvation of the gentiles—he was "while uncircumcised." In this remarkable formulation the two components of his main theme, "to the Jews first, and to the Hellenes," are both present.

What applies to circumcision—which, after all, came much sooner than the 430 years later of the Law—and to the Law, should apply equally well to the coming of the Christian religion over a thousand years later. Paul did try to involve Christ directly in the promise to Abraham in Gal 3:8, "Scripture, foreseeing that the gentiles would be justified by faith, announced to Abraham, 'In you all the gentiles will be blessed,' " and especially in 3:16 with his highly artificial reasoning about the one seed, "The promises were made to Abraham and to his seed. It does not say 'and to his seeds' as if to many, but as to one, 'and to your seed,' who is Christ." In Romans Paul understands Christ's task to have been to secure the promises to the fathers, not to introduce something new, as he states in 15:8, "Christ became a servant of circumcision for the sake of the truth of God, in order to secure the promises of the Fathers." The promise is that the inheritance is not through the Law (4:13) but through faith without the restriction of circumcision and the Law, as Paul states in 4:16, "For that reason it is through faith in order that it would be a generosity, so that the promises would be secure for every seed, not only for the one who is under the Law, but also for the one who is from the faith of Abraham, who is the father of all of us." It was as a gentile, and not as a Jew, that Abraham was justified by his faith, "How was it reckoned? While circumcised or uncircumcised? Not circumcised, but uncircumcised" (4:10).

In 4:19–22 Paul brings into focus the nature of Abraham's faith as the theme of the discussion, and in verses 23–25 he applies it to the faith in God who raised Jesus from the dead. Thematic in both cases is that it is faith in God who makes alive the dead, in the case of Abraham's faith it concerns his own dead body and the dead condition of Sarah's womb (4:19), and in the case of the Christian believer it concerns Christ who had died (4:24).

Even though Paul establishes the relationship between Abraham's faith and the faith of the believer thematically, the thematic coordination of the two manifestations of faith is not his purpose, but the means of coordinating what he had written about Abraham's justification with the Christ-event. That the discussion of Abraham's justification is christologically grounded is apparent in the two highly christological passages by which it is framed, 3:21–26, in which it is grounded, and 4:23–25, which reinforces this grounding. Thus, notwithstanding the remarkably non-christological discussion of the faith of Abraham in Romans compared with Galatians, Romans 4 is no less christological than Galatians.

Transition: 5:1–11

Paul concludes the entire previous reasoning, spelling out its implications, at the same time introducing the discussion which is to follow in 5:12–8:39. What is obviously important for him to convey in 5:1–11 is the assurance of salvation in Christ. He does this by contrasting the previous condition of Jews and gentiles, as described in 1:18–3:20, with the present condition of salvation as described in 3:21–4:25, culminating in 4:11–16 with the discussion of Abraham as the father of all believers. If God reconciled himself with them through the death of Christ while they were still sinners (5:8), alienated from him ("ungodly," ἀσεβῶν, v. 6), how much more can they be confident of that reconciliation now that they are justified (5:6–11).

The contrast drawn between the previous life of alienation from God and the new life of reconciliation with him is reminiscent of the metaphor of the heir coming of age in Gal 4:1–7 and the allegory of Sarah and Hagar in Gal 4:21–31 which has a closer parallel in the metaphor of the married woman in Rom 7:1–3. The theme is developed more positively in Romans than in the polemical allegory of Sarah and Hagar in Gal 4:21–31. Paul concludes the discussion of these contrasts in Romans by interpreting their common meaning paraenetically (7:7–8:17), into which is incorporated, as a semi-independent discussion, the problem of the positive and negative sides of the Law (7:7–8:4).

B. *5:12–8:39—The New Life in Christ*

In this section Paul describes the new life in Christ, continuing the line of thought which he developed in connection with Abraham in chapter 4. After the transition in 5:1–11, the introduction in verse 12, "For this reason (διὰ τοῦτο)" joins what follows with what has preceded. The section 5:12–8:39 can be subdivided into the following subsections: (1) 5:12–7:6, Paul uses four models to underscore the completeness of the transition from a previous life under sin and the Law to the new life in Christ: the Adam and Christ type-antitype (5:12–21); participation in Christ through baptism (6:1–14); slavery to sin and slavery to justice (6:15–23); and the metaphor of the married woman and the law of her husband (7:1–6). A common theme in all four models is that the two sets of circumstances are irreconcilable. (2) 7:7–8:17, paraenetic application of these models to the situation of the readers, into which is incorporated as a semi-independent discussion the problem of the positive and negative sides of the Law (7:7–8:4). (3) 8:18–30, a look into the eschatological future. (4) 8:31–39, an expression of confidence in the new life in Christ.

1. 5:12–7:6—Contrast between earlier and present existence

The four models that emphasize the contrast between an earlier existence under sin and the Law and a new existence in Christ are, as previously stated: (a) 5:12–21, the Adam-Christ type-antitype; (b) 6:1–14, participation in Christ through baptism; (c) 6:15–23, enslavement to sin versus enslavement to justice; and (d) 7:1–6 the metaphor of the married woman. Paul concludes the discussion of the four models by applying them paraenetically to Christian existence in 7:7–8:17, which includes a discussion of the problem of the negative and positive sides of the Law (7:7–8:4). In reality these four subsections are a continuation of what precedes, since Paul is simply expanding on what he wrote in 5:6–11. The continuation of 5:6–11 in 5:12–21 is signalled by the expression "so much more" (πολλῷ μᾶλλον). The expression occurs again in 5:8–10: "God confirmed his love for us in that Christ died for us while we were still sinners: *So much more* will we be saved from wrath now [that we are] justified through his blood. If we were reconciled with God through the death of his son while [still] enemies, *so much more* will we be saved through his life [now that we are] reconciled." And in 5:15: "But with generosity it is not as with the transgression, for if through the transgression of one many died, *so much more* the generosity of God, and the gift in generosity which is of the one man, Jesus Christ, overflows to many." Further, it is repeated in verse 17: "if through the transgression of the one, death reigned through the one, *so much more* those who receive the abundance of generosity and the gift of justification will reign in life through the one, Christ Jesus."

At a more fundamental level the thematic unity of 5:6–11 and the four subsections in 5:12–7:17 is established through the theme of the death of Christ in which the transition from one condition to the other is grounded. Note especially again 5:8–10: "God confirmed his love for us in that Christ died for us while we were still sinners: So much more will we be saved from wrath now [that we are] justified through his blood. If we were reconciled with God through the death of his son while [still] enemies, so much more will we be saved through his life [now that we are] reconciled." This theme is echoed in each of the four models in 5:12–7:6: "if through the transgression of the one, death reigned through the one, so much more those who accept the abundance of generosity and the gift of justification will reign in life through the one, Christ Jesus. Thus, as the transgression of the one man was to the condemnation of all, so the just act of one man is to the justification of all" (5:17–18); "we have been co-buried with him through the baptism into his death, in order that as Christ was raised from the dead through the glory of the Father, so we too might walk in the newness of life" (6:4b); "Praise God that you were slaves of sin, but became obedient from the heart to the teaching that was given to you; having been freed from sin, you have become enslaved to justice" (6:17–18); and, "So, my brothers [and sisters], you too have died to the Law through the body of Christ, in order to belong to another, to him who was raised from the dead, in order to bear fruit for God" (7:4).

This theme also coheres with the next two sections, 7:7–8:4 and 8:5–17, reappearing in 7:24–25: "Wretched person that I am; who will release me from this body of death? Thanks to God, through Jesus Christ our Lord. And so, with regard to myself, I slave for the Law of God with the mind, but with the flesh the Law of sin," and in 8:10–11: "if Christ is in you, the body may be dead through sin, but the spirit is alive through justice. If the spirit of him who raised Jesus from the dead lives in you, he who raised Christ from the dead will make alive your dead bodies through the indwelling of his spirit in you."

There is an important formal and material difference between the first and fourth models compared with the second and third. The first and fourth have meaning almost entirely as illustrations of the fundamental contrast between the two conditions. The nature of the conditions are alluded to only in the conclusion of each section. After the presentation of the Adam-Christ metaphor Paul concludes, "So that, as sin reigned in death, so also generosity would reign through justice to eternal life through Jesus Christ our Lord" (5:21); and after the metaphor of the married woman, we read "For when we were in the flesh, the desires of sin, desires that were [aroused] by the Law, were active in our members to bear fruit for death. But now we have been set free from the Law, having died from that in which we were held captive, so that we slave in the newness of the spirit, and not in the obsoleteness of the letter" (7:5–6). In contrast, the second and third models in chapter 6 illustrate that contrast by describing the conditions themselves. For that reason the second and third can readily be interpreted as discussions which have meanings in themselves, explicitly emphasizing the behavior expected of those who have found salvation in Christ.

It would be a mistake to derive information about Paul's thought from the illustrations of the first and fourth models. Their only meanings are the points they illustrate. Neither of the illustrations are without difficulty. In the case of the Adam-Christ type-antitype Paul expects the illustration to show that what happened in Christ is more than a mere reversal of the fall of Adam: "But not as the transgression is generosity; for if through the transgression of one many died, so much more the generosity of God, and the generous gift which is of the one man, Jesus Christ, overflows to many. And the gift is not as through one who sinned; for the judgment is from the one to condemnation, but the kind act is from many transgressions to a just act" (5:15–16). The metaphor does not reveal why what occurs in Christ is "so much more" than what happens in connection with Adam. In itself the metaphor does not illustrate Paul's point. It can do so only through the meaning which Paul attaches to it in order to accommodate his point. In the case of the illustration of the married woman it is the death of her husband which frees her from her bondage to him by the Law, not her entering into a new relationship with another man. Nevertheless, the latter is the parallel to Christ which Paul has in mind. In both cases Paul's point is clear, but one can recognize it only by noting that it stands in tension with the illustration he uses to express it.

    a. The Adam-Christ type-antitype. Paul's reasoning in 5:12–21 is repetitive, not straightforward, discursive. Through restatement he hopes to make his point clear. We can distinguish the "packets" of his arguments as follows:

[12] For that reason, *as through* one person sin entered into the world, and
        through sin death,
    so also death reached everyone, inasmuch as everyone sinned;

[13] for until the Law came sin was in the world, but sin was not reckoned, there being no Law. [14] But death reigned from Adam until Moses also on those who did not sin in the likeness of Adam's transgression, who is the type of the one to come.

[15] But *not as* the transgression, is kindness;
    for *if through* the transgression of one many died,
        much rather the kindness of God, and the gift in kindness which is
        of the one man, Jesus Christ, overflows to many.
[16] And the gift is *not as* through one sinner;
        for the judgment is from the one to condemnation,
        but the kind act from many transgressions to a just act;

[17] for *if through* the transgression of the one, death reigned through the one,
    much rather those who receive the kindness and the gift of justification will reign in life through the one, Christ Jesus.

[18] Thus, *as through* one person's transgression it came to condemnation of
    everybody,

> so *also through* one person's just act it came to justification and
>   life for everybody;

¹⁹ For *as through* the disobedience of one person many were made sinners,
>   so *also through* the obedience of the one many will be established
>   as just.

²⁰ And so the Law came, in order that transgressions would abound;
>   and where sin abounded, kindness overflowed.

²¹ So that, *as* sin reigned in death,
>   so *also* kindness will reign *through* justice to eternal life *through* Jesus
>   Christ our Lord.

Note the repeated pattern in, respectively, verses 12, 18, 19,
and 21, and verses 15 and 16–17. In verse 21 Paul repeats for the last
time the contrast between what was and what has become, or will be
(as in verses 18 and 19) but with variations worth noting: the formulation is no longer "as through," but simply "as," and "so also"
followed by a twice repeated "through." Note also that in the parallel
formulation in verse 12, "so also" is followed not by a parallel
"through" introducing a contrasting condition, but by a statement of
the result coming from the condition introduced by "as through" in
the first part of the verse.

These differences could be merely stylistic. In reality they
mark a progression in Paul's thought. Verse 12 refers to a condition
that arose through the mediation of Adam. The two intermediate
formulations in verses 18 and 19 refer to a condition mediated by
Christ which reverses the one mediated by Adam. The final contrast
in verse 21 takes the condition established in verse 12 as a given;
there is no further reference to the mediation by Adam, as in verses
12, 15, 17, 18 and 19. Note the parallel formulations: "death reached
everyone, inasmuch as everyone sinned" (v. 12c) and "sin reigned in
death" (v. 21a). Verse 21, drawing the entire series of contrasts to a
conclusion, including those in verses 15–17, reveals Paul's intention.
With the final contrast he moves conclusively forward, away from
the condition in which humanity had been placed by Adam's transgression to the new condition in Christ Jesus, free from the power of
sin and death. Kindness stands over against sin and death. It is
kindness, "the richness of [God's] graciousness, and of his tolerance
and broad-mindedness" (2:4), which frees us from the oppressive-
ness of sin. The statement in verse 21 recalls the peace of God in 5:1:
"Having been justified out of (ἐκ) faith we have peace with God
through (διά) our Lord Jesus Christ."

Verse 20b, "where sin abounds, kindness superabounds,"
raises a question that will concern Paul in both models of the
transition from the previous existence to the new existence in the

next section. It is explicitly recalled in 6:1, "Shall we stay in sin so that kindness can abound?" But both models warn against moral complacency and depravation.

In a remarkable way Paul changes his style in the discussion of the next two models. Romans 6 is divided into two subsections by the parallel formulations in verses 1–2 and 15:

> What then shall we say? Shall we stay in sin so that kindness can abound? By no means!

> What then? Shall we sin because we are not under the Law, but depend on kindness? By no means!

The formulations are not precise parallels, but address the same issue. I will take each up separately.

b. Participation in Christ through baptism. The first subsection, Rom 6:1–14, has an introduction, verses 1 and 2, which states the principle in diatribe form, followed by two further subsections, verses 3–11 which clarifies the point. Verses 12–14 apply it as moral guidance for the readers. Before drawing his conclusion in verse 11, Paul underscores his statement about baptism in verses 3–4 with two parallel arguments (vv. 5–7 and 8–10). The first subsection concludes with a paraenetic principle (v. 14). It does not have the form of an admonition, but states an indicative, which implies an imperative.

[1] What then shall we say? Shall we stay in sin so that kindness can abound? [2] By no means! How can we who died to sin still live in it?

[3] Do you not know that all of us who have been baptized into Christ Jesus were baptized into his death? [4] We were thus buried with him by baptism into death, in order that as Christ was raised from the dead by the glory of the Father, we too might live in newness of life.

> [5] For if we have become co-physical with him in the likeness of his death, we will also be of his resurrection.
> [6] We know this, that our old self was co-crucified with him so that the body of sin might be destroyed, in order no longer to be enslaved to sin.
> [7] For the person who has died is justified from sin.
> [8] But if we have died with Christ, we believe that we shall also live with him.
> [9] For we know that Christ being raised from the dead will never die again; death no longer has dominion over him.
> [10] He who died, died once for all to sin; the life he lives he lives to God.

[11] So you should also consider yourselves dead to sin and alive for God in Christ Jesus.

[12] Let sin therefore not reign in your mortal bodies, to be obedient to their passions. [13] Nor should you submit your members as instruments

of evil to sin, but submit yourselves to God as persons living from death, and your members as instruments of God's justice.

> [14] For sin will not rule over you, for you are not under the Law, but depend on kindness.

c. Enslavement to sin versus enslavement to justice. The structure of Paul's argument in the second subsection (6:15–23), differs from the first. In this case the introduction is a single verse (v. 15) which once more states the principle, followed by a single verse statement of a contradicting principle (v. 16) and then two parenthetic statements (vv. 17–19a) in which Paul applies the contradicting principles to his readers. He then begins a new paragraph (v. 19b) that clarifies in turn the two parenthetic statements, introduced by "for" (γάρ), followed by two further contrasting statements of principle (vv. 20 and 22), each with a supplementary statement (vv. 21 and 23).

[15] What then? Shall we sin because we are not under the Law, but depend on kindness? By no means!

[16] Do you not know that to whom you submit yourself as slaves in obedience, you are slaves to whom you are obedient, either of sin, to death, or of obedience, to justice?

> [17] But thanks to God, you were once slaves of sin, but became obedient from your hearts to the kind of teaching to which you submitted,
> [18] having been freed from sin, you have become slaves of justice.
> [19a] I say this in human terms because of the weakness of your flesh.

[19b] For as you once submitted your members to impurity and to evil for the sake of evil, so you now submit your members to justice for sanctification.

> [20] When you were slaves of sin, you were free from justice.
> > [21] What reward did you have then from the things of which you are now ashamed? The end of such things is death.
> [22] But now, having been set free from sin, becoming slaves of God, you have your fruit to sanctification, with its end, eternal life.
> > [23] For the wages of sin is death, but the gift of God is eternal life in Christ Jesus our Lord.

The question in verse 15, "Shall we sin because we are not under the Law, but depend on kindness?" is prompted by the statement in verse 14 of the previous subsection, "Sin will not rule over you, for you are not under the law, but depend on kindness." Thus, the reasoning of verses 15–23 takes the argument of verses 1–14 a step further.

The structure of the two subsections have a degree of parallelism. Both subsections begin with rhetorical questions that are resolutely negated (vv. 1–2a and 15, respectively), in the first case followed by a supportive second rhetorical question (v. 2b). Then in each case Paul appeals to what the readers are already expected to know in principle (vv. 3–4 and 16). In the first case Paul appeals to their knowledge of baptism in Christ; in the second case to the social institution of slavery. These appeals are the basis for his argument (vv. 5–11 and 17–19a). And in each case this is followed by a conclusion from the basic statements and their supportive arguments in the form of paraenesis (vv. 12–13 and 19b–c). These paraenetic statements are the final answers to the rhetorical questions in verses 1 and 15. In the second subsection Paul lets further supportive arguments follow (vv. 20–22). In terms of the argument, these verses could just as well come before verse 19b–c, since they function in the same way as verses 5–10 in the first subsection, and 17–19a in the second. Both subsections are concluded with more universal statements (vv. 14 and 23).

What concerns Paul in these sections are the final answers in verses 12–13 and 19b–c to the rhetorical questions in verses 1 and 15. The rest of the sections are intended to support these paraenetic calls. The purpose of the chapter, then, is not to expound on baptism and slave relationships; these are simply foundations for paraenesis, which is the purpose of the chapter. The foundations for the arguments can themselves change, baptism or slavery, providing parallel bases for the reasoning. Thus, the foundations themselves are not decisive. They can change. What is decisive is the paraenesis.

d. The metaphor of the married woman. Paul's final model, the woman who is freed from the law of her husband when the husband dies, is straightforward. The analysis of the stylistic structure of the first three models reveals Paul's changing styles of thinking and his remarkable ability to use parallel structures to convey his thoughts. The proposed structures are abstractions. Paradoxically, as abstract structures they aid us in charting the process of Paul's thinking concretely, thereby avoiding the necessity of translating his thoughts into abstract arguments. We will find an even clearer example of this process in his attempt to think through the problem of the positive and negative sides of the Law in 7:7–8:4.

Compared with the first and fourth models, the second and third share a strong, inherently paraenetic character. In them Paul makes his point by means of a discussion of Christian existence itself. His reasoning recalls the opposition in Gal 3:2, "This alone I would like to learn from you, did you receive the spirit through works of the Law or through the obedience of faith?" and 5:16–17, "But I say, walk in the spirit and do not fulfill the desires of the flesh.

For the flesh desires against the spirit, and the spirit against the flesh. They stand opposed to each other, so that you cannot do what you want to." The final statement foreshadows Paul's argument in terms of the rupture in human behavior in Rom 7:7–8:4.

The transition from the previous condition under sin and the Law to the new existence in Christ binds all four models together thematically, and all four of them to 5:1–11, especially verses 6–11. The transition from one condition to the other also connects 5:1–7:6 thematically with 1:18–4:25 in which it is presented in detail as a transition from subjection to the power of sin and the Law (1:18–3:20)—gentiles (1:18–32) as well as Jews (2:1–3:20)—to their common liberation from that condition through faith, exemplified by Abraham (3:21–4:25). In this way, through the link of 5:1–11 and the thematic continuity between 1:18–4:25 and 5:12–8:17, coherence is established throughout the entire first part of Romans. At a deeper level there is another theme, the problem of the Law, which binds the entire section to Paul's main theme that "the gospel . . . is the power of God to salvation for all who believe, to the Jews first, and to the Hellenes" (1:16). In 7:7–8:17 the Law becomes the main topic of discussion. It is never far below the surface in 5:1–7:6, but in 7:7–8:17 Paul can no longer avoid taking it up as a specific issue, similar to the way in which he would no longer be able to avoid the problem of the disbelief of some in Israel in chapters 9–11.

The problem of the Law surfaces in the question in 6:15, "Shall we sin because we are not subject to the Law, but depend on generosity?" This question makes explicit what is implicit with regard to the Law in 6:1, "Shall we sin in order that generosity may abound?" and in 7:6, "we have been set free from the Law, having died from that in which we were held captive, so that we slave in the newness of the spirit, and not the obsoleteness of the letter." The latter text shows that it is not a simple question of abandoning the Law, but of a new form of obedience to it, in the spirit and not in the letter. The statement expresses the same ideals as those in 2:7, "[God will give] to those who, with the patience of good works, seek glory and honor and immortality, eternal life," and in 2:10, "glory and honor and peace to everyone who does good, to the Jew first, and to the gentile." Thus, even though Paul writes that "we are not subject to the Law" (6:15) and "we have been set free from the Law" (7:6) he remains concerned with behavior which is in conformity with the Law. This concern is evident when he asks, "How can we who died to sin still live in it?" (6:2), and, "Do you not realize that to whom you subject yourself in subservience as slaves, you are a slave to whom you are subservient, either of sin to death or of obedience to justice?" (6:16).

In the reasoning of 5:12–21 the Law surfaces already in verse 13 with the reference to the time before the Law, and then, at the end of the section, in the reference to the coming of the Law, "But the Law came in between, in order that transgressions should abound; and where sin abounded, generosity overflowed. So that, as sin reigned in death, so also generosity would reign through justice to eternal life through Jesus Christ our Lord" (5:20–21). This formulation anticipates later discussions, including 7:7–8:17, where it becomes the main topic.

At the surface level it appears as if Paul abandoned submission to the Law; at the deeper level of his intended meaning, however, he remains bound in obedience to it. So, when he admonishes his readers, "Do not let sin reign in your mortal bodies to be obedient to its lusts, nor put your members at the disposal of sin as weapons of evil, but place yourselves at the disposal of God as living from death, and your members as weapons of justice for God" (6:12–13), it recalls his affirmation of the Law in chapter 2, summed up in the statement, "Not the hearers of the Law are just before God, but the doers will be justified" (2:13). Even if he does write, "For sin will not rule over you; for you are not subject to the Law, but depend on generosity" (6:14), the just requirements of the Law remain valid. The next verses leave no doubt about the agreement with chapter 2. This can be seen when one compares Paul's admonition in 6:15–18 with his commendation of obedience to the Law in 2:7–10: "Shall we sin because we are not subject to the Law, but depend on generosity? By no means! Do you not realize that to whom you subject yourself in subservience as slaves, you are a slave to whom you are subservient, either of sin to death or of obedience to justice? Praise God that you were slaves of sin, but became obedient from the heart to the teaching that was given to you; you have become enslaved to justice" (6:15–18), and "[God] will reward each in accordance with his [or her] works: to those who, with the patience of good works, seek glory and honor and immortality, eternal life, but those who [live] from strife and are disobedient to truth but obedient to evil, wrath and anger. Tribulation and pressure on every human being who does evil, on the Jew first, and on the gentile, but glory and honor and peace to everyone who does good, to the Jew first, and to the gentile. There is no favoritism with God" (2:7–10).

One does not have to depend on semiotics to recognize that what Paul says does not exactly correspond with what he means. Bultmann's *Sachkritik* will suffice. Even though Paul repeatedly writes about not being subject to the Law, for example, in 6:15 and 7:4–6, claiming that the Law contributes to sin, "when you were in the flesh, the desires of sin, desires that were [aroused] by the Law, were active in your members" (7:5), he constantly calls for behavior that conforms with the just requirements of the Law, as in 8:3–4: "For [because of] the impotence of the Law which was weak through the flesh, God, having sent his son in the similarity of the sinful flesh and because of sin, condemned sin in the flesh, in order that the just requirement of the Law would be fulfilled in us who do not live in accordance with the flesh, but the spirit." Even if it was because of the impotence of the Law that God sent his son, the purpose of the Son's coming was not to abolish the Law, but "in order that the just requirement of the Law would be fulfilled in us."

Obviously Paul does not intend simply to reject the Law. He was involved in an unresolved struggle concerning the Law, which had for him both a strongly repulsive significance as the basis for Jewish privilege and as a curse, and a powerfully devotional attraction as the expression of the will of God. All doubt that he was engaged in such a struggle is dispelled by 7:7–8:17, where the struggle becomes existential for Paul. What was never far below the surface in 5:12–7:6, and even in 1:18–4:25, now emerges as the main topic. Here the problem of the Law with all its ambiguity for Paul becomes inescapable.

2. 7:7–8:17—The Law of the flesh and the Law of Christ

In this part, one can distinguish two subsections: a. the conflict between two sides of the Law (7:7–8:4), which Paul resolves, and relying upon his solution transforms into b., a conflict between the flesh and the spirit (8:5–17). The second subsection continues the paraenesis already begun in 7:4–6.[9]

7:7–8:4. The conflict between two sides of the Law. In order to have a clear picture of what is at issue one must note the three closely intertwined themes in this subsection. The following three series of figures bring them to expression. First the negative effect of the Law:

7:7–11   What shall we say? The Law is sin? By no means! But I would not have known sin except through the Law; for I would not have known lust, if the Law did not say, you shall not lust. But sin, finding occasion in the commandment, worked all kinds of lust in me. Without the Law sin is dead. I once lived without the Law,

---

[9]For graphic displays of the relationships between the figures expressing Paul's reflections on the Law, see below, Part Two, chapter 5, "Paul's System of Values," IV. "The Problem of the Law and the Opposition between the Spirit and the Flesh."

but with the coming of the Law sin revived and I died; and so it was found that for me the commandment which was for the sake of life became [a cause of] death. For sin, finding occasion in the commandment, misled me, and through it killed [me].

7:13d   sin became extraordinarily sinful through the commandment.

7:21   So I find the Law to be such, that in my wanting to do good, evil is close at hand.

7:23   I see another Law in my members which joins battle with the Law of my mind and takes me captive with the Law of sin in my members.

7:25   with regard to myself (I slave for the Law of God with [my] mind), but with the flesh for the Law of sin.

8:2   (the Law of the spirit of life in Christ Jesus) liberated you from the Law of sin and death.

8:3   because of the impotence of the Law which was weak because of the flesh (God, having sent his son in the similarity of sinful flesh and because of sin, condemned sin in the flesh), . . .

In Paul's reasoning here the negative side of the Law is never considered a characteristic of the Law itself but is due to the power of sin in conjunction with the rupture in human nature. The figures below express the theme of the rupture in human nature. Those already included in the previous listing are not repeated.

7:13   The good then became death for me? By no means! But sin, to be revealed as sin, through the good worked death in me, so that sin became extraordinarily sinful through the commandment.

7:14   (For I know that the Law is spiritual), but I am of the flesh, sold to sin.

7:15–18 I do not know what I do. For I do not do what I want to, but what I hate is what I do. But if what I do not want is what I do, I agree that the Law is good; so now it is no longer I who do it, but sin living in me. For I know that there is no good in me, that is, in my flesh: to want to is close at hand, but not to do what is good.

7:19–21 For I do not do the good that I want to, but the evil that I do not want, that is what I do. If I do what I do not want to, it is no longer I who do it, but sin which dwells in me. So I find the Law that in my wanting to do good, evil is close at hand.

7:24   Wretched person that I am; who will release me from this body of death?

The third theme is the fundamental goodness and holiness of the Law. Paul affirms no less that seven times that the Law is good.

7:12   So the Law is holy, and the commandment holy and just and good.

7:14   For I know that the Law is spiritual . . .

7:16	(if what I do not want is what I do), I agree that the Law is good.
7:22	I delight in the Law of God in my inner being.
7:25	with regard to myself, I slave for the Law of God with [my] mind, (but with the flesh for the Law of sin).
8:2	For the Law of the spirit of life in Christ Jesus liberated you from the Law of sin and death.
8:4	in order that the just requirement of the Law would be fulfilled in us who do not live in accordance with the flesh, but the spirit.

It is noteworthy that in the first part of the section Paul draws his affirmations that the Law is good as conclusions from statements which express the negative side of the Law and the rupture in human nature: "For sin, finding occasion in the commandment, misled me, and through it killed [me]; so the Law is holy, and the commandment holy and just and good" (7:11–12); "sin, to be revealed as sin, through the good worked death in me, so that sin became extraordinarily sinful through the commandment. For I know that the Law is spiritual, but I am of the flesh, sold to sin" (7:13c–14); "if what I do not want is what I do, I agree that the Law is good" (7:16); and, "I find the Law to be such, that in my wanting to do good, evil is close at hand. I delight in the Law of God in my inner being" (7:21–22). With the reference to his delight in the Law of God "in my inner being" Paul begins to resolve the problem. This can also be recognized from the structure of his reasoning.

With his desperate cry in verse 7:24, "Wretched person that I am; who will release me from this body of death?" and his sigh of relief in 25a, "Thanks to God, through Jesus Christ, our Lord," Paul leaves behind the anguish concerning the rupture in human nature. From this juncture on he concerns himself only with the conflict between the two sides of the Law, except for the reaffirmation of his relief in 8:1, "So now there is no condemnation of those who are in Christ Jesus."

Up to that point the theme of the rupture in human nature intervenes between the negative and the positive sides of the Law. From there on the two remain posed directly against each other, but in such a way that the rupture in human nature is absorbed into the opposition between the two sides of the Law: "I slave for the Law of God with [my] mind, but with the flesh for the Law of sin" (7:25d–e); "the Law of the spirit of life in Christ Jesus liberated you from the Law of sin and death" (8:2); and "because of the impotence of the Law which was weak because of the flesh, God . . . condemned sin in the flesh, in order that the just requirement of the Law would be fulfilled in us who do not live in accordance with the flesh, but the spirit" (8:3–4). With the distinction of a life not "in accordance with the flesh, but the spirit," Paul has already moved to the theme of the

next subsection, 8:5–17, in which he converts the conflict between
the two sides of the Law into a conflict between the flesh and the
spirit. In 8:5–17 the theme of the Law surfaces briefly twice more,
first in 8:7, in its positive meaning, "the thoughts of the flesh are
hostility against God, for it does not subject itself to the Law of God,"
and then in 8:15, in a possible hint at the curse of the Law, "you did
not receive a spirit of slavery *to fear once more*." It is worth noting
that what Paul has in mind here, in the aftermath of his struggle with
the conflict between the two opposed sides of the Law, is "the Law
of God" (8:7).

The form of Paul's reasoning in 7:7–8:4 distinguishes itself
markedly from that in other parts of the letter, for example, in chapter
2 or in 3:21–4:25. The theme of chapter 2 is found in statements such
as, "[God] will reward each in accordance with his [or her] works"
(2:6), "There is no favoritism with God" (2:11), and, "Not the hearers
of the Law are just before God, but the doers will be justified" (2:13).
The thesis of the chapter is that before the Law there is no difference
between Jews and gentiles, "There is no favoritism with God" (2:11).
Paul's reasoning in chapter 2 is logical: he provides empirical evidence of the Jews' transgression of the Law in 2:17–25, and proves
by logical inference that the uncircumcised gentile who fulfills the
just requirements of the Law should be considered as in effect
circumcised, putting to shame the Jew who does not obey the Law
(2:25–29).

In the case of 3:21–4:25 the theme is expressed most vividly
in 3:28–30, "For we consider that a person is justified by faith
without works of the Law. Or is God of the Jews only? Not also of the
gentiles? Indeed, also of the gentiles, since it is one God who justifies
the circumcised out of faith, and the uncircumcised through faith."
These verses also convey the thesis of the section, which is that Jews
as well as gentiles are justified by faith. Here too Paul proves his
thesis by logical reasoning, appealing to evidence from scripture
concerning the justification of Abraham, and drawing logically consistent conclusions from it. The heart of his reasoning is in verses
9–12 where he proves that it was as a gentile that Abraham was
justified.

In the discussion of 5:12–6:23 we encountered a way of
reasoning in Paul different from that in 1:18–4:25, especially in
5:12–21 where he presents his arguments in repeated "packages" of
arguments rather then moving forward discursively. In our present
passage, 7:7–8:4, the reasoning is again different. The question Paul
raises in 7:7, followed immediately by its emphatic negation, "What
shall we say? The Law is sin? By no means!" represents a persistent
theme throughout the passage. It expresses at the same time the
thesis to be proved. Paul's reasoning here is not by logical inference,

as we have noted. His positive conclusions about the Law do not flow logically from the evidence on which they are based, for example, "sin, finding occasion in the commandment, misled me, and through it killed [me]; so the Law is holy, and the commandment holy and just and good" (7:11–12). By letting the figures that express the rupture in human nature intervene between the negative and positive statements about the Law, Paul allows the rupture in human nature to resolve the conflict between the opposed sides of the Law, for example, "I slave for the Law of God with [my] mind, but with the flesh for the Law of sin" (7:25d–e). This leads him to the conclusion "that the just requirement of the Law would be fulfilled in us who do not live in accordance with the flesh, but the spirit" (8:4), which appears to resolve the conflict for him. The Law itself is good; its negative side is a result of the power of sin in conjunction with the rupture in human nature. With this understanding, Paul can recognize both the negative and the positive sides of the Law in a way that enables him to affirm the Law for the believer: "the Law of the spirit of life in Christ Jesus liberated you from the Law of sin and death" (8:2). This conclusion reveals the thematic relationship of our section with the statement in 3:31 that we do not destroy the Law by faith, but affirm it. In this way the section picks up the point of that almost parenthetic verse, and clarifies the matter.

The interrelationships between the themes conveyed by the three sets of figures in this passage demonstrate that Paul's intended meaning is not any one of the themes by itself, but an issue that can be found in the interrelationships between them. Whatever other value the many studies of Romans 7 may have,[10] they are not interpretations of what Paul had in mind in the chapter since they make the rupture in human nature the central, if not exclusive, topic of his reflections. Stated in slight exaggeration, it is like making the meaning of a sentence dependent on the meaning of a single word. Since Augustine, there have been conflicting interpretations of the meaning of the rupture in human nature in this passage, specifically with regard to whether the rupture concerns existence before faith, or applies to the existence of the believer as well. Such conflicting interpretations are possible because the distinction did not concern Paul: it was not the point of his reasoning. Some of the past interpretations of the chapter have noted that the idea of the rupture in human nature was not original in Paul but that he took it over from Stoic thought. To that extent they recognized that the rupture in human nature was a component in Paul's reasoning, not the point he

---

[10] For an extensive discussion, see Ulrich Wilckens, *Der Brief an die Römer*, vol. 2 (EKK 4; Zürich: Benziger Verlag / Braunschweig: Neukirchener Verlag, 1987) 101–17.

was trying to make. Unfortunately this insight was lost when the focus turned to the way in which Paul is supposed to have revised the conception. From a text-linguistic point of view the question is not what any one of the identifiable topics in the passage means, but what Paul tried to say by the way he interrelated them in his reasoning.

As we have seen above, the structure of Paul's thinking in this section is characterized by the opposition between the negative and positive sides of the Law, coordinated with the rupture in human nature. We have also seen that in the second part of the subsection the rupture in human nature is absorbed into the opposition between the two sides of the Law. Furthermore, in 8:4 a transition is made in which the conflict between the two sides of the Law is converted into the opposition between the flesh and the spirit. In that way the conflict between the two sides of the Law is left behind in favor of the conflict between the flesh and the spirit, bringing to the fore again the theme of the rupture in human nature. This way of reasoning reveals important similarities to what Claude Lévi–Strauss refers to as mythical, in contrast with positive, thinking. Mythical thinking, according to Lévi–Strauss,[11] does not try to resolve contradictions logically, but coordinates insoluble contradictions in human experience with others that are indisputable and well-recognized, in that way making the insoluble contradictions tolerable without resolving them logically. Paul's reasoning here is similar. By coordinating the contradiction between the negative and positive sides of the Law with the recognized rupture in human nature, he makes the contradiction intelligible without resolving it logically. More, however, is involved in his reasoning in this section.

To begin with, there is more at issue in Paul's thinking about the Law than the conflict between the two sides explicitly mentioned in this section. It is possible to distinguish at least a third side to the Law, that to which he refers in 3:27 as the basis for the pride of the Jew, "What then about pride? It is excluded. By which Law? That of works? No, but by the Law of faith." There does not appear to be anything about the two sides of the Law in 7:7–8:4 that could serve as a ground for Jewish pride. The negative side of the Law, rather than giving reason for pride, can be considered only a ground for despair, as Paul states, "with the coming of the Law sin revived, and I died; and so it was found that for me the commandment which was for the sake of life became [a cause of] death" (7:9b–10). As for the positive side of the Law, according to 3:27 it is precisely the Law of faith which excludes pride. And yet, as our discussion will show, that other, third side of the Law must have been on Paul's mind as well.

---

[11] See especially, "The Structural Study of Myth."

The negative side of the Law in the sense in which Paul writes about it in 7:7–8:4 appears to have had an effect similar to the condemnation of the Jews by the Law in 3:9–20, where he quoted from the Law itself, "what the Law says it says to those who are under the Law" (3:19a), to prove that its purpose was that "every mouth will be shut and the entire world will be subject to God's judgment" (v. 19b). If there is a difference between the two passages, apart from the more personal nature of the present one, it is that 3:9–20 is more conclusive, based as it is on the condemnation by the Law itself.

The sense of the Law in both passages conforms well with Paul's understanding that the purpose of the Law was to increase transgressions in Gal 3:19, "What then about the Law? It was added for the sake of transgressions," and in Rom 4:15, "the Law engenders wrath; where there is no Law, there is also no transgression." If that had indeed been the purpose of the Law, there would be no reason to expect anything else from it other than the despair which Paul describes in our passage. Rather than appearing as wholesome, the Law is seen as a veritable curse, as in Gal 3:10, "those who are from works of the Law are under a curse; for it is written, 'Cursed is everyone who does not remain with everything that is written in the book of the Law, to do it.' " The phrase "those from the Law" must mean the Jews who view the Law as evidence of their justification, that is, their privileged relationship with God. In this verse the side of the Law which leads to despair and the side which serves as the basis for the pride of the Jew appear as a single feature of the Law. The Law on which the Jews rely for their privileged relationship with God is in reality a curse. This contradiction in the Law—at the same time the reason for pride and a curse—may be why Paul, when he affirmed that the Law of works did not negate the pride of the Jew in 3:27, did not seem to remember that he had just previously, in 3:9–20, proved that the Law was in reality a curse which condemned the Jews as sinners.

There is only one ray of light in this dark picture of the negative side of the Law. It was a pedagogue, a custodian, who ensured that Jews did not fall to the depths of gentile depravity (Rom 1:18–32). It is such depravity which made possible the Jewish boast, "We who are by heritage Jews, and not from the gentiles, sinners" (Gal 2:15). "Before faith came we were guarded by the Law, locked up for the revelation of the coming faith. So the Law became our pedagogue (custodian) to Christ, in order that we could be justified by faith" (Gal 3:23–24). The function of the Law here appears to be temporary, "we were . . . locked up for the revelation of the coming truth. . . : with the coming of faith we are no longer under the pedagogue" (vv. 23–25). Paul describes as similarly transitional the Law's purpose to increase transgressions: "[The Law] was added for the sake of transgressions, until the seed would come to whom the promise was made . . ." (Gal 3:19). In these two statements Paul describes in parallel the transitory nature of the Law, in its negative function to increase transgression (3:19), and in its more wholesome function as "our pedagogue" (3:23–25). Both functions of the Law came to an end when Christ freed the Jews from the curse of the Law, "Christ redeemed us from the curse of the Law by having become a curse for our sakes, for it is written, 'Cursed is everyone who is hung from a tree' " (Gal 3:13). In the latter statement there is also more than a hint at that other side of the Law, the basis for Jewish pride in an exclusive relationship with God, which thus also came to an end with Christ.

It is remarkable that Paul describes the removal of the curse of the Law from the Jews as having been for the sake of the salvation of the gentiles, "in order that the blessing of Abraham would reach the gentiles in Christ Jesus; in order that we would receive the promise of the spirit through faith" (Gal 3:14). That this is not an accidental remark, but an important feature in Paul's thinking, is shown by his repetition of the same idea in Rom 15:8–12: "Christ became a servant of circumcision for the sake of the truth of God, in order to secure the promises of the Fathers, and the gentiles praise God because of mercy" (vv. 8–9); subsequent Scripture quotations place the statement in the framework of God's revelation.

The clearest indication of what had been at issue may be 1 Thess 2:16, "[The Jews obstructed] us in speaking to the gentiles in order that they would be saved." Paul's own persecution of the church may have been for the same reason. Removal of the curse of the Law is what freed the proclamation of the gospel for the gentiles as well.

With that we are at the other, positive, side of the Law. In Rom 8:2–4 Paul formulates the liberation from the curse of the Law as a liberation from the Law of sin and death, "For the Law of the spirit of life in Christ Jesus liberated you from the Law of sin and death. For because of the impotence of the Law which was weak because of the flesh, God, having sent his Son in the similarity of sinful flesh, and because of sin, condemned sin in the flesh, in order that the just requirement of the Law would be fulfilled in us who do not live in accordance with the flesh, but the spirit."

Whatever may be said for the Christian interpretation of the positive side of the Law in this passage—it is "the Law of the spirit of life in Christ Jesus [which] liberated you from the Law of sin and death" (8:2)—nowhere does Paul express more eloquently that side of the Law to which he aspires so intensely in this section than in Rom 2:6–10. There he wrote concerning the gentile, the heathen, neither Jew nor Christian, but every human being, "[God] will reward each in accordance with his [or her] works: to those who, with the patience of good works, seek glory and honor and immortality, eternal life," and "glory and honor and peace to everyone who does good, to the Jew first, and to the gentile." Clearly, this is what Paul understands as the Law's positive side, even if his praise also includes its negative side, "to those who [live] from strife, and are disobedient to truth but obedient to evil, wrath and anger. Tribulation and pressure on every human being who does evil, on the Jew first, and on the gentile." Not least in importance is the fact that Paul concludes his chiasm with the observation, "There is no favoritism with God" (v. 11).

As a result of this complexity of Paul's relationship to the Law it should come as no surprise that the cumulative impression left by recent studies concerning Paul and the Law—E. P. Sanders,[12] Hans Hübner,[13] Heikki Räisänen,[14] to mention only three of the most incisive—is that we still have more problems with Paul's understanding of the Law than insights. Thus we do not have a sufficiently clear understanding of this issue to be able to draw from it for our interpretation of the passage. There is however a phenomenon in the functioning of language which, from a linguistic point of view, gives reason not to despair about the situation. Users of a language learn the meanings of most new words, not by being informed about them by others, nor by consulting a lexicon or dictionary, but from the way such words are used in the language. An important distinction of a good dictionary is the use it makes of this phenomenon by clarifying the meanings of words with examples of how they are actually used. Applied to Paul this means that we do not have to depend on knowing his understanding of the Law in order to understand what he is trying to say in our passage. Indeed, the complexity of what is involved suggests that he himself may not have had a precise understanding of what the Law meant for him. A text-linguistic approach to our section will not necessarily answer the question of Paul's understanding of the Law, but it can offer insight into his thinking on the topic and may make it possible to understand why he could make statements about the Law that appear incompatible, for example, his statement in 3:19–20 that the Law condemns every human being as a sinner, but then in 3:27 that "the Law of works" does not negate pride, as if, after 3:9–20, there could still have been reason for pride.

---

[12] *Paul, the Law, and the Jewish People.*
[13] *Das Gesetz bei Paulus. Ein Beitrag zum Werden der paulinischen Theologie* (Göttingen: Vandenhoeck & Ruprecht, 1978, 3d ed. 1982).
[14] *Paul and the Law* (Tübingen: J. C. B. Mohr [Paul Siebeck], 1983; Philadelphia: Fortress, 1986).

In our discussion of the complex nature of Paul's understanding of the Law these aspects of the Law were identified: First with regard to the negative side: α. Due to the power of sin, the effect of the Law is that it leads to sin, rather than to the good, as in our passage. β. This effect of the Law agrees with Paul's statements in Gal 3:19, "What then about the Law? It was added for the sake of transgressions," and in Rom 4:15, "the Law engenders wrath; where there is no Law, there is also no transgression." γ. Together the last two statements express what Paul formulates explicitly in Gal 3:10, "those who are from works of the Law are under a curse; for it is written, 'Cursed is everyone who does not remain with everything that is written in the book of the Law, to do it.' " δ. With the reference to "those from the Law" in the previous statement the specifically Jewish relationship to the Law is revealed. That relationship is characterized by Jewish "pride" in the Law as the expression of a privileged relationship with God which excludes the gentiles. According to 3:27 that pride is denied by "the Law of faith," but is permitted by "the Law of works." ε. Paradoxically, Paul proves in 3:9–20 that Jewish pride is excluded by the Law itself, because the Law condemns the Jews of sin: "What the Law says it says to those who are under the Law. So that every mouth will be shut and the entire world will be subject to God's judgment" (3:19). ζ. On this negative side of the Law belongs finally the understanding of Gal 3:23–24 that the Law was a custodian for the Jews, preventing them from falling into the depths of gentile perversion. Paul's understanding is that, as in the case of all other negative functions of the Law, the custodial function also ended with the coming of faith, as he writes in Gal 3:23–25, "we were . . . locked up for the revelation of the coming truth . . . : with the coming of faith we are no longer under the pedagogue," a statement which has a close parallel in a similar statement concerning the Law's function to increase sin, "[the Law] was added for the sake of transgressions, until the seed would come to those to whom the promise was made" (Gal 3:19).

On the positive side of the Law the situation is less complex. α. In our passage Paul states that through the Law of Christ the believer is freed from the power which sin has over her or him through the Law, "For the Law of the spirit of life in Christ Jesus liberated you from the Law of sin and death" (8:2), with the ultimate purpose "that the just requirement of the Law would be fulfilled in us who do not live in accordance with the flesh, but the spirit" (8:4). β. This liberation has a close parallel in the statement that Christ freed the Jews from the curse of the Law, "Christ redeemed us from the curse of the Law by having become a curse for our sakes—for it is written, 'Cursed is everyone who is hung from a tree' " (Gal 3:13). γ. The ethical implications of this new life of faith, and the believer's calling to fulfill the "just requirement of the Law" (8:4), comes to extensive expression in Romans 6. δ. In Romans 2 Paul expresses a parallel fulfillment of the just requirements of the Law by uncircumcised gentiles: "if an uncircumcised person observes the just requirements of the Law, will his [or her] lack of circumcision not be considered circumcision?" (2:26).

In order to understand what is at issue in Rom 7:7–8:4 we have to move back from the resolution to the issue itself. The rupture in human nature is not at issue. In fact, it is what enables the resolution of the issue, namely, the conflict between the positive and the negative sides of the Law. Many Pauline texts witness to Paul's inability to accept an outright rejection of the Law, explicitly Gal 3:21, "The Law is thus against the promises? By no means! For if a Law with the power to make alive was given, justification would indeed have been through the Law," and Rom 3:31, "Do we destroy the Law with faith? By no means! We affirm it." Note especially 1 Cor 9:21, "to those who are outside the Law [I became] as [one] outside the Law, although not outside the Law of God but under the Law of Christ, in order to win those who are outside the Law."

What is at issue in our section is how the Law could be good, notwithstanding its negative features. Elsewhere in his letters Paul discusses negative as well as positive features of the Law without concerning himself directly with the issue which arises from the conflict between them. The closest he comes to doing so is in Gal 3:21, Rom 3:31, and 1 Cor 9:21 (quoted above), but even in these texts he merely states the issue without dealing with it. It is here in Rom 7:7–8:4 that Paul brings the issue itself into focus, formulated in terms of the Law being good even if it engenders sin. The earlier discussion of the complexity of the issue reveals that although Paul formulates the issue in this way here, there is more to it: to be under the Law is to be under a curse, and yet Paul wants to maintain that the Law is good.

There is no christological reason to affirm that the Law is good. What Paul writes in 8:3b–4 reveals that his affirmation of the Law does not serve his Christology, but, inversely, his Christology serves his affirmation of the Law: "God, having sent his Son in the similarity of the sinful flesh, and because of sin, condemned sin in the flesh, in order that the just requirement of the Law would be fulfilled in us who do not live in accordance with the flesh, but the spirit." Fulfillment of the just requirements of the Law is presented here as the purpose of God's sending of his Son. This purpose makes understandable Paul's deep concern that his readers should live a life in which the just requirements of the Law are fulfilled, as, for example, in Romans 6. Paul maintains the inviolability of the just requirements of the Law, whether it concerns the Jew or the gentile

(Romans 2), or the Christian believer (Romans 6). Note in this regard especially 1 Cor 7:19, "Circumcision counts for nothing, and not being circumcised counts for nothing, but keeping the commandments of God." The fundamental question for an understanding of what is involved in his relationship to the Law is the question of what led Paul to his negative view of the Law.

Of the six negative features of the Law, four constitute a single configuration: α. due to the power of sin, the effect of the Law is that it leads to sin rather than to the good; β. the Law engenders transgressions; γ. those who are from works of the Law are under a curse; and ε. pride is excluded by the Law because it condemns the Jews of sin. Together these features represent the oppressive nature of the Law. The single figure which draws together their common meaning is that it is a curse to be subject to the Law.

The remaining two negative features of the Law each gives expression to its own theme: δ. the Law is the basis of Jewish pride in a privileged relationship with God, and ζ. the Law was a custodian for the Jews, preventing them from falling into the moral depths of gentile perversion. As we have noted, the Law as custodian already moves partly over to a positive meaning. That leaves only two clearly negative features of the Law as determinative for Paul's thinking: that it is a curse to be subject to the Law and that the Law provides the basis for Jewish pride. With that we are back at the contradiction that the Law has become a basis for the Jews' pride in a relationship with God which excludes gentiles, but condemns them as sinners, making them equivalent to gentiles.

In Romans 2 Paul argues that it is not a question of physical circumcision as the sign of being a Jew that counts. Everything is reduced to the question of obedience to the Law, that is, being under the Law in such way that the difference between Jews and gentiles is dissolved. That, however, does not resolve the issue of the conflict between the negative and positive sides of the Law; it merely sharpens the issue by making it applicable to everyone who is subject to the Law, Jew as well as gentile. The Law promises and at the same time condemns. What makes being under the Law a curse is that it does not allow partial fulfillment.

Our passage reveals that is was not on the basis of theoretical reflection that Paul arrived at this understanding, but on the basis of a deep sense of the inability of the Law to free those who rely on it from the power of sin. It is not a question of whether one is actually guilty of this or that transgression; Paul claims that as far as justice under the Law is concerned he was without blemish (Phil 3:6b). But that evidently did not free him from the awareness that he remained subject to the temptation of sin. As a Jew Paul became aware that the pride of being "by heritage a Jew, and not from the gentiles, a sinner"

(Gal 2:15) was a hollow boast. The very Law on which that pride was based condemned the Jew as a sinner, as he proves in Rom 3:9–20, and states summarily in Gal 3:10.

The Law promises the pride of achievement, but at the same time, as a relentless judge, it condemns the transgressor. The curse for Jews is that they can find salvation through the Law only by doing everything that is written in it; there is no middle way, "those who are from works of the Law are under a curse; for it is written, 'Cursed is everyone who does not remain with everything that is written in the book of the Law, to do it' " (Gal 3:10). The same applies to the gentile who aspires to come under the Law, as Paul writes in Gal 5:3, "I testify again to everyone who receives circumcision that he [or she] is bound to keep the whole Law."

And so it appears that the sarcasm with which Paul spurns Peter and the others in Antioch, "We who are by heritage Jews, and not from the gentiles, sinners" (Gal 2:15), finds a parallel expression, this time ironic, in Rom 3:27 when he allows that "the Law of works" does not exclude pride, after he had just earlier in 3:9–20 stated that in fact the Law does not concede pride, but condemns the Jews as sinners. There is no escape from this contradiction in the Law. As a believer in Christ Paul may have tried to avoid it by moving from the Jewish framework into that of the believer in Christ with his statement that "the Law of faith" excludes pride in the Law, but that does not resolve the contradiction which he allows to remain with his statement that "the Law of works" does not do so.

Rom 7:7–8:4 shows that Paul was aware that the contradiction remained also for the believer in Christ, not that he did not try to resolve it. "Wretched person that I am," he writes, "who will release me from this body of death? Thanks to God, through Jesus Christ, our Lord. And so, with regard to myself, I slave for the Law of God with [my] mind, but with the flesh for the Law of sin" (7:24–25). Even as one who had been released from "this body of death" by Jesus Christ, Paul is aware that he is still caught in the contradiction, slaving for the Law of God with his mind, but for the Law of sin with his flesh. In this way, rather than resolve the contradiction, he finds a way of accepting it.

It is remarkable that faith is not mentioned at all in this passage, nor in subsequent passages to the end of chapter 8. There can be no surer indication than in this, also highly christological, passage that faith did not have the crucial significance for Paul that is attributed to it in the interpretation of his thought: "the Law of the spirit of life in Christ Jesus liberated you from the Law of sin and death" (8:2). It is not a justification by faith, but "the Law of the spirit of life in Christ Jesus" which liberates from the Law of sin and death.

8:5–17. The conflict between the flesh and the spirit. Having found the solution of the conflict between the two sides of the Law in the conflict between the flesh and the spirit, Paul continues by posing the spirit against the flesh (vv. 5–11), rounding off his reasoning with a paraenetic appeal (vv. 12–17). In this section he continues the paraenesis which he began in 7:4–6. Note the way in which 8:3, "because of the impotence of the Law which was weak because of the flesh, God, having sent his Son in the similarity of the sinful flesh and because of sin, condemned sin in the flesh," takes up the statement in 7:4, "you too have died to the Law through the body of Christ, in order to belong to another, to him who was raised from the dead, in order to bear fruit for God."

3. 8:18–30—A look into the eschatological future

Aware that all the tensions have not yet been resolved, Paul points to the much greater joy which lies in the future (vv. 18–23). With a remarkable paradoxical statement he asserts that, even though already saved, the believer still looks forward to redemption as a future event, "For in hope we were saved" (8:24a). He reemphasizes the point with: "Hope which sees is not hope: what does the person who sees hope? But if we hope for what we do not see, we anticipate it with patience" (vv. 24b–25).

4. 8:31–39—Expression of confidence in the new life in Christ

With this expression of confidence Paul concludes this first part of his discussion.

With that Paul appears to have rounded off his reasoning that salvation for the Jew first, and for the Hellenes, is achieved through faith, exemplified by Abraham as a model for all believers "who trust in him who raised Jesus our Lord from the dead" (4:24). However, an unresolved issue remains, namely, the question of the disbelief of the Jews which he raised in 3:3a, but did not answer, "What then? If some of them became distrustful." Paul had become distracted by a different issue, the trustworthiness of God, "will not their distrust destroy the trustworthiness of God?" It is an issue which he also did not resolve at that stage. It too remains part of what is under discussion in what now follows in chapters 9–11.

C. 9:1–11:36—The Problem of the Disbelief of Israel

There is a certain structural similarity between the discussion of the Law in 7:7–8:4 and the discussion of the disbelief in Israel in chapters 9–11. Just as Paul recalled in 7:7–8:4 the question concerning the Law that he originally raised in 3:31, so now in chapters 9–11 he recalls the question concerning the distrust of some in Israel that he raised in 3:3a. He recalled the question and answer of 3:31, "Do we destroy the Law with faith? By no means!" in 7:7, "What shall we say? The Law is sin? By no means!" and did not rest his reasoning until he found what must have appeared to him as a resolution of the problem of the Law: "So, with regard to myself, I slave for the Law of God with the mind, but with the flesh the Law of sin" (7:25b), and "For the Law of the spirit of life in Christ Jesus will free you from the Law of sin and death. For [because of] the impotence of the Law which was weak because of the flesh, God, having sent his Son in the similarity of the sinful flesh, and because of sin, condemned sin in the flesh, in order that the just requirement of the Law would be fulfilled in us who do not live in accordance with the flesh, but the spirit" (8:2–4).

Similarly, the problem of the distrust of some in Israel as Paul formulated it in 3:3, "What then? If some of them became distrustful, will not their distrust destroy the trustworthiness of God?" is recalled three times in chapters 9–11: "I speak the truth in Christ, I do not lie, my conscience is my witness in the Holy Spirit, that I have a great sadness and an unceasing heartache. For I pray that I myself would be a curse away from Christ for the sake of my brothers, my kinsmen in the flesh" (9:1–3), "the yearning of my heart and plea to God is for their salvation. I witness concerning them that they have a zeal for God, but without understanding. Ignorant of the justice of God, and seeking to establish their own, they did not submit to the justice of God" (10:1–3), and "I say then: Did God reject his people?" (11:1). Here too Paul does not rest his troubled reasoning before he can conclude that "all of Israel will be saved, as it is written, 'The savior will come from Zion, to turn away ungodliness from Jacob; and this is my covenant with them, when I take away their sins'" (11:26–27).

That the Law was a personal problem for Paul became evident in the discussion of 7:7–25. Similarly the disbelief of some in Israel surfaces as a personal problem for him in chapters 9–11, coming to expression in the same statements in which he recalls the distrust of some in Israel, first in 9:2–3, "I have a great sadness and an unceasing heartache. For I pray that I myself would be a curse away from Christ for the sake of my brothers, my kinsmen in the flesh." Again in 10:1, "the yearning of my heart and plea to God is for their salvation," and finally in 11:1, "I ask then: Did God reject his people? By no means! For I myself am an Israelite, from the seed of Abraham, the tribe of Benjamin."

1. 9:1–33—The doctrine of election

The structure of Romans 9–11 is determined by the three times Paul raises the question of Israel's failure to achieve salvation (in 9:1–5; 10:1–4, and 11:1a). He begins the first round of his reasoning by insisting: "It is not as if God's word failed, for not all who are from Israel belong to Israel" (9:6), and by trying to support this understanding by basing it on God's election of Isaac (vv.7–9) and Jacob (vv. 10–14). But with that Paul finds himself confronted once more, not only with the distrust of some in Israel (3:3), but also with the unresolved problem of God's justice which he raised in 3:5–7, "if our injustice co-establishes the justice of God, what shall we say? Is God who transmits wrath unjust? I speak in human terms. By no means! How then would God judge the world? But if the truth of God overflows to his glory through my falsehood, why am I still judged as a sinner?" It is a problem which he can solve as little here in chapter 9 as he had been able to do in 3:4–8. He gets drawn ever deeper into the insolubility of the problem by reaffirming God's arbitrariness. It is not a matter of "the one who wants to or who runs, but on God who shows mercy" (9:16). Furthermore, the metaphor of the potter (9:20–21), rather than solving the problem, sharpens it, since, in the sense of Paul's metaphor, it is not the jars who criticize the potter's work, but the potter who blames the jars for the way he made them: "Oh man, who are you to answer God? Can the creation say to the creator, 'Why did you make me like this?' Or does the potter not have the right to make from the same clay one vessel for honorable and another for common use?" It is the potter who has no reason to blame his creations for the way they are. Thus also Pharaoh cannot be called to account for his actions: he had no choice in the matter when he was told, "I raised you up for the very purpose of showing my power through you, and that my name might be announced on all the earth" (9:17). It may be correct that God needs both kinds of persons, the good and the evil, but that does not solve the problem of his judgment of them.

Paul evidently wants to put these thoughts in a positive light by emphasizing the beneficent side of God's election: "in order to make known the wealth of his glory on the vessels of mercy, prepared for glory, us whom he called, not only from the Jews, but also from the gentiles" (9:23–24). Within the larger framework of God's redemption of creation, those who are destined for the negative side of God's revelation also have a positive function, as in the case of the disbelief of the Jews, "I ask then, did they stumble so as to fall? Not at all, but through their transgression there is salvation for the gentiles so as to make them jealous. And if their transgression is the good fortune of the world, and their loss the gain of the gentiles, how much more would it not be the case with their fullness" (11:11–12). For further emphasis he then quotes Hosea's affirmation of the inclusion of the gentiles among God's people, "I will call those who are not [my] people, my people, and those whom I did not love, beloved" (9:25, Hos. 2:25). But that is not the point, and Paul senses it. He knows that his problem is not with the elect of Israel and the inclusion of the gentiles, but with those in Israel who do not believe. And so, rather than resolve the problem, he quotes from scripture to draw attention once more to the lost in Israel, culminating with the harsh words of Isaiah 1:9, "If the Lord Sabaoth did not leave us descendants, we would have become like Sodom; would have been like Gomorrah" (9:29).

Thus Paul ends up once more with the disbelief of some in Israel, "What then shall we say? That the gentiles who did not pursue justice received justice, the justice of faith, whereas Israel who followed the Law of righteousness did not attain the Law?" (9:30–31). The reason for Israel's failure remains the same: "because it was not by faith, but through works" (9:32a). When Paul adds that "they stumbled against the stumbling block" (9:32b) it is clear that he understands Israel's disbelief as the rejection of Christ. That "not by faith, but through works" is equivalent to the rejection of Christ, and reveals once more that the works which stand over against faith are not good works, but works as the basis of the Jews' claim to an exclusive relationship with God. Their attempt to establish their own righteousness (10:2) through works was an unwillingness to accept that through faith salvation was offered without distinction to Jews as well as gentiles.

2. 10:1–21—The Jews' attempting to establish their own righteousness

In 10:1 Paul returns to the fundamental issue, now in a highly personal formulation: "the yearning of my heart and plea to God is for their salvation." He has not solved the problem. The equivalence of the Jews' failure to find justice because they sought it "not by faith, but through works" and their stumbling "against the stumbling block" in 9:32 is recalled thematically in 10:2–3, "I witness concerning them that they have a zeal for God, but without understanding. Ignorant of the justice of God, and seeking to establish their own, they did not submit to the justice of God." The righteousness which the Jews sought to establish for themselves was not through good works, but, as we have seen, through works as the basis of an exclusive relationship with God, works in the technical sense of maintaining a privileged relationship with God. The establishment of their own righteousness is their refusal to accept the intended fulfillment in Christ of the promise to Abraham that in him "all the gentiles will be blessed" (Gal 3:8), that he "would become the father of many gentiles" (Rom 4:18). By their rejection of Christ they failed in their trust. Note again 1 Thess 2:16. "[The Jews obstructed] us in speaking to the gentiles in order that they would be saved." Biographically Paul might have recalled that he himself persecuted the church for the same reason.

Then comes a remarkably ambiguous statement: "the end (τέλος) of the Law is Christ [with its objective] the justification of everyone who believes" (10:4). τέλος here means "end" in the same ambiguous sense as in English: Christ is the final purpose and meaning of the Law, and Christ brings the Law to an end. In the sense of fulfilling the purpose of the Law we already know: "We affirm [the Law through faith]" (3:31). At the same time the fulfillment of the purpose of the Law in Christ through faith brings to an end the understanding of the Law as the basis for the Jews' exclusive claim. Not to accept that is what Paul understands as the Jews' ignorance of the justice of God (10:3).

Almost inevitably this leads once more to a discussion of the opposition between the Law and faith (10:4–11), culminating in the reaffirmation that justification through faith is equally available to Jews and gentiles, quoting Joel 3:5, "Everyone who believes in him will not be put to shame" (10:11). Paul concludes: "There is no difference between Jews and Hellenes. The same Lord is [Lord] of all, bestowing riches on all who call on him" (10:12). Yet again the failure of Israel asserts itself: "not all listened to the gospel, for Isaiah says, 'Lord, who believed in our message?' " (10:16). Paul ends with another devastating quotation from Isaiah: "to Israel he announces, 'The whole day I stretched my hands out to a disobedient and obstinate people' " (v. 21). With that Paul is once more at his starting point, the disbelief of "some" in Israel.

3. 11:1–36—The redemption of all of Israel

In chapter 11 for the first time Paul comes to a point where support begins to emerge for his reassertion that "God did not reject his people whom he foreknew" (11:2a). It is a remarkable piece of reasoning. He begins with the assurance that he himself is, after all, a Jew, "I too am an Israelite, from the seed of Abraham, the tribe of Benjamin" (11:1), which calls to mind a similar statement by Elijah. Paul asks, "Do you not know what Scripture says in [the story of] Elijah? How he pleaded with God against Israel, 'Lord, your prophets they killed, your altars they overturned, and I alone am left, and they seek my life' " (11:2b–3, quoting from 1 Kgs 19:10, 14). Elijah's complaint calls forth God's response, "I have left for myself seven thousand who did not bow their knees to Baal" (11:4; 1 Kgs 19:18). On that basis Paul concludes, "And so also in the present a remnant remains through the generosity of [God's] election" (11:5). Even though the remnant to which he refers is not the part of Israel which causes the problem, the reference to "the generosity of [God's] election" is the beginning of the resolution. It begins to occur to Paul that the answer lies, not with human reason, but with God. To be sure, he is aware that he has only arrived at a partial solution: "What Israel sought, it did not find, but the elect found it, and the rest were hardened" (11:7). He follows once more with a series of passages from Scripture which emphasize that the majority of Israel is lost (11:8–10).

Remarkably, from this hopeless situation the solution arises: "if their transgression is the wealth of the world and the diminishing of their numbers the wealth of the gentiles, so much more [would be] their fullness" (11:12). In the reference to the fullness of Israel Paul has still not found the solution, but in that phrase the solution is prepared. What follows is a remarkable reversal. It is now the gentiles who are the beneficiaries of God's kindness. That reversal demands that the question Paul posed earlier concerning the prerogative of the Jews in 3:9, "Do we have something to show?" must now also be applied to the gentiles. Inasmuch as the Jews had nothing to show for themselves because their privilege was a product of God's kindness and not anything they achieved, so gentile Christians too, for the same reason, have nothing to show for themselves. On the one hand, "Branches were cut out in order that I should be grafted in. Right! Through disbelief they were cut out, and it is through faith that you stand: Do not be arrogant, but fear. For if God did not spare the natural branches, he will also not spare you. Behold the graciousness and severity of God: Severity on those who fall, but on you, God's graciousness, if you remain with his graciousness, otherwise you too will be cut out" (11:19–22). On the other hand, inversely, and for the same reason, "They too, if they do not remain in disbelief, will be grafted in" (11:23). And so Paul affirms that also the gentile Christian, and that means every Christian, has nothing to hold forward (cf. 3:9): "For if you were cut out of what was naturally your wild olive tree, and were grafted into the cultured olive, contrary to nature, how much more will these who are naturally [cultured branches] be grafted into their own olive tree" (11:24).

Paul thinks he has solved the problem, but not before appealing to the mystery of God's wisdom. Although the salvation of the gentiles allows that the lost in Israel *can* be saved, it does not prove that they *will* be saved. To be able to affirm that too Paul appeals to the mystery of God's ways, "I do not want you to be uninformed, brothers [and sisters], of this mystery—in order that you should not be conceited—that a hardening came in part over Israel until the fullness of the gentiles came in. And so all of Israel will be saved, as it is written, 'The savior will come from Zion, to turn away ungodliness from Jacob; and this is my covenant with them, when I take away their sins' " (11:25–27). Now Paul is able to draw the conclusion from the positive side of God's election, which is what he tended to emphasize throughout these chapters: "With regard to the gospel they were enemies for your sake: with regard to election, beloved through the Fathers" (11:28–32). Here Paul's reference to the "Fathers" recalls his conviction that the Jews were entrusted with God's revelation (cf. 3:2). That he cannot draw his conclusion on the basis of human insight and reason also becomes plain in his rejoicing statements which follow, quoting from scripture and ending with a doxology (11:33–35).

Paul's remarks in chapter 11 about the Jews also applies in principle to Esau and Pharaoh in 9:6–18. He writes about Pharaoh in 9:17, "For Scripture writes about Pharaoh, 'For this reason I elected you in order to reveal my power in you, and in order to announce my name in the entire world.' " The issue in connection with Esau and Pharaoh is not moral culpability, as Paul emphasizes with regard to Pharaoh in 9:16, "So, it is not a question of wanting to or acting, but of God's being merciful," and 9:18, "So, on whom he wants to he shows mercy, and whom he wants to he hardens." The role played by Esau and Pharaoh in 9:6–18 is taken over by the disobedient in Israel in 11:11–12 and 25–32, concluding with, "God locked everyone in disobedience in order to be merciful on all" (v. 32).

In his reasoning in these chapters Paul does not draw his conclusion about Israel from an interpretation of Scripture and facts concerning Israel's belief. Instead, he appeals to what he understands to be historical facts, and to Scripture as the means of arguing his intended point that in the end all of Israel will be saved. His final conclusion in 11:25–32 is not drawn from the material he mustered; all of that material was introduced for the specific purpose of underscoring his point, and should be interpreted as such. As we have seen, Paul had to make three attempts before he thought he was successful. In his reasoning he was able to show, not only that in the end all of Israel will be saved, but also that the distrust of some in Israel did not destroy the trustworthiness of God (3:3).

D. *Paraenesis: 12:1–15:33*

In 15:8–13, at the end of the paraenetic section, Paul returns a final time to his main theme that "the gospel . . . is the power of God to salvation for all who believe, to the Jews first, and to the

Hellenes" (1:16). Christ secured the promises to the Fathers: "I say, Christ became[15] a servant of circumcision for the sake of the truth of God, in order to secure the promises of the Fathers" (15:8). For Paul, the securing of the promises means that through Christ, faith, and not Jewish privilege, was reaffirmed as the foundation of the promise to Abraham in the sense of Romans 4, "For that reason it is through faith in order that it would be through generosity, so that the promises would be secure for every seed, not only for the one who is under the Law, but also for the one who is from the faith of Abraham, who is the father of all of us" (4:16). The promise to Abraham was that he would become the father of "many *gentiles*"[16] (Rom 4:17, quoting Gen 17:5). It is through the fulfillment of that promise that the gentiles too are able to praise God, with the Jews, "and the gentiles praise God because of mercy. As it is written, 'For that reason I will profess you among the gentiles, and praise your name'; and again [scripture] says, 'Rejoice, O gentiles, with his people'; and again, 'Praise the Lord, all gentiles, and let all the peoples praise him'; and again Isaiah says, 'There will be the root of Jesse, and he who rises up to lead the gentiles; in him will the gentiles hope' " (15:9–12).

CONCLUSION

Our discussion has shown that the theme of Romans, introduced by Paul in 1:16, "[the gospel] is the power of God to salvation for all who believe, to the Jews first, and to the Hellenes," has two components: The gospel is the power of God to salvation for all who believe, and the gospel was entrusted to the Jews, but found its fulfillment in the salvation of the gentiles. The first component occupies Paul's attention throughout the first longer part of the letter, 1:18–8:39. In that part of the letter the other component comes to the surface only briefly in 3:1–8. Only after he exhausted the discussion of the first component in 8:39 does Paul turn his attention to the second.

Compared with the dominating concern with the concrete problem of the readers' desire to become circumcised in Galatians,

---

[15] Paul's statement that Christ "became" (γεγενῆσθαι) a servant of circumcision may mean that he had the preexistent Christ in mind, who was not a Jew to begin with, but, as in the Philippians hymn, became one in order to carry out the act of redemption.

[16] For Paul, ἔθνη in the quotation of Gen 12:3 in Gal 3:8 and Gen 17:5 in Rom 4:17 (ἐθνῶν) does not have the general meaning of "nations"; it means specifically "gentiles." What is at issue for Paul is the distinction between Jews and gentiles.

Paul's reasoning in Romans is more abstract, relaxed, thoughtful. He is obviously not addressing a critical concrete problem as he does in Galatians. In the first part of the letter he allows himself an extended discussion of what occupied him far more briefly in Gal 2:14–5:12. In this extended discussion Paul argues the same point as in Galatians, that salvation is not the privilege of an exclusive community through circumcision, but that through faith it is available for all who believe like the uncircumcised Abraham. Whereas the discussion in Galatians functioned to dissuade Paul's readers from letting themselves become circumcised, the discussion in Romans is a thoughtful reflection on the issue itself.

The second component of Paul's theme in Romans, that the promise of salvation through faith was entrusted to the Jews, is absent in Galatians. More important, the reasoning in Galatians does not seem to allow for this component, but, in its radical formulation, stands in opposition to it. This is especially evident in the allegory of Sarah and Hagar, which represents the opposition between the Law and faith, and which culminates in the harsh quotation from Scripture: "the son of the slave woman will not inherit with the son of the free woman" (Gal 4:30b). In Galatians Paul does not allow for the understanding that salvation through faith is also available to those who are under the Law. However, there are hints in Galatians that this is not the last word. In his report of the agreement in Jerusalem he recognizes a gospel to the Jews as well as to the gentiles, "seeing that I had been entrusted with the gospel to the uncircumcised as Peter had been to the circumcised—for he who worked through Peter for the mission to the circumcised, worked also through me for the gentiles—and recognizing the gift that was given to me, James and Cephas and John, esteemed as pillars, gave me and Barnabas the hand of fellowship so that we would go to the gentiles and they to the circumcised" (2:7–9). In 3:21 Paul refuses to accept a fundamental contradiction between the Law and the promises: "The Law is thus against the promises?" he asks. He replies emphatically, "By no means! For if a Law with the power to make alive was given, justification would indeed have been through the Law." Finally, in 6:15 he negates the importance of the difference between Jew and gentile: "For neither is circumcision anything, nor being uncircumcised, but [being] a new creation."

What appears as a concession in Galatians constitutes one of the two components of Paul's theme in Romans: salvation of the Jews is not only recognized, but understood as the basis of gentile salvation. As Paul argues in Rom 11:17–18, "If some of the branches were cut out, and you, of a wild olive tree, grafted into them, and became participant in the sap of the roots of the olive tree, do not boast against the branches. And if you do boast: it is not you who bear the roots, but the roots you!" What Paul wrote in Romans is not contrary to his views in Galatians, but the critical situation in Galatians spurred him to more radical formulations. Nevertheless, compared with Galatians, Romans, by conceding a priority in salvation to the Jews, may have allowed for a privilege of the Jews which in effect limits the universality of faith. That Paul may not have overcome completely the pride is hinted at in his sarcastic remark, "We who are by heritage Jews, and not from the gentiles, sinners" (Gal 2:15). There is a tension in the formulation of his main theme between salvation by faith for all who believe and the priority of the Jews: the gospel is the power of God to salvation "for *all* who believe," but with the qualification that it is "to the Jews *first*, and to the Hellenes" (Rom 1:16). We may understand better what is involved in Paul's thinking by examining the way in which he takes it up again in Romans after he had raised it in Galatians, reflecting on it, at certain points modifying it or at least sharpening it, and making it clear, that although salvation is promised for all who believe, it is for the Jews first. It is to them that God entrusted his revelation.

4

A Macro-Structure for Galatians and Romans

INTRODUCTION

The discussions of the macro-structures of Galatians and Romans in chapters 2 and 3 above have disclosed a fundamental thematic agreement in the two letters. The following distribution of key concepts in the corpus of generally accepted letters of Paul—1 Thessalonians, Galatians, 1 and 2 Corinthians, Philippians, Romans and Philemon—confirms this close thematic relationship.

Distribution of Key Concepts in Galatians and Romans

	ἀκροβυστία uncircumcised	ἔθνος gentile	Ἕλλην Hellene	Ἰουδαῖος Jew	(ἀ)νόμος Law	περιτομή** circumcision
1 Thess		2	1			
1 Cor	2	3	4	8	14	3
2 Cor		1		1		
Phil					3	2
Phm						
Gal	3	11*	2	5*	32	13
Rom	11	29	6	11	79	15

* In Galatians 1 case of each is, respectively, ἐθνικῶς and Ἰουδαϊκῶς
** Includes the verb περιτέμνειν.

Outside of Galatians and Romans, only 1 Corinthians contains a relatively large number of these key terms, but in that letter they express meanings different from those in Galatians and Romans as the following two examples show: "The Jews ask for signs and the Hellenes seek wisdom, but we proclaim Christ crucified, a scandal for the Jews and foolishness for the gentiles, but for the elect, Jews as well as Hellenes, Christ, the power of God and the wisdom of God" (1 Cor 1:22–24); and, "I became as a Jew for the Jews, in order to win the Jews, to those under the Law as one under the Law—although personally not under the Law—in order to win those who are under the Law, to those who are without the Law as one who is without the Law—although not without the Law of God but under the Law of Christ—in order to win those who are without the Law" (1 Cor 9:20–21). These two passages alone account for one occurrence of "gentile," two of "Hellene," six of "Jew," and nine of the "Law."

A further indication of the close relationship between Galatians and Romans is provided by the semantic parallels in the two letters as presented in Appendixes II and III. Appendix II reveals that in the main section of Galatians, beginning with Paul's report of the Antioch incident in 2:14 and continuing through 5:6, there are only two brief statements, Gal 3:20 and 22, that are not paralleled in some form or another in Romans. In contrast, Appendix III reveals that long stretches of reasoning in Romans have no semantic parallels in Galatians. We may thus conclude hypothetically that Paul reflected further on the subject matter of Galatians in Romans, at the same time expanding on the topic, most notably in the discussions concerning the prerogative of the Jews and their rejection of Christ in 3:1–8 and chapters 9–11. Compared with his impatient argumentation in Galatians, Paul's reasoning in Romans is relaxed and thoughtful.

Many of the parallels in the appendixes are not really verbatim, which means that they are also not exact parallels in meaning. In determining what is meant, the concrete level of the expressions cannot be ignored, but at the same time words alone cannot be considered determinative for the expressed meaning. I understand the passages as parallel expressions of Paul's intended meanings, not as textual parallels. Paul's intended meanings cannot be identified with single expressions, nor with a combination of more than one. Rather, the multiple expressions open a window to his intended meanings.

Some of the parallels are verbally closer than others, but only rarely are they really close, even in phrases. The following texts show the closest verbal parallels: εἰ γὰρ ἐκ νόμου ἡ κληρονομία οὐκέτι ἐξ ἐπαγγελίας, "*if the inheritance is through the Law*, it is no longer through a promise" (Gal 3:18), and εἰ γὰρ οἱ ἐκ νόμου κληρονόμοι, κεκένωται ἡ πίστις καὶ κατήργηται ἡ ἐπαγγελία, "for *if those who are from the Law are inheritors*, faith has become empty, and the promise destroyed" (Rom 4:14). The lack of exact verbal parallels confirms that in Romans Paul did not simply expand on the formulations in Galatians, but reflected further on the subject-matter of the earlier letter.

In this chapter I will investigate what happened in Paul's thinking when he recalled the subject matter of Galatians in Romans. I am not primarily interested in the products of his thinking as they appear in these letters; what interests me is the dynamics of his thinking which resulted in what we find written in them. The focus of the investigation will not be on what material from Galatians reappears in Romans, as in Appendix II, but on what is recalled from Galatians in Romans, as in Appendix III. Therefore, I will begin with Paul's statements in Romans and note how they recall formulations in Galatians. There is hardly any material that is simply repeated. The hypothesis with which I will operate, summarized in the conclusion of the previous chapter, is that the same issue represents the fundamental concern of both letters, namely, that salvation is not the privilege of an exclusive community through circumcision. But whereas it is the entire theme of Galatians, it constitutes only one component of the theme of Romans. The theme of Romans includes a second component, namely, that salvation is linked to the history of the Jews. It appears to stand in opposition to key parts of Galatians, especially 4:21–31, where the Jews seem to be rejected without compromise.

The present chapter has two parts. In the first I will investigate the expressions of shared meanings in Galatians and Romans, in the second, the shared semantic macro-structure of the two letters.

I. EXPRESSIONS OF SHARED MEANINGS IN GALATIANS AND ROMANS

In writing Romans Paul did not have in mind specifically his formulations in Galatians; he probably did not have access to a copy of Galatians when he wrote Romans. He may or may not have remembered that he had identified Abraham's seed as Christ in Galatians. In Galatians the believer becomes a child of Abraham by participation in Abraham's one seed, who is Christ. In Romans the seed is Isaac, but the believer still becomes a child of Abraham through participation in Christ, as in Romans 4, "It was not written only for his sake that 'It was reckoned to him,' but also for our sakes to whom it will be reckoned, [we] who trust in him who raised Jesus our Lord from the dead" (4:23–24).

In the chapter on "A Macro-Structure for Romans" I argued that Rom 1:18–4:25, the first major part of that letter, could be considered as an exposition of Paul's statement in Gal 2:14b–16. This can be seen in the following: In Rom 1:18–32 Paul describes in detail what it means to be "from the gentiles, sinners" (Gal 2:15); in Rom 2:1–3:20 he can be understood as expanding on his challenge to Peter, "If you as a Jew live as a gentile and not a Jew, why do you want to force the gentiles to become Jews?" (Gal 2:14). And in Rom

3:21–4:25 he can be understood as clarifying the meaning of "We who are by heritage Jews . . . , knowing that a person is not justified through works of the Law except through the faith of Jesus Christ, we too believed in Christ Jesus in order to be justified through the faith of Christ and not from works of the Law, for from works of the Law no one will be justified" (Gal 2:15–16).

That a major part of the exposition in Rom 3:21–4:25 is based on Abraham's justification by faith draws into this exposition Gal 3:6–18 as well. Gal 3:6–18 can be considered Paul's earliest endeavor to prove by means of the Abraham story what he wrote in Gal 2:16, that Jews as well as gentiles are justified by faith, and not through Jewish privilege. Rom 1:18–4:25 can thus be understood as an exposition of Gal 2:14b–16 which takes up at the same time the argument of Gal 3:6–18 in support of Gal 2:14b–16.

After 4:25 Romans goes structurally its own way, although it continues to recall large portions of Galatians. For example, a number of figures from the paraenetic section of Galatians, specifically 5:1, 13, 16 and 24–25, are paralleled in Romans 6, confirming the strongly paraenetic character of that chapter. Rom 7:1–6 picks up various portions of Galatians which reflect an issue of central importance in that letter, liberation from the Law through Christ (Gal 2:19–21; 3:10–13, 19, 22–25; 4:1–16, 21–31). Other portions of Romans have little relationship to the reasoning in Galatians (Rom 5:1–21; 7:7–8:4; 8:5–1, 18–30; 9:1–33; 10:1–21). On the one hand, a number of passages from Galatians are sometimes recalled in a few verses in Romans, as in 5:20–21 (Gal 3:10–13, 15, 17–19; 4:4–5), with nothing else recalled in the rest of the section (Rom 5:12–21). Nothing from Galatians is recalled in Romans 11. The summary statement of Rom 15:8–12, on the other hand, recalls crucial parts of the reasoning of Gal 3:8–17.

It is important to distinguish between the recalling of individual figures from Galatians in Romans and the recalling of the actual reasoning from the earlier letter. Note, for example, how the description of gentile depravity in Rom 1:18–32, which forms part of the reasoning of Rom 1:18–4:25, recalls Gal 2:15, "We who are by heritage Jews, and not from the gentiles, sinners," which is an element in the reasoning of Gal 2:14b–16. This can be compared with the recollection of individual, unconnected figures from Gal 4:3, 8, and 5:19–21 in the same section of Romans. If it were not for the recalling of the reasoning of Gal 2:14b–16 and 3:6–18 in Rom 1:18–4:25 the investigation of the relationship between the two letters would be far less significant. The difference this makes can be clearly recognized by comparing the "Semantic Parallels to Galatians in Romans" in Appendix II and the "Galatians Parallels Recalled in Romans" in Appendix III.

In order to make this investigation manageable, the following will be discussed separately: A. the recalling of the reasoning of Gal 2:14b–16 and 3:6–18 in Rom 1:18–4:25; B. the further development of Paul's thoughts on that basis in Rom 5–8; C. the reasoning concerning the priority of the Jews in chapters 9–11, which not only has no parallel reasoning in Galatians, but also develops a theme that appears to be contrary to much of the reasoning in Galatians, especially, 4:21–31; and finally, D. the recalling of crucial parts of the reasoning of Galatians in Rom 15:8–12.

A. *Romans 1:18–4:25—Recalling the Reasoning of Galatians 2:14b–16 and 3:6–18*

The structure of this section in Romans is determined by three sub-topics from Gal 2:14b–16, supplemented by the exposition of justification by faith through the example of the faith of Abraham in Gal 3:6–18, namely: 1. 1:18–32—the depravity of the gentiles; 2. 2:1–3:20—the Jews too are without excuse; and 3. 3:21–4:25—justification through faith for all who believe, with Abraham as the example of faith.

1. *1:18–32—The depravity of the gentiles*

What Paul presents in this section is the assumed background of his sarcastic remark in Gal 2:15 "We who are by heritage Jews, and not from the gentiles, sinners." It is an important starting point for his reasoning. Jews and gentiles do not begin on an equal level. As Paul wrote in Gal 3:23–25, the Jews have the Law which acted as a custodian, preserving them from the depravation of the gentiles, "Before faith came we were guarded by the Law, locked up for the revelation of the coming faith" (v. 23). As the parallels in Gal 4:3 and 8 reveal, the depravity of the gentiles which Paul describes in Rom 1:18–32 was part of his thinking in Galatians as well. Rom 1:23, "they changed the glory of the immortal God to resemble the image of a mortal human being and birds and animals and reptiles," reminds one of Gal 4:8, "not knowing God, you slaved for what were in reality not gods." In Rom 1:23 Paul may nevertheless not recall the actual formulation of Gal 4:8. Both texts express a typical Jewish view of the gentiles, which Paul evidently shared. Both letters indicate that he had not completely given up this bias against the gentiles. His judgment of the gentiles in Rom 1:18–32 is more severe than elsewhere in his letters, but so is his judgment on the Jews which follows in 2:1–3:20.

2. 2:1–3:20—The Jews too are without excuse

In Rom 2:1–3:20 Paul argues extensively and resolutely what he merely hinted at in his sarcastic remark in Gal 2:15, prepared for by his accusation of Peter in Gal 2:14, "I said to Peter in front of everyone, 'If you as a Jew live like a gentile and not a Jew, why do you want to force the gentiles to become Jews?' " The basis for his condemnation of the Jews is that they are preserved from gentile perversion only if they obey the Law, "Circumcision is useful if you practice the Law; if you are a transgressor of the Law your circumcision has become no circumcision" (Rom 2:25). If the Jews transgress the Law they become like gentiles, sinners! Relentlessly, as he challenged Peter in Galatians, he challenges the Jews, "Do you who judge those who do these things, and do so yourself, think that you will escape God's judgment?" (Rom 2:3). He strengthens his challenge in 2:17, "you call yourself a Jew and depend on the Law and pride yourself in God," which is followed by a list of transgressions (vv. 21–23). The argument culminates in an accusation from Scripture, "For the name of God is blasphemed through you among the gentiles" (2:24). The sarcasm of Galatians turns to irony when he states that a gentile who fulfills the just requirements of the Law effectively condemns the Jew as a sinner, "if an uncircumcised person observes the just requirements of the Law, will his [or her] lack of circumcision not be considered circumcision? And the person who is by nature uncircumcised but fulfills the Law judges you who are in the letter and through circumcision a transgressor of the Law" (2:26–27).

Paul went so far with his accusations against the Jews in chapter 2 that he finds himself confronted in 3:1 with the question whether being a Jew retains anything of value, "What then is the prerogative of the Jew, and what the use of circumcision?" His reply that "they were entrusted with God's revelation" (v. 2) supports the second component of his main theme in Romans, "[the gospel is the power of God to salvation for all who believe], *to the Jews first*" (Rom 1:16). It is a meaning not evident in Galatians. On the other hand, Paul was committed to showing in Romans, as he did in Galatians, that with regard to the Law there was no difference between Jews and gentiles. On the other, he had obviously not given up a certain bias in favor of the Jews. Nowhere in Romans does Paul clarify the "prerogative" which he allows the Jews in Rom 3:2. After his brief statement that they were entrusted with God's revelation he finds himself confronted with the problem of their disbelief, "What then? If some of them became distrustful, will not their distrust destroy the trustworthiness of God?" (v. 3). He will address that issue in Romans 9–11. The discussion in Romans 9–11 presupposes that the Jews have a prerogative. The problem with the disbelief of "some of them" (v. 3) would not have arisen if it had not been for such a prerogative. Only in Rom 11:16–24 does the meaning of the Jewish prerogative surface again, and then indirectly, in Paul's statement that gentile salvation is grounded in that of the Jews, "If some of the branches were cut out, and you, of a wild olive tree, grafted into them, and became participant in the sap of the roots of the olive tree, do not boast against the branches. And if you do boast: it is not you who bear the roots, but the roots you!" (vv. 17–18). The issue is raised in Rom 3:1–3 for the first time, but it does not concern Paul further at this stage of the letter.

In 3:9 he reasserts that the Jews have no advantage, notwithstanding the prerogative he attributed to them in verse 2: "Do we have something to show?" he asks. He answers with an emphatic "By no means, for we have already charged everyone to be subject to sin, Jews as well as gentiles." With verse 9 Paul thus returns to the topic of chapter 2, that before the Law there is no distinction between Jews and gentiles. Rom 3:1–8 appears as a mere interlude in his reasoning.

As if the evidence he presented in chapter 2 were not sufficient, in Rom 3:10b–18 Paul adds a series of passages from Scripture to prove his point, culminating in the condemning statement: "We know that what the Law says it says to those who are under the Law. So that every mouth will be shut and the entire world will be subject to God's judgment" (3:19).

With the concluding statements of 3:19b–20, "every mouth will be shut and the entire world will be subject to God's judgment, because through works of the Law no one will be justified before him, for through the Law is the recognition of sin," the first part of Paul's reasoning in Romans is complete: not only the gentiles (1:18–32), but also the Jews are condemned as sinners (2:1–29; 3:9–20). With that he is ready to move to what he argued in Gal 2:15–16, "we who are by heritage Jews . . . , knowing that a person is not justified through works of the Law except through the faith of Jesus Christ, we too believed in Christ Jesus in order to be justified through the faith of Christ and not from works of the Law, for from works of the Law no one will be justified."

3. 3:21–4:25—Justification through faith for all who believe

Paul's statement in Gal 2:15–16 finds a parallel summary expression in Rom 3:21–26. This is followed in 3:27–31 by reflections on related issues, and then in Rom 4:1–25, as in Gal 3:6–9 and 15–17, with an exposition of justification by faith utilizing the Abraham story.

An important feature of the discussion of the Abraham story in Galatians is absent in Romans, namely, the curse of the Law (Gal 3:10–14): "those who are from works of the Law are under a curse; . . . Christ redeemed us from the curse of the Law by having become a curse for our sakes, in order that the blessing of Abraham would reach the gentiles in Christ Jesus, in order that we would receive the promise of the spirit through faith" (vv. 10, 13–14). Even though Paul does not refer to the Law as a curse in Romans, the conception that the Law prevents the Jews from accepting justification by faith is in the background of his thinking throughout the letter. The closest parallel to the conception of the curse of the Law from which Christ frees the Jews is found in Rom 15:8–9a, "Christ became a servant of circumcision for the sake of the truth of God, in order to secure the promises of the Fathers, and the gentiles praise God because of mercy." In Rom 15:8–9a Paul does not say that the Law (or circumcision) was a curse or that Christ became a curse, but the parallel is obvious. In Galatians Christ became a curse in order to free the Jews from the curse of the Law "in order that the blessing of Abraham would reach the gentiles in Christ Jesus" (Gal 3:14a), and in Romans Christ became a servant of circumcision "in order to secure the promises to the Fathers, and the gentiles praise God because of mercy" (Rom 15:8b–9a).

There is a closer parallel, but of a different kind, to Christ's freeing the Jews from the curse of the Law in Rom 5:12–21, according to which, through his obedience, Christ liberated all of humanity from the legacy of Adam's transgression. The move backward in history to Adam's fall, to a point in time before the beginning of Jewish history and the Law, places Paul's thinking in a more universal framework than would have been the case had he limited his exposition to the theme of the Jews and the Law. That the Law was nevertheless on his mind is shown by his concluding remarks, "But the Law came in between, in order that transgressions should abound; and where sin abounded, generosity overflowed, so that, as sin reigned in death, so also generosity would reign through justice to eternal life through Jesus Christ our Lord" (vv. 20–21).

The discussion of the Abraham story in Romans 4 illumines the exegetically disputed meaning of Gal 2:16a, "knowing that a person is not justified through works of the Law if not (ἐὰν μή) through the faith of Jesus Christ." The statement that Abraham is "the father of the circumcised for those who are not only circumcised, but also follow in the footsteps of the faith of the uncircumcised Abraham" (Rom 4:12) recalls Gal 2:16a: the Jews too are not justified if not through a faith such as Abraham's. Paul's meaning in Galatians is that also the Jew, a person who is under the Law, a person who is circumcised, cannot be justified except through faith in Christ. The ἄνθρωπος ἐξ ἔργων νόμου, literally, "a person from the works of the Law," in the clause οὐ δικαιοῦται ἄνθρωπος ἐξ ἔργων νόμου in Gal 2:16 does not refer to a person who seeks to be justified through the doing of good works, but simply to the Jew, to someone who assumes that the distinction of being under the Law is an indication of justification. The meaning is that "[we who are Jews, and not from the gentiles sinners,] knowing that a Jew is not justified if it is not through the faith of Jesus Christ, we too believed in Christ Jesus."

At the same time, Gal 2:16 shows that in that letter too the understanding is that Jews *as Jews* are justified by faith, notwithstanding 4:21–31. But it is in Romans where Paul formulates the issue most clearly, "For we consider that a person is justified by faith without works of the Law. Or is God of the Jews only? Not also of the gentiles? Indeed, also of the gentiles, since it is one God who justifies the circumcised out of faith, and the uncircumcised through faith" (Rom 3:28–30). This parallel justification of "the circumcised out of faith, and the uncircumcised through faith" finds expression in Galatians in the recognition by the Jerusalem apostles that Paul "had been entrusted with the gospel to the uncircumcised as Peter had been to the circumcised" (Gal 2:7), and the agreement that "we would go to the gentiles and they to the circumcised" (Gal 2:9).

Distinctive of Romans is the fact that faith itself becomes thematic in the description of how Abraham came to believe, "he believed in God who made alive the dead and called what is not into being, who in hope against hope believed that he would become the father of many gentiles in accordance with what was said, 'Thus will be your seed,' and not wavering in faith he considered his dead body —being already about a hundred years old—and the barrenness of Sarah's womb; he did not doubt God's promise through distrust, but became strong in his faith, giving honor to God, fully persuaded that what [God] had promised he was also capable of doing. For that reason it was reckoned for him as justification" (Rom 4:17b–22).

Rom 4:17b–22 contains the most conspicuous contradiction of the thought of Galatians. As already mentioned, Abraham's seed is understood in Romans as his own son Isaac; in Galatians the "seed" is Christ, "The promises were made to Abraham and to his seed. It does not say 'and to his seeds' as if to many, but as to one, 'and to your seed,' who is Christ" (Gal 3:16). It is important to note that Paul's reference to Abraham's seed in the two passages is markedly different. In neither case is his purpose specifically to identify the seed of Abraham. In Galatians his intention is to establish that the promise to Abraham was fulfilled not with the Law, but in Christ, in that way establishing at the same time the connection between Christ and the promise to Abraham. In Romans Paul's focus is on the nature of Abraham's faith. His attempt in Galatians to prove by means of the implausible argument about the single seed that the promise was fulfilled not with the Law but with Christ is accomplished far more convincingly in Romans by means of a double argument. First, Paul argues that Abraham was circumcised only after he had already been justified by his faith, "How was [Abraham's faith] reckoned [to him as justification]? While circumcised or uncircumcised? Not circumcised, but uncircumcised. And he received the sign of circumcision, a seal of the justification of faith while uncircumcised" (4:10–11a). He then places in parallel Abraham's trust "in God who made alive the dead" in 4:17b and our trust "in [God] who raised Jesus our Lord from the dead" in 4:24. Paul's intended meaning remains the same; it is simply expressed by means of different figures of the seed in the two letters. This shows that neither expression had meaning in itself; each functioned as part of the expression of a larger meaning. That does not mean that Paul did not intend the figures seriously, but Wrede's caution is worth remembering that we should not "squeeze conceptual capital from every single phrase and every casually chosen expression used by an author."[1]

Paul's main purpose in his appeal to the Abraham story in Galatians and in Romans is to demonstrate that it was not through works of the Law, that is, not as a Jew, that Abraham was justified, but as a gentile. This is explicit in the reasoning in both letters, and is reinforced in Rom 3:28–30, "For we consider that a person is justified by faith without works of the Law. Or is God of the Jews only? Not also of the gentiles? Indeed, also of the gentiles, since it is one God who justifies the circumcised out of faith, and the uncircumcised through faith." In Galatians the argument, in abbreviated form, is as follows: "Scripture, foreseeing that the gentiles would be justified by faith, announced to Abraham, 'In you all the gentiles will be blessed,' so that those who are of faith are blessed with the faith of Abraham. . . . Christ redeemed us from the curse of the Law by having become a curse for our sakes . . . , in order that the blessing of Abraham would reach the gentiles in Christ Jesus, in order that we would receive the promise of the spirit through faith" (Gal 3:6–9, 13–14). In Gal 2:16 Paul had already argued that "we who are by heritage Jews, . . . knowing that a person is not justified through works of the Law except through the faith of Jesus Christ, we too believed in Christ Jesus in order to be justified through the faith of Christ and not from works of the Law." The purpose of his reasoning in Gal 3:6–14 was to prove through the story of Abraham that Jews as well as gentiles are justified by faith.

---

[1] *Über Aufgabe und Methode der sogenannten neutestamentlichen Theologie*, 96; ET, "The Task and Methods of New Testament Theology," 77.

This reasoning is presented in a much briefer form, with greater clarity, in Rom 4:9–13, "This blessing [to which David refers], then, is it on the circumcised, or also on the uncircumcised? For it is said, Faith was reckoned as justice for Abraham. How was it reckoned? While circumcised or uncircumcised? Not circumcised, but uncircumcised. And he received the sign of circumcision, a seal of the justification of faith while uncircumcised, so that he would become the father of all who believe while uncircumcised, that it would be reckoned to them, and the father of the circumcised for those who are not only circumcised, but also follow in the footsteps of the faith of the uncircumcised Abraham. For it was not through the Law that the promise was made to Abraham and to his seed that he would be the inheritor of the world, but through the obedience of faith."

In Rom 4:14—"if those who are from the Law are inheritors, faith had become empty, and the promise destroyed"—a number of figures from Galatians are recalled: "if justification were to be through the Law, then Christ died in vain" (Gal 2:21b); "if the inheritance is through the Law, it is no longer through a promise" (3:18); and "if you receive circumcision, Christ will be of no advantage to you" (5:2). This series of figures reveals a thematic significance, namely, the irreconcilability of justification based on being a Jew and justification by faith. In Rom 9:31–32 Paul recalls that theme, relating it directly to disbelief in Israel, "Israel who followed the Law of righteousness did not attain the Law? Why? Because it was not by faith, but through works: they stumbled against the stumbling block."

B. *Romans 5–8—Exposition of Justification by Faith*

In these four chapters Paul does not recall the reasoning of Galatians. Except for the allegory of Sarah and Hagar, the recollection of the essential reasoning of Galatians is complete with Rom 4:25. The purpose of that allegory is recalled in an altered form in 7:1–6 and in a reversed sense in chapters 9–11. Significant other figures from Galatians are recalled in Paul's further reasoning in Romans, but only as individual elements, not as constitutive parts of his reasoning.

1. *5:1–11—Transition*

In this section Paul concludes his previous reasoning, "Thus, being justified by faith we have peace with God through our Lord Jesus Christ" (v. 1), and moves on to the next. At least one figure from the paraenetic section of Galatians, "We anticipate the hope of justice through the Spirit, in faith" (Gal 5:5), is recalled in Rom 5:2, "through whom we have the entry into this generosity in which we stand, we are proud in the hope of the glory of God."

2. 5:12–21—The Adam-Christ type-antitype

At the level of the expressions, this figure does not recall anything in Galatians, except Rom 5:20, the reference to the Law which came in between (from Gal 3:15–19). In Romans, however, the Law does not come in between the promise to Abraham and its fulfillment, as in Galatians, but between Adam's transgression and Christ's obedience. At the same time, the mentioning of the Law in Rom 5:20–21 to conclude the discussion of Adam and Christ establishes a relationship between Adam and the Law, "the Law came in between, in order that transgressions should abound; and where sin abounded, generosity overflowed. So that, as sin reigned in death, so also generosity would reign through justice to eternal life through Jesus Christ our Lord." The Adam-Christ type-antitype too does not have a meaning of its own, but expresses the problem of the Law. Christ's freeing all of humanity from the legacy of Adam's transgression through his obedience recalls his freeing of the Jews from the curse of the Law (Gal 3:10–14), but it places the issue in a universal framework.

3. 6:1–23—The ethics of the new life in Christ

The first part of this chapter (vv. 1–11) recalls Gal 2:19–20, expanding on it "through the Law I died to the Law in order to live for God. I was crucified with Christ. It is no longer I who live; Christ lives in me. What I live now in the flesh, I live in faith in the son of God who loves me and gave himself for me." Rom 6:15, "What then? Shall we sin because we are not subject to the Law, but depend on generosity?" presupposes the liberation from the Law through being in Christ, a topic that concerns Paul more specifically in the next section (7:1–6).

Romans 6 is heavily paraenetic, drawing conclusions for the believer from the new being in Christ (vv. 1–14), freed from the Law (vv. 15–23). Mainly individual figures are recalled from Galatians, largely from the paraenetic section, as can be expected from the chapter's own strongly paraenetic emphasis. A particularly close parallel to Gal 5:13, "For you are called to freedom, brothers [and sisters], but not the freedom which provides occasion for the flesh, but that which serves each other in love," is Rom 6:15–16, "What then? Shall we sin because we are not subject to the Law, but depend on generosity? By no means! Do you not realize that to whom you subject yourself in subservience as slaves, you are a slave to whom you are subservient, either of sin to death or of obedience to justice?"

4. 7:1–6—The metaphor of the married woman

This section recalls a large number of passages from Galatians which emphasize the transition from a life under the Law to freedom in Christ. Particularly close in meaning is Christ's liberation of the Jews from the curse of the Law in Gal 3:10–13. The topic is less dominant in Romans. The heavier emphasis in Galatians is due to what Paul understood as his readers' intention to subject themselves to the Law by becoming circumcised. The opposition between being under the Law and the freedom in Christ recalls the opposition between slavery and freedom represented by, respectively, Hagar and Sarah in Gal 4:21–31. Note also the parallel figures which introduce the two passages: "I speak to persons who know the Law" (Rom 7:1) recalls Gal 4:21, "Tell me, you who want to be under the Law, do you not hear the Law?"

5. 7:7–8:17—The Law of the flesh and the Law of Christ

In the first part of this section, (i) the problem of the Jewish Law (7:7–8:4), Paul addresses the positive meaning of the Law, an issue which he briefly conceded in Gal 3:21, "The Law is thus against the promises? By no means! For if a Law with the power to make alive was given, justification would indeed have been through the Law." The topic was clearly in the back of his mind already in Galatians; but only here in Romans does he address it as a specific issue.

In the second part, (ii) the law of sin and the law of Christ (8:5–17), Paul continues his thinking of the previous section. In this reasoning too only individual figures from Galatians are recalled. Particularly close in meaning is Gal 5:17–18, "For the flesh desires against the spirit, and the spirit against the flesh. They stand opposed to each other, so that you do not do what you want to. And if you are led by the spirit you are not under the Law." These verses convey what becomes the theme in Rom 8:5–17.

6. 8:18–30—A look into the eschatological future

7. 8:31–39—Concluding expression of confidence in the new life in Christ

Neither of these passages recall figures in Galatians, except for Rom 8:24–25, "For in hope we were saved. Hope which sees is not hope: what does the person who sees hope? But if we hope for what we do not see, we anticipate it with patience," which recalls Gal 5:5, "In faith, we anticipate the hope of justice through the Spirit."

C. Romans 9–11—The Problem of Disbelief in Israel

In these chapters Paul takes up the issue he raised in Rom 3:3, the disbelief of some in Israel, "What then? If some of them became distrustful, will not their distrust destroy the trustworthiness of God?" Nothing is recalled here from Galatians, except individual figures. The topic of these chapters, the salvation of all of Israel, appears to contradict Paul's harsh statement in Gal 4:30–31, "But what does Scripture say? 'Banish the child and his mother, for the son of the slave woman will not inherit with the son of the free woman.' . . . we are not children of the slave woman, but of the free." Note especially the conclusion in Rom 11:26–27, "And so all of Israel will be saved, as it is written, 'The savior will come from Zion, to turn away ungodliness from Jacob; and this is my covenant with them, when I take away their sins.' " In each of the three chapters Paul attempts to overcome the impression that Israel is lost.

1. 9:1–33—The doctrine of election

Paul's first attempt to solve the problem of Jewish disbelief is through the doctrine of divine election. Only two individual figures from Galatians are recalled (Gal 3:23 and 3:18).

Paul is here concerned to clarify not human responsibility, but how God's justice manifests itself in the history of salvation. His ultimate concern in these chapters is the disbelief of some in Israel. In considering Esau and Pharaoh it is important to remember what he says about the disbelief of the Jews, "If their stumbling is the richness of the world, and their loss the richness of the gentiles, how much more their fullness?" (Rom 11:12), and, "In accordance with the promise they were enemies for your sake; in accordance with the election, beloved through the Fathers" (Rom 11:28).

2. 10:1–21—The Jews' attempting to establish their own righteousness

This chapter, more of a condemnation of Israel than an affirmation of its salvation, recalls an important section in Galatians, the Jews under the curse of the Law in Gal 3:10–14. The reference to the mistaken zeal for the Law in verses 2–4 also recalls Paul's own mistaken zeal in Gal 1:14–16a.

3. 11:1–36—The redemption of all of Israel

There is nothing in Galatians that could be recalled in this chapter. Actually the topic stands in a certain tension with Paul's concerns in that letter.

D. *Romans 15:8–12—Salvation of Jews and Gentiles*

This passage, even if it is in the paraenetic section of the letter, concludes the main theme of Romans, "Christ became a servant of circumcision for the sake of the truth of God, in order to secure the promises of the Fathers, and the gentiles praise God because of mercy" (vv. 8–9a). It recalls not only the Abraham story in Galatians and Romans, but also Christ's freeing of the Jews from the curse of the Law. The formulation closely parallels Gal 3:13–14, "Christ redeemed us from the curse of the Law by having become a curse for our sakes . . . , in order that the blessing of Abraham would reach the gentiles in Christ Jesus, in order that we would receive the promise of the spirit through faith." In this way the close thematic relationship between the two letters reemerges, salvation through faith for all who believe, Jews as well as gentiles who are free from the restriction of salvation to those under the Law and circumcision.

II. THE SHARED SEMANTIC MACRO-STRUCTURE OF GALATIANS AND ROMANS

A. *The Common Theme of Galatians and Romans*

The distribution of key concepts from Galatians and Romans in the Pauline letters as presented above—Jew(s), gentile(s), the Law, circumcision, etc.—suggests a close semantic relationship between the two letters. The expressions of shared meanings in these letters, as presented in Appendixes II and III, reaffirm that relationship. More important than the mere expressions of shared meaning is the shared structure of reasoning in Gal 2:14b–16 and 3:6–18 and in Rom 1:18–4:25.

1. The structure of Paul's reasoning in Galatians and in Romans 1:18–4:25

As I suggested previously, the structure of reasoning in Rom 1:18–4:25 recalls the reasoning of Gal 2:14b–16 supplemented by Paul's appeal to the example of Abraham in 3:6–18. In 1:18–32 he describes what it means to be "from the gentiles, sinners" (Gal 2:15), in 2:1–3:20 he clarifies the meaning of his challenge to Peter, "If you as a Jew live as a gentile and not a Jew, why do you want to force the gentiles to become Jews?" (Gal 2:14), and in 3:21–4:25 the meaning of "We who are by heritage Jews . . . , knowing that a person is not justified through works of the Law except through the faith of Jesus Christ, we too believed in Christ Jesus in order to be justified through the faith of Christ and not from works of the Law, for from works of the Law no one will be justified" (Gal 2:15–16).

Furthermore, the contrast between the existence outside of faith and under faith which finds expression in the metaphor of the immature child in Gal 4:1–7 and in the allegory of Sarah and Hagar in 4:21–31 is paralleled by a series of similar contrasts in Rom 5–8, the Adam-Christ type-antitype in 5:12–21, the ethics of the new life in Christ in chapter 6, and the metaphor of the married woman who is freed from the law of her deceased husband in 7:1–5. And in the paraenetic section of Romans, the statement in Gal 5:14 that the Law is fulfilled in the commandment to love your neighbor as yourself is recalled and expanded upon (Rom 13:8–10).

Galatians, on the one hand, by concentrating on a single theme, brings into sharp focus the common central issue of both letters: denial of the restriction of justification to the circumcised, and affirmation of justification by faith for all who believe. It is the single main theme of Galatians, and one of the two components of the main theme of Romans.

Romans, on the other hand, through its careful reasoning, helps clarify the meaning of Paul's thoughts in Galatians, for example, his overstatement of the case against submission to the Law in 4:21–31. Romans opens the perspective to a wider range of issues, in particular the relationship of salvation through faith in Christ to the history of God's revelation to Israel, the second component of the main theme of the letter. Actually, Paul does not specifically address this issue; he does not clarify the relationship between the Jewish prerogative of having been entrusted with God's revelation (Rom 3:2) and his understanding of the gospel. However, the problem which the disbelief of some in Israel poses (Rom 3:3) is the specific topic of chapters 9–11, where, contrary to the impression left by Gal 4:21–31, justification by faith for Jews as well as gentiles is grounded in the particular history of the Jews. Nonetheless, the treatment of Israel's unique history is not allowed to flow into an unrestricted course of universal history as one could be led to believe from Paul's reasoning in Galatians.

If it were not for Rom 3:1–8 there would hardly be any difference in Paul's reasoning in Galatians and the first part of Romans. This passage in any case appears as an interlude in Rom

1:18–4:25. In 3:9 Paul returns to the topic of chapter 2, that the Jews too are without excuse before the Law, reinforcing his reasoning with a series of quotations from Scripture in verses 10–18, and concluding with a final condemnation of the Jews in verse 19, "We know that what the Law says it says to those who are under the Law. So that every mouth will be shut and the entire world will be subject to God's judgment." It seems that Paul was not able to integrate the prerogative of the Jews to which he refers in Rom 3:1–3 into his reasoning in 2:1–3:20. Instead, the subject appears as an interruption in his thought process, and in 3:9 he returns to the original theme of the section, and so remains within the framework of the structure of his reasoning in Galatians.

2. Faith in Christ as an absolute

Notwithstanding differences in the figures Paul uses to convey his understanding of Abraham's faith in Gal 3:6–17 and Rom 4:1–25, his point remains the same: the promise to Abraham was fulfilled in Christ, not through the Law. In Galatians Paul proves his case by making use of the improbable argument that the single seed of the promise to Abraham is Christ. In Romans he does so by the parallel placement of Abraham's faith in "God who made alive the dead and called what is not into being" (Gal 3:16) and the believers' faith "in him who raised Jesus our Lord from the dead" (Rom 4:24). The formulations in Romans 4 make it possible to consider faith as a universal phenomenon, as trust in God. In both cases it is trust in God who makes alive the dead. The semantic parallel in Gal 3:16–17, however, where the promise to Abraham is related directly to Christ as his one seed, suggests that faith in a universal sense is not what Paul has in mind. This is confirmed by the context in which the discussion of Abraham's faith takes place, framed by the two christological passages, 3:21–26 and 4:23–25. The reference to faith in the God who raised "our Lord Jesus" from the dead is not added as a parallel to Abraham's faith, but integrates Abraham's justification by faith and the Christ-event. Semantically Rom 4 expresses the same meaning as Paul's improbable argument about Abraham's one seed in Galatians.

In both letters Abraham's faith is in God's promise that in him "all the gentiles will be blessed" (Gal 3:8), that he would be "the father of many gentiles" (Rom 4:17), which was fulfilled in Christ. Without the fulfillment of the promise in Christ, Abraham's faith has no meaning for Paul. At the same time, the Christ-event is not something new, but the fulfillment of what had been promised to Abraham. It was witnessed to by the Law and the prophets (Rom 3:21). In Rom 15:8 the sole purpose of Christ appears to have been to secure the promises to the Fathers for the sake of the truth of God. Abraham's justification by faith has great significance in Galatians and especially in Rom 4:1–22, where it almost becomes a topic in its own right until Paul reintegrates it into the Christ-event. In these letters neither Abraham's justification by faith nor the Christ-event is understandable without the other. These two conceptions should be conceived of as a single integral event of promise and fulfillment.

At the same time, it is for the sake of interpreting the meaning of the Christ-event that Paul appeals to Abraham's justification by faith in Galatians and Romans. The point which he argues in Galatians and Romans by appealing to Abraham's justification by faith, namely, that salvation is available to Jews as well as gentiles without distinction, is something he already stated in 1 Cor 7:19 without an appeal to Abraham's justification, "Circumcision counts for nothing, and not being circumcised counts for nothing, but keeping the commandments of God."[2] This makes it clear that the earlier letters should not be interpreted in the light of Paul's reasoning in Galatians and Romans, but inversely, Galatians should be interpreted on the basis of the earlier letters, 1 Thessalonians and 1 and 2 Corinthians.

Romans 10 also opens the door to interpreting faith in a universal sense. Paul refers to the Jewish attempt to establish their own righteousness in categories that could be interpreted universally, "they have a zeal for God, but without understanding. Ignorant of the justice of God, and seeking to establish their own, they did not submit to the justice of God" (Rom 10:2–3). One might conclude that the Jews lacked faith in God in a universal sense, without a relationship to faith in Christ. But the very next verse relates their attempt to establish their own righteousness concretely to Christ, "For the end of the Law is Christ for the justification of everyone who believes" (v. 4). The counterposing of righteousness through the Law and justification through faith in Christ which follows in verses 5–13 makes it clear that the Jews' attempt to establish their own righteousness was conceived concretely by Paul as their rejection of Christ. Paul evidently does not distinguish between faith as an expression of a universal trust in God and faith in Christ. Faith in Christ is for him faith itself, not a mere manifestation of a universal faith. Thus, Abraham's faith is not distinguishable from faith in the event of Christ. Paul absolutizes faith in Christ as faith itself.

---

[2]Note the close parallels in Gal 5:6, "For in Christ, neither circumcision is capable of anything, nor not being circumcised, but faith active through love," and Gal 6:15, "For neither is circumcision anything, nor not being circumcised, but a new creature."

3. The fundamental issue in Galatians and Romans

In his reasoning in Gal 2:14c–16 Paul's reaches his point in verse 16, "[even we who are Jews, and not from the gentiles, sinners], knowing that a person is not justified through works of the Law except through the faith of Jesus Christ, we too believed in Christ Jesus in order to be justified through the faith of Christ and not from works of the Law, for from works of the Law no one will be justified." In other words, if even Jews are justified through the faith of Christ, and not by their distinction, through circumcision and the Law, of not being gentile sinners, there is no reason for gentiles to become Jews in order to be justified. The Abraham story in Gal 3:6–17 serves as proof.

In Romans Paul formulates the same point with great clarity in 3:29–30, "Or is God of the Jews only? Not also of the gentiles? Indeed, also of the gentiles, since it is one God who justifies the circumcised out of faith, and the uncircumcised through faith." Rom 3:28–30 defines the issue as a question of whether justification was limited to the Jews or whether gentiles could be justified as well. That is, could gentiles as gentiles, which means sinners in Paul's understanding of Judaism, be justified without first having to become Jews by accepting circumcision and relying on the privileges which the Law provides?

Submission to the Law or the necessity of being Jewish is what Paul rejected with severity in Galatians, where he interpreted the Galatians' willingness to become circumcised as a willingness to become Jewish. As I have argued in chapter 2 concerning "A Macro-Structure for Galatians," he could have misunderstood the Galatians, but it is nevertheless the basis of his reasoning in that letter, and one should interpret it as such. Even if Paul was mistaken about the Galatians' intentions, his reasoning against becoming circumcised in order to be justified has a force of its own, taken as an argument against the hypothetical assumption that salvation is limited to the Jews only. He sometimes gives exaggerated expression to this meaning in Galatians, especially in 4:21–31. By considering the interrelationships between the expressions of the same meaning in the two letters, and taking note of the particular situation in Galatia as (mis)understood by Paul, we may understand better what he meant.

B. *The Expansion and Clarification of the Reasoning of Galatians in Romans*

Romans is not an explicit attempt to clarify Galatians. It represents Paul's further reflection on the reasoning and issues of the earlier letter. There is no reason to exclude the possibility that some of what Paul wrote in Romans contradicts what he wrote in Galatians. On the whole one would have to take what he wrote in Romans, the fruit of more careful reflection, rather than what he wrote in Galatians, as more accurate formulations, although it is also possible that in some cases formulations in Galatians express his intended meanings more accurately than those in Romans. The purpose here is to see what light formulations in the one letter may shed on formulations in the other.

1. Salvation grounded in God's entrusting God's revelation to the Jews

Gentile sinfulness is the implied background of Paul's sarcastic remark in Gal 2:15. The idea surfaces in other parts of Galatians as well, for example, in Paul's reference to the gentile believers' previous enslavement to cosmic powers (4:3) and to beings that are not gods (4:8). But it is in Rom 1:18–32, more than anywhere in Galatians, that Paul makes explicit his Jewish bias against the gentiles. Even if his description of gentile depravity functions as a step in his argument to show that before the Law the Jews too are without excuse, he does not take back what he wrote about the gentiles, but concludes with the sharp condemnation, "Knowing the just requirements of God, that those who commit such acts deserve death, they not only commit them, but approve of [others] doing so" (v. 32). As in Galatians, gentile sinfulness is the background of his thinking.

Just as Paul's condemnation of the gentiles is incomparably more severe in Rom 1:18–32 than in Galatians, so is his condemnation of the Jews in 2:1–3:20. His challenge to Jewish religious-moral superiority in his charge to Peter, "If you as a Jew live like a gentile and not a Jew, why do you want to force the gentiles to become Jews?" (Gal 2:14c), is substantiated in cruel detail in Rom 2:1–3:20. Paul's sarcastic challenge of the Jewish claim to be "by heritage Jews, not from the gentiles, sinners" in Gal 2:15–16 turns to irony in Rom 2:25–29 when he contends that a gentile who fulfills the just requirements of the Law unmasks the Jew who fails to do so as a sinner: "if an uncircumcised person observes the just requirements of the Law, will his [or her] lack of circumcision not be considered circumcision? And the person who is by nature uncircumcised but fulfills the Law judges you who are in the letter and through circumcision a transgressor of the Law" (vv. 26–27).

Notwithstanding this sharp condemnation, Paul's bias against the gentiles is coordinate with his bias in favor of the Jews, based in part on his understanding that salvation for all has its roots in the history of the Jews, which gives them a prerogative, as he writes in Rom 3:2c, "they were entrusted with God's revelation." Nowhere in

Romans does Paul specifically address the issue of the Jewish prerogative, though in chapters 9–11 he returns to the problem which
arises from it, as stated in 3:3, "What then? If some of them became
distrustful, will not their distrust destroy the trustworthiness of
God?" But it is the prerogative of the Jews which makes their rejection of Christ a problem. If they had not been entrusted with God's
revelation, their disbelief would not have presented Paul with the
problem in Romans. The prerogative of the Jews is the assumed
background of Romans 9–11. It comes to the surface in 11:17–25 in
Paul's reasoning that gentile salvation is grounded in that of the Jews.
Thus, the prerogative of the Jews and the problem which arises from
it because of their rejection of Christ is an expansion and qualification of the topic of Galatians, salvation through trust in God for Jews
as well as gentiles. Salvation had been available to the Jews first, as
in the formulation of the main theme of Romans, "[The gospel] is the
power of God to salvation for all who believe, to the Jews first, and
to the Hellenes" (Rom 1:16), and gentile salvation is grounded in the
promise of the salvation that had been entrusted to the Jews, as Paul
argues in Rom 11:17–24. On the other hand, in Paul's reasoning the
beneficiaries of the promise to Abraham were the gentiles, as in his
quotation of Gen 12:3 in Gal 3:8, and Gen 17:5 in Rom 4:17. This
reasoning is what makes the reversal of the sequence "to the Jews
first, and to the gentiles" inevitable in Rom 4:11–12.

In Galatians too there are indications that Paul's rejection of
justification through circumcision and the Law does not exclude
Jewish salvation. His meaning in Gal 4:21–31 cannot be a rejection
of the Jews. In 2:7–9 he allows for a parallel salvation of Jews and
gentiles in his and Peter's parallel missions, "seeing that I had been
entrusted with the gospel to the uncircumcised as Peter had been to
the circumcised—for he who worked through Peter for the mission
to the circumcised, worked also through me for the gentiles— . . .
James and Cephas and John . . . gave me and Barnabas the hand of
friendship, so that we would go to the gentiles and they to the
circumcised." The conception is recalled with great clarity in Rom
3:30, "it is one God who justifies the circumcised out of faith, and
the uncircumcised through faith." Less explicit are Paul's statements
that "in Christ neither circumcision is capable of anything, nor is not
being circumcised, but faith working through love" (Gal 5:6), and
"neither is circumcision anything, nor is being uncircumcised, but a
new creation" (6:15). Coming after 4:21–31, however, there are strong
indications that with these statements Paul qualifies his extreme
formulations concerning existence under the Law. These are not new,
but recall what he wrote in 1 Cor 7:19, "Circumcision is nothing, and
not being circumcised is nothing, but keeping the commandments of
God." What Paul means with 4:21–31 regarding what he perceived

as a critical situation in Galatians was that the gentiles could not expect to find salvation by participating in the Jewish claim to a privileged relationship with God. The purpose of his reasoning with the allegory of Sarah and Hagar is to show that the Law itself—"you who want to be under the Law, do you not hear the Law?" (v. 21)—proves that the claim to a privileged relationship with God, represented by Hagar, mount Sinai, and the present Jerusalem, is negated by the promise, represented by Sarah and the Jerusalem from above.

2. Romans 2 makes explicit the positive side of the Law

An important element interwoven into Paul's reasoning concerning Abraham in Galatians is absent in the discussion in Romans 4, the curse of the Law on the Jews, and Christ freeing them from it (Gal 3:10–14). Paul does write in Romans that "the Law engenders wrath" (Rom 4:15), but he does not identify it as a curse. Noteworthy about the argument in Galatians is that Christ freed the Jews from the curse of the Law "in order that the blessing of Abraham would reach the gentiles in Christ Jesus" (Gal 3:14). Complementary to this argument is Paul's point that, since the Law came later, it was not a factor in the promise of salvation to Abraham (3:15–17). For the latter point there is a semantic parallel in Romans 4, formulated in terms of circumcision. Abraham was justified before he was circumcised (vv. 9–10), "and he received the sign of circumcision, a seal of the justification of faith while uncircumcised" (v. 11a–b). In Romans too the salvation of the gentiles is the ultimate objective of Abraham's faith "so that he would be the father of all who believe while uncircumcised, that it would be reckoned to them" (v. 11c–d), to which Paul adds in Rom 4:12 that it applies to the Jews as well. In verse 13, as in Galatians, he makes explicit the relationship of the Law to the promise to Abraham: "it was not through the Law that the promise was made to Abraham and to his seed that he would be the inheritor of the world, but through the obedience of faith."

In Romans Paul may have intentionally avoided writing about the Law as a curse. What could be considered as a curse from which Christ freed all of humanity through his obedience, even if the term is not used, is the legacy of Adam's transgression in 5:12–21. Of greater significance is the semantic parallel to the curse of the Law in Rom 15:8–9a, "Christ became a servant of circumcision for the sake of the truth of God, in order to secure the promises of the Fathers, and the gentiles praise God because of mercy." The promise to Abraham, referred to here as "the promises to the Fathers," is again related to the salvation of the gentiles. In Galatians Christ became a curse in order to free the Jews from the curse of the Law "so that the blessing of Abraham would reach the gentiles in Christ Jesus" (Gal 3:14a), and in Romans he became a servant of circumcision "in order to secure the promises to the Fathers, and the gentiles praise God because of mercy" (Rom 15:8b–9a). In Rom 4:16 Paul states what the securing of the promise to the Fathers means, once more clarifying the inclusion of Jews and gentiles in relationship to the promise to Abraham: "For that reason it is through faith in order that it would be a generosity, so that the promises would be secure for every seed, not only for the one who is under the Law, but also for the one who is from the faith of Abraham, who is the father of all of us."

Together these statements in Romans help clarify what Paul means by the curse of the Law in Galatians: it prevented the Jews from accepting justification of the sinner through faith, as stated in Rom 10:3–4, "Ignorant of the justice of God, and seeking to establish their own, they did not submit to the justice of God. For the end of the Law is Christ [with its objective] the justification of everyone [Jew or gentile] who believes." Circumcision and the Law distinguished Jews from gentiles, from being sinners: justification through the Law limited justification to the circumcised.

Rom 10:5 makes clear that the curse included the demand that the commandments be fulfilled, "For Moses writes concerning the justification which is through the Law, 'The person who carries out [the commandments] will live by them,' " recalling very closely in meaning the statement of the curse of the Law in Gal 3:10–12, "For those who are from works of the Law are under a curse; for it is written, 'Cursed is everyone who does not remain with everything that is written in the book of the Law, to do it.' That no one is justified through the Law is clear, because 'the just will live by faith'; the Law is not from faith, but 'the person who does [the commandments] will live by them.' "

Paul acknowledges the problem of the Law in both letters when his reasoning reached a point beyond which he was unwilling to go. In Gal 3:21 he questions whether "the Law is thus against the promises?" and in Rom 3:31 he asks whether "we destroy the Law through faith?" In both cases he replies emphatically, "By no means!" His justification in both cases offers little help. In Galatians he gives an explicitly hypothetical reason, "if a Law with the power to make alive was given, justification would indeed have been through the Law." His further exposition in Galatians that the Law was a custodian for the Jews until Christ came (3:23–25) restricts its validity to the Jews, and for only the interim period between the promise to Abraham and its fulfillment in Christ. In Rom 3:31c he announces that the Law's validity extends beyond both of these restrictions: "we affirm [the Law through faith]." Paul obviously knew that his sweeping negations of the Law went beyond his intended meaning, but he did not find it necessary at those points to elaborate.[3] Unable to avoid the issue in Rom 7:7–8:4, he addresses the problem of the Law in its negative and positive meanings as an issue in its own right. In Galatians the problem of the Law has meaning only in relation to other issues, as it does in Romans, until Paul reaches the reasoning of 7:7–8:4.

Paul does not reject the notion that one can be justified for good works either in Galatians or in Romans. In Romans 2 he affirms it as something self-evident, which it probably was for him. An important feature of Romans 2 is his praise for good works and sharp condemnation of evil in verses 6–10, revealing the positive side of the Law for him. Before the Law there is "no favoritism with God. Not the hearers of the Law are just before God, but the doers will be justified" (Rom 2:12–13). Paul does not appear to be aware of a tension between these positive statements concerning the Law and his negative statements that "through works of the Law no one will be justified before [God]" (Rom 3:20). His statements concerning the Law in 2:6–10 have important parallels in the paraenetic sections of all his letters, calling for behavior that fulfills the just requirements of the Law, for example, Gal 5:19–25. In his paraenesis he shows that he expects gentile readers to turn away from their previous sinful existence, for example, in Rom 6:16–18, "Do you not realize that to whom you subject yourselves in subservience as slaves, you are slaves to whom you are subservient, either of sin to death or of obedience to justice? Praise God that you were slaves of sin, but became obedient from the heart to the teaching that was given to you; having been freed from sin, you have become enslaved to justice."

---

[3]This may be one of the most telling examples of what Patte refers to as a conviction which is more fundamental than the arguments that are made in support of it. See, *Paul's Faith*, 9–20.

Part Two ❧
The Semantic Deep Structure of Paul's Thought

In Part One the analysis of the semantic macro-structures of Galatians and Romans revealed that Paul's fundamental concern in these
letters was the opposition between justification through works of the
Law—signifying the limitation of salvation to the circumcised or the
Jews—and justification by faith—signifying that salvation was for
all, the uncircumcised and the circumcised. Our task in Part One was
to determine *what* Paul wanted to say in Galatians and Romans. In
this part our task will be to determine *why* he wanted to say it. In
order to do so I will employ a methodology based on the approach
employed by Claude Lévi-Strauss for the interpretation of myths.[1]
Lévi-Strauss' method of uncovering the meaning expressed in mythical texts is to read them not only syntagmatically, i.e., with the flow
of the stories, but also paradigmatically, by tabulating the recurrences
of similar story elements or mythemes in a myth or a series of myths.
He compares his approach to the reading of a musical score, not only
horizontally for its melody, but also vertically for the harmony of the
various voices of the instruments or singers.[2] The examination of a
sufficient number of story elements enables him to discern structural
patterns of oppositions between groups of mythemes. He illustrates
his method, first with an analysis of the Oedipus myth,[3] and then the
North American Zuni myth of origin and emergence.[4] The method is

---

[1]See "The Structural Study of Myth," *Myth, A Symposium, Journal
of American Folklore* 78 (1955) 428–44. Translated with some additions and
modifications as "La Structure des mythes," *Anthropologie Structurale* (Paris:
Plon, 1958), vol. I, 225–55. ET, *Structural Anthropology* (by Claire Jacobson
and Brooke Grundfest Schoeps, New York: Basic Books, Inc. 1963; paperback:
Doubleday Anchor Book, 1967) vol. 1, 202–28. Page references are to the latter.

[2]"The Structural Study of Myth," 208.

[3]"The Structural Study of Myth," 209–14.

[4]"The Structural Study of Myth," 215–26.

then used on a grand scale in his study of American Indian myths, *Mythologiques*.[5]

More specifically I will employ the method I developed in *Neither on this Mountain nor in Jerusalem*[6] on the basis of the generative trajectory drawn from the semiotic grammar of A. J. Greimas and J. Courtés, *Sémiotique: dictionnaire raisonné de la théorie du langage*.[7]

GENERATIVE TRAJECTORY			
		syntactic component	semantic component
Semio-narrative structures	**deep level**	FUNDAMENTAL SYNTAX	FUNDAMENTAL SEMANTICS
	surface level	SURFACE NARRATIVE SYNTAX	NARRATIVE SEMANTICS
Discourse structures		DISCOURSE SYNTAX Discoursivization actorialization temporalization spatialization	DISCOURSE SEMANTICS Thematization Figurativization

The generative trajectory reveals how meaning is brought to expression in language. It does not concern the actual process through which a text is produced. Rather, it is a grammar in which all the levels are present at the same time.

It is not my intention here to provide a theoretical clarification of the generative trajectory. All that needs to be understood about it will emerge from the discussion of the texts of Galatians and Romans. The generative trajectory will serve as a guide in our analysis of the various levels of meaning in the two letters. For our purposes the generative trajectory has no meaning in itself. It is a theory, a means of understanding, without any meaning of its own.

As the diagram shows, the generative trajectory has two components. The syntactic component draws attention to the way in which expressions in a text are restricted formally at various levels to define their meanings, thus limiting ambiguity. The semantic

---

[5]*Mythologiques* (4 vols.; Paris: Plon, 1964–71).
[6]*Neither on this Mountain nor in Jerusalem: A Study of John 4.* (SBLMS 34, Atlanta: Scholars Press, 1988).
[7]Paris: Hachette, 1979; ET, *Semiotics and Language* (by Larry Crist and Daniel Patte, and others; Bloomington: Indiana University Press, 1982).

component clarifies the various levels of meaning of the text from the concrete expression in figures to the most abstract level of the fundamental semantics, the text's micro-universe. For our purposes it is not necessary to give specific attention to the syntactic component.[8] With regard to the semantic component, the only meanings that are concretely present in the text are the figures or images, at the level of figurativization on the generative trajectory. From an analytical point of view the themes are abstractions, or generalizations, drawn from the common features of series of figures. From a generative point of view the themes are brought to expression by means of series of figures. Our task in this part will be to penetrate to the more abstract levels of Paul's thought, in chapter 5 to his system of values, in chapter 6 to the micro-universe on which his thinking is based.

---

[8]For a complete discussion of the generative trajectory and other features of Greimas' semiotics, see my study on John 4, *Neither on this Mountain, nor in Jerusalem.*

5 ∾

Paul's System of Values

INTRODUCTION

The discussion of Gal 3:18 below illustrates the most significant features of the method for our investigation. At the same time it will allow us to investigate Paul's system of values, by clarifying the relationship between abstract thematic statements and concrete figures in a single verse from Galatians. The abstract, hypothetical statement in Gal 3:18a, "If the inheritance is through the Law, it is no longer through the promise" finds concrete expression in what follows in verse 18b, "God granted it to Abraham as a promise." Other statements in Galatians and Romans also express concretely the abstract, hypothetical opposition between the Law and the promise of Gal 3:18a in a variety of figures:

Galatians:
5:2   If you receive circumcision, Christ will be of no advantage to you.
5:4   Whoever of you are justified through the Law are torn away from
        Christ, you have fallen from grace.

Romans:
4:13   It was not through the Law that the promise was made to
        Abraham and to his seed that he would be the inheritor of the
        world, but through the justification by faith.
4:14   If those who are from the Law are inheritors, faith has become
        empty, and the promise destroyed.

Galatians 3:18a sets two themes—"inheritance through the Law" and "inheritance through the promise"—in opposition to each other: if the one is true the other is not. Placing these two opposed themes on the logical square below reveals all the possible logical relationships between them. On the generative trajectory, these rela-

tionships are part of the syntactic component, located at the level of
the fundamental syntax. Only these relationships are part of the
syntactic component, not the meanings expressed by the themes,
which is a function of the semantic component. The only function of
the various parts of the syntactic component with regard to meaning
is to set limits to its expression, in that way reducing ambiguity.

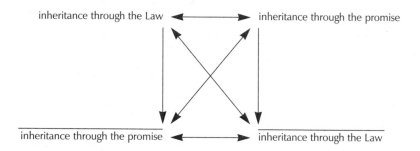

According to Gal 3:18a, "inheritance thought the Law" and
"inheritance through the promise" are *contraries* (indicated by the
horizontal line at the top of the square), that is, either of them can be
true, but not both of them at the same time. The vertical, downward
pointing arrows at the left and right of the square confirms this,
showing that if inheritance is through the Law, then it is not through
the promise, and if inheritance is through the promise, then it is not
through the law. Formulated more technically, inheritance through
the Law implies the negation of inheritance through the promise, and
inheritance through the promise implies the negation of inheritance
through the Law. The lines above "inheritance through the promise"
and "inheritance through the Law" signify negation.

   The bottom horizontal line depicts *subcontraries*, both of
which can be true at the same time: inheritance might be neither
through the promise nor through the Law; there may, in fact, be no
inheritance at all. Whereas the top horizontal line, pointing in both
directions, indicates that either one of the contraries can be true
(even if not both at the same time), and the bottom horizontal line
indicates that both subcontraries can be true at the same time, the
vertical lines, pointing in one direction only, downwards, indicate
that if either of the contraries is true, its subcontrary is also true.

   The diagonal lines depict contradiction, which means that
inheritance either is through the Law or is not; there is no third
alternative to these two. The same applies to the alternatives that
inheritance is either through the promise or is not. The diagonal lines
also point in both directions, indicating the either of the alternatives
could be true.

The logical square does not clarify logical relationships of which Paul was necessarily conscious, but the logical implications of his reasoning. Logically, there is no reason why inheritance through the Law implies that inheritance cannot be through the promise, but if Paul says that is the case, we must proceed from there and trace the logical implications of that reasoning.

Paul's hypothetical statement in Gal 3:18a becomes concrete in v. 18b: "God granted it to Abraham as a promise." With that Paul's thought has moved from the purely theoretical, logical possibilities to what is actually the case: "inheritance through the promise" is actualized, with which "inheritance through the Law" is implicitly negated. A semiotic square can clarify this by showing which of the logical possibilities are actualized. Whereas the logical square presents logical possibilities, regardless of which is actually the case (the diagonal arrows point in both, contradicting directions), the semiotic square shows which of these possibilities are considered to be the case (and so the arrows point in one direction only, toward that which is affirmed).

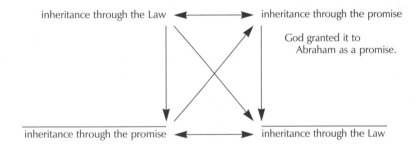

Since the semiotic square shows not what applies in principle but what is considered to be real, we may conclude that if one of the contraries is considered true, its subcontrary is considered true as well. Paul's assertion that God granted the inheritance to Abraham as a promise explicitly affirms only that inheritance is through the promise, but implicitly it also negates that the inheritance is through the Law. For that reason there is also a second diagonal arrow pointing to the negation of inheritance through the Law, even though that has not been made explicit.

This principle does not apply to the subcontraries, both of which can be true at the same time. If Paul merely showed that inheritance was not through the Law it would not necessarily have followed that it was through the promise. Both diagonal arrows could point to the subcontraries, signifying that both are true, and accordingly, that neither contrary is true. Without violating the present logic, it is possible to maintain that there was no inheritance. This has nothing to do with the fact that the subcontraries are stated negatively. As we will see below, in Paul's reasoning justification of the gentiles presupposes, that is, implies justification by faith as its subcontrary. A fine example of the affirmation of both subcontraries is Gal 6:15, "For neither is circumcision anything, nor is not being circumcised, but being a new creature" (cf. 5:6 and 1 Cor 7:19): Paul negates both contraries, circumcision and not being circumcised, introducing being a new creature as a third alternative,

Gal 3:18 is purely theoretical reasoning for which Paul could depend entirely on syllogistic logic to argue his point. Accepting as the major premise that inheritance is either through the Law or through the promise, Paul appeals to God's granting the inheritance to Abraham as a promise for his minor premise from which he could conclude that inheritance is through the promise, and not through the Law. The specific case of Abraham's inheritance as a promise proves the general principle that inheritance is through the promise.

All of Paul's reasoning is not syllogistic. There are cases where he first establishes the subcontrary, that is, the condition presupposed by what he ultimately wants to claim as true, before establishing that truth itself. So, for example, as we will see below, in Gal 3:13–14, he first establishes that justification is by faith before he could assert gentile salvation which implies justification by faith as its subcontrary. All of this may appear far removed from relevance for understanding Paul. Below I will show that not only is it relevant, but, in fact, essential. Showing by means of a semiotic analysis that in order to assert the truth of either one or the other of two contrary claims the implied subcontrary has to be true as well is of utmost importance for establishing a macro-structure for reading Romans and Galatians.

To accomplish this goal, we will move from the concrete level of the figures in the text to the themes they express. From there we will move to the values conveyed by the themes, and finally, in chapter 6, to the deepest level of Paul's micro-universe. The length and complexity of the texts forbid the luxury of a detailed analysis, such as I was able to present in *Neither on this Mountain nor in Jerusalem*. Instead, the analysis will be guided by insights from that earlier investigation.

I. THE OPPOSITION BETWEEN JUSTIFICATION BY FAITH AND JUSTIFICATION THROUGH WORKS OF THE LAW

I begin with that most fundamental of problems in these letters, the opposition between justification through works of the Law and justification by faith, representing the two opposed themes expressed by a large number of figures in Galatians and Romans. We can place them as contraries on a logical square as follows:

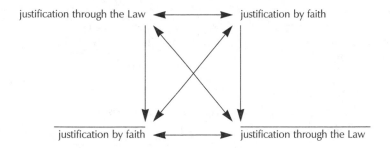

Unlike the author of John 4, Paul almost never uses individual figures, but figures conjoined with their implied negations. So, the figures in Gal 2:21b, "if justification were to be through the Law, then Christ died in vain," give logical expression to justification through the Law and the negation of justification by faith. Gal 2:16b, "in order to be justified through the faith of Christ and not from works of the Law," affirms justification by faith and negates justification through works of the Law. We can now add these figures to the above logical square as follows:

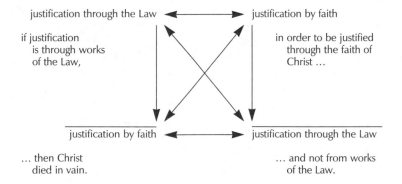

Paul discusses the opposition by means of the figures listed in Appendix IV, "Themes in Galatians and Romans." In the discussion below I list only those that explicitly express the opposition between justification through works of the Law and justification by faith. I also list a few additional figures, in particular those that express the theme, "a child of Abraham."

These figures are intricately related to each other in Paul's thinking. Since justification through works of the Law and justification by faith are contraries, that is, theoretically, if the one is true the other cannot be, it follows that to affirm the one in actuality implies negation of the other. I will first list the figures concerning justification through works of the Law, and then those that concern its contrary, justification by faith.

A. *Figures Expressing Justification through Works of the Law*

These figures express contradictory themes, either affirming or negating justification through works of the Law.

1. Affirming figures:

a. justification through the Law (Gal 2:21; 5:4)
b. doing the commandments (Gal 3:12; Rom 10:5)
c. receiving the spirit through works of the Law (Gal 3:2)
d. providing the spirit through works of the Law (Gal 3:5)
e. inheritance through the Law (Gal 3:18a; Rom 4:14)
f. circumcision (Gal 5:2)
g. the principle of works (Rom 3:27; 4:4)
h. Abraham was justified for works (Rom 4:2)

2. Negating figures:

a. a person is not justified through works of the Law (Gal 2:16a)
b. justification is not through works of the Law (Gal 2:16b)
c. no one is justified through works of the Law (Gal 2:16c; 3:11; Rom 3:20)

d. dying to the Law (Gal 2:19)
e. the Law is a curse (Gal 3:10; 13)
f. the Law does not invalidate the promise (Gal 3:17)
g. the Law does not destroy the promise (Gal 3:17)
h. throwing out the slave woman and her child (Gal 4:30)
i. the child of the slave woman will not inherit (Gal 4:30)
j. the obligation to keep the entire Law (Gal 5:3)
k. justification is revealed without the Law (Rom 3:21a)
l. justification without works of the Law (Rom 3:28)
m. the promise is not through the Law (Rom 4:13)
n. the Law produces wrath (Rom 4:15)
o. a child of the flesh is not a child of God (Rom 9:8)
p. justification is not through works (Rom 11:6)

The significance of the negating figures in the logical system of Paul's thought is that as contradictions of justification through works of the Law they are implied by justification by faith, the contrary of justification through works of the Law. Justification by faith cannot be true unless its contrary, justification through works of the Law, is negated, that is, logically contradicted. The same is of course true for justification through works of the Law, as we will see below.

B. *Figures Expressing Justification by Faith*

As in the case of figures expressing justification through works of the Law, these figures too express contradictory themes, either affirming or negating justification by faith.

1. Affirming figures:

a. justification through the faith of Christ (Gal 2:16a, b)
b. Christ liberates those who are under the curse of the Law (Gal 2:19; 3:13)
c. receiving the spirit through the hearing of the faith (Gal 3:2)
d. providing the spirit through the hearing of the faith (Gal 3:5)
e. faith was reckoned to Abraham as justice (Gal 3:6; Rom 4:3, 9)
f. justification by faith (Gal 3:8; Rom 3:28, 30; 4:15; 10:6: 11:6)
g. the just lives by faith (Gal 3:11)
h. ratification of the testament (Gal 3:17)
i. the principle of faith (Rom 3:27; 4:5)
j. the son of the free woman inherits the promise (Gal 4:30)
k. the promise is through the justification of faith (Rom 4:13)
l. justification as a kindness (Rom 4:15)
m. the promise is secure for every seed (Rom 4:15)
n. children of the promise are considered the seed (of Abraham) (Rom 9:8)

2. Negating figures:

a. the Law is not through faith (Gal 3:12)
b. inheritance is not through the promise (Gal 3:18a)
c. Christ died in vain (Gal 2:21b)
d. Christ is of no advantage (Gal 5:2)
e. being torn away from Christ (Gal 5:4)
f. falling from grace (Gal 5:4)
g. faith is empty (Rom 4:14)
h. the promise is destroyed (Rom 4:14)

With the final group of negating figures the circle of Paul's logical system concerning justification has come full swing to where we started. As contradictions of justification by faith these figures are implied by justification through works of the Law, the contrary of justification by faith. Justification through works of the Law cannot be true unless its contrary, justification by faith is negated, that is, logically contradicted.

As one might expect, negating figures predominate as expressions of justification through works of the Law, and affirming figures as expressions of justification by faith.

In order to view Paul's logic with regard to these figures in a single glance we can place them on a logical square as follows:

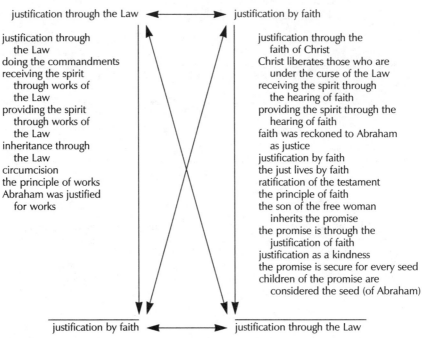

justification through the Law ⟷ justification by faith

justification through
  the Law
doing the commandments
receiving the spirit
  through works of
  the Law
providing the spirit
  through works of
  the Law
inheritance through
  the Law
circumcision
the principle of works
Abraham was justified
  for works

justification through the
  faith of Christ
Christ liberates those who are
  under the curse of the Law
receiving the spirit through
  the hearing of faith
providing the spirit through the
  hearing of faith
faith was reckoned to Abraham
  as justice
justification by faith
the just lives by faith
ratification of the testament
the principle of faith
the son of the free woman
  inherits the promise
the promise is through the
  justification of faith
justification as a kindness
the promise is secure for every seed
children of the promise are
  considered the seed (of Abraham)

justification by faith ⟷ justification through the Law

the Law is not through faith
inheritance is not through the
  promise
Christ died in vain
Christ is of no advantage
being torn away from Christ
falling from grace
faith is empty
the promise is destroyed

a person is not justified through
  works of the Law
justification is not through
  works of the Law
no-one is justified through
  works of the Law
dying to the Law
the Law is a curse
the Law does not invalidate
  the promise
the Law does not destroy the
  promise
throwing out the slave woman
  and her child
the child of the slave woman
  does not inherit
obligation to keep the entire Law
justification is revealed without
  the Law
justification without works of
  the Law
the promise is not through the Law
the Law produces wrath
a child of the flesh is not a child
  of God
justification is not through works

II. JEWISH PRIVILEGE AND GENTILE SALVATION AS CONTRARY VALUES

In order to understand better the role of these figures in Paul's reasoning it will be useful to move briefly to a level of his thought that lies even deeper than that of the themes, namely, the level of their underlying values. From our investigations in Part I it is possible to identify the value expressed in the figures under the theme of justification through the Law as /Jewish privilege/ and the value that comes to expression through the figures under the theme of justification by faith as /gentile salvation/. The slash signs indicate values. We can present the relationship between these values on a logical square as follows:

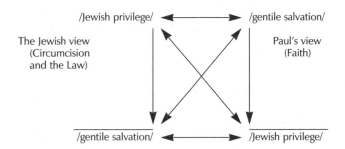

The same logic would also apply for the Jewish position which Paul opposes. The difference is that, according to Paul, the Jewish view affirms the position on the left, that Jewish privilege implicitly negates gentile salvation, whereas Paul himself affirms the position on the right according to which /gentile salvation/ implies the negation of /Jewish privilege/.

The opposition between these two is the root issue in Galatians and Romans. With the writing of Paul's letter to the Galatians the issue of /Jewish privilege/ reached a critical point. The Antioch incident as reported by Paul reveals that there were Jewish Christians who did not understand /gentile salvation/ to negate /Jewish privilege/. We do not have the resources to uncover exactly what happened in Antioch, especially what the brothers "from James," Peter, and Barnabas thought when they refused table fellowship with gentile believers. But Paul's report of the incident in Gal 2:11–16 makes it clear that for them the affirmation of /gentile salvation/ did not imply the negation of /Jewish privilege/. It is even possible that

before the issue came to a head in Galatians, Paul himself did not
see /Jewish privilege/ and /gentile salvation/ in such radical opposition. His report of the Antioch incident brings to the fore what
became the issue for him in Galatia. He probably projected the issue
as it had become clear in Galatia back into the Antioch incident. At
that time Paul may have remained at the concrete level of table
fellowship of Jewish and gentile believers in Christ, without entering
into the abstract issue of Jewish identity. Maintaining the distinctiveness of a Jewish identity even as Christians was what prevented
Peter and the others from full integration in the gentile Christian
community.

Did Paul at that stage already demand the abandonment of
/Jewish privilege/ as radically and clearly as he does in Galatians?
Was he aware of these consequences when he insisted on unrestricted association of Jewish and gentile believers in Antioch? Did
he already then recognize that what he expected of Peter and the
others implicitly negated a distinct Jewish privilege? He may have,
but more probably at that stage of his involvement he remained at
the concrete level of table fellowship with gentile believers, and did
not reflect on the principle involved. Paul's early letters—1 Thessalonians, and 1 and 2 Corinthians—do not reflect Jewish-gentile
relationships as an issue of principle. Paul's position prior to his
writing of Galatians may have been characterized by his assertion in
1 Cor. 7:19, with no indication of controversy, that "circumcision is
nothing and not being circumcised is nothing, but keeping the commandments of God." Before the issue arose in Galatia, Paul's teaching, as reflected in his earlier letters, may not have been distinctly
different from that of the best of Cynic-stoic wandering philosopher-
teachers, promotion of the highest standards of religious morality,
the main difference being that Paul's teaching was rooted in his
Pharisaic upbringing, radically modified by his new-found understanding that keeping the commandments of God was not a prerogative of the Jews alone. That is what he learned through the fateful
encounter with Christ. Whatever the situation may have been before
the issue arose in Galatia, important for our deliberations here is that
in his report of the Antioch incident in Gal 2:11–16 Paul's thinking
moves to the abstract level of a principle. In his further reflections
on the issue in Romans the full extent of what that principle meant
for him becomes clear.

What Paul reports of the attitude of Peter and the others in
Antioch reveals that the affirmation of /gentile salvation/ in itself
does not have to stand in the radical opposition to /Jewish privilege/
in which Paul places it. They could be alternatives: Jews could find
salvation by relying on works of the Law, that is, through circumcision and the Law, and gentiles through faith in Christ, with only

limited submission to the Law, as in Acts 15:28–29. Paul draws a radically different conclusion, however, which he formulates with great precision in Gal 2:16. Even a Jew is not justified except through faith in Christ: "a person is not justified through works of the Law except through the faith of Jesus Christ." Peter and the others tried to maintain an intermediate position between that of the Jews which denied /gentile salvation/, and that of Paul which nullified /Jewish privilege/. The common logic of the Jewish and Pauline systems of values made such an intermediate position untenable. Peter and the others in the Antioch incident were forced to choose between the opposed systems.

What brings these alternatives to a point of radical opposition in Galatians is Paul's, possibly incorrect, understanding that the Galatians considered submitting themselves to the Law by becoming circumcised, which meant for Paul relying once more on /Jewish privilege/ for salvation. He draws the consequences: the affirmation of /Jewish privilege/ negates /gentile salvation/, and by the same logic, /gentile salvation/ implies the negation of /Jewish privilege/. There is no specifically Jewish salvation. All salvation is gentile salvation, as Paul would argue most consistently in Romans with his reasoning that Jewish as well as gentile justification is grounded in Abraham's faith as a gentile, "so that he would be the father of all who believe while uncircumcised, that it would be reckoned to them, and the father of the circumcised for those who are not only circumcised, but also follow in the footsteps of the faith of the uncircumcised Abraham" (Rom 4:11–12).

Since Paul himself, before his conversion, held to the Jewish position we can diagram the change of his position on a semiotic square as follows. Note that the diagonal lines now point only in one direction compared with the bi–directional arrows on the previous logical square which allows the contrary values as alternatives.

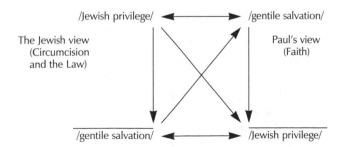

Before Paul can transform the negation of /gentile salvation/ into an affirmation, he has to transform /Jewish privilege/ into the negation of /Jewish privilege/. He cannot do that at the abstract level of the system of values or at the level of the themes. It must take place at the concrete level of the figures. Rom 1:18–4:25 reveals a reasoning that mirrors the above semiotic square. Paul proceeds on the basis of the Jewish negation of /gentile salvation/ by first presenting the depravity of the gentiles which closely reflects the Jewish view (Rom 1:18–33), as presented on the lower left side of the square below. Then, in 2:1–3:20, he transforms the claim of /Jewish privilege/ into its negation, moving from the upper left along the diagonal line of the square to the lower right. Only then, having proven that there is no /Jewish privilege/, "through works of the Law no one will be justified before [God]" (Rom 3:20a), and, "There is no difference, for all have sinned and fall short of the glory of God" (3:22b–23), does Paul transform the negation of /gentile salvation/ into the salvation of Abraham as a gentile, which is the basis of salvation for Jews as well as gentiles (3:21–4:25), as presented on the upper right side of the square.

Paul's reasoning in Gal 2:15–16 and in Rom 1:18–4:25 reflects the development of his own convictions, the fundamental change in his system of values. He himself started off as someone who affirmed /Jewish privilege/, which implied the negation of /gentile salvation/, but then he transformed /Jewish privilege/ into the negation of /Jewish privilege/, represented by the diagonal arrow which points from the upper left corner of the semiotic square to the lower right. Only on that basis was he able to transform the negation of /gentile salvation/ into its affirmation, represented by the diagonal arrow which points from the bottom left to the upper right. To put it simply, Paul could not become a Christian without first surrendering his prerogatives as a Jew (cf. Phil 3:4–7).

Placing Gal 2:15–16 on the same semiotic square reveals the degree to which Paul's reasoning in Rom 1:18–3:20 is a further reflection on the subject matter of the Galatians passage. He does not reason through the issue in Galatians. In each case the contrary affirmations of /Jewish privilege/ (Gal 2:15a) on the upper left corner of the square, and /gentile salvation/ (Gal 2:16ab) on the upper right corner, representing the contraries, implicitly negates their respective subcontraries, the negation of /gentile salvation/ (Gal 2:15b) on the lower left corner of the square, and /Jewish privilege/ (Gal 2:16c–d) on the lower right corner.

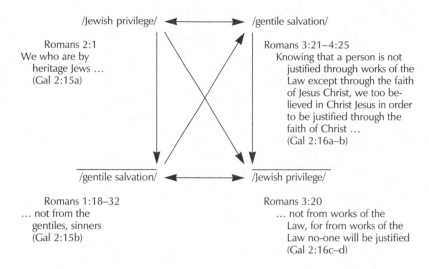

/Jewish privilege/ ⟷ /gentile salvation/

Romans 2:1
We who are by
heritage Jews ...
(Gal 2:15a)

Romans 3:21–4:25
Knowing that a person is not
justified through works of the
Law except through the faith
of Jesus Christ, we too believed in Christ Jesus in order
to be justified through the
faith of Christ ...
(Gal 2:16a–b)

/gentile salvation/ ⟷ /Jewish privilege/

Romans 1:18–32
... not from the
gentiles, sinners
(Gal 2:15b)

Romans 3:20
... not from works of the
Law, for from works of the
Law no-one will be justified
(Gal 2:16c–d)

The semiotic square above reveals the integrity of Paul's reasoning in the first four chapters of Romans. Rom 1:18–3:20, representing the move from the assumed affirmation of /Jewish privilege/ on the upper left corner of the square to its negation on the lower right is essential as the basis for his reasoning in Rom 3:21–4:25 on the upper right corner. The affirmation of /Jewish privilege/ is based on, that is, implies the negation of gentile salvation (Rom 1:18–32), on the lower left corner of the square. Paul makes this explicit in his reference to the condemnation of the gentile perversion of 1:18–32 in 2:1–3. His purpose is to proclaim not merely justification of the sinner, the gentile, by faith, but that of the Jew as well. Before God there is no difference between Jew and gentile, because the Law on which the Jews depend to establish a distinct privilege before God condemns them as sinners, making them equivalent to gentiles (Rom 3:9–20). As Paul wrote in Galatians, a Jew too, is not justified "except through the faith of Jesus Christ" (2:16a).

This network of relationships in Paul's system of values is an abstraction that can serve as a semiotic, grammatical basis for understanding his reasoning in Galatians and Romans. However, only by considering the figures that convey these values are we able to return to the actual concrete level of Paul's reasoning.

The negation of /gentile salvation/ remains a fundamental element in his thinking. Throughout Galatians and Romans, but also elsewhere in his letters, he reminds his gentile readers of their previous existence in alienation from God. Our concern here is only with the figures in Galatians and Romans. Because of the large number of figures it is not possible to list them on the semiotic square on page 184. I list only the themes and sub-themes conveyed by them. The actual figures can be seen in Appendix IV, under "Gentile depravity."

Apart from the thematic discussion of gentile sinfulness in Rom 1:18–32 and the figures under the sub-theme B₁, "the sinful condition of the gentiles," Paul's negation of /gentile salvation/ occurs mainly in the list of sub-themes B₂, "reflected in statements about gentile salvation," and B₃, "gentile salvation in relation to the Jews." Even though the figures of the latter two sub-themes are concerned mainly with gentile salvation and the way in which the destiny of the Jews functions as a basis for gentile salvation, they nevertheless reflect Paul's own negative assessment of the gentiles before their justification through faith in Christ. In a sense those figures belong on a trajectory from the negation of /gentile salvation/ to its affirmation, along the diagonal line from the lower left to the upper right on the semiotic square.

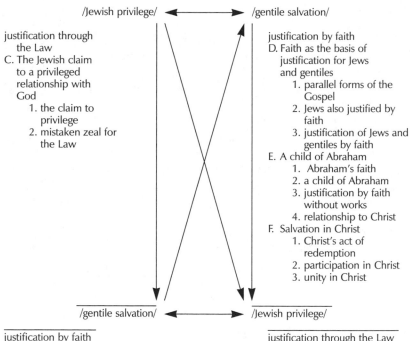

/Jewish privilege/ ⟷ /gentile salvation/

justification through
    the Law
C. The Jewish claim
    to a privileged
    relationship with
    God
        1. the claim to
           privilege
        2. mistaken zeal for
           the Law

justification by faith
D. Faith as the basis of
    justification for Jews
    and gentiles
        1. parallel forms of the
           Gospel
        2. Jews also justified by
           faith
        3. justification of Jews and
           gentiles by faith
E. A child of Abraham
        1. Abraham's faith
        2. a child of Abraham
        3. justification by faith
           without works
        4. relationship to Christ
F. Salvation in Christ
        1. Christ's act of
           redemption
        2. participation in Christ
        3. unity in Christ

/gentile salvation/ ⟷ /Jewish privilege/

justification by faith
B. Gentile depravity
        1. the sinful condi-
           tion of the gentiles
        2. reflected in state-
           ments about [their]
           salvation
        3. gentile salvation
           in relation to Jews
        4. thematic discus-
           sion of gentile
           sinfulness

justification through the Law

C. The Jewish claim
        3. Jewish guilt before the
           Law
        4. equivalence of Jews
           and gentiles before the
           Law

The starting point for Paul's reasoning is the position of the Jews, represented on the left side of the square by /Jewish privilege/ and the implied negation of /gentile salvation/. It is a crucial component in his system of values, and fundamental to his reasoning concerning salvation in general. His affirmation of /gentile salvation/ is not contrary to a supposed justification for the doing of good works, but to /Jewish privilege/ which implies a denial of /gentile salvation/.

As the point of departure in Paul's reasoning, Jewish condemnation of gentiles as depraved sinners, and accordingly, their exclusion from salvation, is essential for understanding the socio-religious transformation which took place when he accepted justification by faith. Affirmation of the value of /Jewish privilege/ is what motivated his persecution of the church. The shift in his understanding of salvation did not signal a step towards a more tolerant attitude to the gentiles, attenuating the Jewish prejudice against them.

And yet, Paul's acceptance of gentile justification through faith does not bring us to the root of what was involved in his thinking. His acceptance of gentile justification by faith is grounded at a deeper level in his rejection of the Jewish claim that as Jews, by virtue of their circumcision and submission to the Law, they are excluded from being condemned as sinners like the gentiles. The square reveals what is also concretely the case: Paul cannot simply transform the negation of /gentile salvation/ to its affirmation, because for him gentile salvation, salvation of the sinner, includes the salvation of the Jews as well. For that reason, semiotically, but also in fact, he first has to transform /Jewish privilege/ into its negation, making it possible for Jews like him, who negate /Jewish privilege/, to share in /gentile salvation/.

Paul rarely affirms /Jewish privilege/ directly, but typically in terms of its already achieved negation, expressed by the figures listed under the theme of "the Jewish claim to a privileged relationship with God." Even the few expressions of "the claim to privilege" in Rom 2:17–20 and especially Gal 2:15 are not outright affirmations, but sarcastic challenges to the Jewish claim to privilege. /Jewish privilege/ is affirmed only as a presupposition for its negation in the figures expressing a "mistaken zeal for the Law," including Paul's own. The Jewish claim to a privileged relationship with God, and with it /Jewish privilege/, is negated in the figures that express "Jewish guilt before the Law," and the "equivalence of Jews and gentiles before the Law."

The negation of /Jewish privilege/ makes it is possible for Paul to affirm that justification by faith is the justification of gentiles, represented by the value /gentile salvation/, which applies to all who believe, Jews as well as gentiles, "there is no difference, for all have sinned and fall short of the glory of God" (Rom 3:22b–23). Paul presents /gentile salvation/ as the salvation of Jews and gentiles with figures expressing "faith as the basis of justification for Jews and gentiles," distinguishable as the figures from Galatians that refer to "parallel forms of the Gospel," and those that emphasize that "Jews [are] also justified by faith." Also significant are the figures from Galatians and Romans that emphasize the "justification of Jews and gentiles by faith," and those that express what it means to be "a child of Abraham," emphasizing "Abraham's faith," being "a child of Abraham," Abraham's "justification by faith without works," as well as those that associate Abraham's justification with a "relationship to Christ." Closely related to the latter sub-theme are figures expressing "salvation in Christ," specifically "Christ's act of redemption," "participation in Christ," and the "unity in Christ." The latter figures once more emphasize that there is no difference between Jews and gentiles in Christ. Finally there are the large number of figures that express "the opposition between justification through the Law and by faith," already listed on the semiotic square on page 178 above.[1]

Paul's starting point, thus, both biographically and systematically, is the negation of /gentile salvation/: biographically that is why he persecuted the church: systematically, it is demanded by his understanding that justification by faith is /gentile salvation/, that is, justification of the sinner who is condemned by the Law. As /gentile salvation/ justification by faith for Paul implies the negation of the Jews' privileged relationship with God, which means that /Jewish privilege/ in his thinking cannot be transformed into some other form of a privileged relationship with God.

Summary

The semiotic squares makes transparent what happens systematically in Paul's thinking. Before he can transform the negation of /gentile salvation/ into its affirmation along the diagonal line from the bottom left to the upper right of the square, he has to transform /Jewish privilege/ into its negation, along the diagonal line from the upper left to the lower right of the square. As long as /Jewish privilege/ is affirmed /gentile salvation/ is negated. /Jewish privi-

---

[1]It is not possible to list those figures again on the previous square on page 178. Apart from their full listing on pages 281–82 in Appendix IV, they are listed in English translation in differentiated categories on pages 176–77, above. I present the sub-themes that those figures express as the first entries under the values that they represent.

lege/ implies the negation of /gentile salvation/. The opposed values /Jewish privilege/ and /gentile salvation/ cannot both be the case. As soon as Paul transforms the affirmation of /Jewish privilege/ into its negation, the negation of /gentile salvation/ is freed to be transformed into its affirmation. The negation of /Jewish privilege/ does not imply the affirmation of /gentile salvation/. Both subcontraries can be the case; it is possible that there is neither /Jewish privilege/ nor /gentile salvation/. But once /Jewish privilege/ has been transformed into the negation of /Jewish privilege/ there is nothing which prevents Paul from transforming the negation of /gentile privilege/ into its affirmation. He does not do so systematically as on the semiotic square, but by means of the concrete figures that bring the values and their negations to expression. The abstraction by means of the semiotic square makes it possible to perceive the systematic consistency of Paul's thinking. His reasoning in Rom 1:18–4:25, which follows a logic closely resembling what is represented on the semiotic square on page 183, reveals how well he was aware of the need to be consistent.

The affirmation of /gentile salvation/ and negation of /Jewish privilege/ are not the only elements in Paul's system of values. There are at least two others without which our understanding of his reasoning in Galatians and Romans would be incomplete, the positive value Paul attaches to good works with its corollary the negative value he attaches to evil works, and the value he attaches to God's revelation to Israel in the past. I will take up the issue of good and evil works first.

III. THE DIFFERENTIATION BETWEEN GOOD AND EVIL

Paul obviously attaches positive value to good works and negative value to evil, but that alone does not bring us very far in untangling his complex understanding of the problem of good and evil. In Appendix IV, I list figures expressing three themes that concern the differentiation between good and evil: G. "The opposition between good and evil," H. "The Law as a problem," and I. "Opposition between the flesh and the spirit."

I list here first the figures under "The opposition between good and evil" in two groups, "the judgment of good and evil" and "the doing of good and evil," differentiated according to their contrasting relationships.

A. The Judgment of Good and Evil

1. Condemnation of evil works

a. The works of the flesh are revealed (Gal 5:19)

b. The person who sows for his own flesh, will reap corruption from the flesh (Gal 6:8a)

c. The wrath of God is revealed on all ungodliness and evil of persons who through evil do not maintain the truth (Rom 1:18)

d. Those who through strife and disobedience do not obey the truth but evil, [will receive] wrath and anger (Rom 2:8)

e. Tribulation and pressure on every human being who does evil, on the Jew first, and on the gentile (Rom 2:9)

f. Those who sin without the Law, will perish without the Law; those who sin under the Law will be judged by the Law (Rom 2:12)

g. When you were slaves of sin you were free from justice; what fruit did you have then for which you are now ashamed? The end of such persons is death (Rom 6:20–21)

h. The rewards of sin is death (Rom 6:23a)

2. Reward for good works

a. The fruit of the spirit is love, etc. (Gal 5:22)

b. The person who sows for the spirit will reap eternal life from the spirit (Gal 6:8b)

c. In due course we will harvest, if we do not relax [in our efforts] (Gal 6:9b)

d. Those who through the patience of good works seek glory and honor and immortality, [will receive] eternal life (Rom 2:7)

e. Glory and honor and peace to everyone who does good, to the Jew first, and to the gentile (Rom 2:10)

f. The doers of the Law will be justified (2:13b)

g. If Abraham was justified for works, he has reason to be proud, but not before God (Rom 4:2)

h. Freed from sin and enslaved to God, you have your fruit to sanctity, and the end, eternal life (Rom 6:22)

i. The gift of God is eternal life in Christ Jesus, our Lord (Rom 6:23b)

3. Negation of reward for those who do evil

a. Those who do [evil] will not inherit the kingdom of God (Gal 5:21)

b. Not the hearers of the Law are just before God (Rom 2:13a)

4. Negation of the condemnation of good works

a. Against [the fruit of the spirit] there is no Law (Gal 5:23)

5. Judgment according to works in general

a. What a person sows, he (or she) will also reap (Gal 6:7c)

b. God will reward each in accordance with [her or] his works (Rom 2:6)

c. There is no favoritism with God (Rom 2:11)

d. God will judge the secrets of humanity according to my gospel through Christ Jesus (Rom 2:16)

B. The Doing of Good or Evil

1. Doing evil

a. (Shall we) remain in sin in order that kindness will abound? (Rom 6:1b)

b. (Shall we) sin because we are not under the Law but under kindness? (Rom 6:15)

2. Doing good

a. Through love slave for each other (Gal 5:13c)

b. The entire Law is fulfilled in one saying, love your neighbor as yourself (Gal 5:14)

c. Walk in the spirit (Gal 5:16a)

d. Do not cease doing good (Gal 6:9a)

e. Practice what is good towards each other, especially towards the community of faith (Gal 6:10b)

f. Make yourselves available to God as persons living from death, and your members as weapons of justice for God (Rom 6:13b)

g. When gentiles, not having the Law by heritage, do the things of the Law, they are a Law to themselves (Rom 2:14)

h. Who show the work of the Law written in their hearts (Rom 2:15a)

i. Consider yourselves dead to sin; alive for God in Christ Jesus (Rom 6:11b–c)

j. Sin will not reign over you, for you are not under the Law, but under [God's] kindness (Rom 6:14)

k. You were slaves of sin, but have become obedient from the heart to the type of teaching to which you have become committed (Rom 6:17b–c)

l. Being freed from sin, you became enslaved to justice (Rom 6:18)

m. Make your members available as slaves of justice to sanctity (Rom 6:19c)

n. Make your members available as a living, holy sacrifice, pleasing to God, your reasonable worship (Rom 12:1)

o. Be transformed to the renewal of the mind in order to discern the will of God: the good and pleasing and perfect (Rom 12:2b–d)

p. Do not owe anyone anything, except to love each other, for whoever loves another has fulfilled the Law (Rom 13:8)

q. Love does not harm the neighbor; thus love is the fulfillment of the Law (Rom 13:10)

3. Negation of doing evil

a. You are called not to freedom as an opportunity for the flesh (Gal 5:13a–b)

b. Do not fulfill the desires of the flesh (Gal 5:16b)

c. Do not let sin reign in your mortal bodies to be obedient to its desires (Rom 6:12)

d. Do not make your members available to sin as weapons of evil (Rom 6:13a)

e. Do not conform with the world (Rom 12:2a)

It is not possible to place both groups of figures, representing the sub-themes, "the judgment of good and evil" and "the doing of good and evil," on a single logical square, because the contrast between the condemnation for evil and the reward for good works is not equivalent to the opposition between good and evil. The opposition between good and evil is neutral towards the contrast—not opposition—between the condemnation of evil and the reward for good works. This is already suggested by the figures that express judgment according to works in general, good as well as evil. The condemnation for evil works affirms /good works/ and negates /evil works/. The same is true of rewards for good works. At this point Paul's understanding of good and evil begins to become clear. Although he attaches positive value to good works and negative value to evil works, rather than attach negative value to the condemnation for evil works, he evaluates both the condemnation for evil and reward for good works positively as expressions of /good works/ and the negation of /evil works/, as the logical square below illustrates. I also list the figures that represent the sub-themes of "the doing of good and evil," that is, the opposed sub-themes, "doing evil" and "doing good," and the sub-theme, negation of "doing evil." There are no figures in Galatians and Romans that express the negation of "doing good."

All of this would be straightforward except for the fact that Paul was unable to assert unequivocally the condemnation for evil works. He does not express this directly in connection with the judgment according to works, but a figure like Rom 7:24 clearly reveals his agony about the condemnation for evil works, "Wretched person that I am; who will release me from this body of death?" His problem with the positive evaluation of the condemnation for evil works comes to its most vivid expression in connection with his attitude to the Law, not as the basis for the Jewish privileged relationship with God, but as the standard for the differentiation between good and evil. That does not mean that Paul negates the condemnation for evil works; his problem is accepting it unequivocally. Our investigation of his problem with the Law will reveal what is involved.

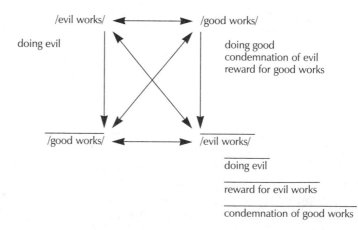

IV. THE PROBLEM OF THE LAW, AND THE OPPOSITION BETWEEN THE SPIRIT AND THE FLESH

A. *The Ambiguity in Paul's Experience of the Law*

That Paul is ambivalent about the Law is reflected in Rom 7:16, "if what I do not want to is what I do, I agree that the Law is good." Against the inability to meet his desire to fulfill the just requirements of the Law, Paul is unable to surrender the unyielding logic of his system of values, according to which the "condemnation of evil" expresses the value /good works/, and the negation of "reward for evil works" expresses negation of the value /evil works/. Thus he writes, "it was found that the commandment which was for the sake of life became for me [a cause of] death" (Rom 7:10b), and calls out in desperation, "Wretched person that I am; who will release me from this body of death?" (7:24). He evaluates the Law negatively in the following figures: "[The Law] was added for the sake of transgressions" (Gal 3:19b); "until the Law came, sin was in the world, but it was not reckoned, there being no Law" (Rom 5:13); the Law "came in to increase transgressions" (Rom 5:20); and "I would not have known sin if it was not for the Law" (Rom 7:7d).

Another indication of his ambivalence about the Law is his finding it necessary to deny that the Law and faith (the promises) are opposed to each other, as expressed in the following two figures: In Gal 3:21 he asks whether the Law is opposed to the promises. He denies this, and then states, "If a Law with the power to make alive had been given, justification would indeed have been through the Law"; in Rom 3:31 he asks, "Do we destroy the Law with faith," which he also denies, and then says, "We affirm the Law."

Paul's ambivalence about the Law can also be seen in the contrast between Rom 3:31, according to which we affirm the Law with faith, and Gal 3:19, 23, 24 and 25, according to which the Law had only a temporary function which ended with the coming of faith: "[The Law] was added for the sake of transgressions, until the seed would come to whom the promise was made" (Gal 3:19), and "Before faith came we were guarded by the Law, locked up for the revelation of the coming faith. So the Law became our pedagogue (custodian) to Christ, in order that we could be justified by faith: with the coming of faith we are no longer under the pedagogue" (Gal 3:23–25).

Paul does not have a systematically developed conception of the Law. His ambivalence results from the ambiguity with which he experiences it. His ultimate purpose in Rom 7:7–8:4 is to come to terms with this ambiguity, but even there his approach does not create systematic clarity. All he can achieve is to become reconciled with the ambiguity in a manner parallel to the mythological sense of Lévi–Strauss' interpretation of myth to which I referred above. As was indicated above in the discussion of Rom 7:7–8:4 (Part One, chapter 3, "A Macro-Structure of Romans"), Paul tries to make understandable his ambiguous relationship to the Law by making use of the rupture in human nature, an idea well recognized in Hellenistic antiquity.

If Paul had tried to solve the problem of the Law in his usual way it would have been possible to clarify his reasoning by means of a semiotic square in which the negative features of the Law are transformed into a negation of those features, and the negation of the positive features are transformed into their affirmation by means of figures that bring that to expression. The following logical square reveals the relationships between the various figures concerning the Law in Rom 7:7–8:4.

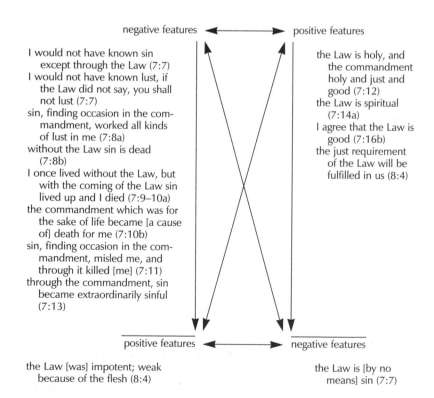

negative features ⟷ positive features

I would not have known sin
  except through the Law (7:7)
I would not have known lust, if
  the Law did not say, you shall
  not lust (7:7)
sin, finding occasion in the commandment, worked all kinds
  of lust in me (7:8a)
without the Law sin is dead
  (7:8b)
I once lived without the Law, but
  with the coming of the Law sin
  lived up and I died (7:9–10a)
the commandment which was for
  the sake of life became [a cause
  of] death for me (7:10b)
sin, finding occasion in the commandment, misled me, and
  through it killed [me] (7:11)
through the commandment, sin
  became extraordinarily sinful
  (7:13)

the Law is holy, and
  the commandment
  holy and just and
  good (7:12)
the Law is spiritual
  (7:14a)
I agree that the Law is
  good (7:16b)
the just requirement
  of the Law will be
  fulfilled in us (8:4)

positive features ⟷ negative features

the Law [was] impotent; weak
  because of the flesh (8:4)

the Law is [by no
  means] sin (7:7)

As the square shows, Paul does not transform the negative features of the Law into a negation of those features, nor does he transform the negation of its positive features into their affirmation, as he does, for example, in the figure in Rom 3:31 that states that we affirm the Law by faith. In Rom 7:7–8:4 the negative and positive features of the Law and their negations are simply placed in the appropriate contradictory relationships to each other, without transformations from one feature to the other.

B. Beyond a Logical Solution

In a manner similar to Lévi-Strauss' mythological reasoning, Paul presents the opposition between the positive and negative features of the Law in parallel to the opposition between the spirit and the flesh. The positive features of the Law stand in opposition to the negative features as the spirit stands in opposition to the flesh:

Positive features : Negative features :: Spirit : Flesh,

as presented graphically in the four parallel columns below. In order to follow the flow of Paul's thinking through the two sets of oppositions it is necessary to read vertically downwards in the columns, as well as horizontally where the text moves to other columns.

Positive features	*Negative features*	*Spirit*	*Flesh*
7[7] The Law is [by no means] sin.	. . . I would not have known sin except through the Law. . . . I would not have known lust, if the Law did not say, you shall not lust. [8] . . . sin, finding occasion in the commandment, worked all kinds of lust in me. . . . without the Law sin is dead. [9] I once lived without the Law, but with the coming of the Law sin lived up, [10] and I died. . . . the commandment that was for the sake of life became [a cause of] death for me. [11] . . . sin, finding occasion in the commandment, misled me, and through it killed [me].		

Positive features	Negative features	Spirit	Flesh
12 . . . the Law is holy, and the commandment holy and just and good.		13 The good [by no means] became death for me.	. . . sin, to be revealed as sin, through the good worked death in me.
	. . . through the commandment, sin became extraordinarily sinful.		
14 . . . the Law is spiritual.			. . . I am of the flesh, sold to sin. 15 I do not know what I do. . . . I do not do what I want to, but what I hate is what I do. 16 . . . what I do not want is what I do.
I agree that the Law is good.			17 . . . it is no longer I who do [what I do not want to], but sin living in me. 18 . . . I know that there is no good in me, that is, in my flesh.
		. . . to want to [do good] is close at hand.	. . . not [close at hand is to do what is good. 19 . . . I do not do the good that I want to, but the evil that I do not want, that is what I do. 20 If I do what I do not want to, it is no longer I who do it, but sin which dwells in me. 21 . . . I find the Law [to be such], that in wanting to do good, evil is close at hand.
		22 I delight in the Law of God in my inner being.	23 . . . another Law [is] in my members, which joins battle with the Law of my mind and takes me captive with the Law of sin in my members. 24 Wretched person that I am; who will release me from this body of death?
		25 . . . [I am released from this body of death] by Christ Jesus our Lord. . . . I slave for the Law of God with [my] mind.	[I slave] with the flesh for the Law of sin.

Positive features	Negative features	Spirit	Flesh
		8[1] . . . there is no condemnation of those who are in Christ Jesus. [2] . . . the Law of the spirit of life in Christ Jesus liberated you from the Law of sin and death.	
	[3] . . . the Law [was] impotent; weak because of the flesh.	God, having sent his son in the similarity of the sinful flesh, and because of sin, condemned sin in the flesh.	
[4] . . . the just requirement of the Law will be fulfilled in us.		[We] do not live in accordance with the flesh, but the spirit.	[5] Those who [live] in accordance with the flesh think the things of the flesh.
		Those [who live] in accordance with the spirit, [think] the things of the spirit.	[6] . . . the thoughts of the flesh are death.
		. . . the thoughts of the spirit are life and peace.	[7] . . . the thoughts of the flesh is hostility towards God, for it does not subject itself to the Law of God, neither can it. [8] Those who [are] of the flesh are unable to please God.
		[9] You are not in the flesh but in the spirit, if indeed the spirit of God dwells in you.	If someone does not have the spirit of Christ, such a person does not belong to him.
		[10] . . . if Christ is in you,	the body may be dead through sin,
		but the spirit is alive through justice. [11] If the spirit of him who raised Jesus from the dead lives in you, he who raised Christ from the dead will make alive your dead bodies through the indwelling of his spirit in you.	

Paul's reasoning in Rom 7:7–8:4 is more than a parallel placement of the oppositions between the positive and negative features of the Law and between the spirit and the flesh. His reasoning moves forward from the opposition between the positive and negative features of the Law to the opposition between the spirit and the flesh. And then, rather than attempt to resolve the opposition between the positive and negative features of the Law, he allows it to be absorbed into the opposition between the spirit and the flesh. This is signaled for the first time by the parallel questions and denials in verses 7 and 11, "The Law is sin? By no means!" and "The good . . . became death for me? By no means!" reformulated above as the parallel figures, "the law is [by no means] sin," and "the good [by no means] became death for me."

C. *Subjection to Sin and the Flesh and Subjection to the Spirit*

Although Paul does not attempt to resolve the opposition between the positive and negative features of the Law, he does resolve the opposition between the flesh and the spirit by means of figures that transform subjection to sin and the flesh into a negation of subjection to sin and the flesh, and negation of subjection to the spirit into affirmation of subjection to the spirit. His reasoning can be clarified by placing the figures he uses for this purpose on a *logical* square, and subsequently, placing on a *semiotic* square those that express the transformation of subjection to sin and the flesh into a negation of subjection to sin and flesh, and the transformation of the negation of submission to the spirit to affirmation of subjection to the spirit. I first list the figures that depict the opposition between subjection to sin and the flesh and subjection to the spirit.

1. Figures expressing subjection to sin and the flesh:

a. Sin works death in me (7:14)
b. I am of the flesh (7:14)
c. I am sold to sin (7:14)
d. I do what I hate (7:15)
e. I do what I do not want to (7:16)
f. Sin dwelling in me does what I do not want to (7:17, 20)
g. I do the evil that I do not want to (7:19)
h. In wanting to do good, evil is close at hand (7:21)
i. Another Law takes me captive with the Law of sin (7:23)
j. I slave with the flesh for the Law of sin (7:25)
k. Those who live in accordance with the flesh think the things of the flesh (8:5)
l. The thoughts of the flesh are death (8:6)
m. The thoughts of the flesh are hostility towards God (8:7)
n. The body is dead through sin (8:10)

(continued on next page)

2. Figures that negate subjection to sin and the flesh:

a. The good has not become death for me (7:13)
b. Release from the body of death (7:24)
c. Christ releases me from this body of death (7:25)
d. There is no condemnation for those who are in Christ (8:1)
e. The Law of the spirit liberates you from the Law of sin and death (8:2)
f. God condemned sin in the flesh (8:3)
g. We do not live in accordance with the flesh (8:4)
h. If the spirit of God dwells in you, you are not in the flesh (8:9)

3. Figures expressing subjection to the spirit:

a. To want to do good is close at hand (7:18)
b. I delight in the Law of God in my inner being (7:22)
c. I slave for the Law of God with my mind (7:25)
d. We live in accordance with the spirit (8:4)
e. Those who live in accordance with the spirit think the things of the spirit (8:5)

f. The thoughts of the spirit are life and peace (8:6)
g. If the spirit of God dwells in you, you are in the spirit (8:9)
h. If Christ is in you, the spirit is alive [in you] through justice (8:10)
i. He who raised Christ from the dead makes alive your dead bodies (8:11)

4. Figures that negate subjection to the spirit:

a. I do not know what I do (7:15)
b. I do not do what I want to (7:15)
c. There is no good in me; in my flesh (7:18)
d. To do good is not close at hand (7:18)
e. I do not do the good that I want to (7:19)
f. The flesh does not subject itself to the Law of God (8:7)
g. The flesh cannot subject itself to the Law of God (8:7)
h. Those who are of the flesh are unable to please God (8:8)
i. Someone who does not have the spirit of Christ does not belong to Christ (8:9)

The logical relationships between these figures are shown by the logical square on the next page.

All of the figures on that square do not express the transformation from assertion of the subjection to sin and the flesh to its negation, and transformation from negation of the subjection to the spirit to its affirmation. The transformations do not begin to take place before Paul's call for liberation from sin and the flesh in 7:24, "Wretched person that I am; who will release me from this body of death?" It has obviously been Paul's intention throughout the passage to overcome the subjection to sin and the flesh, but until 7:24 the figures that express the opposition between the flesh and the spirit, as in the case of those that express the opposition between the negative and positive features of the Law, merely present the opposition as painful reality. The opposition in verses 22–23 between "I delight in the Law of God in my inner being" and "I see another Law in my members that joins battle with the Law of my mind and takes me captive with the Law of sin in my members," already prepares for the transformations which follow in 7:25–8:11.

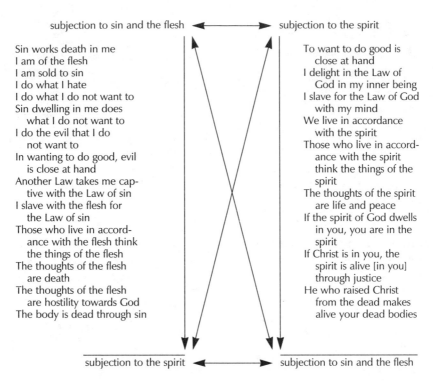

subjection to sin and the flesh ←——→ subjection to the spirit

Sin works death in me
I am of the flesh
I am sold to sin
I do what I hate
I do what I do not want to
Sin dwelling in me does
    what I do not want to
I do the evil that I do
    not want to
In wanting to do good, evil
    is close at hand
Another Law takes me cap-
    tive with the Law of sin
I slave with the flesh for
    the Law of sin
Those who live in accord-
    ance with the flesh think
    the things of the flesh
The thoughts of the flesh
    are death
The thoughts of the flesh
    are hostility towards God
The body is dead through sin

To want to do good is
    close at hand
I delight in the Law of
    God in my inner being
I slave for the Law of God
    with my mind
We live in accordance
    with the spirit
Those who live in accord-
    ance with the spirit
    think the things of the
    spirit
The thoughts of the spirit
    are life and peace
If the spirit of God dwells
    in you, you are in the
    spirit
If Christ is in you, the
    spirit is alive [in you]
    through justice
He who raised Christ
    from the dead makes
    alive your dead bodies

subjection to the spirit ←——→ subjection to sin and the flesh

I do not know what I do
I do not do what I want to
There is no good in me; in
    my flesh
To do good is not close
    at hand
I do not do the good that
    I want to
The flesh does not subject
    itself to the Law of God
The flesh cannot subject
    itself to the Law of God
Those who are of the flesh
    are unable to please God
Someone who does not have
    the spirit of Christ does
    not belong to Christ

The good has not become
    death for me
Who will release me from
    this body of death?
Christ releases me from
    this body of death
There is no condemna-
    tion for those who are
    in Christ
The Law of the spirit
    liberates you from the
    Law of sin and death
God condemned sin in
    the flesh
We do not live in accord-
    ance with the flesh
If the spirit of God dwells
    in you, you are not in
    the flesh

It is possible to distinguish in Paul's reasoning between figures that express the opposition between subjection to sin and the flesh and subjection to the spirit that are purely factual, and figures that depict transformation from subjection to sin and the flesh to liberation from, that is, negation of that subjection, making possible a subjection to the spirit through Christ Jesus. In order to clarify that distinction I will place the respective figures on separate squares. First, I present the figures that express the factual opposition between the flesh and the spirit, representing the rupture in human nature, on the following logical square:

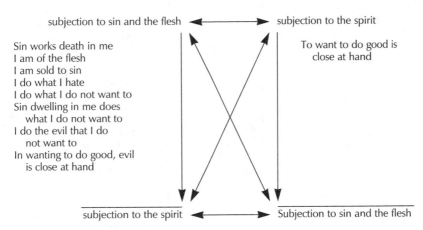

subjection to sin and the flesh ⟷ subjection to the spirit

Sin works death in me
I am of the flesh
I am sold to sin
I do what I hate
I do what I do not want to
Sin dwelling in me does
    what I do not want to
I do the evil that I do
    not want to
In wanting to do good, evil
    is close at hand

To want to do good is
close at hand

subjection to the spirit ⟷ Subjection to sin and the flesh

I do not know what I do
I do not do what I want to
There is no good in me; in
    my flesh
To do good is not close
    at hand
I do not do the good that
    I want to
The flesh does not subject
    itself to the Law of God
The flesh cannot subject
    itself to the Law of God

The good has not become
death for me

Before Paul engages in the reasoning through which he transforms subjection to sin and the flesh into subjection to the spirit, all except two of his figures express subjection to sin and the flesh and negation of subjection to the spirit, with only one figure each for subjection to the spirit and negation of subjection to sin and the flesh.

In Rom 7:22–8:11 Paul no longer accepts the opposition between the spirit and the flesh as a fact of the rupture in human nature, but declares its remedy in Christ Jesus. The following semiotic square clarifies his reasoning:

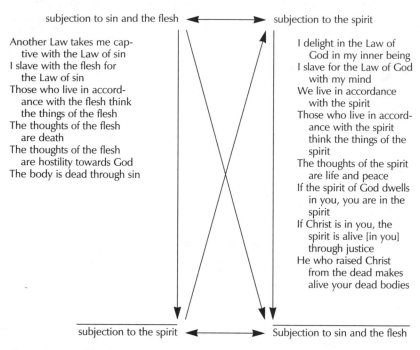

subjection to sin and the flesh ◄────────► subjection to the spirit

Another Law takes me cap-
    tive with the Law of sin
I slave with the flesh for
    the Law of sin
Those who live in accord-
    ance with the flesh think
    the things of the flesh
The thoughts of the flesh
    are death
The thoughts of the flesh
    are hostility towards God
The body is dead through sin

I delight in the Law of
    God in my inner being
I slave for the Law of God
    with my mind
We live in accordance
    with the spirit
Those who live in accord-
    ance with the spirit
    think the things of the
    spirit
The thoughts of the spirit
    are life and peace
If the spirit of God dwells
    in you, you are in the
    spirit
If Christ is in you, the
    spirit is alive [in you]
    through justice
He who raised Christ
    from the dead makes
    alive your dead bodies

subjection to the spirit ◄────────► Subjection to sin and the flesh

Those who are of the flesh
    are unable to please God
Someone who does not have
    the spirit of Christ does
    not belong to Christ

Who will release me from
    this body of death?
Christ releases me from
    this body of death
There is no condemna-
    tion for those who are
    in Christ
The Law of the spirit
    liberates you from the
    Law of sin and death
God condemned sin in
    the flesh
We do not live in accord-
    ance with the flesh
If the spirit of God dwells
    in you, you are not in
    the flesh

The values represented by the opposition between the negative and positive features of the Law and the opposition between the spirit and the flesh are the same as those for the opposition between doing evil works and doing good works, and those that express the condemnation of evil and reward for good works, that is, the opposition between the values /evil works/ and /good works/. Thus it becomes possible to place all the themes that give expression to the differentiation between good and evil on a single square as follows:

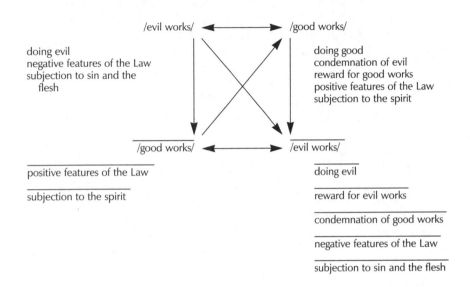

Note that the figures that express the transformation of the subjection to sin and the flesh to its negation and those that express the transformation of the negation of subjection to the spirit to its affirmation do not belong on this square. The reason is that with those transformations Paul leaves behind the opposition between good and evil in favor of an opposition between life and death, as will become clear below in the discussion of his micro-universe. The move from the opposition between good and evil to the opposition between life and death becomes especially clear in his concluding statement, "If the spirit of him who raised Jesus from the dead lives in you, he who raised Christ from the dead will make alive your dead bodies through the indwelling of his spirit in you" (8:11). The close relationship between the opposition between good and evil and between life and death is signaled in other statements as well, for example, "it was found that the commandment that was for the sake of life became for me [a cause of] death" (7:10b), and "sin, finding occasion in the commandment, misled me, and through it killed [me]" (7:11).

   Paul did not resolve the opposition between doing good and evil, or the opposition between the positive and negative features of the Law, or that between subjection to sin and the flesh and subjection to the spirit in Rom 7:22–8:11. He proclaims liberation from the existential rupture in human nature, formulated by means of the figures that express the opposition between the flesh and the spirit, through participation in Christ.

Neither opposition is resolved, but by participating in Christ the believer is liberated from them. The conditional statements in 8:9 show that freedom from the dominion of sin and the flesh is a reality only in Christ, "You are not in the flesh but in the spirit, if indeed the spirit of God dwells in you. If someone does not have the spirit of Christ, such a person does not belong to him." The provisional nature of the being in Christ is vividly captured in statements elsewhere, such as, "in hope we were saved. Hope that sees is not hope. What does the person who sees hope? But if we hope for what we do not see, we anticipate it with patience" (Rom 8:24–25) and "Not that I have already attained it or am already perfected, but I pursue it as if I can take hold of it, inasmuch as I have been taken up by Christ" (Phil 3:12). Participation in Christ does not resolve the oppositions between good and evil, between the positive and negative features of the Law, and not even between the spirit and the flesh, but in Christ the believer is liberated from them: "if Christ is in you, the body may be dead through sin, but the spirit is alive through justice" (8:10).

V. THE REVELATION TO ISRAEL AS THE FOUNDATION OF SALVATION FOR ALL HUMAN BEINGS

Another decisive factor in Paul's understanding of salvation in Christ is that it is grounded in the revelation of God to Israel. In order to understand Paul's thinking it will be necessary to place on a logical square the figures he uses to express this. That will allow us to discern the interrelationships between the figures and the interrelationships between the themes they express. Our first task is again to identify the themes that are expressed by the figures. In this case, because of the complexity of Paul's reasoning concerning the grounding of salvation in God's revelation to Israel, I also distinguish sub-themes on the logical squares, as in Appendix IV. I list first the figures that denote the problem of God's trustworthiness in relationship to the Jewish rejection of Christ. The theme, "Israel entrusted with God's revelation," involves the question of whether Israel was worthy of God's trust, and thus, in Paul's understanding, the trustworthiness of God.

A. The Jews Entrusted with God's Revelation, and Their Disbelief

1. Israel entrusted with God's revelation

a. The Jews were entrusted with God's revelation (Rom 3:2)
b. The disbelief of some in Israel does not destroy the trustworthiness of God (Rom 3:3b–4a)
c. The justice of God was witnessed to by the Law and the prophets (Rom 3:21)
d. To the Jews belong being children, glory, the covenants, the giving of the Law, worship, the promises, and the Fathers (Rom 9:4–5a)
e. Christ in the flesh is from the Jews (Rom 9:5b)
f. The word of God did not become invalid (Rom 9:6a)
g. God did not reject his people (Rom 11:1a–b, 2)

2. Jewish disbelief

a. Some of Israel disbelieved (Rom 3:3a)
b. Israel did not achieve justification, because it was through the Law and not by faith (Rom 9:31–32a)
c. They stumbled against the stumbling block, Christ (Rom 9:32b–33)
d. Israel did not achieve what it sought (Rom 11:7a)
e. The rest of Israel was hardened (Rom 11:7c)

—2. Negation of Jewish disbelief

a. Not all who are from Israel belong to Israel (Rom 9:6b)
b. Not all are children because they are seed of Abraham (Rom 9:7a)
c. In Isaac I will elect your seed (Rom 9:7b)
d. The children of the flesh are not children of God (Rom 9:8a)
e. The children of the promise are considered seed of Abraham (Rom 9:8b)
f. In the present time a remnant remains (Rom 11:5)
g. The elect found what they sought (Rom 11:7b)

The relationships between these themes and figures are clarified on the logical square on the next page. The logic of Paul's understanding is that Jewish disbelief runs counter to their being entrusted with God's revelation. Thus "Israel entrusted with God's revelation" implicitly denies "Jewish disbelief," as shown by the left line of implication. On the other hand, Jewish disbelief is inconsistent with their being entrusted with God's revelation. Their disbelief negates the trust that God had in them (as shown by the right line of implication). Paul does not present evidence that negates Jewish disbelief. The only argument he can use is that Israel is not represented by every Jew, expressed with figures such as, "not all who are from Israel belong to Israel," and "not all are children because they are seed of Abraham," etc. We know only too well that Paul himself was aware that those limited negations of Jewish disbelief were not sufficient to carry the argument; he does not end his discussion of the problem of Jewish disbelief in Romans 9–11 until he can conclude, "and so all of Israel will be saved" (Rom 11:26a).

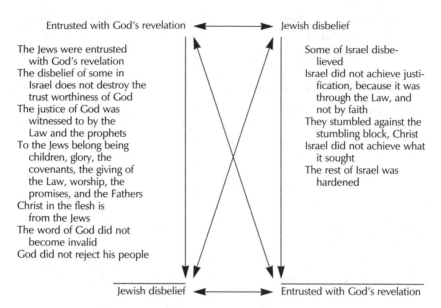

Entrusted with God's revelation ⬅——➡ Jewish disbelief

The Jews were entrusted
with God's revelation
The disbelief of some in
Israel does not destroy the
trust worthiness of God
The justice of God was
witnessed to by the
Law and the prophets
To the Jews belong being
children, glory, the
covenants, the giving of
the Law, worship, the
promises, and the Fathers
Christ in the flesh is
from the Jews
The word of God did not
become invalid
God did not reject his people

Some of Israel disbe-
lieved
Israel did not achieve justification, because it was
through the Law, and
not by faith
They stumbled against the
stumbling block, Christ
Israel did not achieve what
it sought
The rest of Israel was
hardened

Jewish disbelief ⬅——➡ Entrusted with God's revelation

Not all who are from Israel
belong to Israel
Not all are children because
they are seed of Abraham
In Isaac I will elect your seed
The children of the flesh are
not children of God
The children of the promise
are considered seed of
Abraham
In the present time a rem-
nant remains
The elect found what they
sought

The fundamental problem to be resolved regarding God's revelation to Israel and Jewish disbelief is that in Paul's understanding justification by faith and the salvation of the gentiles can be achieved only if the Jews—or at least some of them—are liberated from their subjection to the Law, enabling them to carry the message of the promise to Abraham to the gentiles. The most succinct expression of the series, liberation from the Law, justification by faith, and gentile salvation, is Rom 15:8–9a, "Christ became a servant of circumcision for the sake of the truth of God, in order to secure the promises of the Fathers, and the gentiles praise God because of mercy." Paul portrays the relationship between the Jews' subjection to the Law, justification by faith, and gentile salvation by means of the following figures:

B. *The Jews Liberated from the Law for the Sake of Gentile Salvation*

1. The Jews under the Law

a. Scripture locked everything up under sin (Gal 3:22a)
b. Before the coming of faith we were in the custody of the Law (Gal 3:23a)
c. The Law was our custodian until Christ (Gal 3:24b)
d. Israel sought justification through the Law (Rom 9:32a)
e. Israel stumbled against the stumbling block, Christ (Rom 9:32b–33)
f. God included all under disobedience (Rom 11:32a)

—1. Negation of the Jews under the Law

a. Christ freed us from the curse of the Law (Gal 3:13)
b. We are no longer under the custodian (Gal 3:25b)
c. Christ became a servant of circumcision for the sake of God's truth (Rom 15:8a)

2. Justification by faith

a. We were to receive the promise through faith (Gal 3:14b)
b. The promise was to be given through faith to those who believe (Gal 3:22b)
c. We were locked up for the coming revelation of faith (Gal 3:23b)
d. The Law was our custodian until Christ, in order that we would be justified by faith (Gal 3:24b)

e. The arrival of faith (Gal 3:25a)
f. The promise is from faith in order that it would be through kindness (Rom 4:16)
g. Christ is the end of the Law for the justification of every seed (Rom 10:4)
h. It is through faith that you stand (Rom 11:20)
i. God intends being merciful to all (Rom 11:32b)
j. Christ secured the promises to the Fathers (Rom 15:8b)

—2. Negation of justification by faith

a. Israel did not achieve justification because it was not by faith (Rom 9:31)

3. Gentile salvation

a. The blessing of Abraham went out to the gentiles through Christ (Gal 3:14a)
b. The promise is secure for every seed, for those who are from the Law, as well as those who are from the faith of Abraham (Rom 4:16c–d)
a. Abraham is the father of all of us (Rom 4:16e)
b. The gentiles glorify God (Rom 15:9a).

I will not place the actual figures on the squares which follow. In order to understand Paul's reasoning, it will be sufficient to place the sub-themes on the squares. We can place Paul's reasoning concerning the relationship of the liberation of the Jews from the Law to justification by faith and to gentile salvation on two related logical squares. First the logical relationships between the Jews being under the Law and justification by faith:

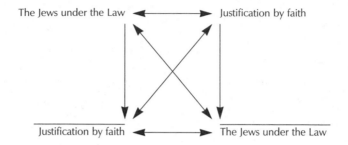

Paul understands justification to imply that Jews are no longer under the Law, as formulated in Gal 3:22–25, "Scripture included everything under sin in order that the promise of faith in Christ Jesus would be given to those who believe. Before faith came we were guarded by the Law, locked up for the revelation of the coming faith. So the Law became our pedagogue until Christ, in order that we could be justified by faith: with the coming of faith we are no longer under the pedagogue."

Before justification by faith was possible the Jews had to be freed from the Law, the curse of the Law (as indicated by the vertical lines of implication). The Jews' being under the Law implies that there is no justification by faith, and salvation by faith implies that Jews are not under the Law. Paul states this explicitly in Gal 3:13–14, "Christ redeemed us from the curse of the Law by having become a curse for our sakes . . . in order that the blessing of Abraham would reach the gentiles in Christ Jesus, in order that we would receive the promise of the spirit through faith." With that statement the relationship between the Jews' being freed from the Law and the salvation of the gentiles by faith is also set forth. The following square illustrates Paul's logic: Gentile salvation implies justification by faith.

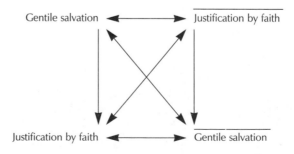

The relationships between the Jews' being freed from the Law, justification by faith, and gentile salvation are demonstrated by the combination these two related semiotic squares as follows:

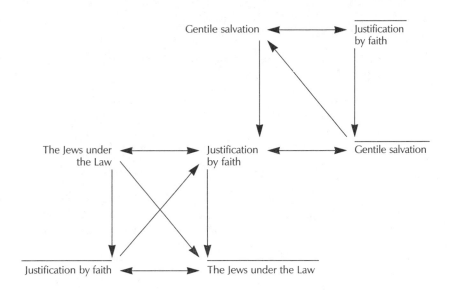

First the Jews are freed from (the curse) of the Law: through Christ's action the Jews' being under the Law is transformed into the negation of the Jews' being under the Law—moving on the lower square along the diagonal line from the left top to the lower right. The negation of the Jews being under (the curse of) the Law makes possible justification by faith which presupposes the Jews' not being under the Law, but under faith. Thus the negation of justification by faith which is presupposed by the Jews' being under the Law is transformed into the affirmation of justification by faith—moving from the bottom left to the top right of the lower square. With the transformation of the negation of justification by faith into its affirmation the condition is already set for the negation of gentile salvation to be transformed into an affirmation of gentile salvation—along the diagonal line from the lower right to the top left of the upper square. I do not draw a diagonal line from the negation of justification by faith to its affirmation on the upper square since that condition has already been met by the transformation on the lower squares. It should nevertheless be noted that the negation of justification by faith implies that there is no gentile salvation.

One way in which Paul tries to solve the problem of the disbelief of the Jews in relationship to their being entrusted with God's revelation is by interpreting it in a positive way in relationship to gentile salvation. It has a secondary feature in Paul's hope to make the Jews jealous of the gentiles because of their justification. This comes to expression in the following figures:

C. *The Disbelief of the Jews and the Salvation of the Gentiles*

1. Jewish disbelief

a. Some of them disbelieved (Rom 3:3a)
b. Israel did not achieve justification because it was not by faith (Rom 9:31)
c. Israel did not achieve what it sought (Rom 11:7a)
d. The rest of Israel was hardened (Rom 11:7c)
e. Israel stumbled (Rom 11:11c)
f. Israel transgressed (Rom 11:12a)
g. Israel fell short (Rom 11:12b)
h. Israel was rejected (Rom 11:15a)
i. Branches were cut out (Rom 11:17a, 19)
j. Through disbelief the Jews were cut out (Rom 11:20a)
k. Hardness came on Israel (Rom 11:25c)
l. Israel became disobedient (Rom 11:31a)
m. They are enemies according to the promises (Rom 11:28a)

2. The gentiles finding salvation

a. The stumbling of Israel was for the salvation of the gentiles (Rom 11:11c)
b. Israel's transgression is the wealth of the world (Rom 11:12a)
c. Israel's shortcoming is the wealth of the gentiles (Rom 11:12b)
d. Israel's rejection is the reconciliation of the world (Rom 11:15a)

e. If the firstfruits are holy, so is the dough (Rom 11:16a)
f. If the roots are holy, so are the branches (Rom 11:16b)
g. The gentiles are grafted in (Rom 11:17b, 19)
h. The gentiles participate in the sap of the olive tree (Rom 11:17b)
i. It is not the gentiles who bear the roots, but the roots the gentiles (Rom 11:18)
j. It is through faith that the gentiles stand (Rom 11:20b)
k. The gentiles were grafted in against nature (Rom 11:24)
l. The fullness of the gentiles enter (Rom 11:25c)
m. Mercy is shown to the gentiles (Rom 11:31ab)
n. They are enemies for our sakes (Rom 11:28a)

3. Jewish jealousy

a. The salvation of the gentiles is to make the Jews jealous (Rom 11:11d)
b. Paul makes the Jews jealous (Rom 11:14a)

4. Saving some of the Jews

a. Paul saves some of the Jews (Rom 11:14b)

The logic of Paul's reasoning assumes that the gentiles do not find salvation except through the disbelief of the Jews. It is a remarkable understanding, but at least gentile salvation as such does not assume that the Jews remain in disbelief. Paul's understanding is that after the "fullness of the gentiles" enter into salvation all of Israel too will be saved (Rom 11:25c–26a). Thus, Jewish disbelief is a presupposition only for the gentiles finding salvation, not for their continued participation in it. The following square makes clear what is involved in the first part of Paul's reasoning.

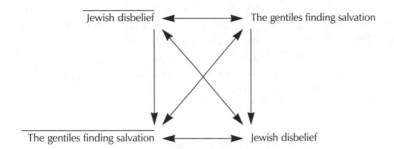

Paul hopes that the salvation of the gentiles would make the Jews jealous, and that in that way at least some of them will be saved. With that the end goal of universal salvation—the fullness of the gentiles and all of Israel—would still not have been reached, but in Paul's expectations it is evidently a step along the way. His reasoning can be clarified on the following series of semiotic squares:

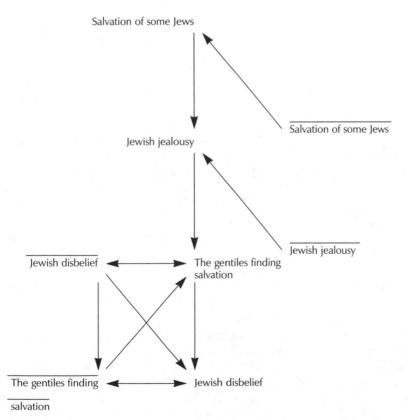

I do not try to clarify on these squares the details of what is involved in the transformation of the negation of Jewish jealousy into its affirmation, and of the transformation of the negation of salvation of some Jews into its affirmation. Paul's thinking on the subject of "somehow [making] those of my flesh jealous and so save some of them" (Rom 11:14) is rather undeveloped. He is grasping at a straw which in the end is insufficient because his longing cannot be stilled by the salvation of "some of his flesh," but only by all of them, which is what he brings to expression in the final group of figures concerning the salvation of all of Israel.

D. *Salvation of All of Israel*

1. The rest of Israel comes to believe

a. Paul would like to save some of his people (Rom 11:14)
b. The Jews do not remain in their disbelief (Rom 11:23a)

2. All of Israel is saved

a. Their fullness is the wealth of the world and of the gentiles (Rom 11:12c)
b. Their inclusion is a resurrection from the dead (Rom 11:15b)
c. The Jews who come to believe are grafted in (Rom 11:23b)
d. The Jews can so much the more be grafted in (Rom 11:24)
e. All of Israel will be saved (Rom 11:26a)
f. By election the Jews are beloved ones through the Fathers (Rom 11:28)
g. Mercy will also be shown to the Jews (Rom 11:31b)

There is a remarkably compact formulation of this longing of Paul in Gal 3:13–14, "Christ bought us free from the curse of the Law by becoming a curse in our place, for it is written, 'Cursed is everyone who hangs from a tree,' in order that the blessing of Abraham would reach the gentiles through (in) Christ Jesus, in order that we would receive the promise of the spirit through faith." It is important to note that it is Christ who mediates the promise of Abraham to the gentiles. Paul understands Christ to have done that by freeing the Jews from the curse of the Law. That part of the statement is repeated in a different formulation in Rom 15:8–9, "I assert that Christ became a servant of circumcision for the sake of the truth of God in order to secure the promises of the Fathers, and the gentiles give glory to God because of mercy." The curse of the Law here in Gal 3:13 appears to be that it prevented the blessing of Abraham from reaching its intended goal in the salvation of the gentiles. Remarkably, an end goal of the blessing of Abraham reaching the gentiles is that the "we" who were freed from the curse of the Law "would receive the promise of the spirit through faith." In Paul's thinking, justification by faith has nothing to do with a negation of being rewarded for the doing of good works. Rather, it functions as a way of arguing that the promise to Abraham was not restricted to the Jews, but meant the salvation of the gentiles, a salvation in which the Jews also participate when they are freed from the accursed restriction that the Law places on them.

Paul's statement in Rom 11:14 that he exalts his ministry "if I can somehow make those of my flesh jealous and so save some of them" is a mere step to his ultimate hope that "[the Jews] too, if they do not remain in disbelief, will be grafted back into" the cultured olive tree. The logic of his reasoning appears rather straightforward, as the following logical square reveals.

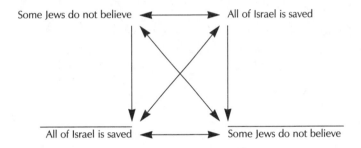

But in reality an intermediate logical step is required: the salvation of all of Israel implies more than the negation of the disbelief of some Jews. Paul's reasoning presupposes that the negation of the disbelief of some Jews means that all Jews come to believe, as shown by the following logic:

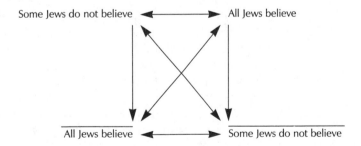

What Paul actually hopes can be shown on the combined semiotic squares on the next page.

When those Jews (some) who do not believe come to believe—following the diagonal line from the left top to the bottom right of the lower square—it makes possible the transformation of "not all Jews believe" into "all Jews believe"—along the diagonal line from the bottom left to the top right of the lower square. With that the presupposition is met for all of Israel to be saved—the transformation from the bottom right to the top left on the upper square. I do not draw the line from the top right to the bottom left of that square since that condition is already met on the lower square.

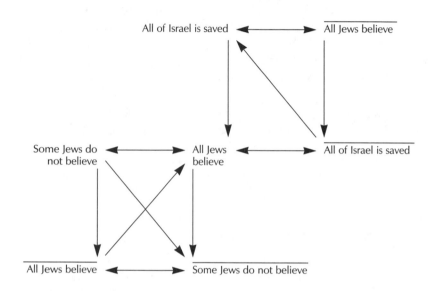

VI. AN ENHANCED UNDERSTANDING OF PAUL'S SYSTEM OF VALUES

Thus Paul comes to the end of what one may call his odyssey, beginning with his insistence on the justification of the gentiles by faith, and concluding with the confidence that all of Israel will also be justified by faith. In this way it becomes possible to extend our previous understanding of his system of values.

It is easy to recognize that the theme of the Jews being liberated from the Law for the sake of gentile salvation brings to expression the opposition between the values /Jewish privilege/, represented by the Jews' subjection to the Law, and /gentile salvation/. The system of values remains the same, but the way it is activated has the added dimension of the Jews having to be freed from their subjection to the Law in order to make gentile salvation possible. Liberation from the curse of the Law does not include all Jews, but those Jews who took it upon themselves to proclaim salvation to the gentiles, certainly Paul himself. In the figures in Galatians expressing the theme of liberation from the curse of the Law, he makes uses of the point to argue that also Peter and the others cannot accept gentile salvation without being freed from the restrictions of the Law.

The situation in connection with the other themes, the Jews entrusted with God's revelation and their disbelief, the disbelief of the Jews and the salvation of the gentiles, and salvation of all of Israel, is more complicated. Individually and together they make it clear that gentile salvation is not an isolated event, but an event which is incomprehensible apart from the context of God's revelation to Israel, brought to expression positively by the theme of the Jews' being entrusted with God's revelation, and negatively by the theme of Jewish disbelief as the foundation of gentile salvation. In addition, Paul is unable to think of gentile salvation as the final event of redemptive history. Justification by faith is not complete before the Jews too find salvation through faith, as expressed through the theme of the salvation of all of Israel. Paul's reasoning in Romans 9–11 reveals a system of values in which an *exclusive* /gentile salvation/ is rejected in parallel to the rejection of /Jewish privilege/ in its opposition to /gentile salvation/ in Galatians and Rom 1:18–4:25. Thus we find the remarkable situation that /gentile salvation/, a positive value for Paul when it stands in opposition to /Jewish privilege/, becomes a negative value when it stands as an isolated event in opposition to /Jewish salvation/, as the following semiotic square shows:

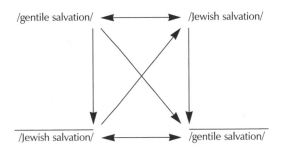

Paul negates /gentile salvation/ when it stands opposed to /Jewish salvation/. Thus we may conclude that for Paul /Jewish privilege/ as well as /gentile salvation/ are negative values when they are understood to represent individually the value /salvation of exclusive groups/, but /gentile salvation/ is a positive value when, along with /Jewish salvation/, it represents /human salvation/. The semiotic square below reveals what is involved.

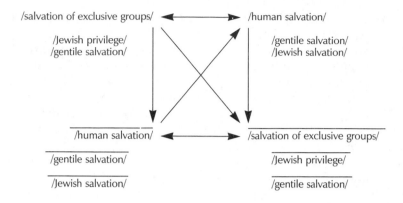

With that the full meaning of Paul's understanding of justification by faith becomes clear. Justification by faith does not mean justification of the gentiles as a means of overcoming the limitations of the Jewish claim to a privileged relationship with God. Salvation by faith means the salvation of all human beings, enciphered in Paul's thinking as the *inclusiveness* of gentile and Jewish salvation. Justification by faith also does not stand in opposition to justification for good works, which, as we have seen, belongs to a different system of values in the totality of Paul's thinking. The relationship between justification by faith and justification for good works can be clarified only by moving to an even deeper level of Paul's thought, his micro-universe.

6 ∿

Paul's Micro-Universe

INTRODUCTION

In their semiotic dictionary, *Sémiotique: dictionnaire rai-sonné de la théorie du langage*, Greimas and Courtés distinguish two micro-universes. One is individual, which is expressed in the polar-ity life/death, and the other is collective or social, which is reflected in the polarity culture/nature.[1] The existential micro-universe is recognizable in the New Testament in the frequent occurrence of the opposition between life and death; the social micro-universe appears in the religious-ethical opposition between good and evil. There are, however, also cases in the New Testament where the social micro-universe occurs at a more abstract level in the opposition between good and bad. The opposition between good and evil is a specific case of the more general opposition between good and bad, which includes, for example, the aesthetic contrast between beautiful and ugly. Thus Paul, in 1 Corinthians 11:3–15, makes a final (bourgeois!) appeal to the aesthetic distinction between good and bad taste to resolve what he takes to be the religious-ethical issue of the veiling of women: "Judge for yourselves: Is it proper for a woman to pray to God unveiled? And does nature itself not teach you that it is degrad-ing for a man to have long hair, but if a woman has long hair it becomes her?" (1 Cor 11:13–15a).

We can recognize the existential and social micro-universes in Barth's distinction between end events—events which occur at every moment in the encounter with the ultimate—and last things which lie on the plane of history. Similarly, we can see them in Bultmann's distinction between eschatology and history, and the

---

[1]See the entries "Micro-univers," and "Sémantique fondamentale," ET, "Micro-universe," and "Semantics, Fundamental."

distinction between the human being as an individual who stands existentially alone before the ultimate, and as a social being for whom engagement with others is constitutive for the meaning of life.

I. THE OPPOSITION BETWEEN THE EXISTENTIAL AND SOCIAL MICRO-UNIVERSES IN THE NEW TESTAMENT

In the New Testament the existential micro-universe is represented in its purest form by the Fourth Gospel, with particular clarity in 5:25, "The hour is coming, and now is, when the dead will hear the voice of the Son of God, and those who hear will live." The author rejects the significance of what happens on the social plane of involvement with others; attention is focussed solely on the voice of the Son of God from beyond the world. The hour which was expected on the temporal plane of history in Jewish eschatology breaks in at every moment of time when the voice of the Son of God is heard. Hearing the voice of the Son of God, paying attention to it, effects a transformation from death to life, from an involvement in the social, historical dimension of existence in this world to incorporation into the community of the Son of God beyond this world.

The contrast between life and death characterizing this existential micro-universe can be presented graphically as a vertical polarity.

Life

Death

Directly opposed to the Fourth Gospel's unconditional break with the social dimension of being human is Matthew's affirmation of this dimension, formulated representatively in the statement: "Not everyone who calls me, 'Lord, Lord,' will enter into the kingdom of heaven, but whoever does the will of my father who is in the heavens" (Matt 7:21). Here the unconditional appeal to the lordship of Christ is rejected. What matters is a person's behavior in the world, that is, whether or not one's deeds demonstrate active submission to the will of God. Matthew's understanding finds vivid expression in his description of the Last Judgment in 25:31–46, where persons are judged on the basis of the deeds they performed—or failed to perform—in aid of fellow human beings, without regard to a conscious relationship to Christ. The opposition between moral good and evil in Matthew's social micro-universe can be presented graphically on a horizontal plane as follows:

Good  Evil

Distinctive of Paul's thinking is that he affirms the validity of both sets of oppositions, those between life and death and those between good and evil, without allowing either to be weakened in its irreconcilably opposed relationship to the other. What are two distinct micro-universes in the Fourth Gospel and Matthew constitute a single micro-universe in Paul. On the one hand, he expresses views which make clear that the two micro-universes are incompatible, for example, in Rom 4:4–5, "For the person who works the reward is not considered a kindness, but is calculated in accordance with what is due: for the person who does not work, but trusts in him who justifies the ungodly, his [or her] trust is reckoned as justice." So also in his statement in Rom 3:27 that pride is excluded by the principle of faith, but not by the principle of works, "What then about boasting? It is excluded. By which Law? That of works? No, but by the Law of faith." On the other hand, and in that same context, in Rom 3:31, Paul reaffirms the complete compatibility of faith and works when he asks, "Do we destroy the Law through faith?" and replies emphatically, "By no means! We affirm it." In his micro-universe the existential and social polarities, life-death and good-bad, stand in irreconcilable opposition to each other, and yet he affirms both. God's kindness stands in irreconcilable opposition to the judgment of good and evil, and yet God himself cannot avoid judgment. Justification is by faith without works (Rom 3:20), and yet, not even God can avoid punishing evil and rewarding good. On the judgment day God will judge the deeds of every human being without paying favors (Rom 2:12–16).

We can present the relationship between these two sets of polarities, between what are distinct micro-universes in John and in Matthew, but a single micro-universe in Paul, in the diagram on the next page.

The vertical polarity does not meet the horizontal at any particular point, but at every point. In that regard the graphic presentation can be misleading. The vertical aspect of Paul's micro-universe is formulated with great clarity by the author of the Fourth Gospel with his "The hour is coming, and now is, when the dead will hear the voice of the Son of God, and those who hear will live" (John 5:25). Whatever happens at any point on the horizontal, social plane of good and evil is irrelevant for what happens on the vertical, existential plane of life and death. God's kindness does not depend in any way on the moral qualities of the human recipient.

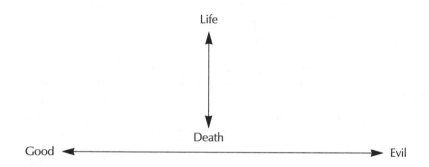

Similarly, according to Paul, what happens on the vertical, existential plane is irrelevant for what happens on the horizontal. In this case Matthew's formulation brings the greatest clarity, "Not everyone who calls me, 'Lord, Lord,' will enter into the kingdom of heaven, but whoever does the will of my father who is in heaven" (Matt 7:21). No appeal to the lordship of Christ can attenuate the judgment on one's works.

II. PAUL'S MICRO-UNIVERSE

The contradiction between the existential and social micro-universes, between discerning the voice of the Son of God and continued allegiance to the world (John), between appeal to the lordship of Christ and active obedience to the Law (Matthew), between faith and works (Paul), constitutes the deepest, most abstract level of New Testament thought. In Matthew and John a fundamental choice has already been made, not as a conscious decision, but as something that is presupposed, resolving the opposition between the social and the existential micro-universes in favor of one and to the exclusion of the other. What characterizes Paul's thought is that no such choice is presupposed. Both of what are distinct micro-universes in Matthew and John are constitutive for his thinking, although he does frequently find himself under pressure to choose in favor of the existential micro-universe, for example, in a statement like, "through works of the Law no one will be justified before him, for through the Law is the recognition of sin" (Rom 3:20). Yet that statement negates not the validity of the social distinction between good and evil, but the Jewish appeal to that opposition as the basis for privilege and the denial of gentile salvation. In Rom 2:1–3:20 Paul appeals to the opposition between good and evil to reject the Jewish claim to a privileged relationship by showing that that opposition denies such a privilege, before he places over against it the opposition between life and death, in Rom 3:21–4:25.

The relationship between the two opposed sets of oppositions at the deepest, most abstract level of Paul's thought makes it possible to recognize as completely consistent his affirmation of both justification by faith (Gal 2:11–5:6; Rom 3:21–4:25; 9:1–11:32) and justification for good works (Rom 1:18–3:20). The relationship between the two sets of oppositions also appears in single formulations, such as Rom 4:2, "if Abraham was justified through works, he would have reason to be proud, but not before God." If Abraham had good works on which he could rely, he would have received recognition for them on the social plane of the opposition between good and evil, but not on the existential plane of the opposition between life and death, not before God! So also in Gal 3:21, "if a Law with the power to make alive was given, justification would indeed have been through the Law." The Law authorizes justification for good works on the plane of the opposition between good and evil—although even on that plane it can be more of a curse than a blessing (Gal 3:10). Its deficiency is its inability to give life. It cannot function on the plane of the opposition between life and death. By its very nature the Law is restricted to the plane of the opposition between good and evil.

And so, what appears to be incongruous, if not contradictory, in Paul's reasoning, that every human being will be rewarded in accordance with her or his achievements but that no one will find life through such achievements, that is, Paul's affirmation of justification by faith without works as well as justification for good works, is shown to be grounded in a coherent system of thought. One may consider it the richness of the New Testament that it includes in its canon both Matthew and John, in that way acknowledging the validity of the opposed social and existential micro-universes which underlie their thinking at the deepest, most abstract levels. But then one should consider Paul's letters as *the* canon, not *a* (distinctive) canon, within the canon. Included in his thinking is the entire range represented by the opposed systems of thought of Matthew and John.

In the contemporary Christian theological setting it has become fashionable to condemn Bultmann's program of existentialist interpretation as short-sighted, incapable of doing justice to the social dimensions of New Testament thought. Bultmann's program was indeed one-sidedly existentialist, as is shown by its culmination in the thought of the Fourth Gospel. But equally one-sided are the contemporary socially oriented interpretations in which the existential dimensions of New Testament thought are close to being completely ignored. Both interpretations, existential as well as social, are motivated by particular historical circumstances, as responses to the needs of the time: Barth and Bultmann by the collapse of culture and the loss of confidence in human destiny; contemporary socially oriented interpretations in response to the demand for human solidarity throughout the world.

The inclusion of Matthew and John in the canon of the New Testament affirms the validity of both forms of interpretation, each in its appropriate circumstances, but emphasis on either of the two at the cost of the other invites a one-sidedness which fails to do justice to what it means to be a human being before God and in the world. If Matthew had been the entire New Testament canon, Christianity may have remained a noble Jewish sect; if John had been the entire canon, Christianity may have deteriorated into a gnostic sect. The inclusion of both Matthew and John avoids such one-sidedness in the canon, even if not in Christian interpretation and practice. The inclusion of both in the canon has the additional advantage that each represents its respective position with forceful clarity. Paul assumes a unique position in the canon, presenting both sets of oppositions with a consistency and clarity equal to that of Matthew and John. By allowing for the opposition between life and death as well as the opposition between good and evil in his system of thought Paul provides the basis for understanding what it means to be a human being *before God* and *in the world* for which there are few parallels in human history.

Conclusion

I. JUSTIFICATION OF THE GENTILES: NEGATION OF RELIGIOUS PRIVILEGE

The text-linguistic part of this study (Part I) has shown as false the traditional conception that fundamental to Paul's thinking in Galatians and Romans was an opposition between justification by faith and justification through works of the Law in the sense of receiving rewards for good works. Paul affirms both justification by faith and justification through works. He himself contributed to the misunderstanding of his thought by using the same expression, justification through works, for two completely different meanings in, respectively, Romans 2 and Romans 3:21–4:25.

In Romans 2 justification through works means to be rewarded for doing good. Paul employs this understanding in Romans 1:18–3:20 to dislodge the Jewish claim to an exclusive relationship with God. In chapter 2 he shows that Jews and gentiles are equal before the Law, because what matters before the Law is not being bound to it through circumcision, but whether or not one carries out its just requirements, "Not the hearers of the Law are just before God, but the doers will be justified" (Rom 2:13). It is not surprising that in the context of this discussion Paul comes to his finest expression of the rewarding of good and the condemnation of evil, "[God] will reward each in accordance with his [or her] works: to those who, with the patience of good works, seek glory and honor and immortality, eternal life, but to those who [live] from strife, and are disobedient to truth but obedient to evil, wrath and anger. Tribulation and pressure on every human being who does evil, on the Jew first, and on the gentile, but glory and honor and peace to everyone who does good, to the Jew first, and to the gentile. There is no favoritism with God" (Rom 2:6–11).

Paul continues this reasoning relentlessly in Romans 3:9–20 by proving from the Law itself that the very Law on which Jews depend for their claim to a privileged relationship with God condemns them as sinners, in that way making them equivalent to gentiles. He concludes with the unyielding statement, "We know that what the Law says it says to those who are under the Law. So that every mouth will be shut and the entire world will be subject to God's judgment" (3:19). In this way Romans 1:18—3:20 can be understood as an extended argument to underscore his sarcastic remark in Galatians 2:15, "We who are by heritage Jews, and not from the gentiles, sinners."

In Romans 3:21–4:25 Paul turns to another understanding of justification through works. The expression now means specifically circumcision and being bound to the Law, signifying a privileged relationship with God, opposed to that of the gentiles who stand condemned as sinners. The issue which Paul addresses in this part of the letter is, as he himself formulates it, whether "God [is] of the Jews only; not also of the gentiles?" (Rom 3:29). Rom 3:21–4:25 functions in effect as an expanded proof for the rest of what he reports of his initial comments to Peter in Antioch, "knowing that a person is not justified as a Jew [literally, 'from the Law'] except through the faith of Jesus Christ, we too believed in Christ Jesus in order to be justified through the faith of Christ, and not from works of the Law, for from works of the Law no one will be justified" (Gal 2:16).

Paul proves the non-existence of such an exclusive relationship with God by pointing out 1) that Abraham was justified, not as a Jew, but as a gentile, an uncircumcised person, and 2) that Jews as well as gentiles are justified by a faith such as the faith of the uncircumcised Abraham: "How was [justification] reckoned [to Abraham]? While he was circumcised or uncircumcised? Not circumcised, but uncircumcised. And he received the sign of circumcision, a seal of the justification of faith while uncircumcised, so that he would be the father of all who believe while uncircumcised, that it would be reckoned to them, and the father of the circumcised for those who are not only circumcised, but also follow in the footsteps of the faith of the uncircumcised Abraham" (Rom 4:10–12). An appeal to Abraham's justification, thus, has to be to a situation before there was a distinction between Jews and gentiles.

Paul's reasoning in Romans 4:10–12 makes more precise the point he made in Galatians: "The Law, which came four hundred and thirty years later, could not invalidate a testament that was ratified by God, so as to destroy the promise" (Gal 3:17). In Romans it is not the Law which came four hundred and thirty years later which stands in opposition to the promise, but Abraham's circumcision which followed almost immediately. Justification by faith does not stand opposed to justification for good works, but to the restriction of justification to the Jews through the Law (Gal 3:17), signified by circumcision (Rom 4:10–12). The negation of that restriction is Paul's main concern in Galatians and in Romans.

Paul proves in Galatians and in Rom 3:21–4:25 that through faith gentiles too are justified, but already in Rom 4:12 he points out that also Jews are justified by faith, that is, by a faith such as that of the uncircumcised Abraham, before there had been a distinction between Jews and gentiles. Jewish disbelief, concretely, the Jewish rejection of Christ, mentioned explicitly for the first time in Rom 3:3a, "What then if some of them became distrustful," becomes a matter of deep concern for Paul, not only because it appears to undermine the trustworthiness of God, "will not their distrust destroy the trustworthiness of God?" (Rom 3:3b), but also because of the solidarity which he continued to have with his own people, as he states, for example, in Rom 9:1–3, "I speak the truth in Christ, I do not lie, my conscience is my witness in the Holy Spirit, that I have a great sadness and an unceasing heartache. For I pray that I myself would be a curse away from Christ for the sake of my brothers, my kinsmen in the flesh."

In Rom 9–11 Jewish disbelief becomes the specific topic of his concern, and he does not rest until he can establish that in the end the Jews too will come to believe, and so find salvation, "They too, if they do not remain in disbelief, will be grafted in. . . . I do not want you to be uninformed, brothers [and sisters], of this mystery— in order that you should not be conceited—that a hardening came in part over Israel until the fullness of the gentiles enter, and so all of Israel will be saved" (Rom 11:23–26a).

The semiotic part of this study (Part Two) has revealed the consistency of Paul's reasoning in Galatians and Romans. The opposition between justification by faith and justification through works, the latter understood as the sign of belonging to a privileged people, finds expression at the level of Paul's system of values in the opposition between /Jewish privilege/ and /gentile salvation/. Paul's meaning becomes clearer when we establish, at a deeper, more abstract level, that the values /gentile salvation/ and /Jewish salvation/ together constitute the more universal value, /human salvation/. This more universal value stands in opposition to /salvation of exclusive groups/, which is constituted by the values /Jewish privilege/ and /gentile salvation/ when the latter stands in opposition to /Jewish salvation/.

Paul's system of values includes a second set of oppositions, between /good works/ and /evil works/, which comes to expression in the themes, justification for good works and condemnation of evil.

Paul did not give up the value of /good works/ and the negation of /evil works/ when he was converted from an exclusivist attitude of Jewish privilege to the acceptance of a justification by faith which removes the distinction between Jews and gentiles. This comes to clear expression already in 1 Cor 7:19, "Circumcision is nothing and not being circumcised is nothing, but keeping the commandments of God."

A conflict appears to occur in Paul's system of values between the configuration /good works/ versus /evil works/, in which /good works/ is evaluated positively, and the configuration /human salvation/ versus /salvation of exclusive groups/, in which /good works/, along with every human mark of distinction, is ignored as a positive value. The reason for this conflict becomes clear at the deepest, most abstract level of Paul's thought, his micro-universe. Here he integrates what are two distinct micro-universes in, respectively, Matthew and John: a social micro-universe in which good and evil are opposed and an existential micro-universe in which life and death are opposed. Characteristic of Paul's thought is its grounding in a micro-universe that includes both the social opposition between good and evil and the existential opposition between life and death. A tension exists between the social and the existential components in Paul's micro-universe because an essential feature of the social component, the opposition between good and evil, is disregarded in the existential component. This tension in Paul's micro-universe explains why, at the level of his system of values, the evaluation of /good works/ and /evil works/ is ignored in the opposition between /human salvation/ and /salvation of exclusive groups/.

The same applies to the existential opposition between life and death. That salvation is by faith, a product of God's kindness, does not remove the judgment of works, as shown in 1 Cor 3:13–15. Everyone will be judged according to her or his works, and "if someone's work is consumed [by the fire of judgment], he or she will bear the loss, but [nevertheless] be saved (receive life), however, as if through fire" (v. 15).

Thus this study shows that at all levels of Paul's thought there is complete coherence between his negation of justification through works of the Law in Galatians and in Rom 3:21–4:25 and his positive statements concerning justification through works of the Law in Romans 2. The affirmation of a justification for good works and the negation of a justification through works of the Law as the sign of having an exclusive relationship with God is coherently grounded in his system of thought, from the most abstract levels of his micro-universe and his system of values to the concrete level of the figures in which they find expression.

II. TRANSFORMATION INTO THE PRESENT

This interpretation can leave the impression that Paul was a dreadful anti-semite. There is a sense in which he is vehemently anti-Jewish. That has bothered me very much since the thought first occurred to me during the year I was involved in the research for this book. I wondered about the advisability of making public a study which could have the effect of nourishing tension in human relationships between religious groups. However, the point that must be emphasized is that what Paul rejects in his denial of the Jewish claim to a privileged relationship with God which excludes gentile salvation is exactly the kind of attitude concerning inter-human relationships in which anti-semitism has its roots. It is an attitude to which Paul refers with sarcasm in his statement to Peter, "We who are by heritage Jews, and not from the gentiles, sinners." An equivalent statement today could be, "We who are by heritage Christians, and not from the heathen, sinners." In the Nazi holocaust it became, "We who are by heritage Christians, and not from the Jews, sinners."

Paul's remark is not specifically anti-Jewish, but is directed against everyone who seeks security by condemning as sinners whoever does not confirm to her or his protected world. In his negation of that state of mind, Paul was not anti-semitic, but was seeking the true meaning of being a Jew. His assertion in Rom 3:9 that "we" Jews have nothing to show, does not negate, but builds on, his affirmation in 3:1–2 that there is a privilege to being a Jew, and circumcision does have a use, because it is the Jews to whom God entrusted his revelation (v. 2b).

With friends I visited the old synagogue in Essen in the Ruhr during the time of my stay in Marburg. It was burned down in the anti-Jewish frenzy of November 9, 1938, the *Reichskristallnacht* during the Nazi period, but has now been restored as a memorial-museum by citizens and the city of Essen. For the current small Jewish population of Essen there is a new synagogue elsewhere in the city. Paul's sarcastic remark in Galatians 2:15 cannot be understood as support for, but is directed against the very sentiment which some Germans felt towards Jews in the period in which these events took place. By misinterpreting Paul's rejection of a righteousness based on "works" as a rejection of justification for good works, Christianity missed Paul's point, and so was not prevented from taking upon itself what Paul denied Judaism, that "we . . . are by heritage Jews, and not from the gentiles, sinners," . . . and in the holocaust turned it against the Jews.

As evidence that this is not an isolated manifestation of the misguided Christian claim to the Jewish privileged relationship with

God, I conclude by quoting the description of our history by the Marburger Professor emeritus Dietrich von Oppen, a history in which he sees fulfilled the prophecies of the twelfth century abbot Joachim of Fiore. Von Oppen's description shows that Hitler's Germany was not an isolated occurrence in the history of the Christian West, even if, as the "Third Reich" it was an "instrument of power which sparked a new climax of terror."[1]

> Someone who is only slightly familiar with world history knows that violence and massacre, slavery and oppression, occurred at all times: Vikings and Huns, Mongolians, Arabs and Turks left bloody trails behind them; the suffering which highly cultured Greek cities inflicted on each other is horrifying. But what the Christian nations did to themselves and to the nations of the world surpasses, in extent and brutality, every comparison. Their actions did not take place as a contradiction of, but most specifically under the banner of their faith, and in its service. Crusades and mass burnings of heretics by the inquisition, countless witch-hunts, including torture and burning at the stake, mass murder and removals in religious wars between western confessions, devastation and the reduction to misery of once great cultures in the wake of discoveries, conquests and the establishment of colonial empires, enslavement, slave hunts, and slave trade in a period covering many centuries, elimination of entire indigenous tribes on other continents, disenfranchisement of those who survived, or restriction to confined reservations, revolutions resulting in streams of shed blood, the exploitation and reduction to misery of factory workers, continued perfecting of modern weapons of war, resulting already in the first world war in millions of battle casualties. It is a horrifying inventory which the Christian nations repressed from their consciousness, and even justified to their Christian consciences. Courageous counter-voices were not absent, but they remained solitary.[2]

---

[1]Dietrich von Oppen, *Marburger Aufzeichnungen zur Krise der modernen Welt* (Stuttgart: Radius-Verlag, 1983) 288.

[2]"Wer die Weltgeschichte auch nur ein wenig kennt, weiß, daß Gewalttat und Massenmord, Verknechtung und Unterdrückung zu allen Zeiten geschehen sind. Wikinger und Hunnen, Mongolen, Araber und Türken haben blutige Spuren auf ihren Wegen hinterlassen. Das Leid, das die hochkultivierten griechischen Städte einander angetan haben, war entsetzlich. Was aber die christlichen Völker sich selbst und den Völkern der Welt angetan haben, das ließ an Ausmaß und Grausamkeit alle Vergleiche hinter sich. Und es geschah nicht trotz ihres Glaubens, sondern meist ausdrücklich in seinem Zeichen und Dienste. Kreuzzüge und Massenverbrennungen von Ketzern durch die Inquisition; unzählbare Hexenprozesse mit Folter und Scheiterhaufen; Massenmorde und -vertreibungen in den Religionskriegen der westlichen Bekenntnisse untereinander; Vernichtung und Verelendung ehemals hoher Kulturvölker im Zuge der Entdeckungen, der Eroberungen und der weltweiten Gründung von Kolonialreichen; Versklavungen, Sklavenjagden

And so, Paul's letters to the Galatians and to the Romans become for us a commentary on our own history, summed up in Rom 10:2–3, "I witness concerning them that they have a zeal for God, but without understanding. Ignorant of God's justice, and seeking to establish their own, they did not subject themselves to the justice of God."

---

und Sklavenhandel über viele Jahrhunderte; Ausrottung ganzer Stämme von Vorbewohnern auf den überseeischen Kontinenten, Rechtlosigkeit der Überlebenden oder ihre Einschließung in enge Reservationen; Revolutionen mit Strömen von vergossenem Blut; Ausbeutung und Verelendung der frühen Fabrikarbeiter; zunehmende Perfektion der technischen Kriegswaffen mit der Folge von Millionenopfern in den Materialschlachten schon des ersten Weltkriegs. Es ist eine grauenvolle Bilanz, die die christlichen Völker im Ganzen freilich aus ihrem Bewußtsein verdrängt haben oder auch vor ihrem christlichen Gewissen zu rechtfertigen wußten. Mutige Gegenstimmen haben nicht gefehlt, doch blieben sie einsam" (*Marburger Aufzeichnungen*, 287–88).

Appendix I: Principles and Procedures in Discourse Analysis

The beginning point for our discussion of the principles and procedures in discourse analysis is the sentence, which we will call S (a statement unit or a colon). It consists of a NP (noun phrase) and a VP (verb phrase), such as:

1. the man (NP) kicked the dog (VP).

The VP could be constituted by a mere verb, such as "fly" in

2. airplanes (NP) fly (VP),

but as Sentence 1 (S_1) indicates a VP is most typically constituted by a NP + VP, "kicked (VP) the dog (NP)." The order of VP and NP is of no significance here.

Additional words or phrases and even clauses can be incorporated into the NP as well as the VP, as in the following sentence, which has a verb phrase into which has been incorporated an entire clause with its own verb: "which [representing 'the little dog'] was walking down the street."

3. the angry man (NP) kicked the little dog which was
   walking down the street very hard (VP).

The way this sentence is constructed leaves it *syntactically* ambiguous: Does "very hard" go with "kicked" or with "walking?" *Semantically*, it is unambiguous, since it is improbable that "walking" could be modified by "very hard."

Notwithstanding its complexity, Sentence 3 (S_3) constitutes a single statement unit. On the other hand, a compound sentence such as,

4. the man kicked the dog and then walked down the road,

constitutes two statement units because the second sentence, constituted by the presupposed NP of the first sentence, "the man," and the VP "walked down the road" is not incorporated, or embedded, to use the technical term, into either the NP or the VP of the first sentence, but is added to it by means of the conjunction "and."

After analyzing the sentence, we must next determine the syntax or grammar of a discourse, i.e., the way the sentences interrelate in a discourse. The problem with such a syntax or grammar of discourse or of a text is that we do not yet have a text grammar, as we do have for sentences.

A description of the syntax of a discourse, as of a sentence, can be done either by bracketing or by means of a branching diagram, for example,

Bracketing

[[The man] [who [was angry]]] [kicked [the dog]]

Diagram 1

Branching

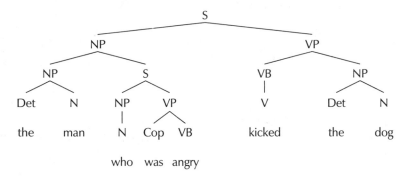

Diagram 2

Each description sorts out the constituents of the sentence. The same can be done in the case of a discourse by sorting out the statement units and diagramming their interrelationships. Both descriptions perform essentially the same function as the diagram shows.

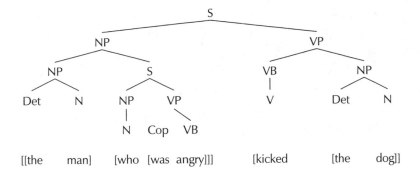

Diagram 3

Every bracket reflects a branching all the way up, except for the last one, which encompasses the entire sentence, but for which a bracket would be redundant.

The disadvantage of bracketing is that the longer the sentence the less revealing the display by means of brackets becomes. This is even more true in the case of discourse where the brackets may stretch over a number of pages. However, for analysis I find bracketing a simpler procedure. For the final display they can then be changed into branching diagrams for the sake of a better overview. I use as an example, Gal 1:13–14. Note that the physical differences in the display of branching is of no significance, for example,

Diagram 4

For discourse, the diagrams have to be turned into a vertical position, with the left hand going on the top in accordance with our custom of reading from the top of the page.

Branching   Bracketing

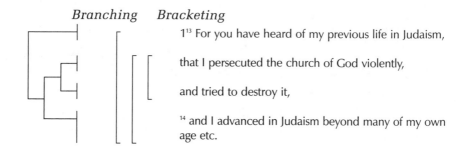

1[13] For you have heard of my previous life in Judaism,

that I persecuted the church of God violently,

and tried to destroy it,

[14] and I advanced in Judaism beyond many of my own age etc.

Diagram 5

Note the structural ambiguity in the following sentence:

5. he said the man was sick.

From the point of view of "he said" it is clear that "the man was sick" is embedded in the VP of a single complex sentence:

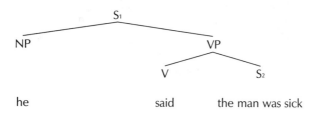

Diagram 6

The embedded sentence (S_2) is a necessary constituent of the VP of S_1. Without it S_1 would be incomplete.

From the point of view of what is said, however, "the man was sick," S_2 is itself a colon. This is even more evident if what "he said" constituted a number of sentences, such as

6. he said the man was sick, and he had to go and help him,
   but he could not do so immediately.

Note, however, that the transformation of direct into indirect reason effects a change of the embedded sentence into a dependent clause, even though it is not recognizable syntactically in English, and even less so in Greek, where ὅτι introduces direct as well as indirect reason.

7. he said that *the man was sick.*

But note in the German, direct reason:

8. er sagt, *der Mann ist krank,*

and indirect reason:

9. er sagt, *daß der Man krank ist.*

Since it can stand by itself as a sentence, *der Mann ist krank* is a colon, but *daß der Man krank ist* cannot stand alone as a sentence and is not a colon.

Thus, in Gal 1:13a, "have heard" and everything that follows is part of the verb phrase of S₁, as the following diagram shows:

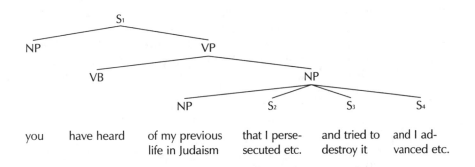

Diagram 7

For display purposes it is necessary to diagram the entire statement vertically, but note that it is diagrammed as a single colon. From the point of view of "you have heard" the entire statement is a single colon, but from the point of view of S₂, S₃, and S₄ these are themselves distinguishable cola, and not merely parts of the verb phrase. The diagram illustrates what happens within the main colon.

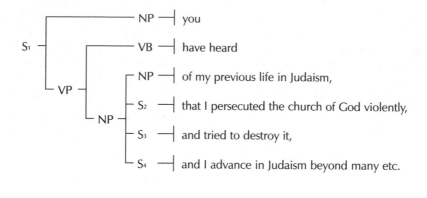

Diagram 8

There is, however, a feature in connection with the three embedded sentences that does not come out in this display. In the first place, they themselves are distinguishable as individual cola, which is not true of the phrase, "of my previous life in Judaism." Secondly, there is also a relationship between S2 and S3 which sets them as a group apart from S4. In S3 Paul still dwells for a moment on the subject matter of S2, before he moves on to something new, although related, in S4. The VPs of S2 and S3 in their deep structure share the same NP, "the church of God," transformed into "it" in the surface structure of S3. Furthermore S2, S3, and S4 are expansions of the NP "of my previous life in Judaism." Thus the branching diagram of the sentence has to be altered as follows in order to be a true presentation of this sentence.

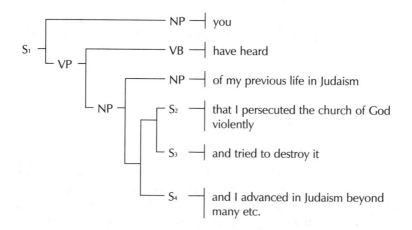

Diagram 9

With that it becomes obvious that we are no longer dealing with sentence structure, but with the structure of discourse. Thus, Gal 1:13–14 has to be analyzed as discourse. Its structure as discourse was described in diagram 5.

A further indication that the structural relationship between S_2, S_3, and S_4 should be taken as discourse is indicated by the repeated recurrence of that structural pattern in Gal., e.g., in 1:10 and 1:12.

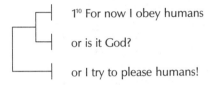

1¹⁰ For now I obey humans

or is it God?

or I try to please humans!

Diagram 10

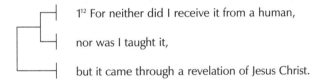

1¹² For neither did I receive it from a human,

nor was I taught it,

but it came through a revelation of Jesus Christ.

Diagram 11

The close cohesion between the first two cola in 1:10 is provided by the shared verb, "obey," which is not repeated in the second colon. In 1:12 the close cohesion is provided by the conjunction, "nor," and the second conjunction, "but," by means of which the third colon is placed in contrast with the first two. In all of these clusters or groupings of cola the same structural pattern recurs. Paul makes a statement, dwells on it for a moment with a second statement, and only then moves on to a third statement that stands over against the first two. In reality the third statement relates back to the first in each case, with the second, almost parenthetically, merely underscoring the first.

The purpose of my analyses is to discover that basic meaning out of which a text becomes comprehensible. It is what Teun van Dijk calls the macro-structure of the text. He defines it as follows: ". . . semantic macro-structures are necessary to explain in sufficiently simple terms how it is possible that throughout a text the selection of lexical items and underlying formation of semantic representations is heavily restricted by some global constraint."[1] The problem is that all we have concretely are the phonetic presentations of the surface structure, and from these the semantic structure has to be derived. Furthermore, as van Dijk observes, everybody constructs "the macro-structure of a text which is relevant for him, personally, and the macro-structures will be different for the same text."[2] The point is that semantic structure and surface structure are not completely coordinate. This can be shown most clearly in the case of ambiguous sentences, especially since the question of ambiguity is so important for discourse. The ambiguity of a sentence, such as,

> 10. flying airplanes can be dangerous,

taken in isolation would hardly be noticed in a discourse because the context in which it occurs determines which meaning is intended.[3]

Transformational grammar makes it possible to show how an ambiguous sentence, such as 10 above, results from combining into an identical sentence two pairs of underlying sentences with different meanings, that is, "Airplanes that fly can be dangerous" and "It is dangerous to fly airplanes." The two pairs of underlying sentences are:

> 11a. airplanes fly.
>   b. airplanes can be dangerous.

and,

> 12a. it can be dangerous.
>   b. X(plur) fly airplanes.

or,

> c. X(sing) flies airplanes.

Sentences 12b and 12c reveal a further ambiguity, which means that the resulting sentence 10 is really triply ambiguous. It is clear that the single, ambiguous, compound sentence cannot be produced except as a result of transformations demanded by the syntax of the English language.

Since it is of further significance for us in connection with discourse, I will outline the transformations of sentences 11a and b in an abbreviated form.

Combining the two sentences in a single one can be diagrammed as follows:

---

[1] *Some Aspects of Text Grammars,* 160.
[2] *Some Aspects of Text Grammars,* 161.
[3] Cf. Chomsky, *Aspects of the Theory of Syntax,* 21.

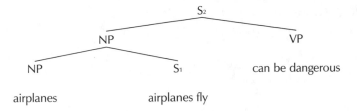

Diagram 12

By the relative clause transformation this becomes:

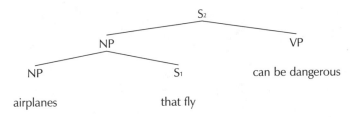

Diagram 13

By the participial transformation it becomes:

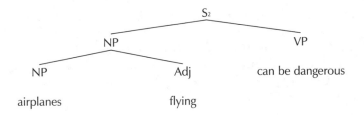

Diagram 14

Note that the participle in this case is adjectival, whereas it is verbal in the sentence which results from the combination of sentences 12a and b or c. That is the distinguishing feature that lies closest to the surface of the resulting ambiguous sentence by which the ambiguity can be resolved.

Finally by the adjectival shift transformation, which in this case is purely stylistic and not grammatically necessary, it becomes:

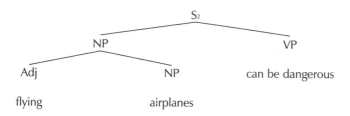

Diagram 15

Note that the pronoun transformation which is the only part of the relative clause transformation that came into operation in our illustration (diagram 13) as a parallel in discourse. When sentences 11a and b form part of a discourse, the NP of 11b is transformed into a pronoun.

> 13a. airplanes fly.
>   b. they can be dangerous.

The rule appears the same in both cases: if an identical NP occurs in the deep structure of a complex sentence (cf. diagram 12), or in sentences that cohere in a discourse, the second occurrence of the NP has to be transformed into an appropriate pronoun.

Note that it is not the NP of the same underlying sentence which is transformed, but in each case the NP of the modifying sentence. Note furthermore, however, that in a less compact way the sentence 11a (= 13a) of the discourse is incorporated into the NP, that is, the pronoun of 13b, similar to the incorporation of the same sentence into the head NP, "(airplanes) that fly," of the complex sentence by means of the relative clause transformation (cf. diagram 13). The transformation of "airplanes" into "they" in sentence 13b of the discourse makes it clear that it is not merely "airplanes" that can be dangerous, but "airplanes (that) fly." The semantic structure of the discourse 13(a,b) and the complex sentence,

> 14. airplanes that fly can be dangerous,

is the same, but as a result of different transformations their surface structures are not.

The discrepancy between surface structure and semantic structure is thus revealed, not only by the ambiguous sentence which has two different sets of deep structure sentences, but also by the four different surface structures that express a single semantic structure: the ambiguous sentence, the discourse 13, the complex sentence 14, and the sentence which was produced up to the stage of the transformation in diagram 14, which, like discourse 13 and sentence 14, is also not ambiguous:

15. airplanes flying can be dangerous.

It appears obvious, therefore, that for a proper understanding of the semantic structure of a sentence or of a discourse it is necessary to distinguish between the contributions of semantics and syntactics in the formation of a surface structure, if not also of phonetics. The structural ambiguity of Gal 1:20, as shown in the diagram on page 240 (Gal 1:18–24), confirms this necessity.

Structure D shows that verse 20 could refer back to verses 18–19; C that it could refer back to only verse 19; and B that it could refer to the entire series of events narrated in 1:15–2:10. These three structures diagram the semantic possibilities, the possibilities of meaning, all of which could have produced the present syntactic structure as diagrammed by means of structure A. The meaning remains ambiguous because syntactically verse 20 fits loosely in its context, as the dotted lines in syntactic structure A indicate. Because of this looseness no appeal can be made to syntax to resolve the ambiguity revealed by the three possible semantic structures B, C, and D. The situation is similar to the three semantic possibilities revealed by the sentences 11a and b, and 12a and b or c, each of which could have produced the ambiguous sentence 10, "flying airplanes can be dangerous." An interpretation of verse 20 cannot afford not to take into consideration that there are three possible semantic structures, B, C, and D, which could have produced it, and that the ambiguity cannot be resolved by the verse's context, because of its lack of syntactic coherence as diagrammed by structure A. Sometimes it is possible to resolve such a problem of coherence by considering an even larger context, but this does not seem possible in the present case.

*Syntactic
Structure*

*Semantic
Structures*

A   B   C   D

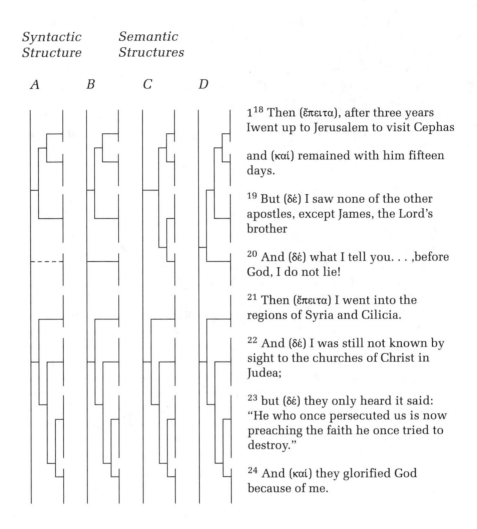

1¹⁸ Then (ἔπειτα), after three years I went up to Jerusalem to visit Cephas

and (καί) remained with him fifteen days.

¹⁹ But (δέ) I saw none of the other apostles, except James, the Lord's brother

²⁰ And (δέ) what I tell you. . . ,before God, I do not lie!

²¹ Then (ἔπειτα) I went into the regions of Syria and Cilicia.

²² And (δέ) I was still not known by sight to the churches of Christ in Judea;

²³ but (δέ) they only heard it said: "He who once persecuted us is now preaching the faith he once tried to destroy."

²⁴ And (καί) they glorified God because of me.

Diagram 16

All of this is not new. Interpreters of Galatians have been aware of these difficulties for a very long time. The task of linguistics, as I understand it, is not to do things that are new, but to clarify and to provide an account of how meaning is factually communicated in language. Its task is to bring to consciousness what the ordinary user of the language, speaker as well as hearer, writer as well as reader, "knows" without being aware of it. The discussions above were attempts to do exactly that.

Appendix II: Semantic Parallels to Galatians in Romans

Galatians

1. Gal 1:14b περισσοτέρως ζηλωτὴς
ὑπάρχων τῶν πατρικῶν μου
παραδόσεων.
2. Gal 2:1–16 Ἔπειτα διὰ
δεκατεσσάρων ἐτῶν πάλιν ἀνέβην
εἰς Ἱεροσόλυμα μετὰ Βαρναβᾶ,
συμπαραλαβὼν καὶ Τίτον· ² ἀνέβην
δὲ κατὰ ἀποκάλυψιν· καὶ ἀνεθέμην
αὐτοῖς τὸ εὐαγγέλιον ὃ κηρύσσω ἐν
τοῖς ἔθνεσιν, κατ' ἰδίαν δὲ τοῖς
δοκοῦσιν, μή πως εἰς κενὸν τρέχω
ἢ ἔδραμον. ³ ἀλλ' οὐδὲ Τίτος ὁ σὺν
ἐμοί, Ἕλλην ὤν, ἠναγκάσθη
περιτμηθῆναι· ⁴ διὰ δὲ τοὺς
παρεισάκτους ψευδαδέλφους, οἵτινες
παρεισῆλθον κατασκοπῆσαι τὴν
ἐλευθερίαν ἡμῶν ἥν ἔχομεν ἐν
Χριστῷ Ἰησοῦ, ἵνα ἡμᾶς
καταδουλώσουσιν· ⁵ οἷς οὐδὲ πρὸς
ὥραν εἴξαμεν τῇ ὑποταγῇ, ἵνα ἡ
ἀλήθεια τοῦ εὐαγγελίου διαμείνῃ
πρὸς ὑμᾶς. ⁶ ἀπὸ δὲ τῶν δοκούντων
εἶναί τι– ὁποῖοί ποτε ἦσαν οὐδέν
μοι διαφέρει· πρόσωπον [ὁ] θεὸς
ἀνθρώπου οὐ λαμβάνει– ἐμοὶ γὰρ οἱ
δοκοῦντες οὐδὲν προσανέθεντο,
⁷ ἀλλὰ τοὐναντίον ἰδόντες ὅτι
πεπίστευμαι τὸ εὐαγγέλιον τῆς
ἀκροβυστίας καθὼς Πέτρος τῆς
περιτομῆς, ⁸ ὁ γὰρ ἐνεργήσας
Πέτρῳ εἰς ἀποστολὴν τῆς
περιτομῆς ἐνήργησεν καὶ ἐμοὶ εἰς

Romans

Rom 10:2 μαρτυρῶ γὰρ αὐτοῖς ὅτι
ζῆλον θεοῦ ἔχουσιν, ἀλλ' οὐ κατ'
ἐπίγνωσιν.

Rom 3:30 εἴπερ εἷς ὁ θεός, ὃς
δικαιώσει περιτομὴν ἐκ πίστεως καὶ
ἀκροβυστίαν διὰ τῆς πίστεως.

τὰ ἔθνη, [9] καὶ γνόντες τὴν χάριν τὴν δοθεῖσάν μοι, Ἰάκωβος καὶ Κηφᾶς καὶ Ἰωάννης, οἱ δοκοῦντες στῦλοι εἶναι, δεξιὰς ἔδωκαν ἐμοὶ καὶ Βαρναβᾷ κοινωνίας, ἵνα ἡμεῖς εἰς τὰ ἔθνη, αὐτοὶ δὲ εἰς τὴν περιτομήν· [10] μόνον τῶν πτωχῶν ἵνα μνημονεύωμεν, ὃ καὶ ἐσπούδασα αὐτὸ τοῦτο ποιῆσαι. [11] Ὅτε δὲ ἦλθεν Κηφᾶς εἰς Ἀντιόχειαν, κατὰ πρόσωπον αὐτῷ ἀντέστην, ὅτι κατεγνωσμένος ἦν. [12] πρὸ τοῦ γὰρ ἐλθεῖν τινας ἀπὸ Ἰακώβου μετὰ τῶν ἐθνῶν συνήσθιεν· ὅτε δὲ ἦλθον, ὑπέστελλεν καὶ ἀφώριζεν ἑαυτόν, φοβούμενος τοὺς ἐκ περιτομῆς. [13] καὶ συνυπεκρίθησαν αὐτῷ [καὶ] οἱ λοιποὶ Ἰουδαῖοι, ὥστε καὶ Βαρναβᾶς συναπήχθη αὐτῶν τῇ ὑποκρίσει. [14] ἀλλ' ὅτε εἶδον ὅτι οὐκ ὀρθοποδοῦσιν πρὸς τὴν ἀλήθειαν τοῦ εὐαγγελίου, εἶπον τῷ Κηφᾷ ἔμπροσθεν πάντων, εἰ σὺ Ἰουδαῖος ὑπάρχων ἐθνικῶς καὶ οὐχὶ Ἰουδαϊκῶς ζῇς, πῶς τὰ ἔθνη ἀναγκάζεις Ἰουδαΐζειν; [15] Ἡμεῖς φύσει Ἰουδαῖοι καὶ οὐκ ἐξ ἐθνῶν ἁμαρτωλοί, [16] εἰδότες [δὲ] ὅτι οὐ δικαιοῦται ἄνθρωπος ἐξ ἔργων νόμου ἐὰν μὴ διὰ πίστεως Ἰησοῦ Χριστοῦ, καὶ ἡμεῖς εἰς τὴν Χριστὸν Ἰησοῦν ἐπιστεύσαμεν, ἵνα δικαιωθῶμεν ἐκ πίστεως Χριστοῦ καὶ οὐκ ἐξ ἔργων νόμου, ὅτι ἐξ ἔργων νόμου οὐ δικαιωθήσεται πᾶσα σάρξ.

Rom 4:11–12 [11] καὶ σημεῖον ἔλαβεν περιτομῆς, σφραγῖδα τῆς δικαιοσύνης τῆς πίστεως τῆς ἐν τῇ ἀκροβυστίᾳ, εἰς τὸ εἶναι αὐτὸν πατέρα πάντων τῶν πιστευόντων δι' ἀκροβυστίας, εἰς τὸ λογισθῆναι [καὶ] αὐτοῖς [τὴν] δικαιοσύνην, [12] καὶ πατέρα περιτομῆς τοῖς οὐκ ἐκ περιτομῆς μόνον ἀλλὰ καὶ τοῖς στοιχοῦσιν τοῖς ἴχνεσιν τῆς ἐν ἀκροβυστίᾳ πίστεως τοῦ πατρὸς ἡμῶν Ἀβραάμ.

Rom 2:1–6 διὸ ἀναπολόγητος εἶ, ὦ ἄνθρωπε πᾶς ὁ κρίνων· ἐν ᾧ γὰρ κρίνεις τὸν ἕτερον, σεαυτὸν κατακρίνεις, τὰ γὰρ αὐτὰ πράσσεις ὁ κρίνων. [2] οἴδαμεν δὲ ὅτι τὸ κρίμα τοῦ θεοῦ ἐστιν κατὰ ἀλήθειαν ἐπὶ τοὺς τὰ τοιαῦτα πράσσοντας. [3] λογίζῃ δὲ τοῦτο, ὦ ἄνθρωπε ὁ κρίνων τοὺς τὰ τοιαῦτα πράσσοντας καὶ ποιῶν αὐτά, ὅτι σὺ ἐκφεύξῃ τὸ κρίμα τοῦ θεοῦ; [4] ἢ τοῦ πλούτου τῆς χρηστότητος αὐτοῦ καὶ τῆς ἀνοχῆς καὶ τῆς μακροθυμίας καταφρονεῖς, ἀγνοῶν ὅτι τὸ χρηστὸν τοῦ θεοῦ εἰς μετάνοιάν σε ἄγει; [5] κατὰ δὲ σκληρότητά σου καὶ ἀμετανόητον καρδίαν θησαυρίζεις σεαυτῷ ὀργὴν ἐν ἡμέρᾳ ὀργῆς καὶ ἀποκαλύψεως δικαιοκρισίας τοῦ θεοῦ, [6] ὃς ἀποδώσει ἑκάστῳ κατὰ τὰ ἔργα αὐτοῦ.

Rom 2:17–24 εἰ δὲ σὺ Ἰουδαῖος ἐπονομάζῃ καὶ ἐπαναπαύῃ νόμῳ καὶ καυχᾶσαι ἐν θεῷ [18] καὶ γινώσκεις τὸ θέλημα καὶ δοκιμάζεις τὰ διαφέροντα κατηχούμενος ἐκ τοῦ νόμου, [19] πέποιθάς τε σεαυτὸν ὁδηγὸν εἶναι τυφλῶν, φῶς τῶν ἐν σκότει, [20] παιδευτὴν ἀφρόνων,

διδάσκαλον νηπίων, ἔχοντα τὴν
μόρφωσιν τῆς γνώσεως καὶ τῆς
ἀληθείας ἐν τῷ νόμῳ— [21] ὁ οὖν
διδάσκων ἕτερον σεαυτὸν οὐ
διδάσκεις; ὁ κηρύσσων μὴ κλέπτειν
κλέπτεις; [22] ὁ λέγων μὴ μοιχεύειν
μοιχεύεις; ὁ βδελυσσόμενος τὰ
εἴδωλα ἱεροσυλεῖς; [23] ὃς ἐν νόμῳ
καυχᾶσαι, διὰ τῆς παραβάσεως τοῦ
νόμου τὸν θεὸν ἀτιμάζεις; [24] τὸ
γὰρ ὄνομα τοῦ θεοῦ δι' ὑμᾶς
βλασφημεῖται ἐν τοῖς ἔθνεσιν,
καθὼς γέγραπται.

Rom 3:19–20 οἴδαμεν δὲ ὅτι ὅσα ὁ
νόμος λέγει τοῖς ἐν τῷ νόμῳ λαλεῖ,
ἵνα πᾶν στόμα φραγῇ καὶ ὑπόδικος
γένηται πᾶς ὁ κόσμος τῷ θεῷ·
[20] διότι ἐξ ἔργων νόμου οὐ
δικαιωθήσεται πᾶσα σὰρξ ἐνώπιον
αὐτοῦ, διὰ γὰρ νόμου ἐπίγνωσις
ἁμαρτίας.

2a. Gal 2:15 ἡμεῖς φύσει Ἰουδαῖοι καὶ
οὐκ ἐξ ἐθνῶν ἁμαρτωλοί.

Rom 1:18–31 Ἀποκαλύπτεται γὰρ
ὀργὴ θεοῦ ἀπ' οὐρανοῦ ἐπὶ πᾶσαν
ἀσέβειαν καὶ ἀδικίαν ἀνθρώπων
τῶν τὴν ἀλήθειαν ἐν ἀδικίᾳ
κατεχόντων κ.τ.λ.

3. Gal 2:17–21 εἰ δὲ ζητοῦντες
δικαιωθῆναι ἐν Χριστῷ εὑρέθημεν
καὶ αὐτοὶ ἁμαρτωλοί, ἄρα Χριστὸς
ἁμαρτίας διάκονος; μὴ γένοιτο. [18] εἰ
γὰρ ἃ κατέλυσα ταῦτα πάλιν
οἰκοδομῶ, παραβάτην ἐμαυτὸν
συνιστάνω.

Rom 7:24–8:2 ταλαίπωρος ἐγὼ
ἄνθρωπος· τίς με ῥύσεται ἐκ τοῦ
σώματος τοῦ θανάτου τούτου;
[25] χάρις δὲ τῷ θεῷ διὰ Ἰησοῦ
Χριστοῦ τοῦ κυρίου ἡμῶν. ἄρα οὖν
αὐτὸς ἐγὼ τῷ μὲν νοῒ δουλεύω
νόμῳ θεοῦ, τῇ δὲ σαρκὶ νόμῳ
ἁμαρτίας. 8[1] Οὐδὲν ἄρα νῦν
κατάκριμα τοῖς ἐν Χριστῷ Ἰησοῦ·
[2] ὁ γὰρ νόμος τοῦ πνεύματος τῆς
ζωῆς ἐν Χριστῷ Ἰησοῦ
ἠλευθέρωσέν σε ἀπὸ τοῦ νόμου τῆς
ἁμαρτίας καὶ τοῦ θανάτου.

[19] ἐγὼ γὰρ διὰ νόμου νόμῳ ἀπέθανον
ἵνα θεῷ ζήσω. Χριστῷ
συνεσταύρωμαι·

Rom 7:1–6 Ἢ ἀγνοεῖτε, ἀδελφοί,
γινώσκουσιν γὰρ νόμον λαλῶ, ὅτι
ὁ νόμος κυριεύει τοῦ ἀνθρώπου ἐφ'
ὅσον χρόνον ζῇ; [2] ἡ γὰρ ὕπανδρος
γυνὴ τῷ ζῶντι ἀνδρὶ δέδεται νόμῳ·
ἐὰν δὲ ἀποθάνῃ ὁ ἀνήρ, κατήργηται
ἀπὸ τοῦ νόμου τοῦ ἀνδρός. [3] ἄρα
οὖν ζῶντος τοῦ ἀνδρὸς μοιχαλὶς

χρηματίσει ἐὰν γένηται ἀνδρὶ ἑτέρῳ·
ἐὰν δὲ ἀποθάνῃ ὁ ἀνήρ, ἐλευθέρα
ἐστὶν ἀπὸ τοῦ νόμου, τοῦ μὴ εἶναι
αὐτὴν μοιχαλίδα γενομένην ἀνδρὶ
ἑτέρῳ. [4] ὥστε, ἀδελφοί μου, καὶ
ὑμεῖς ἐθανατώθητε τῷ νόμῳ διὰ τοῦ
σώματος τοῦ Χριστοῦ, εἰς τὸ
γενέσθαι ὑμᾶς ἑτέρῳ, τῷ ἐκ νεκρῶν
ἐγερθέντι, ἵνα καρποφορήσωμεν τῷ
θεῷ. [5] ὅτε γὰρ ἦμεν ἐν τῇ σαρκί,
τὰ παθήματα τῶν ἁμαρτιῶν τὰ διὰ
τοῦ νόμου ἐνηργεῖτο ἐν τοῖς
μέλεσιν ἡμῶν εἰς τὸ καρποφορῆσαι
τῷ θανάτῳ· [6] νυνὶ δὲ κατηργήθημεν
ἀπὸ τοῦ νόμου, ἀποθανόντες ἐν ᾧ
κατειχόμεθα, ὥστε δουλεύειν ἡμᾶς
ἐν καινότητι πνεύματος καὶ οὐ
παλαιότητι γράμματος.

[20] ζῶ δὲ οὐκέτι ἐγώ, ζῇ δὲ ἐν ἐμοὶ
Χριστός· ὃ δὲ νῦν ζῶ ἐν σαρκί, ἐν
πίστει ζῶ τῇ τοῦ υἱοῦ τοῦ θεοῦ τοῦ
ἀγαπήσαντός με καὶ παραδόντος
ἑαυτὸν ὑπὲρ ἐμοῦ.

Rom 6:3–11 ἢ ἀγνοεῖτε ὅτι ὅσοι
ἐβαπτίσθημεν εἰς Χριστὸν Ἰησοῦν
εἰς τὸν θάνατον αὐτοῦ ἐβαπτίσθημεν; [4] συνετάφημεν οὖν αὐτῷ διὰ
τοῦ βαπτίσματος εἰς τὸν θάνατον,
ἵνα ὥσπερ ἠγέρθη Χριστὸς ἐκ
νεκρῶν διὰ τῆς δόξης τοῦ πατρός,
οὕτως καὶ ἡμεῖς ἐν καινότητι ζωῆς
περιπατήσωμεν. [5] εἰ γὰρ σύμφυτοι
γεγόναμεν τῷ ὁμοιώματι τοῦ
θανάτου αὐτοῦ, ἀλλὰ καὶ τῆς
ἀναστάσεως ἐσόμεθα· [6] τοῦτο
γινώσκοντες, ὅτι ὁ παλαιὸς ἡμῶν
ἄνθρωπος συνεσταυρώθη, ἵνα
καταργηθῇ τὸ σῶμα τῆς ἁμαρτίας,
τοῦ μηκέτι δουλεύειν ἡμᾶς τῇ
ἁμαρτίᾳ· [7] ὁ γὰρ ἀποθανὼν
δεδικαίωται ἀπὸ τῆς ἁμαρτίας. [8] εἰ
δὲ ἀπεθάνομεν σὺν Χριστῷ,
πιστεύομεν ὅτι καὶ συζήσομεν
αὐτῷ· [9] εἰδότες ὅτι Χριστὸς
ἐγερθεὶς ἐκ νεκρῶν οὐκέτι
ἀποθνῄσκει, θάνατος αὐτοῦ οὐκέτι
κυριεύει. [10] ὃ γὰρ ἀπέθανεν, τῇ
ἁμαρτίᾳ ἀπέθανεν ἐφάπαξ· ὃ δὲ ζῇ,
ζῇ τῷ θεῷ. [11] οὕτως καὶ ὑμεῖς
λογίζεσθε ἑαυτοὺς [εἶναι] νεκροὺς
μὲν τῇ ἁμαρτίᾳ ζῶντας δὲ τῷ θεῷ
ἐν Χριστῷ Ἰησοῦ.

²¹ οὐκ ἀθετῶ τὴν χάριν τοῦ θεοῦ· εἰ
γὰρ διὰ νόμου δικαιοσύνη, ἄρα
Χριστὸς δωρεὰν ἀπέθανεν.

Rom 4:14 εἰ γὰρ οἱ ἐκ νόμου κληρονόμοι, κεκένωται ἡ πίστις καὶ
κατήργηται ἡ ἐπαγγελία.

Gal 3:1–5 (Specific to the Galatian situation)

4. Gal 3:6–29 καθὼς Ἀβραὰμ
ἐπίστευσεν τῷ θεῷ, καὶ ἐλογίσθη
αὐτῷ εἰς δικαιοσύνην. ⁷ γινώσκετε
ἄρα ὅτι οἱ ἐκ πίστεως, ⁸ οὗτοι υἱοί
εἰσιν Ἀβραάμ. προϊδοῦσα δὲ ἡ
γραφὴ ὅτι ἐκ πίστεως δικαιοῖ τὰ
ἔθνη ὁ θεὸς προευηγγελίσατο τῷ
Ἀβραὰμ ὅτι ἐνευλογηθήσονται ἐν
σοὶ πάντα τὰ ἔθνη. ⁹ ὥστε οἱ ἐκ
πίστεως εὐλογοῦνται σὺν τῷ πιστῷ
Ἀβραάμ.

Rom 4:9–13 ὁ μακαρισμὸς οὖν οὗτος
ἐπὶ τὴν περιτομὴν ἢ καὶ ἐπὶ τὴν
ἀκροβυστίαν; λέγομεν γάρ,
ἐλογίσθη τῷ Ἀβραὰμ ἡ πίστις εἰς
δικαιοσύνην. ¹⁰ πῶς οὖν ἐλογίσθη;
ἐν περιτομῇ ὄντι ἢ ἐν ἀκροβυστίᾳ;
οὐκ ἐν περιτομῇ ἀλλ' ἐν
ἀκροβυστίᾳ· ¹¹ καὶ σημεῖον ἔλαβεν
περιτομῆς, σφραγῖδα τῆς
δικαιοσύνης τῆς πίστεως τῆς ἐν τῇ
ἀκροβυστίᾳ, εἰς τὸ εἶναι αὐτὸν
πατέρα πάντων τῶν πιστευόντων
δι' ἀκροβυστίας, εἰς τὸ λογισθῆναι
[καὶ] αὐτοῖς [τὴν] δικαιοσύνην,
¹² καὶ πατέρα περιτομῆς τοῖς οὐκ
ἐκ περιτομῆς μόνον ἀλλὰ καὶ τοῖς
στοιχοῦσιν τοῖς ἴχνεσιν τῆς ἐν
ἀκροβυστίᾳ πίστεως τοῦ πατρὸς
ἡμῶν Ἀβραάμ. ¹³ οὐ γὰρ διὰ νόμου
ἡ ἐπαγγελία τῷ Ἀβραὰμ ἢ τῷ
σπέρματι αὐτοῦ, τὸ κληρονόμον
αὐτὸν εἶναι κόσμου, ἀλλὰ διὰ
δικαιοσύνης πίστεως·

¹⁰ ὅσοι γὰρ ἐξ ἔργων νόμου εἰσὶν ὑπὸ
κατάραν εἰσίν· γέγραπται γὰρ ὅτι
ἐπικατάρατος πᾶς ὃς οὐκ ἐμμένει
πᾶσιν τοῖς γεγραμμένοις ἐν τῷ
βιβλίῳ τοῦ νόμου τοῦ ποιῆσαι
αὐτά. ¹¹ ὅτι δὲ ἐν νόμῳ οὐδεὶς
δικαιοῦται παρὰ τῷ θεῷ δῆλον, ὅτι
ὁ δίκαιος ἐκ πίστεως ζήσεται· ¹² ὁ
δὲ νόμος οὐκ ἔστιν ἐκ πίστεως,
ἀλλ' ὁ ποιήσας αὐτὰ ζήσεται ἐν
αὐτοῖς.

Rom 7:1–6 Ἢ ἀγνοεῖτε, ἀδελφοί,
γινώσκουσιν γὰρ νόμον λαλῶ, ὅτι
ὁ νόμος κυριεύει τοῦ ἀνθρώπου ἐφ'
ὅσον χρόνον ζῇ; ² ἡ γὰρ ὕπανδρος
γυνὴ τῷ ζῶντι ἀνδρὶ δέδεται νόμῳ·
ἐὰν δὲ ἀποθάνῃ ὁ ἀνήρ, κατήργηται
ἀπὸ τοῦ νόμου τοῦ ἀνδρός. ³ ἄρα
οὖν ζῶντος τοῦ ἀνδρὸς μοιχαλὶς
χρηματίσει ἐὰν γένηται ἀνδρὶ
ἑτέρῳ· ἐὰν δὲ ἀποθάνῃ ὁ ἀνήρ,
ἐλευθέρα ἐστὶν ἀπὸ τοῦ νόμου, τοῦ
μὴ εἶναι αὐτὴν μοιχαλίδα γενομένην
ἀνδρὶ ἑτέρῳ. ⁴ ὥστε, ἀδελφοί μου,
καὶ ὑμεῖς ἐθανατώθητε τῷ νόμῳ διὰ
τοῦ σώματος τοῦ Χριστοῦ, εἰς τὸ
γενέσθαι ὑμᾶς ἑτέρῳ, τῷ ἐκ νεκρῶν
ἐγερθέντι, ἵνα καρποφορήσωμεν τῷ
θεῷ. ⁵ ὅτε γὰρ ἦμεν ἐν τῇ σαρκί,

τὰ παθήματα τῶν ἁμαρτιῶν τὰ διὰ
τοῦ νόμου ἐνηργεῖτο ἐν τοῖς μέλεσιν
ἡμῶν εἰς τὸ καρποφορῆσαι τῷ
θανάτῳ· [6] νυνὶ δὲ κατηργήθημεν
ἀπὸ τοῦ νόμου, ἀποθανόντες ἐν ᾧ
κατειχόμεθα, ὥστε δουλεύειν ἡμᾶς
ἐν καινότητι πνεύματος καὶ οὐ
παλαιότητι γράμματος.

Rom 10:5–13 Μωϋσῆς γὰρ γράφει
τὴν δικαιοσύνην τὴν ἐκ [τοῦ] νόμου
ὅτι ὁ ποιήσας αὐτὰ ἄνθρωπος
ζήσεται ἐν αὐτοῖς. [6] ἡ δὲ ἐκ
πίστεως δικαιοσύνη οὕτως λέγει,
μὴ εἴπῃς ἐν τῇ καρδίᾳ σου, Τίς
ἀναβήσεται εἰς τὸν οὐρανόν; τοῦτ'
ἔστιν Χριστὸν καταγαγεῖν· [7] ἤ· τίς
καταβήσεται εἰς τὴν ἄβυσσον; τοῦτ'
ἔστιν Χριστὸν ἐκ νεκρῶν
ἀναγαγεῖν. [8] ἀλλὰ τί λέγει; ἐγγύς
σου τὸ ῥῆμά ἐστιν, ἐν τῷ στόματί
σου καὶ ἐν τῇ καρδίᾳ σου· τοῦτ'
ἔστιν τὸ ῥῆμα τῆς πίστεως ὃ
κηρύσσομεν. [9] ὅτι ἐὰν ὁμολογήσῃς
ἐν τῷ στόματί σου κύριον Ἰησοῦν,
καὶ πιστεύσῃς ἐν τῇ καρδίᾳ σου
ὅτι ὁ θεὸς αὐτὸν ἤγειρεν ἐκ
νεκρῶν, σωθήσῃ· [10] καρδίᾳ γὰρ
πιστεύεται εἰς δικαιοσύνην, στόματι
δὲ ὁμολογεῖται εἰς σωτηρίαν.
[11] λέγει γὰρ ἡ γραφή, πᾶς ὁ
πιστεύων ἐπ' αὐτῷ οὐ
καταισχυνθήσεται. [12] οὐ γάρ ἐστιν
διαστολὴ Ἰουδαίου τε καὶ
Ἕλληνος, ὁ γὰρ αὐτὸς κύριος
πάντων, πλουτῶν εἰς πάντας τοὺς
ἐπικαλουμένους αὐτόν· [13]πᾶς γὰρ
ὃς ἂν ἐπικαλέσηται τὸ ὄνομα
κυρίου σωθήσεται.

[13] Χριστὸς ἡμᾶς ἐξηγόρασεν ἐκ τῆς
κατάρας τοῦ νόμου γενόμενος ὑπὲρ
ἡμῶν κατάρα, ὅτι γέγραπται,
ἐπικατάρατος πᾶς ὁ κρεμάμενος ἐπὶ
ξύλου, [14] ἵνα εἰς τὰ ἔθνη ἡ εὐλογία
τοῦ Ἀβραὰμ γένηται ἐν Χριστῷ
Ἰησοῦ, ἵνα τὴν ἐπαγγελίαν τοῦ
πνεύματος λάβωμεν διὰ τῆς
πίστεως. [15] ἀδελφοί, κατὰ
ἄνθρωπον λέγω· ὅμως ἀνθρώπου

Rom 15:8–9a λέγω γὰρ Χριστὸν
διάκονον γεγενῆσθαι περιτομῆς
ὑπὲρ ἀληθείας θεοῦ, εἰς τὸ
βεβαιῶσαι τὰς ἐπαγγελίας τῶν
πατέρων, [9] τὰ δὲ ἔθνη ὑπὲρ ἐλέους
δοξάσαι τὸν θεόν.

Rom 5:20 νόμος δὲ παρεισῆλθεν ἵνα
πλεονάσῃ τὸ παράπτωμα.

κεκυρωμένην διαθήκην οὐδεὶς ἀθετεῖ ἢ ἐπιδιατάσσεται. ¹⁶ τῷ δὲ Ἀβραὰμ ἐρρέθησαν αἱ ἐπαγγελίαι καὶ τῷ σπέρματι αὐτοῦ. οὐ λέγει, καὶ τοῖς σπέρμασιν, ὡς ἐπὶ πολλῶν, ἀλλ᾽ ὡς ἐφ᾽ ἑνός, καὶ τῷ σπέρματί σου, ὅς ἐστιν Χριστός. ¹⁷ τοῦτο δὲ λέγω· διαθήκην προκεκυρωμένην ὑπὸ τοῦ θεοῦ ὁ μετὰ τετρακόσια καὶ τριάκοντα ἔτη γεγονὼς νόμος οὐκ ἀκυροῖ, εἰς τὸ καταργῆσαι τὴν ἐπαγγελίαν.

¹⁸ εἰ γὰρ ἐκ νόμου ἡ κληρονομία, οὐκέτι ἐξ ἐπαγγελίας· τῷ δὲ Ἀβραὰμ δι᾽ ἐπαγγελίας κεχάρισται ὁ θεός. ¹⁹ τί οὖν ὁ νόμος; τῶν παραβάσεων χάριν προσετέθη, ἄχρις οὗ ἔλθῃ τὸ σπέρμα ᾧ ἐπήγγελται, διαταγεὶς δι᾽ ἀγγέλων ἐν χειρὶ μεσίτου.

Rom 15:8–9a λέγω γὰρ Χριστὸν διάκονον γεγενῆσθαι περιτομῆς ὑπὲρ ἀληθείας θεοῦ, εἰς τὸ βεβαιῶσαι τὰς ἐπαγγελίας τῶν πατέρων, ⁹ τὰ δὲ ἔθνη ὑπὲρ ἐλέους δοξάσαι τὸν θεόν.

Rom 4:9 Ὁ μακαρισμὸς οὖν οὗτος ἐπὶ τὴν περιτομὴν ἢ καὶ ἐπὶ τὴν ἀκροβυστίαν; λέγομεν γάρ· ἐλογίσθη τῷ Ἀβραὰμ ἡ πίστις εἰς δικαιοσύνην.

Rom 4:13, 16–18 ¹³ οὐ γὰρ διὰ νόμου ἡ ἐπαγγελία τῷ Ἀβραὰμ ἢ τῷ σπέρματι αὐτοῦ, τὸ κληρονόμον αὐτὸν εἶναι κόσμου, ἀλλὰ διὰ δικαιοσύνης πίστεως· . . . ¹⁶ διὰ τοῦτο ἐκ πίστεως, ἵνα κατὰ χάριν, εἰς τὸ εἶναι βεβαίαν τὴν ἐπαγγελίαν παντὶ τῷ σπέρματι, οὐ τῷ ἐκ τοῦ νόμου μόνον ἀλλὰ καὶ τῷ ἐκ πίστεως Ἀβραάμ, ὅς ἐστιν πατὴρ πάντων ἡμῶν, ¹⁷ καθὼς γέγραπται ὅτι πατέρα πολλῶν ἐθνῶν τέθεικά σε, κατέναντι οὗ ἐπίστευσεν θεοῦ τοῦ ζωοποιοῦντος τοὺς νεκροὺς καὶ καλοῦντος τὰ μὴ ὄντα ὡς ὄντα· ¹⁸ ὃς παρ᾽ ἐλπίδα ἐπ᾽ ἐλπίδι ἐπίστευσεν εἰς τὸ γενέσθαι αὐτὸν πατέρα πολλῶν ἐθνῶν κατὰ τὸ εἰρημένον, οὕτως ἔσται τὸ σπέρμα σου.

Rom 9:32a–b διὰ τί; ὅτι οὐκ ἐκ πίστεως ἀλλ᾽ ὡς ἐξ ἔργων.

Rom 4:14 εἰ γὰρ οἱ ἐκ νόμου κληρονόμοι, κεκένωται ἡ πίστις καὶ κατήργηται ἡ ἐπαγγελία.

Rom 4:15 ὁ γὰρ νόμος ὀργὴν κατεργάζεται· οὗ δὲ οὐκ ἔστιν νόμος, οὐδὲ παράβασις.

Rom 7:7–10 τί οὖν ἐροῦμεν; ὁ νόμος ἁμαρτία; μὴ γένοιτο· ἀλλὰ τὴν ἁμαρτίαν οὐκ ἔγνων εἰ μὴ διὰ νόμου, τήν τε γὰρ ἐπιθυμίαν οὐκ ᾔδειν εἰ μὴ ὁ νόμος ἔλεγεν, οὐκ ἐπιθυμήσεις. ⁸ ἀφορμὴν δὲ λαβοῦσα ἡ ἁμαρτία διὰ τῆς ἐντολῆς κατειργάσατο ἐν ἐμοὶ πᾶσαν ἐπιθυμίαν· χωρὶς γὰρ νόμου ἁμαρτία νεκρά. ⁹ ἐγὼ δὲ ἔζων χωρὶς νόμου

²⁰ ὁ δὲ μεσίτης ἑνὸς οὐκ ἔστιν, ὁ δὲ θεὸς εἷς ἐστιν. ²¹ ὁ οὖν νόμος κατὰ τῶν ἐπαγγελιῶν [τοῦ θεοῦ]; μὴ γένοιτο· εἰ γὰρ ἐδόθη νόμος ὁ δυνάμενος ζῳοποιῆσαι, ὄντως ἐκ νόμου ἂν ἦν ἡ δικαιοσύνη.

²² ἀλλὰ συνέκλεισεν ἡ γραφὴ τὰ πάντα ὑπὸ ἁμαρτίαν ἵνα ἡ ἐπαγγελία ἐκ πίστεως Ἰησοῦ Χριστοῦ δοθῇ τοῖς πιστεύουσιν. ²³πρὸ τοῦ δὲ ἐλθεῖν τὴν πίστιν ὑπὸ νόμον ἐφρουρούμεθα συγκλειόμενοι εἰς τὴν μέλλουσαν πίστιν ἀποκαλυφθῆναι. ²⁴ ὥστε ὁ νόμος παιδαγωγὸς ἡμῶν γέγονεν εἰς Χριστόν, ἵνα ἐκ πίστεως δικαιωθῶμεν· ²⁵ ἐλθούσης δὲ τῆς πίστεως οὐκέτι ὑπὸ παιδαγωγόν ἐσμεν.

ποτέ· ἐλθούσης δὲ τῆς ἐντολῆς ἡ ἁμαρτία ἀνέζησεν, ¹⁰ ἐγὼ δὲ ἀπέθανον, καὶ εὑρέθη μοι ἡ ἐντολὴ ἡ εἰς ζωὴν αὕτη εἰς θάνατον.

Rom 3:31 νόμον οὖν καταργοῦμεν διὰ τῆς πίστεως; μὴ γένοιτο, ἀλλὰ νόμον ἱστάνομεν.

Rom 8:3–4 τὸ γὰρ ἀδύνατον τοῦ νόμου, ἐν ᾧ ἠσθένει διὰ τῆς σαρκός, ὁ θεὸς τὸν ἑαυτοῦ υἱὸν πέμψας ἐν ὁμοιώματι σαρκὸς ἁμαρτίας καὶ περὶ ἁμαρτίας κατέκρινεν τὴν ἁμαρτίαν ἐν τῇ σαρκί, ⁴ ἵνα τὸ δικαίωμα τοῦ νόμου πληρωθῇ ἐν ἡμῖν τοῖς μὴ κατὰ σάρκα περιπατοῦσιν ἀλλὰ κατὰ πνεῦμα.

Rom 7:1–6 Ἢ ἀγνοεῖτε, ἀδελφοί, γινώσκουσιν γὰρ νόμον λαλῶ, ὅτι ὁ νόμος κυριεύει τοῦ ἀνθρώπου ἐφ' ὅσον χρόνον ζῇ; ² ἡ γὰρ ὕπανδρος γυνὴ τῷ ζῶντι ἀνδρὶ δέδεται νόμῳ· ἐὰν δὲ ἀποθάνῃ ὁ ἀνήρ, κατήργηται ἀπὸ τοῦ νόμου τοῦ ἀνδρός. ³ ἄρα οὖν ζῶντος τοῦ ἀνδρὸς μοιχαλὶς χρηματίσει ἐὰν γένηται ἀνδρὶ ἑτέρῳ· ἐὰν δὲ ἀποθάνῃ ὁ ἀνήρ, ἐλευθέρα ἐστὶν ἀπὸ τοῦ νόμου, τοῦ μὴ εἶναι αὐτὴν μοιχαλίδα γενομένην ἀνδρὶ ἑτέρῳ. ⁴ ὥστε, ἀδελφοί μου, καὶ ὑμεῖς ἐθανατώθητε τῷ νόμῳ διὰ τοῦ σώματος τοῦ Χριστοῦ, εἰς τὸ γενέσθαι ὑμᾶς ἑτέρῳ, τῷ ἐκ νεκρῶν ἐγερθέντι, ἵνα καρποφορήσωμεν τῷ θεῷ. ⁵ ὅτε γὰρ ἦμεν ἐν τῇ σαρκί, τὰ παθήματα τῶν ἁμαρτιῶν τὰ διὰ τοῦ νόμου ἐνηργεῖτο ἐν τοῖς μέλεσιν ἡμῶν εἰς τὸ καρποφορῆσαι τῷ θανάτῳ· ⁶ νυνὶ δὲ κατηργήθημεν ἀπὸ τοῦ νόμου, ἀποθανόντες ἐν ᾧ κατειχόμεθα, ὥστε δουλεύειν ἡμᾶς ἐν καινότητι πνεύματος καὶ οὐ παλαιότητι γράμματος.

²⁶ Πάντες γὰρ υἱοὶ θεοῦ ἐστε διὰ τῆς πίστεως ἐν Χριστῷ Ἰησοῦ. ²⁷ ὅσοι γὰρ εἰς Χριστὸν ἐβαπτίσθητε, Χριστὸν ἐνεδύσασθε.

Rom 8:16 αὐτὸ τὸ πνεῦμα συμμαρτυρεῖ τῷ πνεύματι ἡμῶν ὅτι ἐσμὲν τέκνα θεοῦ.

Rom 6:3–10 ἢ ἀγνοεῖτε ὅτι ὅσοι ἐβαπτίσθημεν εἰς Χριστὸν Ἰησοῦν εἰς τὸν θάνατον αὐτοῦ ἐβαπτίσθημεν; ⁴ συνετάφημεν οὖν αὐτῷ διὰ τοῦ βαπτίσματος εἰς τὸν θάνατον, ἵνα ὥσπερ ἠγέρθη Χριστὸς ἐκ νεκρῶν διὰ τῆς δόξης τοῦ πατρός, οὕτως καὶ ἡμεῖς ἐν καινότητι ζωῆς περιπατήσωμεν. ⁵ εἰ γὰρ σύμφυτοι γεγόναμεν τῷ ὁμοιώματι τοῦ θανάτου αὐτοῦ, ἀλλὰ καὶ τῆς ἀναστάσεως ἐσόμεθα· ⁶ τοῦτο γινώσκοντες, ὅτι ὁ παλαιὸς ἡμῶν ἄνθρωπος συνεσταυρώθη, ἵνα καταργηθῇ τὸ σῶμα τῆς ἁμαρτίας, τοῦ μηκέτι δουλεύειν ἡμᾶς τῇ ἁμαρτίᾳ· ⁷ ὁ γὰρ ἀποθανὼν δεδικαίωται ἀπὸ τῆς ἁμαρτίας. ⁸ εἰ δὲ ἀπεθάνομεν σὺν Χριστῷ, πιστεύομεν ὅτι καὶ συζήσομεν αὐτῷ· ⁹ εἰδότες ὅτι Χριστὸς ἐγερθεὶς ἐκ νεκρῶν οὐκέτι ἀποθνήσκει, θάνατος αὐτοῦ οὐκέτι κυριεύει. ¹⁰ ὃ γὰρ ἀπέθανεν, τῇ ἁμαρτίᾳ ἀπέθανεν ἐφάπαξ· ὃ δὲ ζῇ, ζῇ τῷ θεῷ.

²⁸ οὐκ ἔνι Ἰουδαῖος οὐδὲ Ἕλλην, οὐκ ἔνι δοῦλος οὐδὲ ἐλεύθερος, οὐκ ἔνι ἄρσεν καὶ θῆλυ· πάντες γὰρ ὑμεῖς εἷς ἐστε ἐν Χριστῷ Ἰησοῦ. ²⁹ εἰ δὲ ὑμεῖς Χριστοῦ, ἄρα τοῦ Ἀβραὰμ σπέρμα ἐστέ, κατ᾽ ἐπαγγελίαν κληρονόμοι.

Rom 3:22 δικαιοσύνη δὲ θεοῦ διὰ πίστεως Ἰησοῦ Χριστοῦ, εἰς πάντας τοὺς πιστεύοντας· οὐ γάρ ἐστιν διαστολή·

Rom 4:23–25 οὐκ ἐγράφη δὲ δι᾽ αὐτὸν μόνον ὅτι ἐλογίσθη αὐτῷ, ²⁴ ἀλλὰ καὶ δι᾽ ἡμᾶς οἷς μέλλει λογίζεσθαι, τοῖς πιστεύουσιν ἐπὶ τὸν ἐγείραντα Ἰησοῦν τὸν κύριον ἡμῶν ἐκ νεκρῶν, ²⁵ ὃς παρεδόθη διὰ τὰ παραπτώματα ἡμῶν καὶ ἠγέρθη διὰ τὴν δικαίωσιν ἡμῶν.

5. Gal 4:1–7 Λέγω δέ, ἐφ᾽ ὅσον χρόνον ὁ κληρονόμος νήπιός ἐστιν, οὐδὲν διαφέρει δούλου κύριος πάντων ὤν, ² ἀλλὰ ὑπὸ ἐπιτρόπους ἐστὶν καὶ οἰκονόμους ἄχρι τῆς προθεσμίας τοῦ πατρός. ³ οὕτως καὶ ἡμεῖς, ὅτε ἦμεν νήπιοι, ὑπὸ τὰ

Rom 7:1–6 Ἢ ἀγνοεῖτε, ἀδελφοί, γινώσκουσιν γὰρ νόμον λαλῶ, ὅτι ὁ νόμος κυριεύει τοῦ ἀνθρώπου ἐφ᾽ ὅσον χρόνον ζῇ; ² ἡ γὰρ ὕπανδρος γυνὴ τῷ ζῶντι ἀνδρὶ δέδεται νόμῳ· ἐὰν δὲ ἀποθάνῃ ὁ ἀνήρ, κατήργηται ἀπὸ τοῦ νόμου τοῦ ἀνδρός. ³ ἄρα οὖν ζῶντος τοῦ ἀνδρὸς μοιχαλὶς

στοιχεῖα τοῦ κόσμου ἦμεθα
δεδουλωμένοι·

χρηματίσει ἐὰν γένηται ἀνδρὶ ἑτέρῳ·
ἐὰν δὲ ἀποθάνῃ ὁ ἀνήρ, ἐλευθέρα
ἐστὶν ἀπὸ τοῦ νόμου, τοῦ μὴ εἶναι
αὐτὴν μοιχαλίδα γενομένην ἀνδρὶ
ἑτέρῳ. ⁴ ὥστε, ἀδελφοί μου, καὶ
ὑμεῖς ἐθανατώθητε τῷ νόμῳ διὰ τοῦ
σώματος τοῦ Χριστοῦ, εἰς τὸ
γενέσθαι ὑμᾶς ἑτέρῳ, τῷ ἐκ νεκρῶν
ἐγερθέντι, ἵνα καρποφορήσωμεν τῷ
θεῷ. ⁵ ὅτε γὰρ ἦμεν ἐν τῇ σαρκί,
τὰ παθήματα τῶν ἁμαρτιῶν τὰ διὰ
τοῦ νόμου ἐνηργεῖτο ἐν τοῖς
μέλεσιν ἡμῶν εἰς τὸ καρποφορῆσαι
τῷ θανάτῳ· ⁶ νυνὶ δὲ κατηργήθημεν
ἀπὸ τοῦ νόμου, ἀποθανόντες ἐν ᾧ
κατειχόμεθα, ὥστε δουλεύειν ἡμᾶς
ἐν καινότητι πνεύματος καὶ οὐ
παλαιότητι γράμματος.

⁴ ὅτε δὲ ἦλθεν τὸ πλήρωμα τοῦ
χρόνου, ἐξαπέστειλεν ὁ θεὸς τὸν
υἱὸν αὐτοῦ, γενόμενον ἐκ γυναικός,
γενόμενον ὑπὸ νόμον, ⁵ ἵνα τοὺς
ὑπὸ νόμον ἐξαγοράσῃ, ἵνα τὴν
υἱοθεσίαν ἀπολάβωμεν (cf. 4:8,
which shows that he has the
gentiles in mind) ἀλλὰ τότε μὲν
οὐκ εἰδότες θεὸν ἐδουλεύσατε τοῖς
φύσει μὴ οὖσιν θεοῖς (γενόμενον
ὑπὸ νόμον in Gal 4:4 is formulated as διάκονον γεγενῆσθαι
περιτομῆς in Rom 15:8.)
⁶ ὅτι δέ ἐστε υἱοί, ἐξαπέστειλεν ὁ θεὸς
τὸ πνεῦμα τοῦ υἱοῦ αὐτοῦ εἰς τὰς
καρδίας ἡμῶν, κρᾶζον, αββα ὁ
πατήρ. ⁷ ὥστε οὐκέτι εἶ δοῦλος
ἀλλὰ υἱός· εἰ δὲ υἱός, καὶ κληρονόμος διὰ θεοῦ.

Rom 15:8–9a λέγω γὰρ Χριστὸν
διάκονον γεγενῆσθαι περιτομῆς
ὑπὲρ ἀληθείας θεοῦ, εἰς τὸ
βεβαιῶσαι τὰς ἐπαγγελίας τῶν
πατέρων, ⁹ τὰ δὲ ἔθνη ὑπὲρ ἐλέους
δοξάσαι τὸν θεόν.

Rom 8:15–17 οὐ γὰρ ἐλάβετε πνεῦμα
δουλείας πάλιν εἰς φόβον, ἀλλὰ
ἐλάβετε πνεῦμα υἱοθεσίας, ἐν ᾧ
κράζομεν, αββα ὁ πατήρ· ¹⁶ αὐτὸ τὸ
πνεῦμα συμμαρτυρεῖ τῷ πνεύματι
ἡμῶν ὅτι ἐσμὲν τέκνα θεοῦ. ¹⁷ εἰ δὲ
τέκνα, καὶ κληρονόμοι· κληρονόμοι
μὲν θεοῦ, συγκληρονόμοι δὲ Χριστοῦ,
εἴπερ συμπάσχομεν ἵνα καὶ
συνδοξασθῶμεν.

⁸ Ἀλλὰ τότε μὲν οὐκ εἰδότες θεὸν
ἐδουλεύσατε τοῖς φύσει μὴ οὖσιν
θεοῖς· ⁹ νῦν δὲ γνόντες θεόν,
μᾶλλον δὲ γνωσθέντες ὑπὸ θεοῦ,
πῶς ἐπιστρέφετε πάλιν ἐπὶ τὰ
ἀσθενῆ καὶ πτωχὰ στοιχεῖα, οἷς
πάλιν ἄνωθεν δουλεύειν θέλετε;

Rom 1:25 οἵτινες μετήλλαξαν τὴν
ἀλήθειαν τοῦ θεοῦ ἐν τῷ ψεύδει,
καὶ ἐσεβάσθησαν καὶ ἐλάτρευσαν
τῇ κτίσει παρὰ τὸν κτίσαντα, ὅς
ἐστιν εὐλογητὸς εἰς τοὺς αἰῶνας·
ἀμήν.

Rom 6:16–23 οὐκ οἴδατε ὅτι ᾧ
παριστάνετε ἑαυτοὺς δούλους εἰς

¹⁰ ἡμέρας παρατηρεῖσθε καὶ μῆνας
καὶ καιροὺς καὶ ἐνιαυτούς.

ὑπακοήν, δοῦλοί ἐστε ᾧ ὑπακούετε,
ἤτοι ἁμαρτίας εἰς θάνατον ἢ ὑπακοῆς
εἰς δικαιοσύνην; ¹⁷ χάρις δὲ τῷ θεῷ
ὅτι ἦτε δοῦλοι τῆς ἁμαρτίας
ὑπηκούσατε δὲ ἐκ καρδίας εἰς ὃν
παρεδόθητε τύπον διδαχῆς,
¹⁸ ἐλευθερωθέντες δὲ ἀπὸ τῆς
ἁμαρτίας ἐδουλώθητε τῇ
δικαιοσύνῃ· ¹⁹ ἀνθρώπινον λέγω
διὰ τὴν ἀσθένειαν τῆς σαρκὸς
ὑμῶν. ὥσπερ γὰρ παρεστήσατε τὰ
μέλη ὑμῶν δοῦλα τῇ ἀκαθαρσίᾳ καὶ
τῇ ἀνομίᾳ εἰς τὴν ἀνομίαν, οὕτως
νῦν παραστήσατε τὰ μέλη ὑμῶν
δοῦλα τῇ δικαιοσύνῃ εἰς ἁγιασμόν.
²⁰ ὅτε γὰρ δοῦλοι ἦτε τῆς
ἁμαρτίας, ἐλεύθεροι ἦτε τῇ
δικαιοσύνῃ. ²¹ τίνα οὖν καρπὸν
εἴχετε τότε ἐφ' οἷς νῦν
ἐπαισχύνεσθε; τὸ γὰρ τέλος
ἐκείνων θάνατος. ²² νυνὶ δέ,
ἐλευθερωθέντες ἀπὸ τῆς ἁμαρτίας
δουλωθέντες δὲ τῷ θεῷ, ἔχετε τὸν
καρπὸν ὑμῶν εἰς ἁγιασμόν, τὸ δὲ
τέλος ζωὴν αἰώνιον. ²³ τὰ γὰρ
ὀψώνια τῆς ἁμαρτίας θάνατος, τὸ
δὲ χάρισμα τοῦ θεοῦ ζωὴ αἰώνιος
ἐν Χριστῷ Ἰησοῦ τῷ κυρίῳ ἡμῶν.

Rom 7:4–6 ὥστε, ἀδελφοί μου, καὶ
ὑμεῖς ἐθανατώθητε τῷ νόμῳ διὰ τοῦ
σώματος τοῦ Χριστοῦ, εἰς τὸ
γενέσθαι ὑμᾶς ἑτέρῳ, τῷ ἐκ νεκρῶν
ἐγερθέντι, ἵνα καρποφορήσωμεν τῷ
θεῷ. ⁵ ὅτε γὰρ ἦμεν ἐν τῇ σαρκί,
τὰ παθήματα τῶν ἁμαρτιῶν τὰ διὰ
τοῦ νόμου ἐνηργεῖτο ἐν τοῖς
μέλεσιν ἡμῶν εἰς τὸ καρποφορῆσαι
τῷ θανάτῳ· ⁶ νυνὶ δὲ κατηργήθημεν
ἀπὸ τοῦ νόμου, ἀποθανόντες ἐν ᾧ
κατειχόμεθα, ὥστε δουλεύειν ἡμᾶς
ἐν καινότητι πνεύματος καὶ οὐ
παλαιότητι γράμματος.

Gal 4:11–20 (Specific to the Galatian situation)

6. Gal 4:21–31 Λέγετέ μοι, οἱ ὑπὸ
νόμον θέλοντες εἶναι, τὸν νόμον

Rom 7:1–6 Ἢ ἀγνοεῖτε, ἀδελφοί,
γινώσκουσιν γὰρ νόμον λαλῶ, ὅτι

οὐκ ἀκούετε; ²² γέγραπται γὰρ ὅτι Ἀβραὰμ δύο υἱοὺς ἔσχεν, ἕνα ἐκ τῆς παιδίσκης καὶ ἕνα ἐκ τῆς ἐλευθέρας. ²³ ἀλλ' ὁ μὲν ἐκ τῆς παιδίσκης κατὰ σάρκα γεγέννηται, ὁ δὲ ἐκ τῆς ἐλευθέρας δι' ἐπαγγελίας. ²⁴ ἅτινά ἐστιν ἀλληγορούμενα· αὗται γάρ εἰσιν δύο διαθῆκαι, μία μὲν ἀπὸ ὄρους Σινᾶ, εἰς δουλείαν γεννῶσα, ἥτις ἐστὶν Ἁγάρ. ²⁵ τὸ δὲ Ἁγὰρ Σινᾶ ὄρος ἐστὶν ἐν τῇ Ἀραβίᾳ, συστοιχεῖ δὲ τῇ νῦν Ἰερουσαλήμ, δουλεύει γὰρ μετὰ τῶν τέκνων αὐτῆς. ²⁶ ἡ δὲ ἄνω Ἰερουσαλὴμ ἐλευθέρα ἐστίν, ἥτις ἐστὶν μήτηρ ἡμῶν· ²⁷ γέγραπται γάρ, εὐφράνθητι στεῖρα ἡ οὐ τίκτουσα· ῥῆξον καὶ βόησον, ἡ οὐκ ὠδίνουσα· ὅτι πολλὰ τὰ τέκνα τῆς ἐρήμου μᾶλλον ἢ τῆς ἐχούσης τὸν ἄνδρα. ²⁸ ὑμεῖς δέ, ἀδελφοί, κατὰ Ἰσαὰκ ἐπαγγελίας τέκνα ἐστέ. ²⁹ ἀλλ' ὥσπερ τότε ὁ κατὰ σάρκα γεννηθεὶς ἐδίωκεν τὸν κατὰ πνεῦμα, οὕτως καὶ νῦν. ³⁰ ἀλλὰ τί λέγει ἡ γραφή; ἔκβαλε τὴν παιδίσκην καὶ τὸν υἱὸν αὐτῆς, οὐ γὰρ μὴ κληρονομήσει ὁ υἱὸς τῆς παιδίσκης μετὰ τοῦ υἱοῦ τῆς ἐλευθέρας. ³¹ διό, ἀδελφοί, οὐκ ἐσμὲν παιδίσκης τέκνα ἀλλὰ τῆς ἐλευθέρας.

7. Gal 5:1–6 τῇ ἐλευθερίᾳ ἡμᾶς Χριστὸς ἠλευθέρωσεν· στήκετε οὖν καὶ μὴ πάλιν ζυγῷ δουλείας ἐνέχεσθε.

ὁ νόμος κυριεύει τοῦ ἀνθρώπου ἐφ' ὅσον χρόνον ζῇ; ² ἡ γὰρ ὕπανδρος γυνὴ τῷ ζῶντι ἀνδρὶ δέδεται νόμῳ· ἐὰν δὲ ἀποθάνῃ ὁ ἀνήρ, κατήργηται ἀπὸ τοῦ νόμου τοῦ ἀνδρός. ³ ἄρα οὖν ζῶντος τοῦ ἀνδρὸς μοιχαλὶς χρηματίσει ἐὰν γένηται ἀνδρὶ ἑτέρῳ· ἐὰν δὲ ἀποθάνῃ ὁ ἀνήρ, ἐλευθέρα ἐστὶν ἀπὸ τοῦ νόμου, τοῦ μὴ εἶναι αὐτὴν μοιχαλίδα γενομένην ἀνδρὶ ἑτέρῳ. ⁴ ὥστε, ἀδελφοί μου, καὶ ὑμεῖς ἐθανατώθητε τῷ νόμῳ διὰ τοῦ σώματος τοῦ Χριστοῦ, εἰς τὸ γενέσθαι ὑμᾶς ἑτέρῳ, τῷ ἐκ νεκρῶν ἐγερθέντι, ἵνα καρποφορήσωμεν τῷ θεῷ. ⁵ ὅτε γὰρ ἦμεν ἐν τῇ σαρκί, τὰ παθήματα τῶν ἁμαρτιῶν τὰ διὰ τοῦ νόμου ἐνηργεῖτο ἐν τοῖς μέλεσιν ἡμῶν εἰς τὸ καρποφορῆσαι τῷ θανάτῳ· ⁶ νυνὶ δὲ κατηργήθημεν ἀπὸ τοῦ νόμου, ἀποθανόντες ἐν ᾧ κατειχόμεθα, ὥστε δουλεύειν ἡμᾶς ἐν καινότητι πνεύματος καὶ οὐ παλαιότητι γράμματος.

Rom 6:16–23 οὐκ οἴδατε ὅτι ᾧ παριστάνετε ἑαυτοὺς δούλους εἰς ὑπακοήν, δοῦλοί ἐστε ᾧ ὑπακούετε, ἤτοι ἁμαρτίας εἰς θάνατον ἢ ὑπακοῆς εἰς δικαιοσύνην; ¹⁷ χάρις δὲ τῷ θεῷ ὅτι ἦτε δοῦλοι τῆς ἁμαρτίας ὑπηκούσατε δὲ ἐκ καρδίας εἰς ὃν παρεδόθητε τύπον διδαχῆς, ¹⁸ ἐλευθερωθέντες δὲ ἀπὸ τῆς ἁμαρτίας ἐδουλώθητε τῇ δικαιοσύνῃ· ¹⁹ ἀνθρώπινον λέγω διὰ τὴν ἀσθένειαν τῆς σαρκὸς ὑμῶν. ὥσπερ γὰρ παρεστήσατε τὰ μέλη ὑμῶν δοῦλα τῇ ἀκαθαρσίᾳ καὶ τῇ ἀνομίᾳ εἰς τὴν ἀνομίαν, οὕτως νῦν παραστήσατε τὰ μέλη ὑμῶν δοῦλα τῇ δικαιοσύνῃ εἰς ἁγιασμόν. ²⁰ ὅτε γὰρ δοῦλοι ἦτε τῆς ἁμαρτίας, ἐλεύθεροι ἦτε τῇ δικαιοσύνῃ. ²¹ τίνα οὖν καρπὸν εἴχετε τότε ἐφ' οἷς νῦν ἐπαισχύνεσθε; τὸ γὰρ τέλος ἐκείνων θάνατος. ²² νυνὶ δέ, ἐλευθερωθέντες ἀπὸ τῆς ἁμαρτίας δουλωθέντες δὲ τῷ θεῷ, ἔχετε τὸν καρπὸν ὑμῶν εἰς ἁγιασμόν, τὸ δὲ τέλος ζωὴν αἰώνιον. ²³ τὰ γὰρ ὀψώνια τῆς ἁμαρτίας θάνατος, τὸ δὲ χάρισμα τοῦ θεοῦ ζωὴ αἰώνιος ἐν Χριστῷ Ἰησοῦ τῷ κυρίῳ ἡμῶν.

Rom 7:4–6 ὥστε, ἀδελφοί μου, καὶ ὑμεῖς ἐθανατώθητε τῷ νόμῳ διὰ τοῦ σώματος τοῦ Χριστοῦ, εἰς τὸ γενέσθαι ὑμᾶς ἑτέρῳ, τῷ ἐκ νεκρῶν ἐγερθέντι, ἵνα καρποφορήσωμεν τῷ θεῷ. ⁵ ὅτε γὰρ ἦμεν ἐν τῇ σαρκί, τὰ παθήματα τῶν ἁμαρτιῶν τὰ διὰ τοῦ νόμου ἐνηργεῖτο ἐν τοῖς μέλεσιν ἡμῶν εἰς τὸ καρποφορῆσαι τῷ θανάτῳ· ⁶ νυνὶ δὲ κατηργήθημεν ἀπὸ τοῦ νόμου, ἀποθανόντες ἐν ᾧ κατειχόμεθα, ὥστε δουλεύειν ἡμᾶς ἐν καινότητι πνεύματος καὶ οὐ παλαιότητι γράμματος.

² Ἴδε ἐγὼ Παῦλος λέγω ὑμῖν ὅτι ἐὰν περιτέμνησθε Χριστὸς ὑμᾶς οὐδὲν ὠφελήσει. ³ μαρτύρομαι δὲ πάλιν παντὶ ἀνθρώπῳ περιτεμνομένῳ ὅτι ὀφειλέτης ἐστὶν ὅλον τὸν νόμον ποιῆσαι. ⁴ κατηργήθητε ἀπὸ Χριστοῦ οἵτινες ἐν νόμῳ δικαιοῦσθε, τῆς χάριτος ἐξεπέσατε. ⁵ ἡμεῖς γὰρ πνεύματι ἐκ πίστεως ἐλπίδα δικαιοσύνης ἀπεκδεχόμεθα. ⁶ ἐν γὰρ Χριστῷ Ἰησοῦ οὔτε περιτομή τι ἰσχύει οὔτε ἀκροβυστία, ἀλλὰ πίστις δι' ἀγάπης ἐνεργουμένη.

8. Gal 5:13 Ὑμεῖς γὰρ ἐπ' ἐλευθερίᾳ ἐκλήθητε, ἀδελφοί· μόνον μὴ τὴν ἐλευθερίαν εἰς ἀφορμὴν τῇ σαρκί,

Rom 4:14 εἰ γὰρ οἱ ἐκ νόμου κληρονόμοι, κεκένωται ἡ πίστις καὶ κατήργηται ἡ ἐπαγγελία.

Rom 2:25 περιτομὴ μὲν γὰρ ὠφελεῖ ἐὰν νόμον πράσσῃς· ἐὰν δὲ παραβάτης νόμου ᾖς, ἡ περιτομή σου ἀκροβυστία γέγονεν.

Rom 8:24 τῇ γὰρ ἐλπίδι ἐσώθημεν· ἐλπὶς δὲ βλεπομένη οὐκ ἔστιν ἐλπίς· ὃ γὰρ βλέπει τίς ἐλπίζει;

Rom 4:16 διὰ τοῦτο ἐκ πίστεως, ἵνα κατὰ χάριν, εἰς τὸ εἶναι βεβαίαν τὴν ἐπαγγελίαν παντὶ τῷ σπέρματι, οὐ τῷ ἐκ τοῦ νόμου μόνον ἀλλὰ καὶ τῷ ἐκ πίστεως Ἀβραάμ, ὅς ἐστιν πατὴρ πάντων ἡμῶν.

Rom 6:1–2 τί οὖν ἐροῦμεν; ἐπιμένωμεν τῇ ἁμαρτίᾳ, ἵνα ἡ χάρις πλεονάσῃ; ² μὴ γένοιτο. οἵτινες

ἀλλὰ διὰ τῆς ἀγάπης δουλεύετε
ἀλλήλοις.

ἀπεθάνομεν τῇ ἁμαρτίᾳ, πῶς ἔτι
ζήσομεν ἐν αὐτῇ;
Rom 6:12–23 Μὴ οὖν βασιλευέτω ἡ
ἁμαρτία ἐν τῷ θνητῷ ὑμῶν σώματι
εἰς τὸ ὑπακούειν ταῖς ἐπιθυμίαις
αὐτοῦ, [13] μηδὲ παριστάνετε τὰ
μέλη ὑμῶν ὅπλα ἀδικίας τῇ
ἁμαρτίᾳ, ἀλλὰ παραστήσατε
ἑαυτοὺς τῷ θεῷ ὡσεὶ ἐκ νεκρῶν
ζῶντας καὶ τὰ μέλη ὑμῶν ὅπλα
δικαιοσύνης τῷ θεῷ· [14] ἁμαρτία
γὰρ ὑμῶν οὐ κυριεύσει, οὐ γάρ ἐστε
ὑπὸ νόμον ἀλλὰ ὑπὸ χάριν. [15] Τί
οὖν; ἁμαρτήσωμεν ὅτι οὐκ ἐσμὲν
ὑπὸ νόμον ἀλλὰ ὑπὸ χάριν; μὴ
γένοιτο. [16] οὐκ οἴδατε ὅτι ᾧ
παριστάνετε ἑαυτοὺς δούλους εἰς
ὑπακοήν, δοῦλοί ἐστε ᾧ ὑπακούετε,
ἤτοι ἁμαρτίας εἰς θάνατον ἢ
ὑπακοῆς εἰς δικαιοσύνην; [17] χάρις
δὲ τῷ θεῷ ὅτι ἦτε δοῦλοι τῆς
ἁμαρτίας ὑπηκούσατε δὲ ἐκ καρδίας
εἰς ὃν παρεδόθητε τύπον διδαχῆς,
[18] ἐλευθερωθέντες δὲ ἀπὸ τῆς
ἁμαρτίας ἐδουλώθητε τῇ
δικαιοσύνῃ· [19] ἀνθρώπινον λέγω
διὰ τὴν ἀσθένειαν τῆς σαρκὸς
ὑμῶν. ὥσπερ γὰρ παρεστήσατε τὰ
μέλη ὑμῶν δοῦλα τῇ ἀκαθαρσίᾳ καὶ
τῇ ἀνομίᾳ εἰς τὴν ἀνομίαν, οὕτως
νῦν παραστήσατε τὰ μέλη ὑμῶν
δοῦλα τῇ δικαιοσύνῃ εἰς ἁγιασμόν.
[20] ὅτε γὰρ δοῦλοι ἦτε τῆς
ἁμαρτίας, ἐλεύθεροι ἦτε τῇ
δικαιοσύνῃ. [21] τίνα οὖν καρπὸν
εἴχετε τότε ἐφ' οἷς νῦν
ἐπαισχύνεσθε; τὸ γὰρ τέλος
ἐκείνων θάνατος. [22] νυνὶ δέ,
ἐλευθερωθέντες ἀπὸ τῆς ἁμαρτίας
δουλωθέντες δὲ τῷ θεῷ, ἔχετε τὸν
καρπὸν ὑμῶν εἰς ἁγιασμόν, τὸ δὲ
τέλος ζωὴν αἰώνιον. [23] τὰ γὰρ
ὀψώνια τῆς ἁμαρτίας θάνατος, τὸ
δὲ χάρισμα τοῦ θεοῦ ζωὴ αἰώνιος
ἐν Χριστῷ Ἰησοῦ τῷ κυρίῳ ἡμῶν.

9. Gal 5:14 ὁ γὰρ πᾶς νόμος ἐν ἑνὶ
λόγῳ πεπλήρωται, ἐν τῷ ἀγαπήσεις
τὸν πλησίον σου ὡς σεαυτόν.

Rom 13:8–10 μηδενὶ μηδὲν ὀφείλετε,
εἰ μὴ τὸ ἀλλήλους ἀγαπᾶν· ὁ γὰρ
ἀγαπῶν τὸν ἕτερον νόμον
πεπλήρωκεν. [9] τὸ γὰρ οὐ

10. Gal 5:17 ἡ γὰρ σὰρξ ἐπιθυμεῖ κατὰ τοῦ πνεύματος, τὸ δὲ πνεῦμα κατὰ τῆς σαρκός· ταῦτα γὰρ ἀλλήλοις ἀντίκειται, ἵνα μὴ ἃ ἐὰν θέλητε ταῦτα ποιῆτε. ¹⁸ εἰ δὲ πνεύματι ἄγεσθε, οὐκ ἐστὲ ὑπὸ νόμον.

μοιχεύσεις, οὐ φονεύσεις, οὐ κλέψεις, οὐκ ἐπιθυμήσεις, καὶ εἴ τις ἑτέρα ἐντολή, ἐν τῷ λόγῳ τούτῳ ἀνακεφαλαιοῦται, [ἐν τῷ] ἀγαπήσεις τὸν πλησίον σου ὡς σεαυτόν. ¹⁰ ἡ ἀγάπη τῷ πλησίον κακὸν οὐκ ἐργάζεται· πλήρωμα οὖν νόμου ἡ ἀγάπη.

Rom 7:15–8:14 ὃ γὰρ κατεργάζομαι οὐ γινώσκω· οὐ γὰρ ὃ θέλω τοῦτο πράσσω, ἀλλ᾽ ὃ μισῶ τοῦτο ποιῶ. ¹⁶ εἰ δὲ ὃ οὐ θέλω τοῦτο ποιῶ, σύμφημι τῷ νόμῳ ὅτι καλός. ¹⁷ νυνὶ δὲ οὐκέτι ἐγὼ κατεργάζομαι αὐτὸ ἀλλὰ ἡ οἰκοῦσα ἐν ἐμοὶ ἁμαρτία. ¹⁸ οἶδα γὰρ ὅτι οὐκ οἰκεῖ ἐν ἐμοί, τοῦτ᾽ ἔστιν ἐν τῇ σαρκί μου, ἀγαθόν· τὸ γὰρ θέλειν παράκειταί μοι, τὸ δὲ κατεργάζεσθαι τὸ καλὸν οὔ· ¹⁹ οὐ γὰρ ὃ θέλω ποιῶ ἀγαθόν, ἀλλὰ ὃ οὐ θέλω κακὸν τοῦτο πράσσω. ²⁰ εἰ δὲ ὃ οὐ θέλω [ἐγὼ] τοῦτο ποιῶ, οὐκέτι ἐγὼ κατεργάζομαι αὐτὸ ἀλλὰ ἡ οἰκοῦσα ἐν ἐμοὶ ἁμαρτία. ²¹ εὑρίσκω ἄρα τὸν νόμον τῷ θέλοντι ἐμοὶ ποιεῖν τὸ καλὸν ὅτι ἐμοὶ τὸ κακὸν παράκειται· ²² συνήδομαι γὰρ τῷ νόμῳ τοῦ θεοῦ κατὰ τὸν ἔσω ἄνθρωπον, ²³ βλέπω δὲ ἕτερον νόμον ἐν τοῖς μέλεσίν μου ἀντιστρατευόμενον τῷ νόμῳ τοῦ νοός μου καὶ αἰχμαλωτίζοντά με ἐν τῷ νόμῳ τῆς ἁμαρτίας τῷ ὄντι ἐν τοῖς μέλεσίν μου. ²⁴ ταλαίπωρος ἐγὼ ἄνρωπος· τίς με ῥύσεται ἐκ τοῦ σώματος τοῦ θανάτου τούτου; ²⁵ χάρις δὲ τῷ θεῷ διὰ Ἰησοῦ Χριστοῦ τοῦ κυρίου ἡμῶν. ἄρα οὖν αὐτὸς ἐγὼ τῷ μὲν νοΐ δουλεύω νόμῳ θεοῦ, τῇ δὲ σαρκὶ νόμῳ ἁμαρτίας. 8¹ Οὐδὲν ἄρα νῦν κατάκριμα τοῖς ἐν Χριστῷ Ἰησοῦ· ² ὁ γὰρ νόμος τοῦ πνεύματος τῆς ζωῆς ἐν Χριστῷ Ἰησοῦ ἠλευθέρωσέν σε ἀπὸ τοῦ νόμου τῆς ἁμαρτίας καὶ τοῦ θανάτου. ³ τὸ γὰρ ἀδύνατον τοῦ νόμου, ἐν ᾧ ἠσθένει διὰ τῆς σαρκός, ὁ θεὸς τὸν ἑαυτοῦ υἱὸν πέμψας ἐν ὁμοιώματι σαρκὸς ἁμαρτίας καὶ περὶ ἁμαρτίας κατέκρινεν τὴν ἁμαρτίαν ἐν τῇ σαρκί, [4] ἵνα τὸ δικαίωμα τοῦ νόμου πληρωθῇ ἐν ἡμῖν τοῖς μὴ κατὰ σάρκα περιπατοῦσιν ἀλλὰ κατὰ πνεῦμα. οἱ γὰρ κατὰ σάρκα ὄντες τὰ τῆς σαρκὸς φρονοῦσιν, οἱ δὲ κατὰ πνεῦμα τὰ τοῦ πνεύματος. [6] τὸ γὰρ φρόνημα τῆς σαρκὸς θάνατος, τὸ δὲ φρόνημα τοῦ πνεύματος ζωὴ καὶ εἰρήνη· [7] διότι τὸ φρόνημα τῆς σαρκὸς ἔχθρα εἰς θεόν, τῷ γὰρ νόμῳ τοῦ θεοῦ οὐχ ὑποτάσσεται, οὐδὲ γὰρ δύναται· [8] οἱ δὲ ἐν σαρκὶ ὄντες θεῷ ἀρέσαι οὐ δύνανται. [9] ὑμεῖς δὲ οὐκ ἐστὲ ἐν σαρκὶ ἀλλὰ ἐν πνεύματι, εἴπερ πνεῦμα θεοῦ οἰκεῖ ἐν ὑμῖν. εἰ δέ τις πνεῦμα Χριστοῦ οὐκ ἔχει, οὗτος οὐκ ἔστιν αὐτοῦ. [10] εἰ δὲ Χριστὸς ἐν ὑμῖν, τὸ μὲν σῶμα νεκρὸν διὰ ἁμαρτίαν, τὸ δὲ πνεῦμα ζωὴ διὰ δικαιοσύνην. [11] εἰ δὲ τὸ πνεῦμα τοῦ ἐγείραντος τὸν Ἰησοῦν ἐκ νεκρῶν οἰκεῖ ἐν ὑμῖν, ὁ ἐγείρας Χριστὸν ἐκ νεκρῶν ζῳοποιήσει καὶ τὰ θνητὰ σώματα ὑμῶν διὰ τοῦ ἐνοικοῦντος αὐτοῦ πνεύματος ἐν ὑμῖν. [12] Ἄρα οὖν, ἀδελφοί, ὀφειλέται ἐσμέν, οὐ τῇ σαρκὶ τοῦ κατὰ σάρκα ζῆν· [13] εἰ γὰρ κατὰ σάρκα ζῆτε μέλλετε ἀποθνῄσκειν, εἰ δὲ πνεύματι τὰς πράξεις τοῦ σώματος θανατοῦτε ζήσεσθε. [14] ὅσοι γὰρ πνεύματι θεοῦ ἄγονται, οὗτοι υἱοὶ θεοῦ εἰσιν.

11. Gal 5:19–21 φανερὰ δέ ἐστιν τὰ ἔργα τῆς σαρκός, ἅτινά ἐστιν πορνεία, ἀκαθαρσία, ἀσέλγεια, [20] εἰδωλολατρία, φαρμακεία, ἔχθραι, ἔρις, ζῆλος, θυμοί, ἐριθείαι, διχοστασίαι, αἱρέσεις, [21] φθόνοι, μέθαι, κῶμοι, καὶ τὰ ὅμοια τούτοις, ἃ προλέγω ὑμῖν καθὼς προεῖπον ὅτι οἱ τὰ τοιαῦτα πράσσοντες βασιλείαν θεοῦ οὐ κληρονομήσουσιν.

Rom 1:18–31 Ἀποκαλύπτεται γὰρ ὀργὴ θεοῦ ἀπ᾽ οὐρανοῦ ἐπὶ πᾶσαν ἀσέβειαν καὶ ἀδικίαν ἀνθρώπων τῶν τὴν ἀλήθειαν ἐν ἀδικίᾳ κατεχόντων κ.τ.λ.

Appendix III: Galatian Parallels Recalled in Romans

The Galatians passages are given first since they are earlier, but one should read backward to them from the Romans passages in which they are recalled. The complete text of Romans 1:18–11:36 is given in the second column, with only the relevant passages that follow after 11:36.

Galatians

1. Gal 2:15 ἡμεῖς . . . οὐκ ἐξ ἐθνῶν
ἁμαρτωλοί.
Gal 4:3 οὕτως καὶ ἡμεῖς, ὅτε ἦμεν
νήπιοι, ὑπὸ τὰ στοιχεῖα τοῦ

κόσμου ἤμεθα δεδουλωμένοι.
Gal 4:8 Ἀλλὰ τότε μὲν οὐκ εἰδότες
θεὸν ἐδουλεύσατε τοῖς φύσει μὴ
οὖσιν θεοῖς·
Gal 5:19–21 φανερὰ δέ ἐστιν τὰ ἔργα
τῆς σαρκός, ἅτινά ἐστιν πορνεία,
ἀκαθαρσία, ἀσέλγεια,

Romans

Rom 1:18–31 Ἀποκαλύπτεται γὰρ
ὀργὴ θεοῦ ἀπ᾽ οὐρανοῦ ἐπὶ πᾶσαν
ἀσέβειαν καὶ ἀδικίαν ἀνθρώπων
τῶν τὴν ἀλήθειαν ἐν ἀδικίᾳ
κατεχόντων, 19 διότι τὸ γνωστὸν
τοῦ θεοῦ φανερόν ἐστιν ἐν αὐτοῖς·
ὁ θεὸς γὰρ αὐτοῖς ἐφανέρωσεν.
20 τὰ γὰρ ἀόρατα αὐτοῦ ἀπὸ
κτίσεως κόσμου τοῖς ποιήμασιν
νοούμενα καθορᾶται, ἥ τε ἀΐδιος
αὐτοῦ δύναμις καὶ θειότης, εἰς τὸ
εἶναι αὐτοὺς ἀναπολογήτους,
21 διότι γνόντες τὸν θεὸν οὐχ ὡς
θεὸν ἐδόξασαν ἢ ηὐχαρίστησαν,
ἀλλ᾽ ἐματαιώθησαν ἐν τοῖς
διαλογισμοῖς αὐτῶν καὶ ἐσκοτίσθη
ἡ ἀσύνετος αὐτῶν καρδία.
22 φάσκοντες εἶναι σοφοὶ
ἐμωράνθησαν, 23 καὶ ἤλλαξαν τὴν
δόξαν τοῦ ἀφθάρτου θεοῦ ἐν
ὁμοιώματι εἰκόνος φθαρτοῦ
ἀνθρώπου καὶ πετεινῶν καὶ
τετραπόδων καὶ ἑρπετῶν. 24 διὸ
παρέδωκεν αὐτοὺς ὁ θεὸς ἐν ταῖς

²⁰ εἰδωλολατρία, φαρμακεία, ἔχθραι, ἔρις, ζῆλος, θυμοί, ἐριθεῖαι, διχοστασίαι, αἱρέσεις, ²¹ φθόνοι, μέθαι, κῶμοι, καὶ τὰ ὅμοια τούτοις, ἃ προλέγω ὑμῖν καθὼς προεῖπον ὅτι οἱ τὰ τοιαῦτα πράσσοντες βασιλείαν θεοῦ οὐ κληρονομήσουσιν.

ἐπιθυμίαις τῶν καρδιῶν αὐτῶν εἰς ἀκαθαρσίαν τοῦ ἀτιμάζεσθαι τὰ σώματα αὐτῶν ἐν αὐτοῖς, ²⁵ οἵτινες μετήλλαξαν τὴν ἀλήθειαν τοῦ θεοῦ ἐν τῷ ψεύδει, καὶ ἐσεβάσθησαν καὶ ἐλάτρευσαν τῇ κτίσει παρὰ τὸν κτίσαντα, ὅς ἐστιν εὐλογητὸς εἰς τοὺς αἰῶνας· ἀμήν. ²⁶ διὰ τοῦτο παρέδωκεν αὐτοὺς ὁ θεὸς εἰς πάθη ἀτιμίας· αἵ τε γὰρ θήλειαι αὐτῶν μετήλλαξαν τὴν φυσικὴν χρῆσιν εἰς τὴν παρὰ φύσιν, ²⁷ ὁμοίως τε καὶ οἱ ἄρσενες ἀφέντες τὴν φυσικὴν χρῆσιν τῆς θηλείας ἐξεκαύθησαν ἐν τῇ ὀρέξει αὐτῶν εἰς ἀλλήλους, ἄρσενες ἐν ἄρσεσιν τὴν ἀσχημοσύνην κατεργαζόμενοι καὶ τὴν ἀντιμισθίαν ἣν ἔδει. τῆς πλάνης αὐτῶν ἐν ἑαυτοῖς ἀπολαμβάνοντες. ²⁸ καὶ καθὼς οὐκ ἐδοκίμασαν τὸν θεὸν ἔχειν ἐν ἐπιγνώσει, παρέδωκεν αὐτοὺς ὁ θεὸς εἰς ἀδόκιμον νοῦν, ποιεῖν τὰ μὴ καθήκοντα, ²⁹ πεπληρωμένους πάσῃ ἀδικίᾳ πονηρίᾳ πλεονεξίᾳ κακίᾳ, μεστοὺς φθόνου φόνου ἔριδος δόλου κακοηθείας, ψιθυριστὰς, ³⁰ καταλάλους, θεοστυγεῖς, ὑβριστὰς, ὑπερηφάνους, ἀλαζόνας, ἐφευρετὰς κακῶν, γονεῦσιν ἀπειθεῖς, ³¹ ἀσυνέτους ἀσυνθέτους, ἀστόργους, ἀνελεήμονας· ³² οἵτινες τὸ δικαίωμα τοῦ θεοῦ ἐπιγνόντες, ὅτι οἱ τὰ τοιαῦτα πράσσοντες ἄξιοι θανάτου εἰσίν, οὐ μόνον αὐτὰ ποιοῦσιν ἀλλὰ καὶ συνευδοκοῦσιν τοῖς πράσσουσιν.

Gal 2:14 ἀλλ' ὅτε εἶδον ὅτι οὐκ ὀρθοποδοῦσιν πρὸς τὴν ἀλήθειαν τοῦ εὐαγγελίου, εἶπον τῷ Κηφᾷ ἔμπροσθεν πάντων, εἰ σὺ Ἰουδαῖος ὑπάρχων ἐθνικῶς καὶ οὐχὶ Ἰουδαϊκῶς ζῇς, πῶς τὰ ἔθνη ἀναγκάζεις Ἰουδαΐζειν;

Rom 2:1–3:20 διὸ ἀναπολόγητος εἶ, ὦ ἄνθρωπε πᾶς ὁ κρίνων· ἐν ᾧ γὰρ κρίνεις τὸν ἕτερον, σεαυτὸν κατακρίνεις, τὰ γὰρ αὐτὰ πράσσεις ὁ κρίνων. ² οἴδαμεν δὲ ὅτι τὸ κρίμα τοῦ θεοῦ ἐστιν κατὰ ἀλήθειαν ἐπὶ τοὺς τὰ τοιαῦτα πράσσοντας. ³ λογίζῃ δὲ τοῦτο, ὦ ἄνθρωπε ὁ κρίνων τοὺς τὰ τοιαῦτα πράσσοντας καὶ ποιῶν αὐτά, ὅτι σὺ ἐκφεύξῃ τὸ κρίμα τοῦ θεοῦ; ⁴ ἢ

Gal 5:22–25 Ὁ δὲ καρπὸς τοῦ
πνεύματός ἐστιν ἀγάπη, χαρά,
εἰρήνη, μακροθυμία, χρηστότης,
ἀγαθωσύνη, πίστις, [23] πραΰτης,
ἐγκράτεια· κατὰ τῶν τοιούτων οὐκ
ἔστιν νόμος. [24] οἱ δὲ τοῦ Χριστοῦ
[Ἰησοῦ] τὴν σάρκα ἐσταύρωσαν
σὺν τοῖς παθήμασιν καὶ ταῖς
ἐπιθυμίαις. [25] εἰ ζῶμεν πνεύματι,
πνεύματι καὶ στοιχῶμεν.

Gal 5:19–21 φανερὰ δέ ἐστιν τὰ ἔργα
τῆς σαρκός, ἅτινά ἐστιν πορνεία,
ἀκαθαρσία, ἀσέλγεια,
[20] εἰδωλολατρία, φαρμακεία, ἔχθραι,
ἔρις, ζῆλος, θυμοί, ἐριθεῖαι,
διχοστασίαι, αἱρέσεις, [21] φθόνοι,
μέθαι, κῶμοι, καὶ τὰ ὅμοια τούτοις,
ἃ προλέγω ὑμῖν καθὼς προεῖπον
ὅτι οἱ τὰ τοιαῦτα πράσσοντες βασιλείαν θεοῦ οὐ κληρονομήσουσιν.
Gal 6:4 τὸ δὲ ἔργον ἑαυτοῦ
δοκιμαζέτω ἕκαστος, καὶ τότε εἰς
ἑαυτὸν μόνον τὸ καύχημα ἕξει καὶ
οὐκ εἰς τὸν ἕτερον·
Gal 6:8–9 ὅτι ὁ σπείρων εἰς τὴν
σάρκα ἑαυτοῦ ἐκ τῆς σαρκὸς
θερίσει φθοράν, ὁ δὲ σπείρων εἰς
τὸ πνεῦμα ἐκ τοῦ πνεύματος θερίσει
ζωὴν αἰώνιον. [9] τὸ δὲ καλὸν
ποιοῦντες μὴ ἐγκακῶμεν, καιρῷ γὰρ
ἰδίῳ θερίσομεν μὴ ἐκλυόμενοι.

τοῦ πλούτου τῆς χρηστότητος αὐτοῦ
καὶ τῆς ἀνοχῆς καὶ τῆς μακροθυμίας
καταφρονεῖς, ἀγνοῶν ὅτι τὸ χρηστὸν
τοῦ θεοῦ εἰς μετάνοιάν σε ἄγει;
[5] κατὰ δὲ τὴν σκληρότητά σου καὶ
ἀμετανόητον καρδίαν θησαυρίζεις
σεαυτῷ ὀργὴν ἐν ἡμέρᾳ ὀργῆς καὶ
ἀποκαλύψεως δικαιοκρισίας τοῦ
θεοῦ, [6] ὃς ἀποδώσει ἑκάστῳ κατὰ
τὰ ἔργα αὐτοῦ. [7] τοῖς μὲν καθ᾽
ὑπομονὴν ἔργου ἀγαθοῦ δόξαν καὶ
τιμὴν καὶ ἀφθαρσίαν ζητοῦσιν,
ζωὴν αἰώνιον· [8] τοῖς δὲ ἐξ ἐριθείας
καὶ ἀπειθοῦσι τῇ ἀληθείᾳ
πειθομένοις δὲ τῇ ἀδικίᾳ, ὀργὴ καὶ
θυμός. [9] θλῖψις καὶ στενοχωρία ἐπὶ
πᾶσαν ψυχὴν ἀνθρώπου τοῦ
κατεργαζομένου τὸ κακόν, Ἰουδαίου
τε πρῶτον καὶ Ἕλληνος [10] δόξα δὲ
καὶ τιμὴ καὶ εἰρήνη παντὶ τῷ
ἐργαζομένῳ τὸ ἀγαθόν, Ἰουδαίῳ τε
πρῶτον καὶ Ἕλληνι [11] οὐ γάρ
ἐστιν προσωπολημψία παρὰ τῷ
θεῷ. [12] ὅσοι γὰρ ἀνόμως ἥμαρτον,
ἀνόμως καὶ ἀπολοῦνται καὶ ὅσοι ἐν
νόμῳ ἥμαρτον, διὰ νόμου
κριθήσονται· [13] οὐ γὰρ οἱ ἀκροαταὶ
νόμου δίκαιοι παρὰ [τῷ] θεῷ, ἀλλ᾽
οἱ ποιηταὶ νόμου δικαιωθήσονται.
[14] ὅταν γὰρ ἔθνη τὰ μὴ νόμον
ἔχοντα φύσει τὰ τοῦ νόμου
ποιῶσιν, οὗτοι νόμον μὴ ἔχοντες
ἑαυτοῖς εἰσιν νόμος· [15] οἵτινες
ἐνδείκνυνται τὸ ἔργον τοῦ νόμου
γραπτὸν ἐν ταῖς καρδίαις αὐτῶν,
συμμαρτυρούσης αὐτῶν τῆς
συνειδήσεως καὶ μεταξὺ ἀλλήλων
τῶν λογισμῶν κατηγορούντων ἢ
καὶ ἀπολογουμένων, [16] ἐν ἡμέρᾳ
ὅτε κρίνει ὁ θεὸς τὰ κρυπτὰ τῶν
ἀνθρώπων κατὰ τὸ εὐαγγέλιόν μου
διὰ Χριστοῦ Ἰησοῦ. [17] εἰ δὲ σὺ
Ἰουδαῖος ἐπονομάζῃ καὶ ἐπαναπαύῃ
νόμῳ καὶ καυχᾶσαι ἐν θεῷ [18] καὶ
γινώσκεις τὸ θέλημα καὶ δοκιμάζεις
τὰ διαφέροντα κατηχούμενος ἐκ τοῦ
νόμου, [19] πέποιθάς τε σεαυτὸν
ὁδηγὸν εἶναι τυφλῶν, φῶς τῶν ἐν
σκότει, [20] παιδευτὴν ἀφρόνων,

Gal 5:3 μαρτύρομαι δὲ πάλιν παντὶ
ἀνθρώπῳ περιτεμνομένῳ ὅτι
ὀφειλέτης ἐστὶν ὅλον τὸν νόμον
ποιῆσαι.
Gal 6:13 οὐδὲ γὰρ οἱ περιτεμνόμενοι
αὐτοὶ νόμον φυλάσσουσιν, ἀλλὰ
θέλουσιν ὑμᾶς περιτέμνεσθαι ἵνα ἐν
τῇ ὑμετέρᾳ σαρκὶ καυχήσωνται.

διδάσκαλον νηπίων, ἔχοντα τὴν
μόρφωσιν τῆς γνώσεως καὶ τῆς
ἀληθείας ἐν τῷ νόμῳ· 21 ὁ οὖν
διδάσκων ἕτερον σεαυτὸν οὐ
διδάσκεις; ὁ κηρύσσων μὴ κλέπτειν
κλέπτεις; 22 ὁ λέγων μὴ μοιχεύειν
μοιχεύεις; ὁ βδελυσσόμενος τὰ
εἴδωλα ἱεροσυλεῖς; 23 ὃς ἐν νόμῳ
καυχᾶσαι, διὰ τῆς παραβάσεως τοῦ
νόμου τὸν θεὸν ἀτιμάζεις; 24 τὸ
γὰρ ὄνομα τοῦ θεοῦ δι' ὑμᾶς
βλασφημεῖται ἐν τοῖς ἔθνεσιν,
καθὼς γέγραπται. 25 περιτομὴ μὲν
γὰρ ὠφελεῖ ἐὰν νόμον πράσσῃς·
ἐὰν δὲ παραβάτης νόμου ᾖς ἡ
περιτομή σου ἀκροβυστία γέγονεν.
26 ἐὰν οὖν ἡ ἀκροβυστία τὰ
δικαιώματα τοῦ νόμου φυλάσσῃ,
οὐχ ἡ ἀκροβυστία αὐτοῦ εἰς
περιτομὴν λογισθήσεται; 27 καὶ
κρινεῖ ἡ ἐκ φύσεως ἀκροβυστία τὸν
νόμον τελοῦσα σὲ τὸν διὰ
γράμματος καὶ περιτομῆς
παραβάτην νόμου. 28 οὐ γὰρ ὁ ἐν
τῷ φανερῷ Ἰουδαῖός ἐστιν, οὐδὲ ἡ
ἐν τῷ φανερῷ ἐν σαρκὶ περιτομή·
29 ἀλλ' ὁ ἐν τῷ κρυπτῷ Ἰουδαῖος,
καὶ περιτομὴ καρδίας ἐν πνεύματι
οὐ γράμματι, οὗ ὁ ἔπαινος οὐκ ἐξ
ἀνθρώπων ἀλλ' ἐκ τοῦ θεοῦ. 3 1 Τί
οὖν τὸ περισσὸν τοῦ Ἰουδαίου, ἢ
τίς ἡ ὠφέλεια τῆς περιτομῆς; 2 πολὺ
κατὰ πάντα τρόπον. πρῶτον μὲν
[γὰρ] ὅτι ἐπιστεύθησαν τὰ λόγια
τοῦ θεοῦ. 3 τί γὰρ εἰ ἠπίστησάν
τινες; μὴ ἡ ἀπιστία αὐτῶν τὴν
πίστιν τοῦ θεοῦ καταργήσει; 4 μὴ
γένοιτο· γινέσθω δὲ ὁ θεὸς ἀληθής,
πᾶς δὲ ἄνθρωπος ψεύστης, καθὼς
γέγραπται, ὅπως ἂν δικαιωθῇς ἐν
τοῖς λόγοις σου καὶ νικήσεις ἐν τῷ
κρίνεσθαί σε. . . . [vv. 5–8] . . .
9 Τί οὖν; προεχόμεθα; οὐ πάντως,
προῃτιασάμεθα γὰρ Ἰουδαίους τε
καὶ Ἕλληνας πάντας ὑφ' ἁμαρτίαν
εἶναι, 10 καθὼς γέγραπται ὅτι . . .
[vv. 10b–18, Scripture quota-
tions] . . . 19 οἴδαμεν δὲ ὅτι ὅσα ὁ
νόμος λέγει τοῖς ἐν τῷ νόμῳ λαλεῖ,

ἵνα πᾶν στόμα φραγῇ καὶ ὑπόδικος
γένηται πᾶς ὁ κόσμος τῷ θεῷ·
²⁰ διότι ἐξ ἔργων νόμου οὐ
δικαιωθήσεται πᾶσα σὰρξ ἐνώπιον
αὐτοῦ, διὰ γὰρ νόμου ἐπίγνωσις
ἁμαρτίας.

3. Gal 2:15–16 ἡμεῖς φύσει Ἰουδαῖοι
καὶ οὐκ ἐξ ἐθνῶν ἁμαρτωλοί,
¹⁶ εἰδότες [δὲ] ὅτι οὐ δικαιοῦται
ἄνθρωπος ἐξ ἔργων νόμου ἐὰν μὴ
διὰ πίστεως Ἰησοῦ Χριστοῦ, καὶ
ἡμεῖς εἰς Χριστὸν Ἰησοῦν
ἐπιστεύσαμεν, ἵνα δικαιωθῶμεν ἐκ
πίστεως Χριστοῦ καὶ οὐκ ἐξ ἔργων
νόμου, ὅτι ἐξ ἔργων νόμου οὐ
δικαιωθήσεται πᾶσα σάρξ.

Rom 3:21–4:25 Νυνὶ δὲ χωρὶς νόμου
δικαιοσύνη θεοῦ πεφανέρωται,
μαρτυρουμένη ὑπὸ τοῦ νόμου καὶ
τῶν προφητῶν, ²² δικαιοσύνη δὲ
θεοῦ διὰ πίστεως Ἰησοῦ Χριστοῦ,
εἰς πάντας τοὺς πιστεύοντας οὐ γάρ
ἐστιν διαστολή ²³ πάντες γὰρ
ἥμαρτον καὶ ὑστεροῦνται τῆς δόξης
τοῦ θεοῦ, ²⁴ δικαιούμενοι δωρεὰν
τῇ αὐτοῦ χάριτι διὰ τῆς
ἀπολυτρώσεως τῆς ἐν Χριστῷ
Ἰησοῦ· ²⁵ ὃν προέθετο ὁ θεὸς
ἱλαστήριον διὰ [τῆς] πίστεως ἐν τῷ
αὐτοῦ αἵματι εἰς ἔνδειξιν τῆς
δικαιοσύνης αὐτοῦ διὰ τὴν πάρεσιν
τῶν προγεγονότων ἁμαρτημάτων
²⁶ ἐν τῇ ἀνοχῇ τοῦ θεοῦ, πρὸς τὴν
ἔνδειξιν τῆς δικαιοσύνης αὐτοῦ ἐν
τῷ νῦν καιρῷ, εἰς τὸ εἶναι αὐτὸν
δίκαιον καὶ δικαιοῦντα τὸν ἐκ

Gal 6:3–4 εἰ γὰρ δοκεῖ τις εἶναί τι
μηδὲν ὤν, φρεναπατᾷ ἑαυτόν· ⁴ τὸ
δὲ ἔργον ἑαυτοῦ δοκιμαζέτω
ἕκαστος, καὶ τότε εἰς ἑαυτὸν μόνον
τὸ καύχημα ἕξει καὶ οὐκ εἰς τὸν
ἕτερον·

Gal 6:12–14 ὅσοι θέλουσιν
εὐπροσωπῆσαι ἐν σαρκί, οὗτοι
ἀναγκάζουσιν ὑμᾶς περιτέμνεσθαι,
μόνον ἵνα τῷ σταυρῷ τοῦ Χριστοῦ
μὴ διώκωνται· ¹³ οὐδὲ γὰρ οἱ περιτεμνόμενοι αὐτοὶ νόμον
φυλάσσουσιν, ἀλλὰ θέλουσιν ὑμᾶς
περιτέμνεσθαι ἵνα ἐν τῇ ὑμετέρᾳ
σαρκὶ καυχήσωνται. ¹⁴ ἐμοὶ δὲ μὴ
γένοιτο καυχᾶσθαι εἰ μὴ ἐν τῷ
σταυρῷ τοῦ κυρίου ἡμῶν Ἰησοῦ
Χριστοῦ, δι' οὗ ἐμοὶ κόσμος
ἐσταύρωται κἀγὼ κόσμῳ.

Gal 2:7–9 ἀλλὰ τοὐναντίον ἰδόντες
ὅτι πεπίστευμαι τὸ εὐαγγέλιον τῆς
ἀκροβυστίας καθὼς Πέτρος τῆς

πίστεως Ἰησοῦ. ²⁷ Ποῦ οὖν ἡ
καύχησις; ἐξεκλείσθη. διὰ ποίου
νόμου; τῶν ἔργων; οὐχί, ἀλλὰ διὰ
νόμου πίστεως.

²⁸ λογιζόμεθα γὰρ δικαιοῦσθαι πίστει
ἄνθρωπον χωρὶς ἔργων νόμου. ²⁹ ἢ
Ἰουδαίων ὁ θεὸς μόνον; οὐχὶ καὶ
ἐθνῶν; ναὶ καὶ ἐθνῶν, ³⁰ εἴπερ εἷς ὁ

περιτομῆς, [8] ὁ γὰρ ἐνεργήσας
Πέτρῳ εἰς ἀποστολὴν τῆς
περιτομῆς ἐνήργησεν καὶ ἐμοὶ εἰς
τὰ ἔθνη, [9] καὶ γνόντες τὴν χάριν
τὴν δοθεῖσάν μοι, Ἰάκωβος καὶ
Κηφᾶς καὶ Ἰωάννης, οἱ δοκοῦντες
στῦλοι εἶναι, δεξιὰς ἔδωκαν ἐμοὶ
καὶ Βαρναβᾷ κοινωνίας, ἵνα ἡμεῖς
εἰς τὰ ἔθνη, αὐτοὶ δὲ εἰς τὴν
περιτομήν.

Gal 3:21 ὁ οὖν νόμος κατὰ τῶν
ἐπαγγελιῶν [τοῦ θεοῦ]; μὴ γένοιτο·
εἰ γὰρ ἐδόθη νόμος ὁ δυνάμενος
ζῳοποιῆσαι, ὄντως ἐκ νόμου ἂν ἦν
ἡ δικαιοσύνη.

Gal 3:6–9 καθὼς Ἀβραὰμ ἐπίστευσεν
τῷ θεῷ, καὶ ἐλογίσθη αὐτῷ εἰς
δικαιοσύνην. [7] γινώσκετε ἄρα ὅτι
οἱ ἐκ πίστεως, οὗτοι υἱοί εἰσιν
Ἀβραάμ. [8] προϊδοῦσα δὲ ἡ γραφὴ
ὅτι ἐκ πίστεως δικαιοῖ τὰ ἔθνη ὁ
θεὸς προευηγγελίσατο τῷ Ἀβραὰμ
ὅτι ἐνευλογηθήσονται ἐν σοὶ πάντα
τὰ ἔθνη. [9] ὥστε οἱ ἐκ πίστεως
εὐλογοῦνται σὺν τῷ πιστῷ
Ἀβραάμ. [On this follows the passage on the curse of the Law (vv.
10–14). See the parallels to Romans 10:5–13 and 15:8–12.]

Gal 3:17 τοῦτο δὲ λέγω· διαθήκην προκεκυρωμένην ὑπὸ τοῦ θεοῦ ὁ μετὰ
τετρακόσια καὶ τριάκοντα ἔτη
γεγονὼς νόμος οὐκ ἀκυροῖ, εἰς τὸ
καταργῆσαι τὴν ἐπαγγελίαν.

θεός, ὃς δικαιώσει περιτομὴν ἐκ
πίστεως καὶ ἀκροβυστίαν διὰ τῆς
πίστεως.

[31] νόμον οὖν καταργοῦμεν διὰ τῆς
πίστεως; μὴ γένοιτο, ἀλλὰ νόμον
ἱστάνομεν.

[4] [1] Τί οὖν ἐροῦμεν εὑρηκέναι Ἀβραὰμ
τὸν προπάτορα ἡμῶν κατὰ σάρκα;
[2] εἰ γὰρ Ἀβραὰμ ἐξ ἔργων
ἐδικαιώθη, ἔχει καύχημα ἀλλ' οὐ
πρὸς θεόν. [3] τί γὰρ ἡ γραφὴ λέγει;
ἐπίστευσεν δὲ Ἀβραὰμ τῷ θεῷ, καὶ
ἐλογίσθη αὐτῷ εἰς δικαιοσύνην.
[4] τῷ δὲ ἐργαζομένῳ ὁ μισθὸς οὐ
λογίζεται κατὰ χάριν ἀλλὰ κατὰ
ὀφείλημα. [5] τῷ δὲ μὴ ἐργαζομένῳ,
πιστεύοντι δὲ ἐπὶ τὸν δικαιοῦντα
τὸν ἀσεβῆ, λογίζεται ἡ πίστις
αὐτοῦ εἰς δικαιοσύνην, [6] καθάπερ
καὶ Δαυὶδ λέγει τὸν μακαρισμὸν
τοῦ ἀνθρώπου ᾧ ὁ θεὸς λογίζεται
δικαιοσύνην χωρὶς ἔργων,
[7] μακάριοι ὧν ἀφέθησαν αἱ ἀνομίαι
καὶ ὧν ἐπεκαλύφθησαν αἱ ἁμαρτίαι·
[8] μακάριος ἀνὴρ οὗ οὐ μὴ
λογίσηται κύριος ἁμαρτίαν. [9] Ὁ
μακαρισμὸς οὖν οὗτος ἐπὶ τὴν
περιτομὴν ἢ καὶ ἐπὶ τὴν
ἀκροβυστίαν; λέγομεν γάρ,
ἐλογίσθη τῷ Ἀβραὰμ ἡ πίστις εἰς
δικαιοσύνην. [10] πῶς οὖν ἐλογίσθη;
ἐν περιτομῇ ὄντι ἢ ἐν ἀκροβυστίᾳ;
οὐκ ἐν περιτομῇ ἀλλ' ἐν
ἀκροβυστίᾳ [11] καὶ σημεῖον ἔλαβεν
περιτομῆς, σφραγῖδα τῆς
δικαιοσύνης τῆς πίστεως τῆς ἐν τῇ
ἀκροβυστίᾳ, εἰς τὸ εἶναι αὐτὸν
πατέρα πάντων τῶν πιστευόντων
δι' ἀκροβυστίας, εἰς τὸ λογισθῆναι

Gal 2:16 εἰδότες [δὲ] ὅτι οὐ δικαιοῦται ἄνθρωπος ἐξ ἔργων νόμου ἐὰν μὴ διὰ πίστεως Ἰησοῦ Χριστοῦ, καὶ ἡμεῖς εἰς Χριστὸν Ἰησοῦν ἐπιστεύσαμεν, ἵνα δικαιωθῶμεν ἐκ πίστεως Χριστοῦ καὶ οὐκ ἐξ ἔργων νόμου, ὅτι ἐξ ἔργων νόμου οὐ δικαιωθήσεται πᾶσα σάρξ.

Gal 5:6 ἐν γὰρ Χριστῷ Ἰησοῦ οὔτε περιτομή τι ἰσχύει οὔτε ἀκροβυστία, ἀλλὰ πίστις δι' ἀγάπης ἐνεργουμένη.

Gal 3:15–18 Ἀδελφοί, κατὰ ἄνθρωπον λέγω· ὅμως ἀνθρώπου κεκυρωμένην διαθήκην οὐδεὶς ἀθετεῖ ἢ ἐπιδιατάσσεται. ¹⁶ τῷ δὲ Ἀβραὰμ ἐρρέθησαν αἱ ἐπαγγελίαι καὶ τῷ σπέρματι αὐτοῦ. οὐ λέγει, καὶ τοῖς σπέρμασιν, ὡς ἐπὶ πολλῶν, ἀλλ' ὡς ἐφ' ἑνός, καὶ τῷ σπέρματί σου, ὅς ἐστιν Χριστός. ¹⁷ τοῦτο δὲ λέγω· διαθήκην προκεκυρωμένην ὑπὸ τοῦ θεοῦ ὁ μετὰ τετρακόσια καὶ τριάκοντα ἔτη γεγονὼς νόμος οὐκ ἀκυροῖ, εἰς τὸ καταργῆσαι τὴν ἐπαγγελίαν. ¹⁸ εἰ γὰρ ἐκ νόμου ἡ κληρονομία, οὐκέτι ἐξ ἐπαγγελίας· τῷ δὲ Ἀβραὰμ δι' ἐπαγγελίας κεχάρισται ὁ θεός.

Gal 2:21 οὐκ ἀθετῶ τὴν χάριν τοῦ θεοῦ· εἰ γὰρ διὰ νόμου δικαιοσύνη, ἄρα Χριστὸς δωρεὰν ἀπέθανεν.

Gal 5:2 Ἴδε ἐγὼ Παῦλος λέγω ὑμῖν ὅτι ἐὰν περιτέμνησθε Χριστὸς ὑμᾶς οὐδὲν ὠφελήσει.

Gal 5:4 κατηργήθητε ἀπὸ Χριστοῦ οἵτινες ἐν νόμῳ δικαιοῦσθε, τῆς χάριτος ἐξεπέσατε.

Gal 3:16 τῷ δὲ Ἀβραὰμ ἐρρέθησαν αἱ ἐπαγγελίαι καὶ τῷ σπέρματι αὐτοῦ. οὐ λέγει, καὶ τοῖς σπέρμασιν, ὡς ἐπὶ πολλῶν, ἀλλ' ὡς ἐφ' ἑνός, καὶ τῷ σπέρματί σου, ὅς ἐστιν Χριστός.

[καὶ] αὐτοῖς [τὴν] δικαιοσύνην, ¹² καὶ πατέρα περιτομῆς τοῖς οὐκ ἐκ περιτομῆς μόνον ἀλλὰ καὶ τοῖς στοιχοῦσιν τοῖς ἴχνεσιν τῆς ἐν ἀκροβυστίᾳ πίστεως τοῦ πατρὸς ἡμῶν Ἀβραάμ.

¹³ Οὐ γὰρ διὰ νόμου ἡ ἐπαγγελία τῷ Ἀβραὰμ ἢ τῷ σπέρματι αὐτοῦ, τὸ κληρονόμον αὐτὸν εἶναι κόσμου, ἀλλὰ διὰ δικαιοσύνης πίστεως.

¹⁴ εἰ γὰρ οἱ ἐκ νόμου κληρονόμοι, κεκένωται ἡ πίστις καὶ κατήργηται ἡ ἐπαγγελία· ¹⁵ ὁ γὰρ νόμος ὀργὴν κατεργάζεται οὗ δὲ οὐκ ἔστιν νόμος, οὐδὲ παράβασις. ¹⁶ διὰ τοῦτο ἐκ πίστεως, ἵνα κατὰ χάριν, εἰς τὸ εἶναι βεβαίαν τὴν ἐπαγγελίαν παντὶ τῷ σπέρματι, οὐ τῷ ἐκ τοῦ νόμου μόνον ἀλλὰ καὶ τῷ ἐκ πίστεως Ἀβραάμ, ὅς ἐστιν πατὴρ πάντων ἡμῶν, ¹⁷ καθὼς γέγραπται ὅτι πατέρα πολλῶν ἐθνῶν τέθεικά σε, κατέναντι οὗ ἐπίστευσεν θεοῦ τοῦ ζῳοποιοῦντος τοὺς νεκροὺς καὶ καλοῦντος τὰ μὴ ὄντα ὡς ὄντα· ¹⁸ ὃς παρ' ἐλπίδα ἐπ' ἐλπίδι ἐπίστευσεν εἰς τὸ γενέσθαι αὐτὸν πατέρα πολλῶν ἐθνῶν κατὰ τὸ εἰρημένον, οὕτως ἔσται τὸ σπέρμα σου ¹⁹ καὶ μὴ ἀσθενήσας τῇ πίστει κατενόησεν τὸ ἑαυτοῦ σῶμα [ἤδη] νενεκρωμένον, ἑκατονταέτης που ὑπάρχων, καὶ τὴν νέκρωσιν τῆς μήτρας Σάρρας, ²⁰ εἰς δὲ τὴν

Gal 3:29 εἰ δὲ ὑμεῖς Χριστοῦ, ἄρα τοῦ Ἀβραὰμ σπέρμα ἐστέ, κατ' ἐπαγγελίαν κληρονόμοι.

4.

Gal 5:5 ἡμεῖς γὰρ πνεύματι ἐκ πίστεως ἐλπίδα δικαιοσύνης ἀπεκδεχόμεθα.

ἐπαγγελίαν τοῦ θεοῦ οὐ διεκρίθη τῇ ἀπιστίᾳ ἀλλ' ἐνεδυναμώθη τῇ πίστει, δοὺς δόξαν τῷ θεῷ ²¹ καὶ πληροφορηθεὶς ὅτι ὃ ἐπήγγελται δυνατός ἐστιν καὶ ποιῆσαι. ²² διὸ [καὶ] ἐλογίσθη αὐτῷ εἰς δικαιοσύνην. ²³ Οὐκ ἐγράφη δὲ δι' αὐτὸν μόνον ὅτι ἐλογίσθη αὐτῷ, ²⁴ ἀλλὰ καὶ δι' ἡμᾶς οἷς μέλλει λογίζεσθαι, τοῖς πιστεύουσιν ἐπὶ τὸν ἐγείραντα Ἰησοῦν τὸν κύριον ἡμῶν ἐκ νεκρῶν, ²⁵ ὃς παρεδόθη διὰ τὰ παραπτώματα ἡμῶν καὶ ἠγέρθη διὰ τὴν δικαίωσιν ἡμῶν.

Rom 5:1–11 Δικαιωθέντες οὖν ἐκ πίστεως εἰρήνην ἔχομεν πρὸς τὸν θεὸν διὰ τοῦ κυρίου ἡμῶν Ἰησοῦ Χριστοῦ, ² δι' οὗ καὶ τὴν προσαγωγὴν ἐσχήκαμεν [τῇ πίστει] εἰς τὴν χάριν ταύτην ἐν ᾗ ἑστήκαμεν, καὶ καυχώμεθα ἐπ' ἐλπίδι τῆς δόξης τοῦ θεοῦ. ³ οὐ μόνον δέ, ἀλλὰ καὶ καυχώμεθα ἐν ταῖς θλίψεσιν, εἰδότες ὅτι ἡ θλῖψις ὑπομονὴν κατεργάζεται, ⁴ ἡ δὲ ὑπομονὴ δοκιμήν, ἡ δὲ δοκιμὴ ἐλπίδα ⁵ ἡ δὲ ἐλπὶς οὐ καταισχύνει, ὅτι ἡ ἀγάπη τοῦ θεοῦ ἐκκέχυται ἐν ταῖς καρδίαις ἡμῶν διὰ πνεύματος ἁγίου τοῦ δοθέντος ἡμῖν, ⁶ ἔτι γὰρ Χριστὸς ὄντων ἡμῶν ἀσθενῶν ἔτι κατὰ καιρὸν ὑπὲρ ἀσεβῶν ἀπέθανεν. ⁷ μόλις γὰρ ὑπὲρ δικαίου τις ἀποθανεῖται ὑπὲρ γὰρ τοῦ ἀγαθοῦ τάχα τις καὶ τολμᾷ ἀποθανεῖν ⁸ συνίστησιν δὲ τὴν ἑαυτοῦ ἀγάπην εἰς ἡμᾶς ὁ θεὸς ὅτι ἔτι ἁμαρτωλῶν ὄντων ἡμῶν Χριστὸς ὑπὲρ ἡμῶν ἀπέθανεν. ⁹ πολλῷ οὖν μᾶλλον δικαιωθέντες νῦν ἐν τῷ αἵματι αὐτοῦ σωθησόμεθα δι' αὐτοῦ ἀπὸ τῆς ὀργῆς. ¹⁰ εἰ γὰρ ἐχθροὶ ὄντες κατηλλάγημεν τῷ θεῷ διὰ τοῦ θανάτου τοῦ υἱοῦ αὐτοῦ, πολλῷ μᾶλλον καταλλαγέντες σωθησόμεθα ἐν τῇ ζωῇ αὐτοῦ· ¹¹ οὐ μόνον δέ, ἀλλὰ καὶ καυχώμενοι ἐν τῷ θεῷ διὰ τοῦ κυρίου ἡμῶν Ἰησοῦ

Χριστοῦ, δι' οὖ νῦν τὴν καταλλαγὴν ἐλάβομεν.

5.

Rom 5:12–21 Διὰ τοῦτο ὥσπερ δι' ἑνὸς ἀνθρώπου ἡ ἁμαρτία εἰς τὸν κόσμον εἰσῆλθεν καὶ διὰ τῆς ἁμαρτίας ὁ θάνατος, καὶ οὕτως εἰς πάντας ἀνθρώπους ὁ θάνατος διῆλθεν, ἐφ' ᾧ πάντες ἥμαρτον· ¹³ ἄχρι γὰρ νόμου ἁμαρτία ἦν ἐν κόσμῳ, ἁμαρτία δὲ οὐκ ἐλλογεῖται μὴ ὄντος νόμου. ¹⁴ ἀλλὰ ἐβασίλευσεν ὁ θάνατος ἀπὸ Ἀδὰμ μέχρι Μωϋσέως καὶ ἐπὶ τοὺς μὴ ἁμαρτήσαντας ἐπὶ τῷ ὁμοιώματι τῆς παραβάσεως Ἀδάμ, ὅς ἐστιν τύπος τοῦ μέλλοντος. ¹⁵ Ἀλλ' οὐχ ὡς τὸ παράπτωμα, οὕτως καὶ τὸ χάρισμα· εἰ γὰρ τῷ τοῦ ἑνὸς παραπτώματι οἱ πολλοὶ ἀπέθανον, πολλῷ μᾶλλον ἡ χάρις τοῦ θεοῦ καὶ ἡ δωρεὰ ἐν χάριτι τῇ τοῦ ἑνὸς ἀνθρώπου Ἰησοῦ Χριστοῦ εἰς τοὺς πολλοὺς ἐπερίσσευσεν. ¹⁶ καὶ οὐχ ὡς δι' ἑνὸς ἁμαρτήσαντος τὸ δώρημα· τὸ μὲν γὰρ κρίμα ἐξ ἑνὸς εἰς κατάκριμα, τὸ δὲ χάρισμα ἐκ πολλῶν παραπτωμάτων εἰς δικαίωμα. ¹⁷ εἰ γὰρ τῷ τοῦ ἑνὸς παραπτώματι ὁ θάνατος ἐβασίλευσεν διὰ τοῦ ἑνός, πολλῷ μᾶλλον οἱ τὴν περισσείαν τῆς χάριτος καὶ τῆς δωρεᾶς τῆς δικαιοσύνης λαμβάνοντες ἐν ζωῇ βασιλεύσουσιν διὰ τοῦ ἑνὸς Ἰησοῦ Χριστοῦ. ¹⁸ Ἄρα οὖν ὡς δι' ἑνὸς παραπτώματος εἰς πάντας ἀνθρώπους εἰς κατάκριμα, οὕτως καὶ δι' ἑνὸς δικαιώματος εἰς πάντας ἀνθρώπους εἰς δικαίωσιν ζωῆς· ¹⁹ ὥσπερ γὰρ διὰ τῆς παρακοῆς τοῦ ἑνὸς ἀνθρώπου ἁμαρτωλοὶ κατεστάθησαν οἱ πολλοί, οὕτως καὶ διὰ τῆς ὑπακοῆς τοῦ ἑνὸς δίκαιοι κατασταθήσονται οἱ πολλοί. ²⁰ νόμος δὲ παρεισῆλθεν ἵνα πλεονάσῃ τὸ παράπτωμα· οὖ δὲ ἐπλεόνασεν ἡ ἁμαρτία, ὑπερεπερίσσευσεν ἡ χάρις, ²¹ ἵνα ὥσπερ ἐβασίλευσεν ἡ ἁμαρτία ἐν

Gal 3:19 Τί οὖν ὁ νόμος; τῶν παραβάσεων χάριν προσετέθη, ἄχρις οὗ ἔλθῃ τὸ σπέρμα ᾧ ἐπήγγελται, διαταγεὶς δι' ἀγγέλων ἐν χειρὶ μεσίτου.

Gal 3:10–14 ὅσοι γὰρ ἐξ ἔργων
νόμου εἰσὶν ὑπὸ κατάραν εἰσίν·
γέγραπται γὰρ ὅτι ἐπικατάρατος
πᾶς ὃς οὐκ ἐμμένει πᾶσιν τοῖς
γεγραμμένοις ἐν τῷ βιβλίῳ τοῦ
νόμου τοῦ ποιῆσαι αὐτά. [11] ὅτι δὲ
ἐν νόμῳ οὐδεὶς δικαιοῦται παρὰ τῷ
θεῷ δῆλον, ὅτι ὁ δίκαιος ἐκ
πίστεως ζήσεται· [12] ὁ δὲ νόμος οὐκ
ἔστιν ἐκ πίστεως, ἀλλ' ὁ ποιήσας
αὐτὰ ζήσεται ἐν αὐτοῖς. [13] Χριστὸς
ἡμᾶς ἐξηγόρασεν ἐκ τῆς κατάρας
τοῦ νόμου γενόμενος ὑπὲρ ἡμῶν
κατάρα, ὅτι γέγραπται,
ἐπικατάρατος πᾶς ὁ κρεμάμενος ἐπὶ
ξύλου.
Gal 3:15, 17–18 ἀδελφοί, κατὰ
ἄνθρωπον λέγω· ὅμως ἀνθρώπου
κεκυρωμένην διαθήκην οὐδεὶς ἀθετεῖ
ἢ ἐπιδιατάσσεται. . . . [17] τοῦτο δὲ
λέγω· διαθήκην προκεκυρωμένην
ὑπὸ τοῦ θεοῦ ὁ μετὰ τετρακόσια
καὶ τριάκοντα ἔτη γεγονὼς νόμος
οὐκ ἀκυροῖ, εἰς τὸ καταργῆσαι τὴν
ἐπαγγελίαν. [18] εἰ γὰρ ἐκ νόμου ἡ
κληρονομία, οὐκέτι ἐξ ἐπαγγελίας·
τῷ δὲ Ἀβραὰμ δι' ἐπαγγελίας
κεχάρισται ὁ θεός.
Gal 4:4–5 ὅτε δὲ ἦλθεν τὸ πλήρωμα
τοῦ χρόνου, ἐξαπέστειλεν ὁ θεὸς
τὸν υἱὸν αὐτοῦ, γενόμενον ἐκ
γυναικός, γενόμενον ὑπὸ νόμον,
[5] ἵνα τοὺς ὑπὸ νόμον ἐξαγοράσῃ,
ἵνα τὴν υἱοθεσίαν ἀπολάβωμεν.

6. Gal 5:13 Ὑμεῖς γὰρ ἐπ' ἐλευθερίᾳ
ἐκλήθητε, ἀδελφοί· μόνον μὴ τὴν
ἐλευθερίαν εἰς ἀφορμὴν τῇ σαρκί,
ἀλλὰ διὰ τῆς ἀγάπης δουλεύετε
ἀλλήλοις.
Gal 5:16 Λέγω δέ, πνεύματι περιπατεῖτε καὶ ἐπιθυμίαν σαρκὸς οὐ μὴ
τελέσητε.
Gal 2:20 ζῶ δὲ οὐκέτι ἐγώ, ζῇ δὲ ἐν
ἐμοὶ Χριστός· ὃ δὲ νῦν ζῶ ἐν
σαρκί, ἐν πίστει ζῶ τῇ τοῦ υἱοῦ
τοῦ θεοῦ τοῦ ἀγαπήσαντός με καὶ
παραδόντος ἑαυτὸν ὑπὲρ ἐμοῦ.

τῷ θανάτῳ, οὕτως καὶ ἡ χάρις
βασιλεύσῃ διὰ δικαιοσύνης εἰς ζωὴν
αἰώνιον διὰ Ἰησοῦ Χριστοῦ τοῦ
κυρίου ἡμῶν.

Rom 6:1–23 τί οὖν ἐροῦμεν;
ἐπιμένωμεν τῇ ἁμαρτίᾳ, ἵνα ἡ χάρις
πλεονάσῃ; [2] μὴ γένοιτο· οἵτινες
ἀπεθάνομεν τῇ ἁμαρτίᾳ, πῶς ἔτι
ζήσομεν ἐν αὐτῇ; [3] ἢ ἀγνοεῖτε ὅτι
ὅσοι ἐβαπτίσθημεν εἰς Χριστὸν
Ἰησοῦν εἰς τὸν θάνατον αὐτοῦ
ἐβαπτίσθημεν; [4] συνετάφημεν οὖν
αὐτῷ διὰ τοῦ βαπτίσματος εἰς τὸν
θάνατον, ἵνα ὥσπερ ἠγέρθη
Χριστὸς ἐκ νεκρῶν διὰ τῆς δόξης
τοῦ πατρός, οὕτως καὶ ἡμεῖς ἐν
καινότητι ζωῆς περιπατήσωμεν.

Gal 3:27 ὅσοι γὰρ εἰς Χριστὸν
ἐβαπτίσθητε, Χριστὸν ἐνεδύσασθε.
Gal 5:24–25 οἱ δὲ τοῦ Χριστοῦ
[Ἰησοῦ] τὴν σάρκα ἐσταύρωσαν
σὺν τοῖς παθήμασιν καὶ ταῖς
ἐπιθυμίαις. 25 εἰ ζῶμεν πνεύματι,
πνεύματι καὶ στοιχῶμεν.

Gal 5:1 τῇ ἐλευθερίᾳ ἡμᾶς Χριστὸς
ἠλευθέρωσεν· στήκετε οὖν καὶ μὴ
πάλιν ζυγῷ δουλείας ἐνέχεσθε.
Gal 5:13 Ὑμεῖς γὰρ ἐπ' ἐλευθερίᾳ
ἐκλήθητε, ἀδελφοί· μόνον μὴ τὴν
ἐλευθερίαν εἰς ἀφορμὴν τῇ σαρκί,
ἀλλὰ διὰ τῆς ἀγάπης δουλεύετε
ἀλλήλοις. 14 ὁ γὰρ πᾶς νόμος ἐν
ἑνὶ λόγῳ πεπλήρωται, ἐν τῷ
ἀγαπήσεις τὸν πλησίον σου ὡς
σεαυτόν.
Gal 5:16 Λέγω δέ, πνεύματι περιπατεῖτε καὶ ἐπιθυμίαν σαρκὸς οὐ μὴ
τελέσητε.
Gal 4:8–10 Ἀλλὰ τότε μὲν οὐκ
εἰδότες θεὸν ἐδουλεύσατε τοῖς
φύσει μὴ οὖσιν θεοῖς· 9 νῦν δὲ
γνόντες θεόν, μᾶλλον δὲ
γνωσθέντες ὑπὸ θεοῦ, πῶς
ἐπιστρέφετε πάλιν ἐπὶ τὰ ἀσθενῆ
καὶ πτωχὰ στοιχεῖα, οἷς πάλιν
ἄνωθεν δουλεύειν θέλετε; 10 ἡμέρας
παρατηρεῖσθε καὶ μῆνας καὶ
καιροὺς καὶ ἐνιαυτούς.

5 εἰ γὰρ σύμφυτοι γεγόναμεν τῷ
ὁμοιώματι τοῦ θανάτου αὐτοῦ, ἀλλὰ
καὶ τῆς ἀναστάσεως ἐσόμεθα·
6 τοῦτο γινώσκοντες, ὅτι ὁ παλαιὸς
ἡμῶν ἄνθρωπος συνεσταυρώθη, ἵνα
καταργηθῇ τὸ σῶμα τῆς ἁμαρτίας,
τοῦ μηκέτι δουλεύειν ἡμᾶς τῇ
ἁμαρτίᾳ· 7 ὁ γὰρ ἀποθανὼν
δεδικαίωται ἀπὸ τῆς ἁμαρτίας. 8 εἰ
δὲ ἀπεθάνομεν σὺν Χριστῷ,
πιστεύομεν ὅτι καὶ συζήσομεν
αὐτῷ· 9 εἰδότες ὅτι Χριστὸς
ἐγερθεὶς ἐκ νεκρῶν οὐκέτι
ἀποθνήσκει, θάνατος αὐτοῦ οὐκέτι
κυριεύει. 10 ὃ γὰρ ἀπέθανεν, τῇ
ἁμαρτίᾳ ἀπέθανεν ἐφάπαξ· ὃ δὲ ζῇ,
ζῇ τῷ θεῷ. 11 οὕτως καὶ ὑμεῖς
λογίζεσθε ἑαυτοὺς [εἶναι] νεκροὺς
μὲν τῇ ἁμαρτίᾳ ζῶντας δὲ τῷ θεῷ
ἐν Χριστῷ Ἰησοῦ. 12 Μὴ οὖν
βασιλευέτω ἡ ἁμαρτία ἐν τῷ θνητῷ
ὑμῶν σώματι εἰς τὸ ὑπακούειν ταῖς
ἐπιθυμίαις αὐτοῦ, 13 μηδὲ
παριστάνετε τὰ μέλη ὑμῶν ὅπλα
ἀδικίας τῇ ἁμαρτίᾳ, ἀλλὰ
παραστήσατε ἑαυτοὺς τῷ θεῷ ὡσεὶ
ἐκ νεκρῶν ζῶντας καὶ τὰ μέλη
ὑμῶν ὅπλα δικαιοσύνης τῷ θεῷ·
14 ἁμαρτία γὰρ ὑμῶν οὐ κυριεύσει,
οὐ γάρ ἐστε ὑπὸ νόμον ἀλλὰ ὑπὸ
χάριν. 15 Τί οὖν; ἁμαρτήσωμεν ὅτι
οὐκ ἐσμὲν ὑπὸ νόμον ἀλλὰ ὑπὸ
χάριν; μὴ γένοιτο. 16 οὐκ οἴδατε
ὅτι ᾧ παριστάνετε ἑαυτοὺς δούλους
εἰς ὑπακοήν, δοῦλοί ἐστε ᾧ
ὑπακούετε, ἤτοι ἁμαρτίας εἰς
θάνατον ἢ ὑπακοῆς εἰς
δικαιοσύνην; 17 χάρις δὲ τῷ θεῷ
ὅτι ἦτε δοῦλοι τῆς ἁμαρτίας
ὑπηκούσατε δὲ ἐκ καρδίας εἰς ὃν
παρεδόθητε τύπον διδαχῆς,
18 ἐλευθερωθέντες δὲ ἀπὸ τῆς
ἁμαρτίας ἐδουλώθητε τῇ
δικαιοσύνῃ· 19 ἀνθρώπινον λέγω
διὰ τὴν ἀσθένειαν τῆς σαρκὸς
ὑμῶν. ὥσπερ γὰρ παρεστήσατε τὰ
μέλη ὑμῶν δοῦλα τῇ ἀκαθαρσίᾳ καὶ
τῇ ἀνομίᾳ εἰς τὴν ἀνομίαν, οὕτως
νῦν παραστήσατε τὰ μέλη ὑμῶν

7. Gal 2:19–21 ἐγὼ γὰρ διὰ νόμου
νόμῳ ἀπέθανον ἵνα θεῷ ζήσω.
Χριστῷ συνεσταύρωμαι· ²⁰ ζῶ δὲ
οὐκέτι ἐγώ, ζῇ δὲ ἐν ἐμοὶ Χριστός·
ὃ δὲ νῦν ζῶ ἐν σαρκί, ἐν πίστει ζῶ
τῇ τοῦ υἱοῦ τοῦ θεοῦ τοῦ
ἀγαπήσαντός με καὶ παραδόντος
ἑαυτὸν ὑπὲρ ἐμοῦ. ²¹ οὐκ ἀθετῶ
τὴν χάριν τοῦ θεοῦ· εἰ γὰρ διὰ
νόμου δικαιοσύνη, ἄρα Χριστὸς
δωρεὰν ἀπέθανεν.
Gal 3:10–13 ὅσοι γὰρ ἐξ ἔργων νόμου
εἰσὶν ὑπὸ κατάραν εἰσίν· γέγραπται
γὰρ ὅτι ἐπικατάρατος πᾶς ὃς οὐκ
ἐμμένει πᾶσιν τοῖς γεγραμμένοις ἐν
τῷ βιβλίῳ τοῦ νόμου τοῦ ποιῆσαι
αὐτά. ¹¹ ὅτι δὲ ἐν νόμῳ οὐδεὶς
δικαιοῦται παρὰ τῷ θεῷ δῆλον, ὅτι
ὁ δίκαιος ἐκ πίστεως ζήσεται· ¹² ὁ
δὲ νόμος οὐκ ἔστιν ἐκ πίστεως,
ἀλλ' ὁ ποιήσας αὐτὰ ζήσεται ἐν
αὐτοῖς. ¹³ Χριστὸς ἡμᾶς
ἐξηγόρασεν ἐκ τῆς κατάρας τοῦ
νόμου γενόμενος ὑπὲρ ἡμῶν
κατάρα, ὅτι γέγραπται,
ἐπικατάρατος πᾶς ὁ κρεμάμενος ἐπὶ
ξύλου.
Gal 3:19 Τί οὖν ὁ νόμος; τῶν
παραβάσεων χάριν προσετέθη,
ἄχρις οὗ ἔλθῃ τὸ σπέρμα ᾧ
ἐπήγγελται, διαταγεὶς δι' ἀγγέλων
ἐν χειρὶ μεσίτου.
Gal 3:22–25 ἀλλὰ συνέκλεισεν ἡ
γραφὴ τὰ πάντα ὑπὸ ἁμαρτίαν ἵνα

δοῦλα τῇ δικαιοσύνῃ εἰς ἁγιασμόν.
²⁰ ὅτε γὰρ δοῦλοι ἦτε τῆς
ἁμαρτίας, ἐλεύθεροι ἦτε τῇ
δικαιοσύνῃ. ²¹ τίνα οὖν καρπὸν
εἴχετε τότε ἐφ' οἷς νῦν
ἐπαισχύνεσθε; τὸ γὰρ τέλος
ἐκείνων θάνατος. ²² νυνὶ δέ,
ἐλευθερωθέντες ἀπὸ τῆς ἁμαρτίας
δουλωθέντες δὲ τῷ θεῷ, ἔχετε τὸν
καρπὸν ὑμῶν εἰς ἁγιασμόν, τὸ δὲ
τέλος ζωὴν αἰώνιον. ²³ τὰ γὰρ
ὀψώνια τῆς ἁμαρτίας θάνατος, τὸ
δὲ χάρισμα τοῦ θεοῦ ζωὴ αἰώνιος
ἐν Χριστῷ Ἰησοῦ τῷ κυρίῳ ἡμῶν.
Rom 7:1–6 Ἢ ἀγνοεῖτε, ἀδελφοί,
γινώσκουσιν γὰρ νόμον λαλῶ, ὅτι
ὁ νόμος κυριεύει τοῦ ἀνθρώπου ἐφ'
ὅσον χρόνον ζῇ; ² ἡ γὰρ ὕπανδρος
γυνὴ τῷ ζῶντι ἀνδρὶ δέδεται νόμῳ·
ἐὰν δὲ ἀποθάνῃ ὁ ἀνήρ, κατήργηται
ἀπὸ τοῦ νόμου τοῦ ἀνδρός. ³ ἄρα
οὖν ζῶντος τοῦ ἀνδρὸς μοιχαλὶς
χρηματίσει ἐὰν γένηται ἀνδρὶ
ἑτέρῳ· ἐὰν δὲ ἀποθάνῃ ὁ ἀνήρ,
ἐλευθέρα ἐστὶν ἀπὸ τοῦ νόμου, τοῦ
μὴ εἶναι αὐτὴν μοιχαλίδα γενομένην
ἀνδρὶ ἑτέρῳ ⁴ ὥστε, ἀδελφοί μου,
καὶ ὑμεῖς ἐθανατώθητε τῷ νόμῳ διὰ
τοῦ σώματος τοῦ Χριστοῦ, εἰς τὸ
γενέσθαι ὑμᾶς ἑτέρῳ, τῷ ἐκ νεκρῶν
ἐγερθέντι, ἵνα καρποφορήσωμεν τῷ
θεῷ. ⁵ ὅτε γὰρ ἦμεν ἐν τῇ σαρκί,
τὰ παθήματα τῶν ἁμαρτιῶν τὰ διὰ
τοῦ νόμου ἐνηργεῖτο ἐν τοῖς
μέλεσιν ἡμῶν εἰς τὸ καρποφορῆσαι
τῷ θανάτῳ· ⁶ νυνὶ δὲ κατηργήθημεν
ἀπὸ τοῦ νόμου, ἀποθανόντες ἐν ᾧ
κατειχόμεθα, ὥστε δουλεύειν ἡμᾶς
ἐν καινότητι πνεύματος καὶ οὐ
παλαιότητι γράμματος

ἡ ἐπαγγελία ἐκ πίστεως Ἰησοῦ
Χριστοῦ δοθῇ τοῖς πιστεύουσιν.
²³ πρὸ τοῦ δὲ ἐλθεῖν τὴν πίστιν
ὑπὸ νόμον ἐφρουρούμεθα συγκλειόμενοι εἰς τὴν μέλλουσαν
πίστιν ἀποκαλυφθῆναι. ²⁴ ὥστε ὁ
νόμος παιδαγωγὸς ἡμῶν γέγονεν εἰς
Χριστόν, ἵνα ἐκ πίστεως
δικαιωθῶμεν· ²⁵ ἐλθούσης δὲ τῆς
πίστεως οὐκέτι ὑπὸ παιδαγωγόν
ἐσμεν.

Gal 4:1–10 Λέγω δέ, ἐφ' ὅσον χρόνον
ὁ κληρονόμος νήπιός ἐστιν, οὐδὲν
διαφέρει δούλου κύριος πάντων ὢν,
² ἀλλὰ ὑπὸ ἐπιτρόπους ἐστὶν καὶ
οἰκονόμους ἄχρι τῆς προθεσμίας
τοῦ πατρός. ³ οὕτως καὶ ἡμεῖς, ὅτε
ἦμεν νήπιοι, ὑπὸ τὰ στοιχεῖα τοῦ
κόσμου ἤμεθα δεδουλωμένοι· ⁴ ὅτε
δὲ ἦλθεν τὸ πλήρωμα τοῦ χρόνου,
ἐξαπέστειλεν ὁ θεὸς τὸν υἱὸν
αὐτοῦ, γενόμενον ἐκ γυναικός,
γενόμενον ὑπὸ νόμον, ⁵ ἵνα τοὺς
ὑπὸ νόμον ἐξαγοράσῃ, ἵνα τὴν
υἱοθεσίαν ἀπολάβωμεν. ⁶ Ὅτι δέ
ἐστε υἱοί, ἐξαπέστειλεν ὁ θεὸς τὸ
πνεῦμα τοῦ υἱοῦ αὐτοῦ εἰς τὰς
καρδίας ἡμῶν, κρᾶζον, Αββα ὁ
πατήρ. ⁷ ὥστε οὐκέτι εἶ δοῦλος
ἀλλὰ υἱός· εἰ δὲ υἱός, καὶ κληρονόμος διὰ θεοῦ. ⁸ Ἀλλὰ τότε μὲν
οὐκ εἰδότες θεὸν ἐδουλεύσατε τοῖς
φύσει μὴ οὖσιν θεοῖς· ⁹ νῦν δὲ
γνόντες θεόν, μᾶλλον δὲ
γνωσθέντες ὑπὸ θεοῦ, πῶς
ἐπιστρέφετε πάλιν ἐπὶ τὰ ἀσθενῆ
καὶ πτωχὰ στοιχεῖα, οἷς πάλιν
ἄνωθεν δουλεύειν θέλετε; ¹⁰ ἡμέρας
παρατηρεῖσθε καὶ μῆνας καὶ
καιροὺς καὶ ἐνιαυτούς.

Gal 4:21–31 Λέγετέ μοι, οἱ ὑπὸ νόμον
θέλοντες εἶναι, τὸν νόμον οὐκ
ἀκούετε; ²² γέγραπται γὰρ ὅτι
Ἀβραὰμ δύο υἱοὺς ἔσχεν, ἕνα ἐκ
τῆς παιδίσκης καὶ ἕνα ἐκ τῆς
ἐλευθέρας. ²³ ἀλλ' ὁ μὲν ἐκ τῆς
παιδίσκης κατὰ σάρκα γεγέννηται,
ὁ δὲ ἐκ τῆς ἐλευθέρας δι'
ἐπαγγελίας. ²⁴ ἅτινά ἐστιν

ἀλληγορούμενα· αὗται γάρ εἰσιν δύο
διαθῆκαι, μία μὲν ἀπὸ ὄρους Σινᾶ, εἰς
δουλείαν γεννῶσα, ἥτις ἐστὶν Ἀγάρ.
²⁵ τὸ δὲ Ἀγὰρ Σινᾶ ὄρος ἐστὶν ἐν
τῇ Ἀραβίᾳ, συστοιχεῖ δὲ τῇ νῦν
Ἰερουσαλήμ, δουλεύει γὰρ μετὰ τῶν
τέκνων αὐτῆς. ²⁶ ἡ δὲ ἄνω
Ἰερουσαλὴμ ἐλευθέρα ἐστίν, ἥτις
ἐστὶν μήτηρ ἡμῶν· ²⁷ γέγραπται
γάρ, εὐφράνθητι, στεῖρα ἡ οὐ
τίκτουσα, ῥῆξον καὶ βόησον, ἡ οὐκ
ὠδίνουσα· ὅτι πολλὰ τὰ τέκνα τῆς
ἐρήμου μᾶλλον ἢ τῆς ἐχούσης τὸν
ἄνδρα. ²⁸ ὑμεῖς δέ, ἀδελφοί, κατὰ
Ἰσαὰκ ἐπαγγελίας τέκνα ἐστέ.
²⁹ ἀλλ' ὥσπερ τότε ὁ κατὰ σάρκα
γεννηθεὶς ἐδίωκεν τὸν κατὰ πνεῦμα,
οὕτως καὶ νῦν. ³⁰ ἀλλὰ τί λέγει ἡ
γραφή; ἔκβαλε τὴν παιδίσκην καὶ
τὸν υἱὸν αὐτῆς, οὐ γὰρ μὴ
κληρονομήσει ὁ υἱὸς τῆς παιδίσκης
μετὰ τοῦ υἱοῦ τῆς ἐλευθέρας. ³¹ διό,
ἀδελφοί, οὐκ ἐσμὲν παιδίσκης
τέκνα ἀλλὰ τῆς ἐλευθέρας.
Gal 5:1 τῇ ἐλευθερίᾳ ἡμᾶς Χριστὸς
ἠλευθέρωσεν· στήκετε οὖν καὶ μὴ
πάλιν ζυγῷ δουλείας ἐνέχεσθε.

8. Gal 3:19 Τί οὖν ὁ νόμος; τῶν
παραβάσεων χάριν προσετέθη,
ἄχρις οὗ ἔλθῃ τὸ σπέρμα ᾧ
ἐπήγγελται, διαταγεὶς δι' ἀγγέλων
ἐν χειρὶ μεσίτου.

Rom 7:7–8:4 τί οὖν ἐροῦμεν; ὁ νόμος
ἁμαρτία; μὴ γένοιτο· ἀλλὰ τὴν
ἁμαρτίαν οὐκ ἔγνων εἰ μὴ διὰ
νόμου, τήν τε γὰρ ἐπιθυμίαν οὐκ
ᾔδειν εἰ μὴ ὁ νόμος ἔλεγεν, οὐκ
ἐπιθυμήσεις. ⁸ ἀφορμὴν δὲ λαβοῦσα
ἡ ἁμαρτία διὰ τῆς ἐντολῆς
κατειργάσατο ἐν ἐμοὶ πᾶσαν
ἐπιθυμίαν· χωρὶς γὰρ νόμου ἁμαρτία
νεκρά. ⁹ ἐγὼ δὲ ἔζων χωρὶς νόμου
ποτέ· ἐλθούσης δὲ τῆς ἐντολῆς ἡ
ἁμαρτία ἀνέζησεν, ¹⁰ ἐγὼ δὲ
ἀπέθανον, καὶ εὑρέθη μοι ἡ ἐντολὴ
ἡ εἰς ζωὴν αὕτη εἰς θάνατον. ¹¹ ἡ
γὰρ ἁμαρτία ἀφορμὴν λαβοῦσα διὰ
τῆς ἐντολῆς ἐξηπάτησέν με καὶ δι'
αὐτῆς ἀπέκτεινεν. ¹² ὥστε ὁ μὲν
νόμος ἅγιος, καὶ ἡ ἐντολὴ ἁγία καὶ
δικαία καὶ ἀγαθή. ¹³ Τὸ οὖν ἀγαθὸν
ἐμοὶ ἐγένετο θάνατος; μὴ γένοιτο·
ἀλλὰ ἡ ἁμαρτία, ἵνα φανῇ ἁμαρτία,

διὰ τοῦ ἀγαθοῦ μοι κατεργαζομένη
θάνατον· ἵνα γένηται καθ' ὑπερβολὴν
ἁμαρτωλὸς ἡ ἁμαρτία διὰ τῆς
ἐντολῆς. ¹⁴ οἴδαμεν γὰρ ὅτι ὁ νόμος
πνευματικός ἐστιν· ἐγὼ δὲ σάρκινός
εἰμι, πεπραμένος ὑπὸ τὴν ἁμαρτίαν.
¹⁵ ὃ γὰρ κατεργάζομαι οὐ γινώσκω·
οὐ γὰρ ὃ θέλω τοῦτο πράσσω, ἀλλ'
ὃ μισῶ τοῦτο ποιῶ. ¹⁶ εἰ δὲ ὃ οὐ
θέλω τοῦτο ποιῶ, σύμφημι τῷ νόμῳ
ὅτι καλός. ¹⁷ νυνὶ δὲ οὐκέτι ἐγὼ
κατεργάζομαι αὐτὸ ἀλλὰ ἡ οἰκοῦσα
ἐν ἐμοὶ ἁμαρτία. ¹⁸ οἶδα γὰρ ὅτι
οὐκ οἰκεῖ ἐν ἐμοί, τοῦτ' ἔστιν ἐν τῇ
σαρκί μου, ἀγαθόν· τὸ γὰρ θέλειν
παράκειταί μοι, τὸ δὲ
κατεργάζεσθαι τὸ καλὸν οὔ· ¹⁹ οὐ
γὰρ ὃ θέλω ποιῶ ἀγαθόν, ἀλλὰ ὃ
οὐ θέλω κακὸν τοῦτο πράσσω. ²⁰ εἰ
δὲ ὃ οὐ θέλω [ἐγὼ] τοῦτο ποιῶ,
οὐκέτι ἐγὼ κατεργάζομαι αὐτὸ ἀλλὰ
ἡ οἰκοῦσα ἐν ἐμοὶ ἁμαρτία.
²¹ εὑρίσκω ἄρα τὸν νόμον τῷ
θέλοντι ἐμοὶ ποιεῖν τὸ καλὸν ὅτι
ἐμοὶ τὸ κακὸν παράκειται·
²² συνήδομαι γὰρ τῷ νόμῳ τοῦ θεοῦ
κατὰ τὸν ἔσω ἄνθρωπον, ²³ βλέπω
δὲ ἕτερον νόμον ἐν τοῖς μέλεσίν
μου ἀντιστρατευόμενον τῷ νόμῳ
τοῦ νοός μου καὶ αἰχμαλωτίζοντά
με ἐν τῷ νόμῳ τῆς ἁμαρτίας τῷ
ὄντι ἐν τοῖς μέλεσίν μου.
²⁴ ταλαίπωρος ἐγὼ ἄνθρωπος· τίς
με ῥύσεται ἐκ τοῦ σώματος τοῦ
θανάτου τούτου; ²⁵ χάρις δὲ τῷ θεῷ
διὰ Ἰησοῦ Χριστοῦ τοῦ κυρίου
ἡμῶν. ἄρα οὖν αὐτὸς ἐγὼ τῷ μὲν
νοῒ δουλεύω νόμῳ θεοῦ, τῇ δὲ
σαρκὶ νόμῳ ἁμαρτίας. 8¹ Οὐδὲν
ἄρα νῦν κατάκριμα τοῖς ἐν Χριστῷ
Ἰησοῦ· ² ὁ γὰρ νόμος τοῦ
πνεύματος τῆς ζωῆς ἐν Χριστῷ
Ἰησοῦ ἠλευθέρωσέν σε ἀπὸ τοῦ
νόμου τῆς ἁμαρτίας καὶ τοῦ
θανάτου. ³ τὸ γὰρ ἀδύνατον τοῦ
νόμου, ἐν ᾧ ἠσθένει διὰ τῆς
σαρκός, ὁ θεὸς τὸν ἑαυτοῦ υἱὸν
πέμψας ἐν ὁμοιώματι σαρκὸς
ἁμαρτίας καὶ περὶ ἁμαρτίας

Gal 5:17 ἡ γὰρ σὰρξ ἐπιθυμεῖ κατὰ
τοῦ πνεύματος, τὸ δὲ πνεῦμα κατὰ
τῆς σαρκός· ταῦτα γὰρ ἀλλήλοις
ἀντίκειται, ἵνα μὴ ἃ ἐὰν θέλητε
ταῦτα ποιῆτε.

Gal 5:18 εἰ δὲ πνεύματι ἄγεσθε, οὐκ
ἐστὲ ὑπὸ νόμον.

Gal 2:17–18 εἰ δὲ ζητοῦντες
δικαιωθῆναι ἐν Χριστῷ εὑρέθημεν
καὶ αὐτοὶ ἁμαρτωλοί, ἄρα Χριστὸς
ἁμαρτίας διάκονος; μὴ γένοιτο.
¹⁸ εἰ γὰρ ἃ κατέλυσα ταῦτα πάλιν
οἰκοδομῶ, παραβάτην ἐμαυτὸν
συνιστάνω.

Gal 3:21 ὁ οὖν νόμος κατὰ τῶν
ἐπαγγελιῶν [τοῦ θεοῦ]; μὴ γένοιτο·
εἰ γὰρ ἐδόθη νόμος ὁ δυνάμενος
ζωοποιῆσαι, ὄντως ἐκ νόμου ἂν ἦν
ἡ δικαιοσύνη.

κατέκρινεν τὴν ἁμαρτίαν ἐν τῇ
σαρκί, [4] ἵνα τὸ δικαίωμα τοῦ νόμου
πληρωθῇ ἐν ἡμῖν τοῖς μὴ κατὰ
σάρκα περιπατοῦσιν ἀλλὰ κατὰ
πνεῦμα.

9. Gal 5:17–18 ἡ γὰρ σὰρξ ἐπιθυμεῖ
κατὰ τοῦ πνεύματος, τὸ δὲ πνεῦμα
κατὰ τῆς σαρκός· ταῦτα γὰρ
ἀλλήλοις ἀντίκειται, ἵνα μὴ ἃ ἐὰν
θέλητε ταῦτα ποιῆτε. [18] εἰ δὲ
πνεύματι ἄγεσθε, οὐκ ἐστὲ ὑπὸ
νόμον.

Rom 8:5–17 οἱ γὰρ κατὰ σάρκα ὄντες
τὰ τῆς σαρκὸς φρονοῦσιν, οἱ δὲ
κατὰ πνεῦμα τὰ τοῦ πνεύματος.
[6] τὸ γὰρ φρόνημα τῆς σαρκὸς
θάνατος, τὸ δὲ φρόνημα τοῦ
πνεύματος ζωὴ καὶ εἰρήνη· [7] διότι
τὸ φρόνημα τῆς σαρκὸς ἔχθρα εἰς
θεόν, τῷ γὰρ νόμῳ τοῦ θεοῦ οὐχ
ὑποτάσσεται, οὐδὲ γὰρ δύναται·
[8] οἱ δὲ ἐν σαρκὶ ὄντες θεῷ ἀρέσαι
οὐ δύνανται. [9] ὑμεῖς δὲ οὐκ ἐστὲ ἐν
σαρκὶ ἀλλὰ ἐν πνεύματι, εἴπερ
πνεῦμα θεοῦ οἰκεῖ ἐν ὑμῖν. εἰ δέ τις
πνεῦμα Χριστοῦ οὐκ ἔχει, οὗτος
οὐκ ἔστιν αὐτοῦ. [10] εἰ δὲ Χριστὸς
ἐν ὑμῖν, τὸ μὲν σῶμα νεκρὸν διὰ
ἁμαρτίαν, τὸ δὲ πνεῦμα ζωὴ διὰ
δικαιοσύνην. [11] εἰ δὲ τὸ πνεῦμα
τοῦ ἐγείραντος τὸν Ἰησοῦν ἐκ
νεκρῶν οἰκεῖ ἐν ὑμῖν, ὁ ἐγείρας
Χριστὸν ἐκ νεκρῶν ζῳοποιήσει καὶ
τὰ θνητὰ σώματα ὑμῶν διὰ τοῦ
ἐνοικοῦντος αὐτοῦ πνεύματος ἐν
ὑμῖν. [12] Ἄρα οὖν, ἀδελφοί,
ὀφειλέται ἐσμέν, οὐ τῇ σαρκὶ τοῦ
κατὰ σάρκα ζῆν· [13] εἰ γὰρ κατὰ
σάρκα ζῆτε μέλλετε ἀποθνήσκειν, εἰ
δὲ πνεύματι τὰς πράξεις τοῦ
σώματος θανατοῦτε ζήσεσθε.
[14] ὅσοι γὰρ πνεύματι θεοῦ ἄγονται,
οὗτοι υἱοὶ θεοῦ εἰσιν. [15] οὐ γὰρ
ἐλάβετε πνεῦμα δουλείας πάλιν εἰς
φόβον, ἀλλὰ ἐλάβετε πνεῦμα
υἱοθεσίας, ἐν ᾧ κράζομεν, Αββα ὁ
πατήρ· [16] αὐτὸ τὸ πνεῦμα συμμαρτυρεῖ τῷ πνεύματι ἡμῶν ὅτι ἐσμὲν
τέκνα θεοῦ. [17] εἰ δὲ τέκνα, καὶ κλη-
ρονόμοι· κληρονόμοι μὲν θεοῦ, συγκληρονόμοι δὲ Χριστοῦ, εἴπερ
συμπάσχομεν ἵνα καὶ
συνδοξασθῶμεν.

Gal 3:26 πάντες γὰρ υἱοὶ θεοῦ ἐστε
διὰ τῆς πίστεως ἐν Χριστῷ Ἰησοῦ.
Gal 4:6–7 ὅτι δὲ ἐστε υἱοί,
ἐξαπέστειλεν ὁ θεὸς τὸ πνεῦμα τοῦ
υἱοῦ αὐτοῦ εἰς τὰς καρδίας ἡμῶν,
κρᾶζον, Αββα ὁ πατήρ. [7] ὥστε
οὐκέτι εἶ δοῦλος ἀλλὰ υἱός· εἰ δὲ
υἱός, καὶ κληρονόμος διὰ θεοῦ.

10.

Rom 8:18–30 Λογίζομαι γὰρ ὅτι οὐκ
ἄξια τὰ παθήματα τοῦ νῦν καιροῦ
πρὸς τὴν μέλλουσαν δόξαν

ἀποκαλυφθῆναι εἰς ἡμᾶς. [19] ἡ γὰρ
ἀποκαραδοκία τῆς κτίσεως τὴν
ἀποκάλυψιν τῶν υἱῶν τοῦ θεοῦ
ἀπεκδέχεται· [20] τῇ γὰρ ματαιότητι ἡ
κτίσις ὑπετάγη, οὐχ ἑκοῦσα ἀλλὰ
διὰ τὸν ὑποτάξαντα, ἐφ' ἑλπίδι
[21] ὅτι καὶ αὐτὴ ἡ κτίσις
ἐλευθερωθήσεται ἀπὸ τῆς δουλείας
τῆς φθορᾶς εἰς τὴν ἐλευθερίαν τῆς
δόξης τῶν τέκνων τοῦ θεοῦ.
[22] οἴδαμεν γὰρ ὅτι πᾶσα ἡ κτίσις
συστενάζει καὶ συνωδίνει ἄχρι τοῦ
νῦν· [23] οὐ μόνον δέ, ἀλλὰ καὶ αὐτοὶ
τὴν ἀπαρχὴν τοῦ πνεύματος ἔχοντες
ἡμεῖς καὶ αὐτοὶ ἐν ἑαυτοῖς
στενάζομεν υἱοθεσίαν
ἀπεκδεχόμενοι, τὴν ἀπολύτρωσιν

Gal 5:5 ἡμεῖς γὰρ πνεύματι ἐκ πίστεως   τοῦ σώματος ἡμῶν. [24] τῇ γὰρ ἑλπίδι
ἐλπίδα δικαιοσύνης ἀπεκδεχόμεθα.   ἐσώθημεν· ἐλπὶς δὲ βλεπομένη οὐκ
ἔστιν ἐλπίς· ὃ γὰρ βλέπει τίς
ἐλπίζει; [25] εἰ δὲ ὃ οὐ βλέπομεν
ἐλπίζομεν, δι' ὑπομονῆς
ἀπεκδεχόμεθα. [26] Ὡσαύτως δὲ καὶ
τὸ πνεῦμα συναντιλαμβάνεται τῇ
ἀσθενείᾳ ἡμῶν· τὸ γὰρ τί
προσευξώμεθα καθὸ δεῖ οὐκ
οἴδαμεν, ἀλλὰ αὐτὸ τὸ πνεῦμα
ὑπερεντυγχάνει στεναγμοῖς
ἀλαλήτοις· [27] ὁ δὲ ἐραυνῶν τὰς
καρδίας οἶδεν τί τὸ φρόνημα τοῦ
πνεύματος, ὅτι κατὰ θεὸν
ἐντυγχάνει ὑπὲρ ἁγίων. [28] οἴδαμεν
δὲ ὅτι τοῖς ἀγαπῶσιν τὸν θεὸν
πάντα συνεργεῖ εἰς ἀγαθόν, τοῖς
κατὰ πρόθεσιν κλητοῖς οὖσιν.
[29] ὅτι οὓς προέγνω, καὶ προώρισεν
συμμόρφους τῆς εἰκόνος τοῦ υἱοῦ
αὐτοῦ, εἰς τὸ εἶναι αὐτὸν
πρωτότοκον ἐν πολλοῖς ἀδελφοῖς·
[30] οὓς δὲ προώρισεν, τούτους καὶ
ἐκάλεσεν· καὶ οὓς ἐκάλεσεν,
τούτους καὶ ἐδικαίωσεν· οὓς δὲ
11.   ἐδικαίωσεν, τούτους καὶ ἐδόξασεν.

Rom 8:31–39 Τί οὖν ἐροῦμεν πρὸς
ταῦτα; εἰ ὁ θεὸς ὑπὲρ ἡμῶν, τίς
καθ' ἡμῶν; [32] ὅς γε τοῦ ἰδίου υἱοῦ
οὐκ ἐφείσατο, ἀλλὰ ὑπὲρ ἡμῶν
πάντων παρέδωκεν αὐτόν, πῶς οὐχὶ
καὶ σὺν αὐτῷ τὰ πάντα ἡμῖν

12.

Gal 3:23 Πρὸ τοῦ δὲ ἐλθεῖν τὴν πίστιν ὑπὸ νόμον ἐφρουρούμεθα συγκλειόμενοι εἰς τὴν μέλλουσαν πίστιν ἀποκαλυφθῆναι. ²⁴ ὥστε ὁ νόμος παιδαγωγὸς ἡμῶν γέγονεν εἰς Χριστόν, ἵνα ἐκ πίστεως δικαιωθῶμεν·

χαρίσεται; ³³ τίς ἐγκαλέσει κατὰ ἐκλεκτῶν θεοῦ; θεὸς ὁ δικαιῶν· ³⁴ τίς ὁ κατακρινῶν; Χριστὸς [Ἰησοῦς] ὁ ἀποθανών, μᾶλλον δὲ ἐγερθείς, ὃς καί ἐστιν ἐν δεξιᾷ τοῦ θεοῦ, ὃς καὶ ἐντυγχάνει ὑπὲρ ἡμῶν. ³⁵ τίς ἡμᾶς χωρίσει ἀπὸ τῆς ἀγάπης τοῦ Χριστοῦ; θλῖψις ἢ στενοχωρία ἢ διωγμὸς ἢ λιμὸς ἢ γυμνότης ἢ κίνδυνος ἢ μάχαιρα; ³⁶ καθὼς γέγραπται ὅτι ἕνεκεν σοῦ θανατούμεθα ὅλην τὴν ἡμέραν, ἐλογίσθημεν ὡς πρόβατα σφαγῆς. ³⁷ ἀλλ' ἐν τούτοις πᾶσιν ὑπερνικῶμεν διὰ τοῦ ἀγαπήσαντος ἡμᾶς. ³⁸ πέπεισμαι γὰρ ὅτι οὔτε θάνατος οὔτε ζωὴ οὔτε ἄγγελοι οὔτε ἀρχαὶ οὔτε ἐνεστῶτα οὔτε μέλλοντα οὔτε δυνάμεις ³⁹ οὔτε ὕψωμα οὔτε βάθος οὔτε τις κτίσις ἑτέρα δυνήσεται ἡμᾶς χωρίσαι ἀπὸ τῆς ἀγάπης τοῦ θεοῦ τῆς ἐν Χριστῷ Ἰησοῦ τῷ κυρίῳ ἡμῶν.

Rom 9:1–33 Ἀλήθειαν λέγω ἐν Χριστῷ, οὐ ψεύδομαι, συμμαρτυρούσης μοι τῆς συνειδήσεώς μου ἐν πνεύματι ἁγίῳ, ² ὅτι λύπη μοί ἐστιν μεγάλη καὶ ἀδιάλειπτος ὀδύνη τῇ καρδίᾳ μου. ³ ηὐχόμην γὰρ ἀνάθεμα εἶναι αὐτὸς ἐγὼ ἀπὸ τοῦ Χριστοῦ ὑπὲρ τῶν ἀδελφῶν μου τῶν συγγενῶν μου κατὰ σάρκα, ⁴ οἵτινές εἰσιν Ἰσραηλῖται, ὧν ἡ υἱοθεσία καὶ ἡ δόξα καὶ αἱ διαθῆκαι καὶ ἡ νομοθεσία καὶ ἡ λατρεία καὶ αἱ ἐπαγγελίαι. ⁵ ὧν οἱ πατέρες, καὶ ἐξ ὧν ὁ Χριστὸς τὸ κατὰ σάρκα· ὁ ὢν ἐπὶ πάντων θεὸς εὐλογητὸς εἰς τοὺς αἰῶνας, ἀμήν. ⁶ Οὐχ οἷον δὲ ὅτι ἐκπέπτωκεν ὁ λόγος τοῦ θεοῦ. οὐ γὰρ πάντες οἱ ἐξ Ἰσραήλ, οὗτοι Ἰσραήλ· ⁷ οὐδ' ὅτι εἰσὶν σπέρμα Ἀβραάμ, πάντες τέκνα, ἀλλ', ἐν Ἰσαὰκ κληθήσεταί σοι σπέρμα. ⁸ τοῦτ' ἔστιν, οὐ τὰ τέκνα τῆς σαρκὸς ταῦτα τέκνα τοῦ θεοῦ, ἀλλὰ τὰ τέκνα τῆς ἐπαγγελίας λογίζεται εἰς σπέρμα· ⁹ ἐπαγγελίας γὰρ ὁ

λόγος οὗτος, κατὰ τὸν καιρὸν τοῦτον
ἐλεύσομαι καὶ ἔσται τῇ Σάρρᾳ υἱός.
¹⁰ οὐ μόνον δέ, ἀλλὰ καὶ Ῥεβέκκα
ἐξ ἑνὸς κοίτην ἔχουσα, Ἰσαὰκ τοῦ
πατρὸς ἡμῶν· ¹¹ μήπω γὰρ
γεννηθέντων μηδὲ πραξάντων τι
ἀγαθὸν ἢ φαῦλον, ἵνα ἡ κατ᾽
ἐκλογὴν πρόθεσις τοῦ θεοῦ μένῃ,
¹² οὐκ ἐξ ἔργων ἀλλ᾽ ἐκ τοῦ
καλοῦντος, ἐρρέθη αὐτῇ ὅτι ὁ
μείζων δουλεύσει τῷ ἐλάσσονι·
¹³ καθὼς γέγραπται, τὸν Ἰακὼβ
ἠγάπησα, τὸν δὲ Ἡσαῦ ἐμίσησα.
¹⁴ Τί οὖν ἐροῦμεν; μὴ ἀδικία παρὰ
τῷ θεῷ; μὴ γένοιτο· ¹⁵ τῷ Μωϋσεῖ
γὰρ λέγει, ἐλεήσω ὃν ἂν ἐλεῶ, καὶ
οἰκτιρήσω ὃν ἂν οἰκτίρω. ¹⁶ ἄρα
οὖν οὐ τοῦ θέλοντος οὐδὲ τοῦ
τρέχοντος, ἀλλὰ τοῦ ἐλεῶντος θεοῦ.
¹⁷ λέγει γὰρ ἡ γραφὴ τῷ Φαραὼ ὅτι
εἰς αὐτὸ τοῦτο ἐξήγειρά σε ὅπως
ἐνδείξωμαι ἐν σοὶ τὴν δύναμίν μου,
καὶ ὅπως διαγγελῇ τὸ ὄνομά μου ἐν
πάσῃ τῇ γῇ. ¹⁸ ἄρα οὖν ὃν θέλει
ἐλεεῖ, ὃν δὲ θέλει σκληρύνει.
¹⁹ Ἐρεῖς μοι οὖν, τί [οὖν] ἔτι
μέμφεται; τῷ γὰρ βουλήματι αὐτοῦ
τίς ἀνθέστηκεν; ²⁰ ὦ ἄνθρωπε,
μενοῦνγε σὺ τίς εἶ ὁ
ἀνταποκρινόμενος τῷ θεῷ; μὴ ἐρεῖ
τὸ πλάσμα τῷ πλάσαντι, τί με
ἐποίησας οὕτως; ²¹ ἢ οὐκ ἔχει
ἐξουσίαν ὁ κεραμεὺς τοῦ πηλοῦ ἐκ
τοῦ αὐτοῦ φυράματος ποιῆσαι ὃ μὲν
εἰς τιμὴν σκεῦος, ὃ δὲ εἰς ἀτιμίαν;
²² εἰ δὲ θέλων ὁ θεὸς ἐνδείξασθαι
τὴν ὀργὴν καὶ γνωρίσαι τὸ δυνατὸν
αὐτοῦ ἤνεγκεν ἐν πολλῇ
μακροθυμίᾳ σκεύη ὀργῆς κατηρ-
τισμένα εἰς ἀπώλειαν, ²³ καὶ ἵνα
γνωρίσῃ τὸν πλοῦτον τῆς δόξης
αὐτοῦ ἐπὶ σκεύη ἐλέους, ἃ προ-
ητοίμασεν εἰς δόξαν, ²⁴ οὓς καὶ
ἐκάλεσεν ἡμᾶς οὐ μόνον ἐξ
Ἰουδαίων ἀλλὰ καὶ ἐξ ἐθνῶν; ²⁵ ὡς
καὶ ἐν τῷ Ὡσηὲ λέγει, καλέσω τὸν
οὐ λαόν μου λαόν μου καὶ τὴν οὐκ
ἠγαπημένην ἠγαπημένην· ²⁶ καὶ
ἔσται ἐν τῷ τόπῳ οὗ ἐρρέθη αὐτοῖς,

Gal 3:18 εἰ γὰρ ἐκ νόμου ἡ
κληρονομία, οὐκέτι ἐξ ἐπαγγελίας·
τῷ δὲ Ἀβραὰμ δι' ἐπαγγελίας
κεχάρισται ὁ θεός.

13.

Gal 1:14–16a καὶ προέκοπτον ἐν
τῷ Ἰουδαϊσμῷ ὑπὲρ πολλοὺς
συνηλικιώτας ἐν τῷ γένει μου,
περισσοτέρως ζηλωτὴς ὑπάρχων
τῶν πατρικῶν μου παραδόσεων.
[15] ὅτε δὲ εὐδόκησεν [ὁ θεὸς] ὁ
ἀφορίσας με ἐκ κοιλίας μητρός μου
καὶ καλέσας διὰ τῆς χάριτος αὐτοῦ
[16] ἀποκαλύψαι τὸν υἱὸν αὐτοῦ ἐν
ἐμοὶ ἵνα εὐαγγελίζωμαι αὐτὸν ἐν
τοῖς ἔθνεσιν, . . .

Gal 3:10–14 ὅσοι γὰρ ἐξ ἔργων
νόμου εἰσὶν ὑπὸ κατάραν εἰσίν·
γέγραπται γὰρ ὅτι ἐπικατάρατος
πᾶς ὃς οὐκ ἐμμένει πᾶσιν τοῖς
γεγραμμένοις ἐν τῷ βιβλίῳ τοῦ
νόμου τοῦ ποιῆσαι αὐτά. [11] ὅτι δὲ
ἐν νόμῳ οὐδεὶς δικαιοῦται παρὰ τῷ
θεῷ δῆλον, ὅτι ὁ δίκαιος ἐκ
πίστεως ζήσεται· [12] ὁ δὲ νόμος οὐκ
ἔστιν ἐκ πίστεως, ἀλλ' ὁ ποιήσας

οὐ λαός μου ὑμεῖς, ἐκεῖ κληθήσονται
υἱοὶ θεοῦ ζῶντος. [27] Ἠσαΐας δὲ
κράζει ὑπὲρ τοῦ Ἰσραήλ, ἐὰν ᾖ ὁ
ἀριθμὸς τῶν υἱῶν Ἰσραὴλ ὡς ἡ
ἄμμος τῆς θαλάσσης, τὸ ὑπόλειμμα
σωθήσεται· [28] λόγον γὰρ συντελῶν
καὶ συντέμνων ποιήσει κύριος ἐπὶ
τῆς γῆς. [29] καὶ καθὼς προείρηκεν
Ἠσαΐας, εἰ μὴ κύριος Σαβαὼθ
ἐγκατέλιπεν ἡμῖν σπέρμα, ὡς
Σόδομα ἂν ἐγενήθημεν καὶ ὡς
Γόμορρα ἂν ὡμοιώθημεν. [30] Τί οὖν
ἐροῦμεν; ὅτι ἔθνη τὰ μὴ διώκοντα
δικαιοσύνην κατέλαβεν
δικαιοσύνην, δικαιοσύνην δὲ τὴν ἐκ
πίστεως· [31] Ἰσραὴλ δὲ διώκων
νόμον δικαιοσύνης εἰς νόμον οὐκ
ἔφθασεν. [32] διὰ τί; ὅτι οὐκ ἐκ
πίστεως ἀλλ' ὡς ἐξ ἔργων·
προσέκοψαν τῷ λίθῳ τοῦ
προσκόμματος, [33] καθὼς γέγραπται,
ἰδοὺ τίθημι ἐν Σιὼν λίθον
προσκόμματος καὶ πέτραν
σκανδάλου, καὶ ὁ πιστεύων ἐπ'
αὐτῷ οὐ καταισχυνθήσεται.

Rom 10:1–21 Ἀδελφοί, ἡ μὲν εὐδοκία
τῆς ἐμῆς καρδίας καὶ ἡ δέησις πρὸς
τὸν θεὸν ὑπὲρ αὐτῶν εἰς σωτηρίαν.
[2] μαρτυρῶ γὰρ αὐτοῖς ὅτι ζῆλον
θεοῦ ἔχουσιν, ἀλλ' οὐ κατ'
ἐπίγνωσιν· [3] ἀγνοοῦντες γὰρ τὴν
τοῦ θεοῦ δικαιοσύνην, καὶ τὴν ἰδίαν
[δικαιοσύνην] ζητοῦντες στῆσαι, τῇ
δικαιοσύνῃ τοῦ θεοῦ οὐχ
ὑπετάγησαν· [4] τέλος γὰρ νόμου
Χριστὸς εἰς δικαιοσύνην παντὶ τῷ
πιστεύοντι.

[5] Μωϋσῆς γὰρ γράφει τὴν δικαιοσύνην
τὴν ἐκ [τοῦ] νόμου ὅτι ὁ ποιήσας
αὐτὰ ἄνθρωπος ζήσεται ἐν αὐτοῖς.
[6] ἡ δὲ ἐκ πίστεως δικαιοσύνη
οὕτως λέγει, μὴ εἴπῃς ἐν τῇ καρδίᾳ
σου, Τίς ἀναβήσεται εἰς τὸν
οὐρανόν; τοῦτ' ἔστιν Χριστὸν κατα-
γαγεῖν· [7] ἤ, τίς καταβήσεται εἰς τὴν
ἄβυσσον; τοῦτ' ἔστιν Χριστὸν ἐκ
νεκρῶν ἀναγαγεῖν. [8] ἀλλὰ τί λέγει;

αὐτὰ ζήσεται ἐν αὐτοῖς. ¹³ Χριστὸς
ἡμᾶς ἐξηγόρασεν ἐκ τῆς κατάρας
τοῦ νόμου γενόμενος ὑπὲρ ἡμῶν
κατάρα, ὅτι γέγραπται,
ἐπικατάρατος πᾶς ὁ κρεμάμενος ἐπὶ
ξύλου. ¹⁴ ἵνα εἰς τὰ ἔθνη ἡ εὐλογία
τοῦ Ἀβραὰμ γένηται ἐν Χριστῷ
Ἰησοῦ, ἵνα τὴν ἐπαγγελίαν τοῦ
πνεύματος λάβωμεν διὰ τῆς
πίστεως.

ἐγγύς σου τὸ ῥῆμά ἐστιν, ἐν τῷ
στόματί σου καὶ ἐν τῇ καρδίᾳ σου·
τοῦτ' ἔστιν τὸ ῥῆμα τῆς πίστεως ὃ
κηρύσσομεν. ⁹ ὅτι ἐὰν ὁμολογήσῃς
ἐν τῷ στόματί σου κύριον Ἰησοῦν,
καὶ πιστεύσῃς ἐν τῇ καρδίᾳ σου
ὅτι ὁ θεὸς αὐτὸν ἤγειρεν ἐκ
νεκρῶν, σωθήσῃ· ¹⁰ καρδίᾳ γὰρ
πιστεύεται εἰς δικαιοσύνην, στόματι
δὲ ὁμολογεῖται εἰς σωτηρίαν.
¹¹ λέγει γὰρ ἡ γραφή, πᾶς ὁ
πιστεύων ἐπ' αὐτῷ οὐ
καταισχυνθήσεται. ¹² οὐ γάρ ἐστιν
διαστολὴ Ἰουδαίου τε καὶ
Ἕλληνος, ὁ γὰρ αὐτὸς κύριος
πάντων, πλουτῶν εἰς πάντας τοὺς
ἐπικαλουμένους αὐτόν· ¹³ πᾶς γὰρ
ὃς ἂν ἐπικαλέσηται τὸ ὄνομα
κυρίου σωθήσεται. ¹⁴ πῶς οὖν
ἐπικαλέσωνται εἰς ὃν οὐκ
ἐπίστευσαν; πῶς δὲ πιστεύσωσιν
οὗ οὐκ ἤκουσαν; πῶς δὲ ἀκούσωσιν
χωρὶς κηρύσσοντος; ¹⁵ πῶς δὲ
κηρύξωσιν ἐὰν μὴ ἀποσταλῶσιν;
καθὼς γέγραπται, ὡς ὡραῖοι οἱ
πόδες τῶν εὐαγγελιζομένων [τὰ]
ἀγαθά. ¹⁶ ἀλλ' οὐ πάντες
ὑπήκουσαν τῷ εὐαγγελίῳ· Ἡσαΐας
γὰρ λέγει, κύριε, τίς ἐπίστευσεν τῇ
ἀκοῇ ἡμῶν; ¹⁷ ἄρα ἡ πίστις ἐξ
ἀκοῆς, ἡ δὲ ἀκοὴ διὰ ῥήματος
Χριστοῦ. ¹⁸ ἀλλὰ λέγω, μὴ οὐκ
ἤκουσαν; μενοῦνγε, εἰς πᾶσαν τὴν
γῆν ἐξῆλθεν ὁ φθόγγος αὐτῶν, καὶ
εἰς τὰ πέρατα τῆς οἰκουμένης τὰ
ῥήματα αὐτῶν. ¹⁹ ἀλλὰ λέγω, μὴ
Ἰσραὴλ οὐκ ἔγνω; πρῶτος Μωϋσῆς
λέγει, ἐγὼ παραζηλώσω ὑμᾶς ἐπ'
οὐκ ἔθνει, ἐπ' ἔθνει ἀσυνέτῳ
παροργιῶ ὑμᾶς. ²⁰ Ἡσαΐας δὲ
ἀποτολμᾷ καὶ λέγει, εὑρέθην [ἐν]
τοῖς ἐμὲ μὴ ζητοῦσιν, ἐμφανὴς
ἐγενόμην τοῖς ἐμὲ μὴ ἐπερωτῶσιν.
²¹ πρὸς δὲ τὸν Ἰσραὴλ λέγει, ὅλην
τὴν ἡμέραν ἐξεπέτασα τὰς χεῖράς
μου πρὸς λαὸν ἀπειθοῦντα καὶ
ἀντιλέγοντα.

14.

Rom 11:1–32 Λέγω οὖν, μὴ ἀπώσατο
ὁ θεὸς τὸν λαὸν αὐτοῦ; μὴ γένοιτο·

καὶ γὰρ ἐγὼ Ἰσραηλίτης εἰμί, ἐκ
σπέρματος Ἀβραάμ, φυλῆς Βενιαμίν.
² οὐκ ἀπώσατο ὁ θεὸς τὸν λαὸν
αὐτοῦ ὃν προέγνω. ἢ οὐκ οἴδατε ἐν
Ἠλίᾳ τί λέγει ἡ γραφή; ὡς
ἐντυγχάνει τῷ θεῷ κατὰ τοῦ
Ἰσραήλ, ³ κύριε, τοὺς προφήτας
σου ἀπέκτειναν, τὰ θυσιαστήριά
σου κατέσκαψαν, κἀγὼ ὑπελείφθην
μόνος, καὶ ζητοῦσιν τὴν ψυχήν μου.
⁴ ἀλλὰ τί λέγει αὐτῷ ὁ χρημα-
τισμός; κατέλιπον ἐμαυτῷ
ἑπτακισχιλίους ἄνδρας, οἵτινες οὐκ
ἔκαμψαν γόνυ τῇ Βάαλ. ⁵ οὕτως
οὖν καὶ ἐν τῷ νῦν καιρῷ λεῖμμα
κατ᾽ ἐκλογὴν χάριτος γέγονεν· ⁶ εἰ
δὲ χάριτι, οὐκέτι ἐξ ἔργων, ἐπεὶ ἡ
χάρις οὐκέτι γίνεται χάρις. ⁷ τί οὖν;
ὃ ἐπιζητεῖ Ἰσραήλ, τοῦτο οὐκ
ἐπέτυχεν, ἡ δὲ ἐκλογὴ ἐπέτυχεν· οἱ
δὲ λοιποὶ ἐπωρώθησαν, ⁸ καθὼς
γέγραπται, ἔδωκεν αὐτοῖς ὁ θεὸς
πνεῦμα κατανύξεως, ὀφθαλμοὺς τοῦ
μὴ βλέπειν καὶ ὦτα τοῦ μὴ ἀκούειν,
ἕως τῆς σήμερον ἡμέρας. ⁹ καὶ
Δαυὶδ λέγει, γενηθήτω ἡ τράπεζα
αὐτῶν εἰς παγίδα καὶ εἰς θήραν καὶ
εἰς σκάνδαλον καὶ εἰς ἀνταπόδομα
αὐτοῖς, ¹⁰ σκοτισθήτωσαν οἱ
ὀφθαλμοὶ αὐτῶν τοῦ μὴ βλέπειν,
καὶ τὸν νῶτον αὐτῶν διὰ παντὸς
σύγκαμψον. ¹¹ Λέγω οὖν, μὴ
ἔπταισαν ἵνα πέσωσιν; μὴ γένοιτο·
ἀλλὰ τῷ αὐτῶν παραπτώματι ἡ
σωτηρία τοῖς ἔθνεσιν, εἰς τὸ
παραζηλῶσαι αὐτούς. ¹² εἰ δὲ τὸ
παράπτωμα αὐτῶν πλοῦτος κόσμου
καὶ τὸ ἥττημα αὐτῶν πλοῦτος
ἐθνῶν, πόσῳ μᾶλλον τὸ πλήρωμα
αὐτῶν. ¹³ Ὑμῖν δὲ λέγω τοῖς
ἔθνεσιν. ἐφ᾽ ὅσον μὲν οὖν εἰμι ἐγὼ
ἐθνῶν ἀπόστολος, τὴν διακονίαν
μου δοξάζω, ¹⁴ εἴ πως παραζηλώσω
μου τὴν σάρκα καὶ σώσω τινὰς ἐξ
αὐτῶν. ¹⁵ εἰ γὰρ ἡ ἀποβολὴ αὐτῶν
καταλλαγὴ κόσμου, τίς ἡ
πρόσλημψις εἰ μὴ ζωὴ ἐκ νεκρῶν;
¹⁶ εἰ δὲ ἡ ἀπαρχὴ ἁγία, καὶ τὸ
φύραμα· καὶ εἰ ἡ ῥίζα ἁγία, καὶ οἱ

κλάδοι. ¹⁷ Εἰ δέ τινες τῶν κλάδων
ἐξεκλάσθησαν, σὺ δὲ ἀγριέλαιος ὢν
ἐνεκεντρίσθης ἐν αὐτοῖς καὶ συγκοινωνὸς τῆς ῥίζης τῆς πιότητος
τῆς ἐλαίας ἐγένου, ¹⁸ μὴ κατακαυχῶ
τῶν κλάδων· εἰ δὲ κατακαυχᾶσαι,
οὐ σὺ τὴν ῥίζαν βαστάζεις ἀλλὰ ἡ
ῥίζα σέ. ¹⁹ ἐρεῖς οὖν, ἐξεκλάσθησαν
κλάδοι ἵνα ἐγὼ ἐγκεντρισθῶ.
²⁰ καλῶς· τῇ ἀπιστίᾳ
ἐξεκλάσθησαν, σὺ δὲ τῇ πίστει
ἕστηκας. μὴ ὑψηλὰ φρόνει, ἀλλὰ
φοβοῦ· ²¹ εἰ γὰρ ὁ θεὸς τῶν κατὰ
φύσιν κλάδων οὐκ ἐφείσατο, [μὴ
πως] οὐδὲ σοῦ φείσεται. ²² ἴδε οὖν
χρηστότητα καὶ ἀποτομίαν θεοῦ·
ἐπὶ μὲν τοὺς πεσόντας ἀποτομία,
ἐπὶ δὲ σὲ χρηστότης θεοῦ, ἐὰν
ἐπιμένῃς τῇ χρηστότητι, ἐπεὶ καὶ
σὺ ἐκκοπήσῃ. ²³ κἀκεῖνοι δέ, ἐὰν
μὴ ἐπιμένωσιν τῇ ἀπιστίᾳ,
ἐγκεντρισθήσονται· δυνατὸς γάρ
ἐστιν ὁ θεὸς πάλιν ἐγκεντρίσαι
αὐτούς. ²⁴ εἰ γὰρ σὺ ἐκ τῆς κατὰ
φύσιν ἐξεκόπης ἀγριελαίου καὶ
παρὰ φύσιν ἐνεκεντρίσθης εἰς
καλλιέλαιον, πόσῳ μᾶλλον οὗτοι οἱ
κατὰ φύσιν ἐγκεντρισθήσονται τῇ
ἰδίᾳ ἐλαίᾳ. ²⁵ Οὐ γὰρ θέλω ὑμᾶς
ἀγνοεῖν, ἀδελφοί, τὸ μυστήριον
τοῦτο, ἵνα μὴ ἦτε [παρ'] ἑαυτοῖς
φρόνιμοι, ὅτι πώρωσις ἀπὸ μέρους
τῷ Ἰσραὴλ γέγονεν ἄχρις οὗ τὸ
πλήρωμα τῶν ἐθνῶν εἰσέλθῃ, ²⁶ καὶ
οὕτως πᾶς Ἰσραὴλ σωθήσεται·
καθὼς γέγραπται, ἥξει ἐκ Σιὼν ὁ
ῥυόμενος, ἀποστρέψει ἀσεβείας ἀπὸ
Ἰακώβ· ²⁷ καὶ αὕτη αὐτοῖς ἡ παρ'
ἐμοῦ διαθήκη, ὅταν ἀφέλωμαι τὰς
ἁμαρτίας αὐτῶν. ²⁸ κατὰ μὲν τὸ
εὐαγγέλιον ἐχθροὶ δι' ὑμᾶς, κατὰ δὲ
τὴν ἐκλογὴν ἀγαπητοὶ διὰ τοὺς
πατέρας· ²⁹ ἀμεταμέλητα γὰρ τὰ
χαρίσματα καὶ ἡ κλῆσις τοῦ θεοῦ.
³⁰ ὥσπερ γὰρ ὑμεῖς ποτε
ἠπειθήσατε τῷ θεῷ, νῦν δὲ
ἠλεήθητε τῇ τούτων ἀπειθείᾳ,
³¹ οὕτως καὶ οὗτοι νῦν ἠπείθησαν
τῷ ὑμετέρῳ ἐλέει ἵνα καὶ αὐτοὶ

[νῦν] ἐλεηθῶσιν· ³² συνέκλεισεν
γὰρ ὁ θεὸς τοὺς πάντας εἰς
ἀπείθειαν ἵνα τοὺς πάντας ἐλεήσῃ.

15.

Rom 11:33–36 Ὦ βάθος πλούτου καὶ
σοφίας καὶ γνώσεως θεοῦ· ὡς
ἀνεξεραύνητα τὰ κρίματα αὐτοῦ καὶ
ἀνεξιχνίαστοι αἱ ὁδοὶ αὐτοῦ. ³⁴ τίς
γὰρ ἔγνω νοῦν κυρίου; ἢ τίς
σύμβουλος αὐτοῦ ἐγένετο; ³⁵ ἢ τίς
προέδωκεν αὐτῷ, καὶ ἀνταποδο-
θήσεται αὐτῷ; ³⁶ ὅτι ἐξ αὐτοῦ καὶ
δι αὐτοῦ καὶ εἰς αὐτὸν τὰ πάντα·
αὐτῷ ἡ δόξα εἰς τοὺς αἰῶνας· ἀμήν.

16. Gal 5:14 ὁ γὰρ πᾶς νόμος ἐν ἑνὶ
λόγῳ πεπλήρωται, ἐν τῷ ἀγαπήσεις
τὸν πλησίον σου ὡς σεαυτόν.

Rom 13:8 Μηδενὶ μηδὲν ὀφείλετε, εἰ
μὴ τὸ ἀλλήλους ἀγαπᾶν· ὁ γὰρ
ἀγαπῶν τὸν ἕτερον νόμον
πεπλήρωκεν. ⁹ τὸ γὰρ οὐ
μοιχεύσεις, οὐ φονεύσεις, οὐ
κλέψεις, οὐκ ἐπιθυμήσεις, καὶ εἴ τις
ἑτέρα ἐντολή, ἐν τῷ λόγῳ τούτῳ
ἀνακεφαλαιοῦται, [ἐν τῷ] ἀγαπήσεις
τὸν πλησίον σου ὡς σεαυτόν. ¹⁰ ἡ
ἀγάπη τῷ πλησίον κακὸν οὐκ
ἐργάζεται· πλήρωμα οὖν νόμου ἡ
ἀγάπη.

17. Gal 3:8–10 προϊδοῦσα δὲ ἡ γραφὴ
ὅτι ἐκ πίστεως δικαιοῖ τὰ ἔθνη ὁ
θεὸς προευηγγελίσατο τῷ Ἀβραὰμ
ὅτι ἐνευλογηθήσονται ἐν σοὶ πάντα
τὰ ἔθνη. ⁹ ὥστε οἱ ἐκ πίστεως
εὐλογοῦνται σὺν τῷ πιστῷ
Ἀβραάμ. ¹⁰ ὅσοι γὰρ ἐξ ἔργων
νόμου εἰσὶν ὑπὸ κατάραν εἰσίν·
γέγραπται γὰρ ὅτι ἐπικατάρατος
πᾶς ὃς οὐκ ἐμμένει πᾶσιν τοῖς
γεγραμμένοις ἐν τῷ βιβλίῳ τοῦ
νόμου τοῦ ποιῆσαι αὐτά.
Gal 3:13–14 Χριστὸς ἡμᾶς
ἐξηγόρασεν ἐκ τῆς κατάρας τοῦ
νόμου γενόμενος ὑπὲρ ἡμῶν κατάρα,
ὅτι γέγραπται, ἐπικατάρατος πᾶς ὁ
κρεμάμενος ἐπὶ ξύλου. ¹⁴ ἵνα εἰς
τὰ ἔθνη ἡ εὐλογία τοῦ Ἀβραὰμ
γένηται ἐν Χριστῷ Ἰησοῦ, ἵνα τὴν
ἐπαγγελίαν τοῦ πνεύματος λάβωμεν
διὰ τῆς πίστεως.

Rom 15:8–12 λέγω γὰρ Χριστὸν
διάκονον γεγενῆσθαι περιτομῆς
ὑπὲρ ἀληθείας θεοῦ, εἰς τὸ
βεβαιῶσαι τὰς ἐπαγγελίας τῶν
πατέρων, ⁹ τὰ δὲ ἔθνη ὑπὲρ ἐλέους
δοξάσαι τὸν θεόν· καθὼς γέγραπται,
διὰ τοῦτο ἐξομολογήσομαί σοι ἐν
ἔθνεσιν, καὶ τῷ ὀνόματί σου ψαλῶ.
¹⁰ καὶ πάλιν λέγει, εὐφράνθητε,
ἔθνη, μετὰ τοῦ λαοῦ αὐτοῦ. ¹¹ καὶ
πάλιν αἰνεῖτε, πάντα τὰ ἔθνη, τὸν
κύριον, καὶ ἐπαινεσάτωσαν αὐτὸν
πάντες οἱ λαοί. ¹² καὶ πάλιν
Ἡσαΐας λέγει, ἔσται ἡ ῥίζα τοῦ
Ἰεσσαί καὶ ὁ ἀνιστάμενος ἄρχειν
ἐθνῶν, ἐπ' αὐτῷ ἔθνη ἐλπιοῦσιν.

Appendix IV:
Themes in Galatians and Romans

A. Opposition between justification through the Law and by faith

Gal 2:16a οὐ δικαιοῦται ἄνθρωπος ἐξ ἔργων νόμου ἐὰν μὴ διὰ πίστεως Ἰησοῦ Χριστοῦ.

Gal 2:16b . . . ἵνα δικαιωθῶμεν ἐκ πίστεως Χριστοῦ καὶ οὐκ ἐξ ἔργων νόμου.

Gal 2:16c ἐξ ἔργων νόμου οὐ δικαιωθήσεται πᾶσα σάρξ.

Gal 2:19a ἐγὼ γὰρ διὰ νόμου νόμῳ ἀπέθανον ἵνα θεῷ ζήσω.

Gal 2:21b εἰ . . . διὰ νόμου δικαιοσύνη, ἄρα Χριστὸς δωρεὰν ἀπέθανεν.

Gal 3:2 ἐξ ἔργων νόμου τὸ πνεῦμα ἐλάβετε ἢ ἐξ ἀκοῆς πίστεως;

Gal 3:5 ὁ . . . ἐπιχορηγῶν ὑμῖν τὸ πνεῦμα καὶ ἐνεργῶν δυνάμεις ἐν ὑμῖν ἐξ ἔργων νόμου ἢ ἐξ ἀκοῆς πίστεως;

Gal 3:10a ὅσοι γὰρ ἐξ ἔργων νόμου εἰσὶν ὑπὸ κατάραν εἰσίν·

Gal 3:11 ὅτι . . . ἐν νόμῳ οὐδεὶς δικαιοῦται παρὰ τῷ θεῷ δῆλον, ὅτι ὁ δίκαιος ἐκ πίστεως ζήσεται·

Gal 3:12 ὁ . . . νόμος οὐκ ἔστιν ἐκ πίστεως, ἀλλ' ὁ ποιήσας αὐτὰ ζήσεται ἐν αὐτοῖς.

Gal 3:13a–b Χριστὸς ἡμᾶς ἐξηγόρασεν ἐκ τῆς κατάρας τοῦ νόμου γενόμενος ὑπὲρ ἡμῶν κατάρα

Gal 3:17 διαθήκην προκεκυρωμένην ὑπὸ τοῦ θεοῦ ὁ μετὰ τετρακόσια καὶ τριάκοντα ἔτη γεγονὼς νόμος οὐκ ἀκυροῖ, εἰς τὸ καταργῆσαι τὴν ἐπαγγελίαν.

Gal 3:18a εἰ . . . ἐκ νόμου ἡ κληρονομία, οὐκέτι ἐξ ἐπαγγελίας.

Gal 4:30 τί λέγει ἡ γραφή; ἔκβαλε τὴν παιδίσκην καὶ τὸν υἱὸν αὐτῆς, οὐ γὰρ μὴ κληρονομήσει ὁ υἱὸς τῆς παιδίσκης μετὰ τοῦ υἱοῦ τῆς ἐλευθέρας.

Gal 5:2 ἐὰν περιτέμνησθε Χριστὸς ὑμᾶς οὐδὲν ὠφελήσει.

Gal 5:3 μαρτύρομαι . . . παντὶ ἀνθρώπῳ περιτεμνομένῳ ὅτι ὀφειλέτης ἐστὶν ὅλον τὸν νόμον ποιῆσαι.

Gal 5:4 κατηργήθητε ἀπὸ Χριστοῦ οἵτινες ἐν νόμῳ δικαιοῦσθε, τῆς χάριτος ἐξεπέσατε.

Gal 5:18 εἰ δὲ πνεύματι ἄγεσθε, οὐκ ἐστὲ ὑπὸ νόμον.

Rom 3:20 διότι ἐξ ἔργων νόμου οὐ δικαιωθήσεται πᾶσα σὰρξ ἐνώπιον αὐτοῦ, διὰ γὰρ νόμου ἐπίγνωσις ἁμαρτίας.

Rom 3:21a χωρὶς νόμου δικαιοσύνη θεοῦ πεφανέρωται.

Rom 3:27 ποῦ οὖν ἡ καύχησις; ἐξεκλείσθη. διὰ ποίου νόμου; τῶν ἔργων; οὐχί, ἀλλὰ διὰ νόμου πίστεως.

Rom 3:28 λογιζόμεθα γὰρ δικαιοῦσθαι πίστει ἄνθρωπον χωρὶς ἔργων νόμου.

Rom 4:4 τῷ δὲ ἐργαζομένῳ ὁ μισθὸς οὐ λογίζεται κατὰ χάριν ἀλλὰ κατὰ ὀφείλημα·

Rom 4:5 τῷ δὲ μὴ ἐργαζομένῳ, πιστεύοντι δὲ ἐπὶ τὸν δικαιοῦντα τὸν ἀσεβῆ, λογίζεται ἡ πίστις αὐτοῦ εἰς δικαιοσύνην.

Rom 4:13 οὐ . . . διὰ νόμου ἡ ἐπαγγελία τῷ Ἀβραὰμ ἢ τῷ σπέρματι αὐτοῦ, τὸ κληρονόμον αὐτὸν εἶναι κόσμου, ἀλλὰ διὰ δικαιοσύνης πίστεως·

Rom 4:14 εἰ . . . οἱ ἐκ νόμου κληρονόμοι, κεκένωται ἡ πίστις καὶ κατήργηται ἡ ἐπαγγελία·

Rom 4:15–16 ὁ . . . νόμος ὀργὴν κατεργάζεται· οὗ δὲ οὐκ ἔστιν νόμος, οὐδὲ παράβασις. διὰ τοῦτο ἐκ πίστεως, ἵνα κατὰ χάριν, εἰς τὸ εἶναι βεβαίαν τὴν ἐπαγγελίαν παντὶ τῷ σπέρματι.

Rom 9:8 οὐ τὰ τέκνα τῆς σαρκὸς ταῦτα τέκνα τοῦ θεοῦ, ἀλλὰ τὰ τέκνα τῆς ἐπαγγελίας λογίζεται εἰς σπέρμα·

Rom 10:4 τέλος γὰρ νόμου Χριστὸς εἰς δικαιοσύνην παντὶ τῷ πιστεύοντι.

Rom 10:5–13 Μωϋσῆς γὰρ γράφει τὴν δικαιοσύνην τὴν ἐκ [τοῦ] νόμου ὅτι ὁ ποιήσας αὐτὰ ἄνθρωπος ζήσεται ἐν αὐτοῖς. ἡ δὲ ἐκ πίστεως δικαιοσύνη οὕτως λέγει, . . . ἐγγύς σου τὸ ῥῆμά ἐστιν, ἐν τῷ στόματί σου καὶ ἐν τῇ καρδίᾳ σου· τοῦτ᾽ ἔστιν τὸ ῥῆμα τῆς πίστεως ὃ κηρύσσομεν. . . . πᾶς γὰρ ὃς ἂν ἐπικαλέσηται τὸ ὄνομα κυρίου σωθήσεται.

Rom 11:6 εἰ . . . χάριτι, οὐκέτι ἐξ ἔργων, ἐπεὶ ἡ χάρις οὐκέτι γίνεται χάρις.

Rom 15:8 λέγω γὰρ Χριστὸν διάκονον γεγενῆσθαι περιτομῆς ὑπὲρ ἀληθείας θεοῦ, εἰς τὸ βεβαιῶσαι τὰς ἐπαγγελίας τῶν πατέρων.

B. Gentile depravity

1. The sinful condition of the gentiles

Gal 2:15 Ἡμεῖς φύσει Ἰουδαῖοι καὶ οὐκ ἐξ ἐθνῶν ἁμαρτωλοί.

Gal 4:3 οὕτως καὶ ἡμεῖς, ὅτε ἦμεν νήπιοι, ὑπὸ τὰ στοιχεῖα τοῦ κόσμου ἤμεθα δεδουλωμένοι.

Gal 4:8 τότε οὐκ εἰδότες θεὸν ἐδουλεύσατε τοῖς φύσει μὴ οὖσιν θεοῖς.

Rom 6:19b ὥσπερ παρεστήσατε τὰ μέλη ὑμῶν δοῦλα τῇ ἀκαθαρσίᾳ καὶ τῇ ἀνομίᾳ εἰς τὴν ἀνομίαν.

Rom 6:20 ὅτε δοῦλοι ἦτε τῆς ἁμαρτίας, ἐλεύθεροι ἦτε τῇ δικαιοσύνῃ.

Rom 6:21 τίνα καρπὸν εἴχετε τότε ἐφ' οἷς νῦν ἐπαισχύνεσθε; τὸ γὰρ τέλος ἐκείνων θάνατος.

Rom 7:5 ὅτε ἦμεν ἐν τῇ σαρκί, τὰ παθήματα τῶν ἁμαρτιῶν τὰ διὰ τοῦ νόμου ἐνηργεῖτο ἐν τοῖς μέλεσιν ἡμῶν εἰς τὸ καρποφορῆσαι τῷ θανάτῳ.

Rom 11:30 ὥσπερ ὑμεῖς ποτε ἠπειθήσατε τῷ θεῷ.

2. As reflected in statements about gentile salvation

Gal 4:9 νῦν γνόντες θεόν, μᾶλλον γνωσθέντες ὑπὸ θεοῦ, πῶς ἐπιστρέφετε πάλιν ἐπὶ τὰ ἀσθενῆ καὶ πτωχὰ στοιχεῖα, οἷς πάλιν ἄνωθεν δουλεύειν θέλετε;

Gal 5:1 τῇ ἐλευθερίᾳ ἡμᾶς Χριστὸς ἠλευθέρωσεν· στήκετε οὖν καὶ μὴ πάλιν ζυγῷ δουλείας ἐνέχεσθε.

Rom 6:19 ὥσπερ παρεστήσατε τὰ μέλη ὑμῶν δοῦλα τῇ ἀκαθαρσίᾳ οὕτως νῦν παραστήσατε τὰ μέλη ὑμῶν δοῦλα τῇ δικαιοσύνῃ εἰς ἁγιασμόν.

3. Gentile salvation in relation to the Jews

Gal 3:13–14 Χριστὸς ἡμᾶς ἐξηγόρασεν ἐκ τῆς κατάρας τοῦ νόμου . . . ἵνα εἰς τὰ ἔθνη ἡ εὐλογία τοῦ Ἀβραὰμ γένηται ἐν Χριστῷ Ἰησοῦ.

Rom 4:16 διὰ τοῦτο ἐκ πίστεως, ἵνα κατὰ χάριν, εἰς τὸ εἶναι βεβαίαν τὴν ἐπαγγελίαν παντὶ τῷ σπέρματι, οὐ τῷ ἐκ τοῦ νόμου μόνον ἀλλὰ καὶ τῷ ἐκ πίστεως Ἀβραάμ, ὅς ἐστιν πατὴρ πάντων ἡμῶν.

Rom 9:30 ἔθνη τὰ μὴ διώκοντα δικαιοσύνην κατέλαβεν δικαιοσύνην, δικαιοσύνην δὲ τὴν ἐκ πίστεως.

Rom 11:11 τῷ αὐτῶν παραπτώματι ἡ σωτηρία τοῖς ἔθνεσιν.

Rom 11:17 σὺ ἀγριέλαιος ὢν ἐνεκεντρίσθης ἐν αὐτοῖς καὶ συγκοινωνὸς τῆς ῥίζης τῆς πιότητος τῆς ἐλαίας ἐγένου.

Rom 11:24 σὺ ἐκ τῆς κατὰ φύσιν ἐξεκόπης ἀγριελαίου καὶ παρὰ φύσιν ἐνεκεντρίσθης εἰς καλλιέλαιον.

Rom 11:25 πώρωσις ἀπὸ μέρους τῷ Ἰσραὴλ γέγονεν ἄχρις οὗ τὸ πλήρωμα τῶν ἐθνῶν εἰσέλθῃ.

Rom 11:30 ὑμεῖς ποτε ἠπειθήσατε τῷ θεῷ, νῦν δὲ ἠλεήθητε τῇ τούτων ἀπειθείᾳ.

Rom 15:8–9a Χριστὸν διάκονον γεγενῆσθαι περιτομῆς ὑπὲρ ἀληθείας θεοῦ, εἰς τὸ βεβαιῶσαι τὰς ἐπαγγελίας τῶν πατέρων, τὰ δὲ ἔθνη ὑπὲρ ἐλέους δοξάσαι τὸν θεόν.

4. Thematic discussion of gentile sinfulness

Rom 1:18–32 Ἀποκαλύπτεται ὀργὴ θεοῦ ἀπ' οὐρανοῦ ἐπὶ πᾶσαν ἀσέβειαν καὶ ἀδικίαν ἀνθρώπων τῶν τὴν ἀλήθειαν ἐν ἀδικίᾳ κατεχόντων, διότι τὸ γνωστὸν τοῦ θεοῦ φανερόν ἐστιν ἐν αὐτοῖς· ὁ θεὸς γὰρ αὐτοῖς ἐφανέρωσεν. τὰ γὰρ ἀόρατα αὐτοῦ ἀπὸ κτίσεως κόσμου τοῖς ποιήμασιν νοούμενα καθορᾶται, ἥ τε ἀΐδιος αὐτοῦ δύναμις καὶ θειότης, εἰς τὸ εἶναι αὐτοὺς ἀναπολογήτους, διότι γνόντες τὸν θεὸν οὐχ ὡς θεὸν ἐδόξασαν ἢ ηὐχαρίστησαν, ἀλλ' ἐματαιώθησαν ἐν τοῖς διαλογισμοῖς αὐτῶν καὶ ἐσκοτίσθη ἡ ἀσύνετος αὐτῶν καρδία. φάσκοντες εἶναι σοφοὶ ἐμωράνθησαν, καὶ ἤλλαξαν τὴν δόξαν τοῦ ἀφθάρτου θεοῦ ἐν ὁμοιώματι εἰκόνος φθαρτοῦ ἀνθρώπου καὶ πετεινῶν καὶ τετραπόδων καὶ ἑρπετῶν.

Διὸ παρέδωκεν αὐτοὺς ὁ θεὸς ἐν ταῖς ἐπιθυμίαις τῶν καρδιῶν αὐτῶν εἰς ἀκαθαρσίαν τοῦ ἀτιμάζεσθαι τὰ σώματα αὐτῶν ἐν αὐτοῖς, οἵτινες μετήλλαξαν τὴν ἀλήθειαν τοῦ θεοῦ ἐν τῷ ψεύδει, καὶ ἐσεβάσθησαν καὶ ἐλάτρευσαν τῇ κτίσει παρὰ τὸν κτίσαντα, ὅς ἐστιν εὐλογητὸς εἰς τοὺς αἰῶνας· ἀμήν.

διὰ τοῦτο παρέδωκεν αὐτοὺς ὁ θεὸς εἰς πάθη ἀτιμίας· αἵ τε γὰρ θήλειαι αὐτῶν μετήλλαξαν τὴν φυσικὴν χρῆσιν εἰς τὴν παρὰ φύσιν, ὁμοίως τε καὶ οἱ ἄρσενες ἀφέντες τὴν φυσικὴν χρῆσιν τῆς θηλείας ἐξεκαύθησαν ἐν τῇ ὀρέξει αὐτῶν εἰς ἀλλήλους, ἄρσενες ἐν ἄρσεσιν τὴν ἀσχημοσύνην κατεργαζόμενοι καὶ τὴν ἀντιμισθίαν ἣν ἔδει τῆς πλάνης αὐτῶν ἐν ἑαυτοῖς ἀπολαμβάνοντες.

καὶ καθὼς οὐκ ἐδοκίμασαν τὸν θεὸν ἔχειν ἐν ἐπιγνώσει, παρέδωκεν αὐτοὺς ὁ θεὸς εἰς ἀδόκιμον νοῦν, ποιεῖν τὰ μὴ καθήκοντα, πεπληρωμένους πάσῃ ἀδικίᾳ πονηρίᾳ πλεονεξίᾳ κακίᾳ, μεστοὺς φθόνου φόνου ἔριδος δόλου κακοηθείας, ψιθυριστάς, καταλάλους, θεοστυγεῖς, ὑβριστάς, ὑπερηφάνους, ἀλαζόνας, ἐφευρετὰς κακῶν, γονεῦσιν ἀπειθεῖς, ἀσυνέτους ἀσυνθέτους, ἀστόργους, ἀνελεήμονας· οἵτινες τὸ δικαίωμα τοῦ θεοῦ ἐπιγνόντες, ὅτι οἱ τὰ τοιαῦτα πράσσοντες ἄξιοι θανάτου εἰσίν, οὐ μόνον αὐτὰ ποιοῦσιν ἀλλὰ καὶ συνευδοκοῦσιν τοῖς πράσσουσιν.

C. The Jewish claim to a privileged relationship with God

1. The claim to privilege

Gal 2:15 Ἡμεῖς φύσει Ἰουδαῖοι καὶ οὐκ ἐξ ἐθνῶν ἁμαρτωλοί.

Rom 2:17–20 εἰ δὲ σὺ Ἰουδαῖος ἐπονομάζῃ
　　　　ἐπαναπαύῃ νόμῳ
　　　　καυχᾶσαι ἐν θεῷ
　　　　γινώσκεις τὸ θέλημα
　　　　δοκιμάζεις τὰ διαφέροντα κατηχούμενος ἐκ τοῦ νόμου,
　　　　πέποιθάς τε σεαυτὸν ὁδηγὸν εἶναι τυφλῶν,
　　　　φῶς τῶν ἐν σκότει,
　　　　παιδευτὴν ἀφρόνων,
　　　　διδάσκαλον νηπίων,
　　　　ἔχοντα τὴν μόρφωσιν τῆς γνώσεως καὶ τῆς ἀληθείας ἐν τῷ νόμῳ·

2. Mistaken zeal for the Law

Gal 1:13a καθ' ὑπερβολὴν ἐδίωκον τὴν ἐκκλησίαν τοῦ θεοῦ καὶ ἐπόρθουν αὐτήν.

Gal 1:13b προέκοπτον ἐν τῷ Ἰουδαϊσμῷ ὑπὲρ πολλοὺς συνηλικιώτας ἐν τῷ γένει μου.

Gal 1:13c περισσοτέρως ζηλωτὴς ὑπάρχων τῶν πατρικῶν μου παραδόσεων.

Gal 1:23 ὁ διώκων ἡμᾶς ποτε νῦν εὐαγγελίζεται τὴν πίστιν ἥν ποτε ἐπόρθει.

Rom 10:2 ζῆλον θεοῦ ἔχουσιν, ἀλλ' οὐ κατ' ἐπίγνωσιν.

Rom 10:3 ἀγνοοῦντες γὰρ τὴν τοῦ θεοῦ δικαιοσύνην, καὶ τὴν ἰδίαν [δικαιοσύνην] ζητοῦντες στῆσαι, τῇ δικαιοσύνῃ τοῦ θεοῦ οὐχ ὑπετάγησαν.

3. Jewish guilt before the Law

Rom 2:1 ἀναπολόγητος εἶ, ὦ ἄνθρωπε πᾶς ὁ κρίνων· ἐν ᾧ γὰρ κρίνεις τὸν ἕτερον, σεαυτὸν κατακρίνεις, τὰ γὰρ αὐτὰ πράσσεις ὁ κρίνων.

Rom 2:3 λογίζῃ δὲ τοῦτο, ὦ ἄνθρωπε ὁ κρίνων τοὺς τὰ τοιαῦτα πράσσοντας καὶ ποιῶν αὐτά, ὅτι σὺ ἐκφεύξῃ τὸ κρίμα τοῦ θεοῦ;

Rom 2:4 τοῦ πλούτου τῆς χρηστότητος αὐτοῦ καὶ τῆς ἀνοχῆς καὶ τῆς μακροθυμίας καταφρονεῖς, ἀγνοῶν ὅτι τὸ χρηστὸν τοῦ θεοῦ εἰς μετάνοιάν σε ἄγει;

Rom 2:5 κατὰ δὲ τὴν σκληρότητά σου καὶ ἀμετανόητον καρδίαν θησαυρίζεις σεαυτῷ ὀργὴν ἐν ἡμέρᾳ ὀργῆς καὶ ἀποκαλύψεως δικαιοκρισίας τοῦ θεοῦ.

Rom 2:21–24 ὁ διδάσκων ἕτερον σεαυτὸν οὐ διδάσκεις;
ὁ κηρύσσων μὴ κλέπτειν κλέπτεις;
ὁ λέγων μὴ μοιχεύειν μοιχεύεις;
ὁ βδελυσσόμενος τὰ εἴδωλα ἱεροσυλεῖς;
ὃς ἐν νόμῳ καυχᾶσαι, διὰ τῆς παραβάσεως τοῦ νόμου τὸν θεὸν ἀτιμάζεις;
τὸ γὰρ ὄνομα τοῦ θεοῦ δι' ὑμᾶς βλασφημεῖται ἐν τοῖς ἔθνεσιν, καθὼς γέγραπται.

Rom 2:25 περιτομὴ μὲν γὰρ ὠφελεῖ ἐὰν νόμον πράσσῃς· ἐὰν δὲ παραβάτης νόμου ᾖς ἡ περιτομή σου ἀκροβυστία γέγονεν.

Rom 2:27 κρινεῖ ἡ ἐκ φύσεως ἀκροβυστία τὸν νόμον τελοῦσα σὲ τὸν διὰ γράμματος καὶ περιτομῆς παραβάτην νόμου.

Rom 3:19 οἴδαμεν δὲ ὅτι ὅσα ὁ νόμος λέγει τοῖς ἐν τῷ νόμῳ λαλεῖ, ἵνα πᾶν στόμα φραγῇ καὶ ὑπόδικος γένηται πᾶς ὁ κόσμος τῷ θεῷ.

4. Equivalence of Jews and gentiles before the Law

Rom 2:26 ἐὰν ἡ ἀκροβυστία τὰ δικαιώματα τοῦ νόμου φυλάσσῃ, οὐχ ἡ ἀκροβυστία αὐτοῦ εἰς περιτομὴν λογισθήσεται;

Rom 2:28 οὐ ὁ ἐν τῷ φανερῷ Ἰουδαῖός ἐστιν, οὐδὲ ἡ ἐν τῷ φανερῷ ἐν σαρκὶ περιτομή.

Rom 2:29 ὁ ἐν τῷ κρυπτῷ Ἰουδαῖος, καὶ περιτομὴ καρδίας ἐν πνεύματι οὐ γράμματι, οὗ ὁ ἔπαινος οὐκ ἐξ ἀνθρώπων ἀλλ' ἐκ τοῦ θεοῦ.

Rom 3:9a προεχόμεθα; οὐ πάντως.

Rom 3:9c Ἰουδαίους τε καὶ Ἕλληνας πάντας ὑφ' ἁμαρτίαν εἶναι.

D. Faith as the basis of justification for Jews and gentiles

1. Parallel forms of the Gospel

Gal 2:7 ἀλλὰ τοὐναντίον ἰδόντες ὅτι πεπίστευμαι τὸ εὐαγγέλιον τῆς ἀκροβυστίας καθὼς Πέτρος τῆς περιτομῆς,

Gal 2:8 ὁ γὰρ ἐνεργήσας Πέτρῳ εἰς ἀποστολὴν τῆς περιτομῆς ἐνήργησεν καὶ ἐμοὶ εἰς τὰ ἔθνη,

Gal 2:9d-f δεξιὰς ἔδωκαν ἐμοὶ καὶ Βαρναβᾷ κοινωνίας, ἵνα ἡμεῖς εἰς τὰ ἔθνη, αὐτοὶ δὲ εἰς τὴν περιτομήν·

2. Jews also justified by faith

Gal 2:16a εἰδότες [δὲ] ὅτι οὐ δικαιοῦται ἄνθρωπος ἐξ ἔργων νόμου ἐὰν μὴ διὰ πίστεως Ἰησοῦ Χριστοῦ,

Gal 2:16b-d καὶ ἡμεῖς εἰς Χριστὸν Ἰησοῦν ἐπιστεύσαμεν, ἵνα δικαιωθῶμεν ἐκ πίστεως Χριστοῦ καὶ οὐκ ἐξ ἔργων νόμου.

Rom 4:12 καὶ πατέρα περιτομῆς τοῖς οὐκ ἐκ περιτομῆς μόνον ἀλλὰ καὶ τοῖς στοιχοῦσιν τοῖς ἴχνεσιν τῆς ἐν ἀκροβυστίᾳ πίστεως τοῦ πατρὸς ἡμῶν Ἀβραάμ.

3. Justification of Jews and gentiles by faith

Gal 3:13–14 Χριστὸς ἡμᾶς ἐξηγόρασεν ἐκ τῆς κατάρας τοῦ νόμου . . . ἵνα εἰς τὰ ἔθνη ἡ εὐλογία τοῦ Ἀβραὰμ γένηται ἐν Χριστῷ Ἰησοῦ, ἵνα τὴν ἐπαγγελίαν τοῦ πνεύματος λάβωμεν διὰ τῆς πίστεως.

Gal 3:27–28a ὅσοι γὰρ εἰς Χριστὸν ἐβαπτίσθητε, Χριστὸν ἐνεδύσασθε· οὐκ ἔνι Ἰουδαῖος οὐδὲ Ἕλλην

Rom 1:16 Οὐ γὰρ ἐπαισχύνομαι τὸ εὐαγγέλιον, δύναμις γὰρ θεοῦ ἐστιν εἰς σωτηρίαν παντὶ τῷ πιστεύοντι, Ἰουδαίῳ τε πρῶτον καὶ Ἕλληνι·

Rom 3:29–30 ἢ Ἰουδαίων ὁ θεὸς μόνον; οὐχὶ καὶ ἐθνῶν; ναὶ καὶ ἐθνῶν, εἴπερ εἷς ὁ θεός, ὃς δικαιώσει περιτομὴν ἐκ πίστεως καὶ ἀκροβυστίαν διὰ τῆς πίστεως.

Rom 4:9–12 Ὁ μακαρισμὸς οὖν οὗτος ἐπὶ τὴν περιτομὴν ἢ καὶ ἐπὶ τὴν ἀκροβυστίαν; λέγομεν γάρ, ἐλογίσθη τῷ Ἀβραὰμ ἡ πίστις εἰς δικαιοσύνην.

πῶς οὖν ἐλογίσθη; ἐν περιτομῇ ὄντι ἢ ἐν ἀκροβυστίᾳ; οὐκ ἐν περιτομῇ ἀλλ' ἐν ἀκροβυστίᾳ· καὶ σημεῖον ἔλαβεν περιτομῆς, σφραγῖδα τῆς δικαιοσύνης τῆς πίστεως τῆς ἐν τῇ ἀκροβυστίᾳ, εἰς τὸ εἶναι αὐτὸν πατέρα πάντων τῶν πιστευόντων δι' ἀκροβυστίας, εἰς τὸ λογισθῆναι [καὶ] αὐτοῖς [τὴν] δικαιοσύνην, καὶ πατέρα περιτομῆς τοῖς οὐκ ἐκ περιτομῆς μόνον ἀλλὰ καὶ τοῖς στοιχοῦσιν τοῖς ἴχνεσιν τῆς ἐν ἀκροβυστίᾳ πίστεως τοῦ πατρὸς ἡμῶν Ἀβραάμ.

Rom 4:16 διὰ τοῦτο ἐκ πίστεως, ἵνα κατὰ χάριν, εἰς τὸ εἶναι βεβαίαν τὴν ἐπαγγελίαν παντὶ τῷ σπέρματι, οὐ τῷ ἐκ τοῦ νόμου μόνον ἀλλὰ καὶ τῷ ἐκ πίστεως Ἀβραάμ, ὅς ἐστιν πατὴρ πάντων ἡμῶν,

Rom 10:11–13 λέγει γὰρ ἡ γραφή, πᾶς ὁ πιστεύων ἐπ' αὐτῷ οὐ καταισχυνθήσεται. οὐ γάρ ἐστιν διαστολὴ Ἰουδαίου τε καὶ Ἕλληνος, ὁ γὰρ αὐτὸς κύριος πάντων, πλουτῶν εἰς πάντας τοὺς ἐπικαλουμένους αὐτόν· πᾶς γὰρ ὃς ἂν ἐπικαλέσηται τὸ ὄνομα κυρίου σωθήσεται.

Rom 15:8–9a λέγω γὰρ Χριστὸν διάκονον γεγενῆσθαι περιτομῆς ὑπὲρ ἀληθείας θεοῦ, εἰς τὸ βεβαιῶσαι τὰς ἐπαγγελίας τῶν πατέρων, τὰ δὲ ἔθνη ὑπὲρ ἐλέους δοξάσαι τὸν θεόν.

E. A child of Abraham

1. Abraham's faith

Gal 3:6 καθὼς Ἀβραὰμ ἐπίστευσεν τῷ θεῷ, καὶ ἐλογίσθη αὐτῷ εἰς δικαιοσύνην.

Rom 4:3 τί ἡ γραφὴ λέγει; ἐπίστευσεν δὲ Ἀβραὰμ τῷ θεῷ, καὶ ἐλογίσθη αὐτῷ εἰς δικαιοσύνην.

Rom 4:17b ἐπίστευσεν θεοῦ τοῦ ζῳοποιοῦντος τοὺς νεκροὺς καὶ καλοῦντος τὰ μὴ ὄντα ὡς ὄντα·

Rom 4:18 ὃς παρ' ἐλπίδα ἐπ' ἐλπίδι ἐπίστευσεν εἰς τὸ γενέσθαι αὐτὸν πατέρα πολλῶν ἐθνῶν κατὰ τὸ εἰρημένον, οὕτως ἔσται τὸ σπέρμα σου.

Rom 4:19 μὴ ἀσθενήσας τῇ πίστει κατενόησεν τὸ ἑαυτοῦ σῶμα [ἤδη] νενεκρωμένον, ἑκατονταετής που ὑπάρχων, καὶ τὴν νέκρωσιν τῆς μήτρας Σάρρας.

Rom 4:20–21 εἰς δὲ τὴν ἐπαγγελίαν τοῦ θεοῦ οὐ διεκρίθη τῇ ἀπιστίᾳ ἀλλ' ἐνεδυναμώθη τῇ πίστει, δοὺς δόξαν τῷ θεῷ καὶ πληροφορηθεὶς ὅτι ὃ ἐπήγγελται δυνατός ἐστιν καὶ ποιῆσαι. διὸ [καὶ] ἐλογίσθη αὐτῷ εἰς δικαιοσύνην.

2. A child of Abraham

Gal 3:7 οἱ ἐκ πίστεως, οὗτοι υἱοί εἰσιν Ἀβραάμ.

Gal 3:8 προϊδοῦσα δὲ ἡ γραφὴ ὅτι ἐκ πίστεως δικαιοῖ τὰ ἔθνη ὁ θεὸς προ-ευηγγελίσατο τῷ Ἀβραὰμ ὅτι ἐνευλογηθήσονται ἐν σοὶ πάντα τὰ ἔθνη.

Gal 3:9 οἱ ἐκ πίστεως εὐλογοῦνται σὺν τῷ πιστῷ Ἀβραάμ.

Gal 3:13–14 Χριστὸς ἡμᾶς ἐξηγόρασεν ἐκ τῆς κατάρας τοῦ νόμου . . . ἵνα εἰς τὰ ἔθνη ἡ εὐλογία τοῦ Ἀβραὰμ γένηται ἐν Χριστῷ Ἰησοῦ, ἵνα τὴν ἐπαγγελίαν τοῦ πνεύματος λάβωμεν διὰ τῆς πίστεως.

Gal 3:29 εἰ δὲ ὑμεῖς Χριστοῦ, ἄρα τοῦ Ἀβραὰμ σπέρμα ἐστέ, κατ᾽ ἐπαγγελίαν κληρονόμοι.

Rom 4:11–12 σημεῖον ἔλαβεν περιτομῆς, σφραγῖδα τῆς δικαιοσύνης τῆς πίστεως τῆς ἐν τῇ ἀκροβυστίᾳ, εἰς τὸ εἶναι αὐτὸν πατέρα πάντων τῶν πιστευόντων δι᾽ ἀκροβυστίας, εἰς τὸ λογισθῆναι [καὶ] αὐτοῖς [τὴν] δικαιοσύνην, καὶ πατέρα περιτομῆς τοῖς οὐκ ἐκ περιτομῆς μόνον ἀλλὰ καὶ τοῖς στοιχοῦσιν τοῖς ἴχνεσιν τῆς ἐν ἀκροβυστίᾳ πίστεως τοῦ πατρὸς ἡμῶν Ἀβραάμ.

Rom 4:16e (Ἀβραάμ), ὅς ἐστιν πατὴρ πάντων ἡμῶν, καθὼς γέγραπται ὅτι πατέρα πολλῶν ἐθνῶν τέθεικά σε.

Rom 4:18 ὃς παρ᾽ ἐλπίδα ἐπ᾽ ἐλπίδι ἐπίστευσεν εἰς τὸ γενέσθαι αὐτὸν πατέρα πολλῶν ἐθνῶν κατὰ τὸ εἰρημένον, οὕτως ἔσται τὸ σπέρμα σου.

Rom 9:6b–7 οὐ πάντες οἱ ἐξ Ἰσραήλ, οὗτοι Ἰσραήλ· οὐδ᾽ ὅτι εἰσὶν σπέρμα Ἀβραάμ, πάντες τέκνα, ἀλλ᾽, ἐν Ἰσαὰκ κληθήσεταί σοι σπέρμα.

3. Justification by faith without works

Gal 3:18 εἰ ἐκ νόμου ἡ κληρονομία, οὐκέτι ἐξ ἐπαγγελίας· τῷ δὲ Ἀβραὰμ δι᾽ ἐπαγγελίας κεχάρισται ὁ θεός.

Rom 4:1 τί οὖν ἐροῦμεν εὑρηκέναι Ἀβραὰμ τὸν προπάτορα ἡμῶν κατὰ σάρκα; εἰ γὰρ Ἀβραὰμ ἐξ ἔργων ἐδικαιώθη, ἔχει καύχημα· ἀλλ᾽ οὐ πρὸς θεόν.

Rom 4:9 ὁ μακαρισμὸς οὖν οὗτος ἐπὶ τὴν περιτομὴν ἢ καὶ ἐπὶ τὴν ἀκροβυστίαν; λέγομεν γάρ, ἐλογίσθη τῷ Ἀβραὰμ ἡ πίστις εἰς δικαιοσύνην.

Rom 4:10 πῶς ἐλογίσθη; ἐν περιτομῇ ὄντι ἢ ἐν ἀκροβυστίᾳ; οὐκ ἐν περιτομῇ ἀλλ᾽ ἐν ἀκροβυστίᾳ.

Rom 4:13 οὐ γὰρ διὰ νόμου ἡ ἐπαγγελία τῷ Ἀβραὰμ ἢ τῷ σπέρματι αὐτοῦ, τὸ κληρονόμον αὐτὸν εἶναι κόσμου, ἀλλὰ διὰ δικαιοσύνης πίστεως.

Rom 4:16a–d διὰ τοῦτο ἐκ πίστεως, ἵνα κατὰ χάριν, εἰς τὸ εἶναι βεβαίαν τὴν ἐπαγγελίαν παντὶ τῷ σπέρματι, οὐ τῷ ἐκ τοῦ νόμου μόνον ἀλλὰ καὶ τῷ ἐκ πίστεως Ἀβραάμ.

4. Relationship to Christ

Gal 3:16 τῷ Ἀβραὰμ ἐρρέθησαν αἱ ἐπαγγελίαι καὶ τῷ σπέρματι αὐτοῦ. οὐ λέγει, καὶ τοῖς σπέρμασιν, ὡς ἐπὶ πολλῶν, ἀλλ᾽ ὡς ἐφ᾽ ἑνός, καὶ τῷ σπέρματί σου, ὅς ἐστιν Χριστός.

Gal 3:29 εἰ δὲ ὑμεῖς Χριστοῦ, ἄρα τοῦ Ἀβραὰμ σπέρμα ἐστέ, κατ᾽ ἐπαγγελίαν κληρονόμοι.

Rom 4:23–24 οὐκ ἐγράφη δὲ δι᾽ αὐτὸν μόνον ὅτι ἐλογίσθη αὐτῷ, ἀλλὰ καὶ δι᾽ ἡμᾶς οἷς μέλλει λογίζεσθαι, τοῖς πιστεύουσιν ἐπὶ τὸν ἐγείραντα Ἰησοῦν τὸν κύριον ἡμῶν ἐκ νεκρῶν.

F. Salvation in Christ

1. Christ's act of redemption

Gal 1:4 (χάρις ἀπὸ κυρίου Ἰησοῦ Χριστοῦ) τοῦ δόντος ἑαυτὸν ὑπὲρ τῶν ἁμαρτιῶν ἡμῶν ὅπως ἐξέληται ἡμᾶς ἐκ τοῦ αἰῶνος τοῦ ἐνεστῶτος πονηροῦ κατὰ τὸ θέλημα τοῦ θεοῦ καὶ πατρὸς ἡμῶν.

Gal 4:4–5 ὅτε δὲ ἦλθεν τὸ πλήρωμα τοῦ χρόνου, ἐξαπέστειλεν ὁ θεὸς τὸν υἱὸν αὐτοῦ, γενόμενον ἐκ γυναικός, γενόμενον ὑπὸ νόμον, ἵνα τοὺς ὑπὸ νόμον ἐξαγοράσῃ, ἵνα τὴν υἱοθεσίαν ἀπολάβωμεν.

Gal 4:6 ὅτι δέ ἐστε υἱοί, ἐξαπέστειλεν ὁ θεὸς τὸ πνεῦμα τοῦ υἱοῦ αὐτοῦ εἰς τὰς καρδίας ἡμῶν, κρᾶζον, αββα ὁ πατήρ.

Rom 5:6 ἔτι γὰρ Χριστὸς ὄντων ἡμῶν ἀσθενῶν ἔτι κατὰ καιρὸν ὑπὲρ ἀσεβῶν ἀπέθανεν.

Rom 5:8 συνίστησιν τὴν ἑαυτοῦ ἀγάπην εἰς ἡμᾶς ὁ θεὸς ὅτι ἔτι ἁμαρτωλῶν ὄντων ἡμῶν Χριστὸς ὑπὲρ ἡμῶν ἀπέθανεν.

Rom 5:19 ὥσπερ γὰρ διὰ τῆς παρακοῆς τοῦ ἑνὸς ἀνθρώπου ἁμαρτωλοὶ κατεστάθησαν οἱ πολλοί, οὕτως καὶ διὰ τῆς ὑπακοῆς τοῦ ἑνὸς δίκαιοι κατασταθήσονται οἱ πολλοί.

Rom 5:21 ἵνα ὥσπερ ἐβασίλευσεν ἡ ἁμαρτία ἐν τῷ θανάτῳ, οὕτως καὶ ἡ χάρις βασιλεύσῃ διὰ δικαιοσύνης εἰς ζωὴν αἰώνιον διὰ Ἰησοῦ Χριστοῦ τοῦ κυρίου ἡμῶν.

Rom 6:7 ὁ ἀποθανὼν δεδικαίωται ἀπὸ τῆς ἁμαρτίας.

Rom 6:9 Χριστὸς ἐγερθεὶς ἐκ νεκρῶν οὐκέτι ἀποθνήσκει, θάνατος αὐτοῦ οὐκέτι κυριεύει.

Rom 6:10 ὃ ἀπέθανεν, τῇ ἁμαρτίᾳ ἀπέθανεν ἐφάπαξ· ὃ δὲ ζῇ, ζῇ τῷ θεῷ.

Rom 8:32 (θεὸς) ὅς τοῦ ἰδίου υἱοῦ οὐκ ἐφείσατο, ἀλλὰ ὑπὲρ ἡμῶν πάντων παρέδωκεν αὐτόν.

2. Participation in Christ

Gal 2:20a ζῶ δὲ οὐκέτι ἐγώ, ζῇ δὲ ἐν ἐμοὶ Χριστός.

Gal 2:20b ὃ δὲ νῦν ζῶ ἐν σαρκί, ἐν πίστει ζῶ τῇ τοῦ υἱοῦ τοῦ θεοῦ τοῦ ἀγαπήσαντός με καὶ παραδόντος ἑαυτὸν ὑπὲρ ἐμοῦ.

Gal 3:26 πάντες υἱοὶ θεοῦ ἐστε διὰ τῆς πίστεως ἐν Χριστῷ Ἰησοῦ.

Gal 3:27 ὅσοι εἰς Χριστὸν ἐβαπτίσθητε, Χριστὸν ἐνεδύσασθε.

Gal 3:29 εἰ ὑμεῖς Χριστοῦ, ἄρα τοῦ Ἀβραὰμ σπέρμα ἐστέ, κατ' ἐπαγγελίαν κληρονόμοι.

Gal 5:1 τῇ ἐλευθερίᾳ ἡμᾶς Χριστὸς ἠλευθέρωσεν

Gal 6:14 ἐμοὶ μὴ γένοιτο καυχᾶσθαι εἰ μὴ ἐν τῷ σταυρῷ τοῦ κυρίου ἡμῶν Ἰησοῦ Χριστοῦ, δι' οὗ ἐμοὶ κόσμος ἐσταύρωται κἀγὼ κόσμῳ.

Gal 6:17 ἐγὼ τὰ στίγματα τοῦ Ἰησοῦ ἐν τῷ σώματί μου βαστάζω.

Rom 4:23–25 οὐκ ἐγράφη δὲ δι' αὐτὸν μόνον ὅτι ἐλογίσθη αὐτῷ, ἀλλὰ καὶ δι' ἡμᾶς οἷς μέλλει λογίζεσθαι, τοῖς πιστεύουσιν ἐπὶ τὸν ἐγείραντα Ἰησοῦν τὸν κύριον ἡμῶν ἐκ νεκρῶν, ὃς παρεδόθη διὰ τὰ παραπτώματα ἡμῶν καὶ ἠγέρθη διὰ τὴν δικαίωσιν ἡμῶν.

Rom 5:1–2 δικαιωθέντες ἐκ πίστεως εἰρήνην ἔχομεν πρὸς τὸν θεὸν διὰ τοῦ κυρίου ἡμῶν Ἰησοῦ Χριστοῦ, δι' οὗ καὶ τὴν προσαγωγὴν ἐσχήκαμεν [τῇ πίστει] εἰς τὴν χάριν ταύτην ἐν ᾗ ἑστήκαμεν, καὶ καυχώμεθα ἐπ' ἐλπίδι τῆς δόξης τοῦ θεοῦ.

Rom 5:9 πολλῷ μᾶλλον δικαιωθέντες νῦν ἐν τῷ αἵματι αὐτοῦ σωθησόμεθα δι' αὐτοῦ ἀπὸ τῆς ὀργῆς.

Rom 5:10 εἰ γὰρ ἐχθροὶ ὄντες κατηλλάγημεν τῷ θεῷ διὰ τοῦ θανάτου τοῦ υἱοῦ αὐτοῦ, πολλῷ μᾶλλον καταλλαγέντες σωθησόμεθα ἐν τῇ ζωῇ αὐτοῦ.

Rom 5:11 οὐ μόνον δέ, ἀλλὰ καὶ καυχώμενοι ἐν τῷ θεῷ διὰ τοῦ κυρίου ἡμῶν Ἰησοῦ Χριστοῦ, δι' οὗ νῦν τὴν καταλλαγὴν ἐλάβομεν.

Rom 6:3 ἢ ἀγνοεῖτε ὅτι ὅσοι ἐβαπτίσθημεν εἰς Χριστὸν Ἰησοῦν εἰς τὸν θάνατον αὐτοῦ ἐβαπτίσθημεν;

Rom 6:4 συνετάφημεν αὐτῷ διὰ τοῦ βαπτίσματος εἰς τὸν θάνατον, ἵνα ὥσπερ ἠγέρθη Χριστὸς ἐκ νεκρῶν διὰ τῆς δόξης τοῦ πατρός, οὕτως καὶ ἡμεῖς ἐν καινότητι ζωῆς περιπατήσωμεν.

Rom 6:5 εἰ σύμφυτοι γεγόναμεν τῷ ὁμοιώματι τοῦ θανάτου αὐτοῦ, ἀλλὰ καὶ τῆς ἀναστάσεως ἐσόμεθα.

Rom 6:8 εἰ ἀπεθάνομεν σὺν Χριστῷ, πιστεύομεν ὅτι καὶ συζήσομεν αὐτῷ.

Rom 7:4 ὥστε ὑμεῖς ἐθανατώθητε τῷ νόμῳ διὰ τοῦ σώματος τοῦ Χριστοῦ, εἰς τὸ γενέσθαι ὑμᾶς ἑτέρῳ, τῷ ἐκ νεκρῶν ἐγερθέντι, ἵνα καρποφορήσωμεν τῷ θεῷ.

Rom 7:24–25a τίς με ῥύσεται ἐκ τοῦ σώματος τοῦ θανάτου τούτου; χάρις δὲ τῷ θεῷ διὰ Ἰησοῦ Χριστοῦ τοῦ κυρίου ἡμῶν.

Rom 8:1 οὐδὲν κατάκριμα τοῖς ἐν Χριστῷ Ἰησοῦ.

Rom 8:3 τὸ ἀδύνατον τοῦ νόμου, ἐν ᾧ ἠσθένει διὰ τῆς σαρκός, ὁ θεὸς τὸν ἑαυτοῦ υἱὸν πέμψας ἐν ὁμοιώματι σαρκὸς ἁμαρτίας καὶ περὶ ἁμαρτίας κατέκρινεν τὴν ἁμαρτίαν ἐν τῇ σαρκί.

Rom 8:11 εἰ τὸ πνεῦμα τοῦ ἐγείραντος τὸν Ἰησοῦν ἐκ νεκρῶν οἰκεῖ ἐν ὑμῖν, ὁ ἐγείρας Χριστὸν ἐκ νεκρῶν ζῳοποιήσει καὶ τὰ θνητὰ σώματα ὑμῶν διὰ τοῦ ἐνοικοῦντος αὐτοῦ πνεύματος ἐν ὑμῖν.

Rom 8:17 εἰ τέκνα, καὶ κληρονόμοι· κληρονόμοι μὲν θεοῦ, συγκληρονόμοι δὲ Χριστοῦ, εἴπερ συμπάσχομεν ἵνα καὶ συνδοξασθῶμεν.

Rom 8:34 τίς ὁ κατακρινῶν; Χριστὸς ['Ιησοῦς] ὁ ἀποθανών, μᾶλλον δὲ ἐγερθείς, ὃς καί ἐστιν ἐν δεξιᾷ τοῦ θεοῦ, ὃς καὶ ἐντυγχάνει ὑπὲρ ἡμῶν.

3. Unity in Christ

Gal 3:28 οὐκ ἔνι 'Ιουδαῖος οὐδὲ "Ελλην, οὐκ ἔνι δοῦλος οὐδὲ ἐλεύθερος, οὐκ ἔνι ἄρσεν καὶ θῆλυ· πάντες γὰρ ὑμεῖς εἷς ἐστε ἐν Χριστῷ 'Ιησοῦ.

Gal 5:6 ἐν Χριστῷ 'Ιησοῦ οὔτε περιτομή τι ἰσχύει οὔτε ἀκροβυστία, ἀλλὰ πίστις δι' ἀγάπης ἐνεργουμένη.

Rom 3:21–22 χωρὶς νόμου δικαιοσύνη θεοῦ πεφανέρωται, μαρτυρουμένη ὑπὸ τοῦ νόμου καὶ τῶν προφητῶν, δικαιοσύνη δὲ θεοῦ διὰ πίστεως 'Ιησοῦ Χριστοῦ, εἰς πάντας τοὺς πιστεύοντας· οὐ γάρ ἐστιν διαστολή.

Rom 3:23–24 πάντες ἥμαρτον καὶ ὑστεροῦνται τῆς δόξης τοῦ θεοῦ, δικαιούμενοι δωρεὰν τῇ αὐτοῦ χάριτι διὰ τῆς ἀπολυτρώσεως τῆς ἐν Χριστῷ 'Ιησοῦ.

G. The opposition between good and evil

1. The judgment of good and evil

Gal 5:19–21 φανερὰ ἐστιν τὰ ἔργα τῆς σαρκός, . . . οἱ τὰ τοιαῦτα πράσσοντες βασιλείαν θεοῦ οὐ κληρονομήσουσιν.

Gal 5:22–23 ὁ καρπὸς τοῦ πνεύματός ἐστιν ἀγάπη, . . . κατὰ τῶν τοιούτων οὐκ ἔστιν νόμος.

Gal 6:7c ὃ ἐὰν σπείρῃ ἄνθρωπος, τοῦτο καὶ θερίσει·

Gal 6:8a ὁ σπείρων εἰς τὴν σάρκα ἑαυτοῦ ἐκ τῆς σαρκὸς θερίσει φθοράν,

Gal 6:8b ὁ σπείρων εἰς τὸ πνεῦμα ἐκ τοῦ πνεύματος θερίσει ζωὴν αἰώνιον.

Gal 6:9b καιρῷ ἰδίῳ θερίσομεν μὴ ἐκλυόμενοι.

Rom 1:18 ἀποκαλύπτεται ὀργὴ θεοῦ ἀπ' οὐρανοῦ ἐπὶ πᾶσαν ἀσέβειαν καὶ ἀδικίαν ἀνθρώπων τῶν τὴν ἀλήθειαν ἐν ἀδικίᾳ κατεχόντων.

Rom 2:6 [θεὸς] ὃς ἀποδώσει ἑκάστῳ κατὰ τὰ ἔργα αὐτοῦ.

Rom 2:7 τοῖς καθ' ὑπομονὴν ἔργου ἀγαθοῦ δόξαν καὶ τιμὴν καὶ ἀφθαρσίαν ζητοῦσιν, ζωὴν αἰώνιον·

Rom 2:8 τοῖς ἐξ ἐριθείας καὶ ἀπειθοῦσι τῇ ἀληθείᾳ πειθομένοις δὲ τῇ ἀδικίᾳ, ὀργὴ καὶ θυμός.

Rom 2:9 θλῖψις καὶ στενοχωρία ἐπὶ πᾶσαν ψυχὴν ἀνθρώπου τοῦ κατεργαζομένου τὸ κακόν, 'Ιουδαίου τε πρῶτον καὶ "Ελληνος.

Rom 2:10 δόξα καὶ τιμὴ καὶ εἰρήνη παντὶ τῷ ἐργαζομένῳ τὸ ἀγαθόν, 'Ιουδαίῳ τε πρῶτον καὶ "Ελληνι·

Rom 2:11 οὐ ἐστιν προσωπολημψία παρὰ τῷ θεῷ.

Rom 2:12 ὅσοι ἀνόμως ἥμαρτον, ἀνόμως καὶ ἀπολοῦνται· καὶ ὅσοι ἐν νόμῳ ἥμαρτον, διὰ νόμου κριθήσονται·

Rom 2:13a οὐ οἱ ἀκροαταὶ νόμου δίκαιοι παρὰ [τῷ] θεῷ,

Rom 2:13b οἱ ποιηταὶ νόμου δικαιωθήσονται.

Rom 2:15b συμμαρτυρούσης αὐτῶν τῆς συνειδήσεως καὶ μεταξὺ ἀλλήλων τῶν λογισμῶν κατηγορούντων ἢ καὶ ἀπολογουμένων,

Rom 2:16 κρίνει ὁ θεὸς τὰ κρυπτὰ τῶν ἀνθρώπων κατὰ τὸ εὐαγγέλιόν μου διὰ Χριστοῦ Ἰησοῦ.

Rom 4:2 εἰ Ἀβραὰμ ἐξ ἔργων ἐδικαιώθη, ἔχει καύχημα· ἀλλ' οὐ πρὸς θεόν.

Rom 6:20–21 ὅτε γὰρ δοῦλοι ἦτε τῆς ἁμαρτίας, ἐλεύθεροι ἦτε τῇ δικαιοσύνῃ. τίνα οὖν καρπὸν εἴχετε τότε ἐφ' οἷς νῦν ἐπαισχύνεσθε; τὸ γὰρ τέλος ἐκείνων θάνατος.

Rom 6:22 ἐλευθερωθέντες ἀπὸ τῆς ἁμαρτίας δουλωθέντες δὲ τῷ θεῷ, ἔχετε τὸν καρπὸν ὑμῶν εἰς ἁγιασμόν, τὸ δὲ τέλος ζωὴν αἰώνιον.

Rom 6:23a τὰ ὀψώνια τῆς ἁμαρτίας θάνατος,

Rom 6:23b τὸ χάρισμα τοῦ θεοῦ ζωὴ αἰώνιος ἐν Χριστῷ Ἰησοῦ τῷ κυρίῳ ἡμῶν.

2. Doing good or evil

Gal 5:13a–b Ὑμεῖς . . . ἐκλήθητε . . . μὴ τὴν ἐλευθερίαν εἰς ἀφορμὴν τῇ σαρκί.

Gal 5:13c διὰ τῆς ἀγάπης δουλεύετε ἀλλήλοις.

Gal 5:14 ὁ πᾶς νόμος ἐν ἑνὶ λόγῳ πεπλήρωται, ἐν τῷ ἀγαπήσεις τὸν πλησίον σου ὡς σεαυτόν.

Gal 5:16a πνεύματι περιπατεῖτε

Gal 5:16b ἐπιθυμίαν σαρκὸς οὐ μὴ τελέσητε.

Gal 6:9a τὸ καλὸν ποιοῦντες μὴ ἐγκακῶμεν.

Gal 6:10b ἐργαζώμεθα τὸ ἀγαθὸν πρὸς πάντας, μάλιστα δὲ πρὸς τοὺς οἰκείους τῆς πίστεως.

Rom 2:14 ὅταν ἔθνη τὰ μὴ νόμον ἔχοντα φύσει τὰ τοῦ νόμου ποιῶσιν, οὗτοι νόμον μὴ ἔχοντες ἑαυτοῖς εἰσιν νόμος·

Rom 2:15a οἵτινες ἐνδείκνυνται τὸ ἔργον τοῦ νόμου γραπτὸν ἐν ταῖς καρδίαις αὐτῶν,

Rom 6:1b ἐπιμένωμεν τῇ ἁμαρτίᾳ, ἵνα ἡ χάρις πλεονάσῃ;

Rom 6:11b–c λογίζεσθε ἑαυτοὺς [εἶναι] νεκροὺς μὲν τῇ ἁμαρτίᾳ ζῶντας δὲ τῷ θεῷ ἐν Χριστῷ Ἰησοῦ.

Rom 6:12 μὴ βασιλευέτω ἡ ἁμαρτία ἐν τῷ θνητῷ ὑμῶν σώματι εἰς τὸ ὑπακούειν ταῖς ἐπιθυμίαις αὐτοῦ.

Rom 6:13a μὴ παριστάνετε τὰ μέλη ὑμῶν ὅπλα ἀδικίας τῇ ἁμαρτίᾳ.

Rom 6:13b παραστήσατε ἑαυτοὺς τῷ θεῷ ὡσεὶ ἐκ νεκρῶν ζῶντας καὶ τὰ μέλη ὑμῶν ὅπλα δικαιοσύνης τῷ θεῷ·

Rom 6:14 ἁμαρτία ὑμῶν οὐ κυριεύσει, οὐ γάρ ἐστε ὑπὸ νόμον ἀλλὰ ὑπὸ χάριν.

Rom 6:15 ἁμαρτήσωμεν ὅτι οὐκ ἐσμὲν ὑπὸ νόμον ἀλλὰ ὑπὸ χάριν; μὴ γένοιτο.

Rom 6:17b–c ἦτε δοῦλοι τῆς ἁμαρτίας ὑπηκούσατε δὲ ἐκ καρδίας εἰς ὃν παρεδόθητε τύπον διδαχῆς.

Rom 6:18 ἐλευθερωθέντες ἀπὸ τῆς ἁμαρτίας ἐδουλώθητε τῇ δικαιοσύνῃ.

Rom 6:19c παραστήσατε τὰ μέλη ὑμῶν δοῦλα τῇ δικαιοσύνῃ εἰς ἁγιασμόν.

Rom 12:1 παραστῆσαι τὰ σώματα ὑμῶν θυσίαν ζῶσαν ἁγίαν εὐάρεστον τῷ θεῷ, τὴν λογικὴν λατρείαν ὑμῶν.

Rom 12:2a μὴ συσχηματίζεσθε τῷ αἰῶνι τούτῳ.

Rom 12:2b μεταμορφοῦσθε τῇ ἀνακαινώσει τοῦ νοός, εἰς τὸ δοκιμάζειν ὑμᾶς τί τὸ θέλημα τοῦ θεοῦ, τὸ ἀγαθὸν καὶ εὐάρεστον καὶ τέλειον.

Rom 13:8 Μηδενὶ μηδὲν ὀφείλετε, εἰ μὴ τὸ ἀλλήλους ἀγαπᾶν· ὁ γὰρ ἀγαπῶν τὸν ἕτερον νόμον πεπλήρωκεν.

Rom 13:10 ἡ ἀγάπη τῷ πλησίον κακὸν οὐκ ἐργάζεται· πλήρωμα οὖν νόμου ἡ ἀγάπη.

H. The Law as a problem

Gal 3:19 τί ὁ νόμος; τῶν παραβάσεων χάριν προσετέθη, ἄχρις οὗ ἔλθῃ τὸ σπέρμα ᾧ ἐπήγγελται, διαταγεὶς δι' ἀγγέλων ἐν χειρὶ μεσίτου.

Gal 3:19 τί ὁ νόμος; τῶν παραβάσεων χάριν προσετέθη, ἄχρις οὗ ἔλθῃ τὸ σπέρμα ᾧ ἐπήγγελται, διαταγεὶς δι' ἀγγέλων ἐν χειρὶ μεσίτου.

Gal 3:21 ὁ οὖν νόμος κατὰ τῶν ἐπαγγελιῶν [τοῦ θεοῦ]; μὴ γένοιτο· εἰ γὰρ ἐδόθη νόμος ὁ δυνάμενος ζῳοποιῆσαι, ὄντως ἐκ νόμου ἂν ἦν ἡ δικαιοσύνη.

Gal 3:23 πρὸ τοῦ ἐλθεῖν τὴν πίστιν ὑπὸ νόμον ἐφρουρούμεθα συγκλειόμενοι εἰς τὴν μέλλουσαν πίστιν ἀποκαλυφθῆναι.

Gal 3:24 ὁ νόμος παιδαγωγὸς ἡμῶν γέγονεν εἰς Χριστόν, ἵνα ἐκ πίστεως δικαιωθῶμεν.

Gal 3:25 ἐλθούσης τῆς πίστεως οὐκέτι ὑπὸ παιδαγωγόν ἐσμεν.

Gal 5:14 ὁ πᾶς νόμος ἐν ἑνὶ λόγῳ πεπλήρωται, ἐν τῷ ἀγαπήσεις τὸν πλησίον σου ὡς σεαυτόν.

Rom 3:31 νόμον καταργοῦμεν διὰ τῆς πίστεως; μὴ γένοιτο, ἀλλὰ νόμον ἱστάνομεν.

Rom 5:13 ἄχρι νόμου ἁμαρτία ἦν ἐν κόσμῳ, ἁμαρτία δὲ οὐκ ἐλλογεῖται μὴ ὄντος νόμου.

Rom 5:20 νόμος παρεισῆλθεν ἵνα πλεονάσῃ τὸ παράπτωμα.

Rom 7:7 τί ἐροῦμεν; ὁ νόμος ἁμαρτία; μὴ γένοιτο· ἀλλὰ τὴν ἁμαρτίαν οὐκ ἔγνων εἰ μὴ διὰ νόμου, τήν τε ἐπιθυμίαν οὐκ ᾔδειν εἰ μὴ ὁ νόμος ἔλεγεν, οὐκ ἐπιθυμήσεις.

Rom 7:8a ἀφορμὴν λαβοῦσα ἡ ἁμαρτία διὰ τῆς ἐντολῆς κατειργάσατο ἐν ἐμοὶ πᾶσαν ἐπιθυμίαν.

Rom 7:8b χωρὶς νόμου ἁμαρτία νεκρά.

Rom 7:9–10a ἐγὼ ἔζων χωρὶς νόμου ποτέ· ἐλθούσης δὲ τῆς ἐντολῆς ἡ ἁμαρτία ἀνέζησεν, ἐγὼ δὲ ἀπέθανον.

Rom 7:10b εὑρέθη μοι ἡ ἐντολὴ ἡ εἰς ζωὴν αὕτη εἰς θάνατον·

Rom 7:11 ἡ ἁμαρτία ἀφορμὴν λαβοῦσα διὰ τῆς ἐντολῆς ἐξηπάτησέν με καὶ δι᾽ αὐτῆς ἀπέκτεινεν.

Rom 7:12 ὁ νόμος ἅγιος, καὶ ἡ ἐντολὴ ἁγία καὶ δικαία καὶ ἀγαθή.

Rom 7:13 ἡ ἁμαρτία, ἵνα φανῇ ἁμαρτία, διὰ τοῦ ἀγαθοῦ μοι κατεργαζομένη θάνατον· ἵνα γένηται καθ᾽ ὑπερβολὴν ἁμαρτωλὸς ἡ ἁμαρτία διὰ τῆς ἐντολῆς.

Rom 7:14 οἴδαμεν ὅτι ὁ νόμος πνευματικός ἐστιν· ἐγὼ δὲ σάρκινός εἰμι, πεπραμένος ὑπὸ τὴν ἁμαρτίαν.

Rom 7:16 εἰ δὲ ὃ οὐ θέλω τοῦτο ποιῶ, σύμφημι τῷ νόμῳ ὅτι καλός.

Rom 7:21 εὑρίσκω τὸν νόμον τῷ θέλοντι ἐμοὶ ποιεῖν τὸ καλὸν ὅτι ἐμοὶ τὸ κακὸν παράκειται.

Rom 7:22–23 συνήδομαι τῷ νόμῳ τοῦ θεοῦ κατὰ τὸν ἔσω ἄνθρωπον, βλέπω δὲ ἕτερον νόμον ἐν τοῖς μέλεσίν μου ἀντιστρατευόμενον τῷ νόμῳ τοῦ νοός μου καὶ αἰχμαλωτίζοντά με ἐν τῷ νόμῳ τῆς ἁμαρτίας τῷ ὄντι ἐν τοῖς μέλεσίν μου.

Rom 7:25b αὐτὸς ἐγὼ τῷ μὲν νοΐ δουλεύω νόμῳ θεοῦ, τῇ δὲ σαρκὶ νόμῳ ἁμαρτίας.

Rom 8:2 ὁ νόμος τοῦ πνεύματος τῆς ζωῆς ἐν Χριστῷ Ἰησοῦ ἠλευθέρωσέν σε ἀπὸ τοῦ νόμου τῆς ἁμαρτίας καὶ τοῦ θανάτου.

Rom 8:3–4 τὸ ἀδύνατον τοῦ νόμου, ἐν ᾧ ἠσθένει διὰ τῆς σαρκός, ὁ θεὸς τὸν ἑαυτοῦ υἱὸν πέμψας ἐν ὁμοιώματι σαρκὸς ἁμαρτίας καὶ περὶ ἁμαρτίας κατέκρινεν τὴν ἁμαρτίαν ἐν τῇ σαρκί, ἵνα τὸ δικαίωμα τοῦ νόμου πληρωθῇ ἐν ἡμῖν τοῖς μὴ κατὰ σάρκα περιπατοῦσιν ἀλλὰ κατὰ πνεῦμα.

Rom 13:8b–10a ὁ ἀγαπῶν τὸν ἕτερον νόμον πεπλήρωκεν. τὸ γὰρ οὐ μοιχεύσεις, οὐ φονεύσεις, οὐ κλέψεις, οὐκ ἐπιθυμήσεις, καὶ εἴ τις ἑτέρα ἐντολή, ἐν τῷ λόγῳ τούτῳ ἀνακεφαλαιοῦται, [ἐν τῷ] ἀγαπήσεις τὸν πλησίον σου ὡς σεαυτόν. ἡ ἀγάπη τῷ πλησίον κακὸν οὐκ ἐργάζεται.

Rom 13:10b πλήρωμα οὖν νόμου ἡ ἀγάπη.

I. Opposition between the flesh and the spirit

Gal 5:17 ἡ σὰρξ ἐπιθυμεῖ κατὰ τοῦ πνεύματος, τὸ δὲ πνεῦμα κατὰ τῆς σαρκός· ταῦτα γὰρ ἀλλήλοις ἀντίκειται, ἵνα μὴ ἃ ἐὰν θέλητε ταῦτα ποιῆτε.

Gal 5:18 εἰ πνεύματι ἄγεσθε, οὐκ ἐστὲ ὑπὸ νόμον.

Gal 5:19–21 φανερὰ ἐστιν τὰ ἔργα τῆς σαρκός, ἅτινά ἐστιν πορνεία, κ.τ.λ.

Gal 5:22–23 ὁ καρπὸς τοῦ πνεύματός ἐστιν ἀγάπη, κ.τ.λ. κατὰ τῶν τοιούτων οὐκ ἔστιν νόμος.

Gal 5:24 οἱ τοῦ Χριστοῦ [Ἰησοῦ] τὴν σάρκα ἐσταύρωσαν σὺν τοῖς παθήμασιν καὶ ταῖς ἐπιθυμίαις.

Gal 5:25 εἰ ζῶμεν πνεύματι, πνεύματι καὶ στοιχῶμεν.

Gal 6:8 ὁ σπείρων εἰς τὴν σάρκα ἑαυτοῦ ἐκ τῆς σαρκὸς θερίσει φθοράν, ὁ δὲ σπείρων εἰς τὸ πνεῦμα ἐκ τοῦ πνεύματος θερίσει ζωὴν αἰώνιον.

Rom 6:19 ὥσπερ παρεστήσατε τὰ μέλη ὑμῶν δοῦλα τῇ ἀκαθαρσίᾳ καὶ τῇ ἀνομίᾳ εἰς τὴν ἀνομίαν, οὕτως νῦν παραστήσατε τὰ μέλη ὑμῶν δοῦλα τῇ δικαιοσύνῃ εἰς ἁγιασμόν.

Rom 6:20–21 ὅτε δοῦλοι ἦτε τῆς ἁμαρτίας, ἐλεύθεροι ἦτε τῇ δικαιοσύνῃ. τίνα οὖν καρπὸν εἴχετε τότε ἐφ᾽ οἷς νῦν ἐπαισχύνεσθε; τὸ γὰρ τέλος ἐκείνων θάνατος.

Rom 7:5 ὅτε ἦμεν ἐν τῇ σαρκί, τὰ παθήματα τῶν ἁμαρτιῶν τὰ διὰ τοῦ νόμου ἐνηργεῖτο ἐν τοῖς μέλεσιν ἡμῶν εἰς τὸ καρποφορῆσαι τῷ θανάτῳ.

Rom 7:22–23 συνήδομαι τῷ νόμῳ τοῦ θεοῦ κατὰ τὸν ἔσω ἄνθρωπον, βλέπω δὲ ἕτερον νόμον ἐν τοῖς μέλεσίν μου ἀντιστρατευόμενον τῷ νόμῳ τοῦ νοός μου καὶ αἰχμαλωτίζοντά με ἐν τῷ νόμῳ τῆς ἁμαρτίας τῷ ὄντι ἐν τοῖς μέλεσίν μου.

Rom 7:25b αὐτὸς ἐγὼ τῷ μὲν νοῒ δουλεύω νόμῳ θεοῦ, τῇ δὲ σαρκὶ νόμῳ ἁμαρτίας.

Rom 8:2 ὁ νόμος τοῦ πνεύματος τῆς ζωῆς ἐν Χριστῷ Ἰησοῦ ἠλευθέρωσέν σε ἀπὸ τοῦ νόμου τῆς ἁμαρτίας καὶ τοῦ θανάτου.

Rom 8:3–4 τὸ ἀδύνατον τοῦ νόμου, ἐν ᾧ ἠσθένει διὰ τῆς σαρκός, ὁ θεὸς τὸν ἑαυτοῦ υἱὸν πέμψας ἐν ὁμοιώματι σαρκὸς ἁμαρτίας καὶ περὶ ἁμαρτίας κατέκρινεν τὴν ἁμαρτίαν ἐν τῇ σαρκί, ἵνα τὸ δικαίωμα τοῦ νόμου πληρωθῇ ἐν ἡμῖν τοῖς μὴ κατὰ σάρκα περιπατοῦσιν ἀλλὰ κατὰ πνεῦμα.

Rom 8:5 οἱ κατὰ σάρκα ὄντες τὰ τῆς σαρκὸς φρονοῦσιν, οἱ δὲ κατὰ πνεῦμα τὰ τοῦ πνεύματος.

Rom 8:6 τὸ φρόνημα τῆς σαρκὸς θάνατος, τὸ δὲ φρόνημα τοῦ πνεύματος ζωὴ καὶ εἰρήνη.

Rom 8:7 τὸ φρόνημα τῆς σαρκὸς ἔχθρα εἰς θεόν, τῷ γὰρ νόμῳ τοῦ θεοῦ οὐχ ὑποτάσσεται, οὐδὲ γὰρ δύναται.

Rom 8:8 οἱ ἐν σαρκὶ ὄντες θεῷ ἀρέσαι οὐ δύνανται.

Rom 8:9a ὑμεῖς οὐκ ἐστὲ ἐν σαρκὶ ἀλλὰ ἐν πνεύματι, εἴπερ πνεῦμα θεοῦ οἰκεῖ ἐν ὑμῖν.

Rom 8:9b εἰ τις πνεῦμα Χριστοῦ οὐκ ἔχει, οὗτος οὐκ ἔστιν αὐτοῦ.

Rom 8:10 εἰ Χριστὸς ἐν ὑμῖν, τὸ μὲν σῶμα νεκρὸν διὰ ἁμαρτίαν, τὸ δὲ πνεῦμα ζωὴ διὰ δικαιοσύνην.

Rom 8:11 εἰ τὸ πνεῦμα τοῦ ἐγείραντος τὸν Ἰησοῦν ἐκ νεκρῶν οἰκεῖ ἐν ὑμῖν, ὁ ἐγείρας Χριστὸν ἐκ νεκρῶν ζῳοποιήσει καὶ τὰ θνητὰ σώματα ὑμῶν διὰ τοῦ ἐνοικοῦντος αὐτοῦ πνεύματος ἐν ὑμῖν.

Rom 8:12 ὀφειλέται ἐσμέν, οὐ τῇ σαρκὶ τοῦ κατὰ σάρκα ζῆν.

Rom 8:13a εἰ κατὰ σάρκα ζῆτε μέλλετε ἀποθνήσκειν.

Rom 8:13b εἰ πνεύματι τὰς πράξεις τοῦ σώματος θανατοῦτε ζήσεσθε.

Rom 8:14 ὅσοι πνεύματι θεοῦ ἄγονται, οὗτοι υἱοὶ θεοῦ εἰσιν.

Rom 8:15 οὐ ἐλάβετε πνεῦμα δουλείας πάλιν εἰς φόβον, ἀλλὰ ἐλάβετε πνεῦμα υἱοθεσίας, ἐν ᾧ κράζομεν, αββα ὁ πατήρ.

Rom 8:16–17 αὐτὸ τὸ πνεῦμα συμμαρτυρεῖ τῷ πνεύματι ἡμῶν ὅτι ἐσμὲν τέκνα θεοῦ. εἰ δὲ τέκνα, καὶ κληρονόμοι· κληρονόμοι μὲν θεοῦ, συγκληρονόμοι δὲ Χριστοῦ, εἴπερ συμπάσχομεν ἵνα καὶ συνδοξασθῶμεν.

J. The Jewish prerogative as the foundation of justification by faith

Because of the complexity of the relationships between the figures in connection with this theme, and because frequently more than one figure is used in a single sentence, I differentiate further between sub-themes in columns. The – sign indicates negation. The figures should be read from the top to the bottom in the columns, not by skipping from column to column.

1. The Jews entrusted with God's revelation and their disbelief

	Israel entrusted with God's revelation	Jewish disbelief
Rom 3:2	ἐπιστεύθησαν τὰ λόγια τοῦ θεοῦ	
Rom 3:3a		τί γὰρ εἰ ἠπίστησάν τινες;
Rom 3:3b–4a		– μὴ ἡ ἀπιστία αὐτῶν τὴν πίστιν τοῦ θεοῦ καταργήσει; μὴ γένοιτο
Rom 3:21	(χωρὶς νόμου δικαιοσύνη θεοῦ πεφανέρωται), μαρτυρουμένη ὑπὸ τοῦ νόμου καὶ τῶν προφητῶν	
Rom 9:4	οἵτινές εἰσιν Ἰσραηλῖται, ὧν ἡ υἱοθεσία καὶ ἡ δόξα καὶ αἱ διαθῆκαι καὶ ἡ νομοθεσία καὶ ἡ λατρεία καὶ αἱ ἐπαγγελίαι	

Rom 9:5a	ὧν οἱ πατέρες	
Rom 9:5b	ἐξ ὧν ὁ Χριστὸς τὸ κατὰ σάρκα	
Rom 9:6b		– οὐ γὰρ πάντες οἱ ἐξ Ἰσραήλ, οὗτοι Ἰσραήλ.
Rom 9:7a		– οὐδ' ὅτι εἰσὶν σπέρμα Ἀβραάμ, πάντες τέκνα.
Rom 9:8		– τοῦτ' ἔστιν, οὐ τὰ τέκνα τῆς σαρκὸς ταῦτα τέκνα τοῦ θεοῦ, ἀλλὰ τὰ τέκνα τῆς ἐπαγγελίας λογίζεται εἰς σπέρμα·
Rom 9:31–32a		Ἰσραὴλ διώκων νόμον δικαιοσύνης εἰς νόμον οὐκ ἔφθασεν. διὰ τί; ὅτι οὐκ ἐκ πίστεως ἀλλ' ὡς ἐξ ἔργων
Rom 9:32b		προσέκοψαν τῷ λίθῳ τοῦ προσκόμματος
Rom 11:7a		ὃ ἐπιζητεῖ Ἰσραήλ, τοῦτο οὐκ ἐπέτυχεν.
Rom 11:7b		(ἡ δὲ ἐκλογὴ ἐπέτυχεν·) οἱ δὲ λοιποὶ ἐπωρώθησαν.

2. The Jews liberated from the Law for the sake of gentile salvation

The Jews under the Law	Salvation by faith	Gentile salvation
Gal 3:13–14 – Χριστὸς ἡμᾶς ἐξηγόρασεν ἐκ τῆς κατάρας τοῦ νόμου γενόμενος ὑπὲρ ἡμῶν κατάρα.		
		ἵνα εἰς τὰ ἔθνη ἡ εὐλογία τοῦ Ἀβραὰμ γένηται ἐν Χριστῷ Ἰησοῦ,
	ἵνα τὴν ἐπαγγελίαν τοῦ πνεύματος λάβωμεν διὰ τῆς πίστεως.	

Gal 3:22	συνέκλεισεν ἡ γραφὴ τὰ πάντα ὑπὸ ἁμαρτίαν		
		ἵνα ἡ ἐπαγγελία ἐκ πίστεως Ἰησοῦ Χριστοῦ δοθῇ τοῖς πιστεύουσιν	
Gal 3:23	πρὸ τοῦ δὲ ἐλθεῖν τὴν πίστιν ὑπὸ νόμον ἐφρουρούμεθα συγ-κλειόμενοι εἰς τὴν μέλλουσαν πίστιν ἀποκαλυφθῆναι		
Gal 3:24	ὁ νόμος παιδαγωγὸς ἡμῶν γέγονεν εἰς Χριστόν,		
		ἵνα ἐκ πίστεως δικαιωθῶμεν	
Gal 3:25		ἐλθούσης δὲ τῆς πίστεως	
	— οὐκέτι ὑπὸ παιδαγωγόν ἐσμεν		
Rom 4:16		διὰ τοῦτο ἐκ πίστεως, ἵνα κατὰ χάριν,	
			εἰς τὸ εἶναι βεβαίαν τὴν ἐπαγγελίαν παντὶ τῷ σπέρματι, οὐ τῷ ἐκ τοῦ νόμου μόνον ἀλλὰ καὶ τῷ ἐκ πίστεως Ἀβραάμ, ὅς ἐστιν πατὴρ πάντων ἡμῶν
Rom 9:31–32a		(Ἰσραὴλ διώκων νόμον δικαιοσύνης εἰς νόμον οὐκ ἔφθασεν. διὰ τί;) — ὅτι οὐκ ἐκ πίστεως	
	ἀλλ᾽ ὡς ἐξ ἔργων		
Rom 9:32b	προσέκοψαν τῷ λίθῳ τοῦ προσκόμματος		

Rom 10:4	τέλος γὰρ νόμου Χριστὸς εἰς δικαιοσύνην παντὶ τῷ πιστεύοντι	
Rom 11:20	(τῇ ἀπιστίᾳ ἐξεκλάσ- θησαν), σὺ δὲ τῇ πίστει ἕστηκας	
Rom 11:32	συνέκλεισεν γὰρ ὁ θεὸς τοὺς πάντας εἰς ἀπείθειαν	
	ἵνα τοὺς πάντας ἐλεήσῃ	
Rom 15:8	– Χριστὸν διάκονον γεγενῆσθαι περι τομῆς	
	ὑπὲρ ἀληθείας θεοῦ, εἰς τὸ βεβαιῶσαι τὰς ἐπαγγελίας τῶν πατέρων,	
		τὰ δὲ ἔθνη ὑπὲρ ἐλέους δοξάσαι τὸν θεόν

3. The disbelief of the Jews and the salvation of the gentiles

	The disbelief of the Jews	Salvation of the gentiles	Making the Jews jealous
Rom 3:3	τί γὰρ εἰ ἠπίστησάν τινες; (μὴ ἡ ἀπιστία αὐτῶν τὴν πίστιν τοῦ θεοῦ καταργήσει;)		
Rom 9:31–32	Ἰσραὴλ διώκων νόμον δικαιοσύνης εἰς νόμον οὐκ ἔφθασεν.		
Rom 11:7a	ὃ ἐπιζητεῖ Ἰσραήλ, τοῦτο οὐκ ἐπέτυχεν.		
Rom 11:7b	(ἡ δὲ ἐκλογὴ ἐπέτυχεν)· οἱ δὲ λοιποὶ ἐπωρώθησαν.		
Rom 11:11a–b	– μὴ ἔπταισαν ἵνα πέσωσιν; μὴ γένοιτο·		

Rom 11:11c-d τῷ αὐτῶν παραπτώματι

ἡ σωτηρία τοῖς
ἔθνεσιν,

εἰς τὸ παραζηλῶσαι
αὐτούς.

Rom 11:12a–b . . . τὸ παράπτωμα
αὐτῶν

πλοῦτος κόσμου

καὶ τὸ ἥττημα αὐτῶν

πλοῦτος ἐθνῶν.

Rom 11:14

εἴ πως παραζηλώσω
μου τὴν σάρκα (καὶ
σώσω τινὰς ἐξ
αὐτῶν).

Rom 11:15   . . . ἡ ἀποβολὴ αὐτῶν

καταλλαγὴ κόσμου.

Rom 11:16

εἰ ἡ ἀπαρχὴ ἁγία,
καὶ τὸ φύραμα·
καὶ εἰ ἡ ῥίζα ἁγία,
καὶ οἱ κλάδοι.

Rom 11:17   εἰ δέ τινες τῶν κλάδων
ἐξεκλάσθησαν,

σὺ δὲ ἀγριέλαιος ὢν
ἐνεκεντρίσθης ἐν
αὐτοῖς καὶ συγ-
κοινωνὸς τῆς ῥίζης
τῆς πιότητος τῆς
ἐλαίας ἐγένου.

Rom 11:18

οὐ σὺ τὴν ῥίζαν
βαστάζεις ἀλλὰ ἡ
ῥίζα σέ.

Rom 11:19   ἐξεκλάσθησαν κλάδοι

ἵνα ἐγὼ ἐγκεντρισθῶ.

Rom 11:20   τῇ ἀπιστίᾳ
ἐξεκλάσθησαν,

σὺ δὲ τῇ πίστει
ἕστηκας.

Rom 11:24   εἰ σὺ ἐκ τῆς κατὰ
φύσιν ἐξεκόπης ἀγρι-

ελαίου καὶ παρὰ
φύσιν ἐνεκεντρίσθης
εἰς καλλιέλαιον,
(πόσῳ μᾶλλον οὗτοι
οἱ κατὰ φύσιν
ἐγκεντρισθήσονται
τῇ ἰδίᾳ ἐλαίᾳ).

Rom 11:25b   πώρωσις ἀπὸ μέρους τῷ
                Ἰσραὴλ γέγονεν

                           ἄχρις οὗ τὸ
                           πλήρωμα τῶν ἐθνῶν
                           εἰσέλθῃ.

Rom 11:28   κατὰ μὲν τὸ εὐαγγέλιον
                ἐχθροὶ

                           δι' ὑμᾶς

Rom 11:31   οὕτως καὶ οὗτοι νῦν
                ἠπείθησαν

                           τῷ ὑμετέρῳ ἐλέει.

4. The trustworthiness of God and the elect from Israel

	The trustworthiness of God	Not all from Israel belong to Israel	The elect from Israel
Rom 3:3–4a	(τί γὰρ εἰ ἠπίστησάν τινες;) μὴ ἡ ἀπιστία αὐτῶν τὴν πίστιν τοῦ θεοῦ καταργήσει; μὴ γένοιτο		
Rom 9:6–8	οὐχ οἷον δὲ ὅτι ἐκπέπτωκεν ὁ λόγος τοῦ θεοῦ.		
		οὐ γὰρ πάντες οἱ ἐξ Ἰσραήλ, οὗτοι Ἰσραήλ. οὐδ' ὅτι εἰσὶν σπέρμα Ἀβραάμ, πάντες τέκνα.	
			ἐν Ἰσαὰκ κληθήσεταί σοι σπέρμα

τοῦτ' ἔστιν, οὐ τὰ
τέκνα τῆς σαρκὸς
ταῦτα τέκνα τοῦ
θεοῦ,

     ἀλλὰ τὰ τέκνα τῆς
     ἐπαγγελίας λογίζεται
     εἰς σπέρμα·

Rom 11:1a–b μὴ ἀπώσατο ὁ θεὸς τὸν
     λαὸν αὐτοῦ; μὴ γένοιτο

Rom 11:2 οὐκ ἀπώσατο ὁ θεὸς
     τὸν λαὸν αὐτοῦ ὃν
     προέγνω.

Rom 11:5   οὕτως οὖν καὶ ἐν τῷ
           νῦν καιρῷ λεῖμμα
           κατ' ἐκλογὴν
           χάριτος γέγονεν·

Rom 11:7b   ἡ δὲ ἐκλογὴ
           ἐπέτυχεν·

     οἱ δὲ λοιποὶ
     ἐπωρώθησαν.

5. Salvation of all of Israel

	The rest of Israel comes to believe	**All of Israel is saved**
Rom 11:12c		(εἰ τὸ παράπτωμα αὐτῶν πλοῦτος κόσμου καὶ τὸ ἥττημα αὐτῶν πλοῦτος ἐθνῶν), πόσῳ μᾶλλον τὸ πλήρωμα αὐτῶν.
Rom 11:14	(εἴ πως παραζηλώσω μου τὴν σάρκα) καὶ σώσω τινὰς ἐξ αὐτῶν.	
Rom 11:15b		τίς ἡ πρόσλημψις εἰ μὴ ζωὴ ἐκ νεκρῶν;
Rom 11:23	κἀκεῖνοι δέ, ἐὰν μὴ ἐπιμένωσιν τῇ ἀπιστίᾳ, ἐγκεντρισθήσονται	
Rom 11:24		(εἰ σὺ ἐκ τῆς κατὰ φύσιν ἐξεκόπης ἀγριελαίου καὶ παρὰ φύσιν ἐνεκεντρίσθης εἰς καλλιέλαιον),

                       πόσῳ μᾶλλον οὗτοι οἱ κατὰ
                       φύσιν ἐγκεντρισθήσονται τῇ
                       ἰδίᾳ ἐλαίᾳ.

Rom 11:25c–26a   (πώρωσις ἀπὸ μέρους τῷ
                       Ἰσραὴλ γέγονεν ἄχρις οὗ τὸ
                       πλήρωμα τῶν ἐθνῶν εἰσέλθῃ),
                       καὶ οὕτως πᾶς Ἰσραὴλ
                       σωθήσεται.

Rom 11:28   (κατὰ μὲν τὸ εὐαγγέλιον
                       ἐχθροὶ δι' ὑμᾶς), κατὰ δὲ τὴν
                       ἐκλογὴν ἀγαπητοὶ διὰ τοὺς
                       πατέρας·

Rom 11:31   (οὕτως καὶ οὗτοι νῦν
                       ἠπείθησαν τῷ ὑμετέρῳ ἐλέει)
                       ἵνα καὶ αὐτοὶ [νῦν] ἐλεηθῶσιν·

Bibliography

Barth, Karl. *Die Auferstehung der Toten.* Zollikon-Zürich: Evangelischer Verlag, 4. Auflage, 1953. ET, *The Resurrection of the Dead.* Translated by H. J. Stenning. New York: Fleming H. Revell, 1933.

_____. *Der Römerbrief.* Zürich: EVZ-Verlag, 1919; Zollikon-Zürich: Evangelischer Verlag. 8th repr. of the 2d rev. ed., 1947. ET, *The Epistle to the Romans.* Translated by Edwyn C. Hoskyns. London: Oxford, 1933.

Bauer, Walter. *Wörterbuch zum Neuen Testament.* Berlin: Verlag Alfred Töpelmann, 4th ed., 1952.

Beekman, John, and John Callow. *Translating the Word of God.* Grand Rapids: Zondervan Publishing House, 1974.

Beker, J. Christiaan. "The Method of Recasting Pauline Theology: The Coherence-Contingency Scheme as Interpretive Model." Pages 596–602. In *Society of Biblical Literature 1986 Seminar Papers.* Edited by Kent Harold Richards. Scholars Press: Atlanta, Georgia, 1986.

_____. *Paul the Apostle: The Triumph of God in Life and Thought.* Philadelphia: Fortress, 1980.

Betz, Hans Dieter. *Der Apostel Paulus und die sokratische Tradition.* Tübingen: J. C. B. Mohr (Paul Siebeck), 1972.

_____. "2 Cor 6:14–7:1: An Anti-Pauline Fragment." *JBL* 92 (1973) 88–108.

_____. *Galatians: A Commentary on Paul's Letter to the Churches in Galatia.* Hermeneia. Philadelphia: Fortress, 1979.

_____. "Geist, Freiheit, und Gesetz: Die Botschaft des Paulus und die Gemeinde in Galatien." *ZThK* 71 (1974) 78–93. English version, "Spirit, Freedom, and the Law: Paul's Message to the Galatians." *SEÅ* 39 (1974) 145–60.

_____. "In Defense of the Spirit: Paul's Letter to the Galatians as a Document of Early Christian Apologetics." In *Aspects of Religious Propaganda in Judaism and Early Christianity.* Edited by Elizabeth Schüssler-Fiorenza. Pages 99–114. Notre Dame, Ind.: University of Notre Dame Press, 1976.

_____. "The Literary Composition and Function of Paul's Letter to the Galatians." *NTS* 21 (1975) 353–79.

Bjerkelund, Carl J. Παρακαλῶ: *Form, Funktion und Sinn der παρακαλῶ-Sätzen in den paulinischen Briefe.* Bibliotheca Theologica Norvegica 1. Oslo: Universitetsvorlaget, 1967.

Boers, Hendrikus. "The Form Critical Study of Paul's Letters: I Thessalonians as a Case Study." *NTS* 22 (1976) 140–58.

_____. "The Foundations of Paul's Thought: A Methodological Investigation—The Problem of a Coherent Center of Paul's Thought." *ST* 42 (1988) 55–68.

_____. "Interpreting Paul: Demythologizing in Reverse." In *The Philosophy of Order: Essays on History, Consciousness and Politics in Honor of Eric Voegelin.* Edited by Peter J. Opitz and Gregor Sebba. Pages 153–72. Stuttgart: Klett-Cotta, 1980.

_____. *Neither on this Mountain, nor in Jerusalem. A Study of John 4.* SBLMS 34. Atlanta: Scholars Press, 1988.

Bousset, Wilhelm. *Jesu Predigt in ihrem Gegensatz zum Judentum: Ein religionsgeschichtlicher Vergleich.* Göttingen: Vandenhoeck & Ruprecht, 1892.

_____. *Kyrios Christos: Geschichte des Christusglaubens von den Anfängen des Christentums bis Irenaeus.* Göttingen: Vandenhoeck & Ruprecht, 1913. 5th ed. 1965. ET, *Kyrios Christos: A History of the Belief in Christ from the Beginnings of Christianity to Irenaeus.* Translated by John E. Steely. Nashville: Abingdon Press, 1970.

Bultmann, Rudolf. "Karl Barth, "Die Auferstehung der Toten.'" *TBl* 5 (1926). Repr. in *Glauben und Verstehen: Gesammelte Aufsätze.* 4th ed. Tübingen: J. C. B. Mohr (Paul Siebeck), 1961. 1.38–64. ET, "Karl Barth, The Resurrection of the Dead." Pages 66–94. In *Faith and Understanding.* Translated by L. P. Smith. New York: Harper and Row, 1969.

_____. "Karl Barth's 'Römerbrief' in zweiter Auflage." *ChW* 36 (1922) cols. 320–34, 358–61, and 369–73. Repr. in Jürgen Moltmann (ed.). *Anfänge der dialektischen Theologie.* Munich: Chr. Kaiser Verlag, 1962. Vol. 1, 119–42. ET, "Karl Barth's *Epistle to the Romans* in its Second Edition." Pages 100–120. In James M. Robinson (ed.). *The Beginnings of Dialectical Theology.* Translated by Keith R. Crim. Richmond, Virginia: John Knox Press, 1968.

_____. "Neues Testament und Mythologie." Pages 15–48. In Hans-Werner Bartsch. *Kerygma und Mythos: Ein Theologisches Gespräch.* Hamburg-Bergstedt: Herbert Reich-Evangelischer Verlag, 1948. 2d ed. 1951. ET, "New Testament and Mythology." Pages 1–44. In *Kerygma and Myth.* Translated by Reginald Fuller. London: SPCK, 1957.

Chomsky, Noam. *Aspects of the Theory of Syntax.* Cambridge: Massachusetts Institute of Technology, 1965.

_____. *Syntactic Structures.* Paris: The Hague, 1971.

Dahl, Nils A. "Paul's Letter to the Galatians: Epistolary Genre, Content, and Structure" (unpublished).

de Beaugrande, Robert-Alain and Wolfgang Dressler. *Introduction to Text-linguistics.* London: Longmans, 1981. German edition: *Einführung in die Textlinguistik.* Konzepte der Sprach- und Literaturwissenschaft. Tübingen: Max Niemeyer Verlag, 1981.

de Saussure, Ferdinand. *Cours de linguistique générale.* Posthumously collected and published by his students, Charles Bally and Charles Albert Sechehaye. Paris: Payot 1916. ET, *Course in General Linguistics.* Translated by Wade Baskin. New York: Philosophical Library, 1959.

Doty, William G. "Response to 'The Structural Analysis of Philemon,' by John L. White." n.p., n.d.

du Toit, A. B. "Dikaiosyne in Röm 6. Beobachtungen zur ethischen Dimension der paulinischen Gerechtigkeitsauffassung." *ZTK* 76 (1979) 261–91.

Fillmore, Charles J. "The Case for Case." Pages 1–90. In *Universals in Linguistic Theory.* Edited by Emmon Bach and Robert T. Harms. New York/ Chicago/etc.: Holt, Rinehart and Winston Inc., 1968.

Funk, Robert W. "The Apostolic *Parousia*: Form and Significance." In *Christian History and Interpretation: Studies Presented to John Knox.* Edited by W. R. Farmer, C. F. D. Moule and R. R. Niebuhr. Cambridge: The University Press, 1967.

Greimas, A. J. and J. Courtés. *Sémiotique: Dictionnaire raisonné de la théorie du langage.* Paris: Hachette, 1979. ET, *Semiotics and Language.* Translated by Larry Crist and Daniel Patte, and others. Bloomington: Indiana University Press, 1982.

Hall, Robert G. "The Rhetorical Outline of Galatians: A Reconsideration." *JBL* 106 (1987) 277–87.

Halliday, M. A. K. *Explorations in the Functions of Language.* London: Edward Arnold, 1973.

Harris, Zellig S. "Discourse Analysis." *Language* 28 (1952) 1–30.

_____. "Discourse Analysis: A Sample Text." *Language* 28 (1952) 474–94.

Heiligenthal, Roman. *Werke als Zeichen. Untersuchungen zur Bedeutung der menschlichen Taten im Frühjudentum, Neues Testament und Frühchristentum.* WUNT 2. Reihe 9. Tübingen: J. C. B. Mohr (Paul Siebeck) 1983.

Hester, James C. "The Rhetorical Structure of Galatians 1:11–2:14." *JBL* 103 (1984) 223–33.

Hübner, Hans. *Das Gesetz bei Paulus: Ein Beitrag zum Werden der paulinischen Theologie.* Göttingen: Vandenhoeck & Ruprecht, 1978. 3d ed. 1982.

Hurd, John C. "Concerning the Structure of 1 Thessalonians" (unpublished).

Käsemann, Ernst. "Das Problem des historischen Jesus." *ZThK* 15 (1954), 125–53. Pages 187–213. Repr. in vol. 1. *Exegetische Versuche und Besinnungen.* Göttingen: Vandenhoeck & Ruprecht, 1960. ET, "The Problem of the Historical Jesus." Pages 15–47. *Essays on New Testament Themes.* Translated by W. J. Montague. London: SCM Press Ltd., 1964.

_____. "Die Anfänge christlicher Theologie." *ZThK* 57 (1960), 162–85. Pages 82–104. Repr. in vol. 2. *Exegetische Versuche und Besinnungen.* Göttingen: Vandenhoeck & Ruprecht, 1960. ET, "The Beginnings of Christian Theology." Pages 82–107. In *New Testament Questions of Today.* Translated by W. J. Montague. London: SCM Press Ltd., 1969.

_____. *Paulinische Perspektiven.* Tübingen: J. C. B. Mohr (Paul Siebeck), 1969. ET, *Perspectives on Paul.* Philadelphia: Fortress, 1971.

_____. "Sackgassen im Streit um den historischen Jesus." *EVuB.* Vol. 2, 1964, 31–69. ET, "Blind Alleys in the 'Jesus of History' Controversy." Pages 23–65. In *New Testament Questions of Today.* Translated by W. J. Montague. London: SCM Press Ltd., 1969.

_____. "Zum Thema der urchristlichen Apokalyptik." *ZThK* 59 (1962) 257–84. Repr. in *EVuB*, vol. 2., 105–31. ET, "On the Subject of Primitive Christian Apocalyptic." Pages 108–37. In *New Testament Questions of Today.*

Kennedy, G. A. *New Testament Interpretation through Rhetorical Criticism.* Chapel Hill: University of North Carolina Press, 1984.

Kennedy, H. A. A. "The Significance and Range of the Covenant Conception in the New Testament." *The Expositor* 10 (1915) 385–410.

Kim, Chan-Hie. *The Familiar Letter of Recommendation.* SBLDS 4. Missoula, Montana: Society of Biblical Literature, 1972.

Kintsch, W. "On Comprehending Stories." In *Cognitive Processes in Comprehension.* Edited by Marcel Adam Just and Patricia A. Carpenter. Pages 33–62. Hillsdale, N.J.: Lawrence Erlbaum Associates, 1977.

Kintsch, W., and T. A. van Kijk. "Comment on se rapelle et on résume des histoires." *Langages* 40 (1975) 98–116.

Koskenniemi, Heikki. *Studien zur Idee und Phraseologie des griechischen Briefes bis 400 n.Chr.* Annales Academiae Scientiarum Fennicae, Sarja-Ser. B, Nide-Tom. 102, 2. Helsinki, 1956.

Lévi-Strauss, Claude, "The Structural Study of Myth." *Myth. A Symposium, Journal of American Folklore* 78 (1955) 428–44. Translated with some additions and modifications as "La Structure des mythes." In *Anthropologie Structurale.* Paris: Plon, 1958. 1.225–55. ET. Pages 202–28. In vol. 1. *Structural Anthropology.* Translated by Claire Jacobson and Brooke Grundfest Schoeps, New York: Basic Books, Inc., 1963. Paperback: Doubleday Anchor Book, 1967.

Louw, Johannes P. "Discourse Analysis and the Greek New Testament." *BT* 24 (1937) 101–18.

_____. *Semantics of New Testament Greek.* Philadelphia/Chico: Fortress/ Scholars Press, 1982. From the Afrikaans, *Semantiek van Nuwe Testamentiese Grieks.* Pretoria, South Africa, 1976.

Louw, Johannes P. and Eugene A. Nida. *Greek-English Lexicon of the New Testament Based on Semantic Domains.* New York: United Bible Societies, 1988.

Malherbe, Abraham J. " 'Gentle as a Nurse.' The Cynic Background to I Thess ii." *NovT* 12 (1970) 203–17.

_____. "I Thessalonians as a Paraenetic Letter" (unpublished 1972 SBL Seminar paper).

Michel, Otto. *Der Brief an die Römer.* MeyerK 4. 12th Edition. Göttingen: Vandenhoeck & Ruprecht, 1963.

Nida, Eugene A. *Exploring Semantic Structures.* Munich: Wilhelm Fink Verlag, 1975.

Patte, Daniel. *Paul's Faith and the Power of the Gospel: A Structural Introduction to the Pauline Letters.* Philadelphia: Fortress, 1983.

Propp, V. *Morphology of the Folktale*. Austin and London: University of Texas Press, 1968.

Räisänen, Heikki. *Paul and the Law*. Tübingen: J. C. B. Mohr (Paul Siebeck), 1983. Philadelphia: Fortress, 1986.

Reder, Lynne M. "The Role of Elaboration in the Comprehension and Retention of Prose: A Critical Review." *Review of Educational Research* 50 (1980) 27.

Sanders, E. P. *Paul and Palestinian Judaism: A Comparison of Patterns of Religion*. Philadelphia: Fortress, 1977.

_____. *Paul, the Law, and the Jewish People*. Philadelphia: Fortress, 1983.

Schubert, Paul. *Form and Function of the Pauline Thanksgiving*. ZNW Beihefte 19/20. Berlin: Alfred Töpelmann, 1939.

Smit, Joop. "Hoe kun je de heidenen verplichten als joden to leven? Paulus en de torah in Galaten 2,11–21." *Bijdragen* 46 (1985) 118–40.

_____. "The Letter of Paul to the Galatians: A Deliberative Speech." *NTS* 35 (1989) 1–26.

_____. "Naar een nieuwe benadering von Paulus' brieven: De historische bewijsvoering in Gal. 3,1–4,11." *TTh* 24 (1984) 207–34.

_____. "Paulus, de Galaten en het judaisme: een narrative analyse van Galaten 1–2." *TTh* 25 (1985) 337–62.

_____. "Redactie in de brief aan de Galaten: retorische analyse van Gal 4,12–6,18." *TTh* 26 (1986) 113–44.

Standaert, Benoît. "La Rhétorique antique et l'épître aux Galates." *FoiVie* 84 (1985) 33–40.

van Dijk, Teun. *Some Aspects of Text Grammars: A Study in Theoretical Linguistics and Poetics*. Janua Linguarum, Series Maior 63. The Hague/ Paris: Mouton 1972.

von Oppen, Dietrich. *Marburger Aufzeichnungen zur Krise der modernen Welt*. Stuttgart: Radius, 1983.

Vouga, François. "Zur rhetorischen Gattung des Galaterbriefes." *ZNW* 79 (1988) 291–92.

Weiß, Johannes. *Die Predigt Jesus vom Reiche Gottes*. Göttingen: Vandenhoeck & Ruprecht, 1892.

White, John L. *The Body of the Greek Letter*. SBLDS 2. Missoula, Montana: Society of Biblical Literature, 1972.

_____. *The Form and Structure of the Official Petition*. SBLDS 5. Missoula, Montana: Society of Biblical Literature, 1972.

_____. "The Structural Analysis of Philemon: A Point of Departure in the Formal Analysis of the Pauline Letter." Pages 1–47. In *The Society of Biblical Literature One Hundred Seventh Annual Meeting Seminar Papers*. Society of Biblical Literature, 1971.

Whitehead, Alfred North. *Process and Reality: An Essay in Cosmology*. New York: Harper & Row, 1960.

Wilckens, Ulrich. *Der Brief an die Römer*. EKK 4. Zürich: Benziger Verlag / Braunschweig: Neukirchener Verlag, 3 vols., 2d rev. ed., vols. 1 and 2, 1987, vol. 3, 1989.

Wrede, William. *Paulus*. Religionsgeschichtliche Volksbücher I 5–6. Gebauer-Schwetschke: Halle, 1904. Pages 1–97. Repr. in Karl Heinrich Rengstorf (ed.). *Das Paulusbild in der neueren deutschen Forschung*.

Wege der Forschung 24. Darmstadt: Wissenschaftliche Buchgesellschaft, 1964. ET *Paul.* London: Philip Green, 1907.

_____. *Über Aufgabe und Methode der sogenannten neutestamentlichen Theologie.* Göttingen: Vandenhoeck & Ruprecht, 1897. Pages 81–154. Repr. in Georg Strecker (ed.). *Das Problem der Theologie des neuen Testaments.* Darmstadt: Wissenschaftliche Bucgesellschaft, 1975. ET, "The Task and Methods of New Testament Theology." Pages 68–116. In Robert Morgan. *The Nature of New Testament Theology.* London: SCM Press/Naperville, Ill.: Alec R. Allenson, 1973.

Wuellner, Wilhelm. "Paul's Rhetoric of Argumentation in Romans: An Alternative to the Donfried-Karris Debate over Romans." Pages 128–46. In *The Romans Debate.* Edited by Karl P. Donfried. Minneapolis: Augsburg Publishing House, 1977. 2d revised and expanded edition. Peabody, Mass: Hendrickson, 1991.

Index of Subjects

Index of Modern Authors

Index of Greek Terms

Index of Ancient and Biblical Texts